The Bone Peddlers

Also by Wm. R. Fix:

Pyramid Odyssey
Star Maps

WM. R. FIX

THE BONE PEDDLERS

Selling Evolution

MACMILLAN PUBLISHING COMPANY
New York

Macmillan Publishing Company
866 Third Avenue, New York, N.Y. 10022
Collier Macmillan Canada, Inc.

Macmillan books are available at special discounts for bulk purchases for sales promotions, premiums, fund-raising, or educational use. Special editions or book excerpts can also be created to specification. For details, contact:

Special Sales Director
Macmillan Publishing Company
866 Third Avenue
New York, New York 10022

Library of Congress Cataloging in Publication Data
Fix, William R., 1941–
   The bone peddlers.
   Bibliography: p.
   Includes index.
   1. Human evolution.   2. Man—Origin.   I. Title.
GN281.F58   1984   573.2ʹ   83-19954
ISBN 0-02-538480-5

10   9   8   7   6   5   4   3   2   1

Printed in the United States of America

Toward the evolution of a holistic conception of the nature of man.

Any profession that does not supply its own criticism and iconoclasm will discover that someone else will do the job, and usually in a way it does not like.

—NORMAN MACBETH
Darwin Retried: An Appeal to Reason

CONTENTS

Acknowledgments

No writer of a work such as this with over 200 bibliographic entries can be insensible of the debt he owes to others. It is therefore first appropriate to thank the many writers, scholars and scientists upon whose works I have drawn—even those with whom I most strongly disagree—for without the accumulated writings of many men this work would not have been possible, nor, conceivably, necessary.

Second, I wish to thank Allan Stormont, publisher and literary agent of Toronto, whose faith in this project over many months did much to sustain the writer in his task.

Finally, I wish to thank my highly literate wife, Dianne Ellen Fix, who did much research and continuity editing, executed most of the drawings, and, perhaps most difficult of all, kept our extremely inquisitive little boy out of the office so his father could work.

Proposed Ancestors of Man: A Chronology

THE BONE PEDDLERS

Proposed ancestors of man:	Year discovered or first proposed:	Promoted by:	Career as missing link:
Neanderthal	1856	Most early evolutionists	Abandoned as ancestral species by many anthropologists in 1960s and 1970s
Home erectus (Java man, Peking man)	1891	Eugene Dubois Teilhard de Chardin Franz Weidenreich	Ancestral status made highly questionable by discovery of skull 1470 in 1972
Piltdown man	1912	Arthur Keith and most evolutionists	Exposed as hoax in 1953
Hesperopithecus	1922	Harold Cook	Found to be an extinct pig in 1927
Australopithecus africanus	1924	Raymond Dart Robert Ardrey Maitland Edey	Disqualified by the discovery of skull 1470 in 1972
Australopithecus robustus	1938	Robert Broom	Disqualified by discovery of Homo habilis in 1960s
Gigantopithecus	1946	Franz Weidenreich	Dropped by most anthropologists as too improbable by 1950
Zinjanthropus	1959	Louis Leakey	Displaced by Leakey's discovery of Homo habilis in 1960s
Homo habilis	1960	Louis and Richard Leakey	Ancestral status still indeterminate
Ramapithecus	1964	David Pilbeam and Elwyn Simons	Found to be the ancestor of Orangutan in 1979
Lothagam man	1967	Bryan Patterson	Disqualified by new measurement in 1977
Australopithecus afarensis "Lucy"	1979	Donald Johanson Timothy White Maitland Edey	Beset by many problems and mounting controversy in early 1980s

Introduction: Wandering into the Accident Factory

I.

I WAS an innocent bystander in the argument between the creationists and evolutionists until the night of January 6, 1981, when I happened to be watching *The CBS Evening News* with Dan Rather at the anchor desk. Rather related how during the presidential campaign the previous autumn Ronald Reagan had told an audience in Texas that he had "a great many questions about evolutionary theory" and asserted that the theory "is not believed in the scientific community to be as infallible as it once was believed." This statement was obviously designed to appeal to voters in the nation's Bible Belt. Since Reagan had alleged that the scientific community itself no longer held evolutionary theory to be "as infallible as it once was believed," it was not surprising that members of the community should wish to comment.

On January 6, spokesmen for the American Association for the Advancement of Science (AAAS) finally issued a reply. According to Rather they characterized Reagan's statement as "tremendously unfortunate." One Association scientist asserted that the 100 million fossils identified and dated in the world's museums "constitute 100 million facts that prove evolution beyond any doubt whatever."

Perhaps to many people this report was the least important or interesting item in the news, merely the kind of polemic issued by one group of ax grinders against another, which has become so common of late. I, on the other hand, found it astonishing. The ax grinders in this case are the most important scientific association in the United States. The AAAS publishes *Science*, the most prestigious periodical of its kind in the country. The style and content of this magazine is virtually the definition of what it means to be scientific in twentieth-century America. Putting it another way, this association stands somewhat in the same relation to American scientists as the pope and the College of Cardinals stand to Roman Catholics.

Customarily, authorities of this giddy elevation speak publicly only in careful and considered terms. I was in a position to know. For the last decade I had been immersed in the history of science. I had read so much scientific literature that I had achieved a sensitivity to professional innuendo roughly comparable to that of certain Kremlin watchers who can tell from the pronunciation of particular syllables whether the Soviet leader merely has indigestion or is about to invade Poland. Similarly, if these statements by the Association spokesmen were as careful and considered as they could manage, I suspected that Reagan had touched a nerve.

It seemed reasonable that if the AAAS spokesmen felt the president-elect (as he then was) had misrepresented the position of the majority of scientists, they could have said just that. But it was beyond me to understand how Reagan's statement could really be "tremendously unfortunate." One would have thought Reagan had said something truly outrageous, like, "Anyone who believes in evolution is a perverted atheist" or "Evolution is a fraud, and if elected I will terminate all federal funding that supports the teaching of evolution." That Reagan merely had "a great many doubts about evolutionary theory" did not seem so unusual to me.

The other part of the response was even more remarkable: 100 million fossils constitute "100 million facts that prove evolution beyond any doubt whatever." At the time of the offense on the evening of January 6, I was not particularly well read on evolution. It had been twenty years since I had studied the subject for a semester or two in college. But even in my dim recollections I could recall having been taught that the fossil record was ambiguous on many points and that there were many scientists who acknowledged these problems and mysteries. To say that 100 million fossils in the world's museums constitute "100 million facts that prove evolution beyond any doubt whatever" has about as much credibility as an election in one of those theoretical "democracies" where 99 percent of the vote goes for the party leader and the other 1 percent are taken out and shot.

Few things in life are this clear-cut. Yet taking the statement at face value, one would think that among those 100 million fossils there was not a single contrary indication of any kind, that the evolutionary scorecard was even better than the vote for the party leader. It would not have mattered if these were merely the rantings of an inebriated undergraduate debating man's origin with a fundamentalist classmate. But this was a spokesman for the leading scientific association in the United States whose remarks were being relayed to tens of millions of people. For anyone really interested in the advancement of science, or even in truth in advertising, this had approximately the same level of interest as an announcement from the Vatican that the pope would walk on water next Sunday.

If I had been inundated with such exaggerated rhetoric month after month, the episode might have seemed less bizarre. As it was, I viewed the situation from a rather detached perspective. I had not been in the country during the 1980 presidential campaign and had returned to the United States only a few weeks before the AAAS response was reported by CBS. I was aware that the political power of the nation's Bible Belt was on the rise and that the scientific community found this threatening, but that in itself did not adequately explain the AAAS response.

At this juncture I should explain my own approach to the question of evolution. Until I became aroused by those peculiar articulations and began to inquire after the reigning wisdom in the field, my study of the subject had more or less ceased in my college days. Like most of my classmates, I cared little about the evolution of the horse or the bat; what really concerned us was the origin of man. For a fleeting moment around 1960 my knowledge of paleoanthropology (the study of fossil man) was completely up to date—or so I thought. Louis Leakey, then the world's top paleoanthropologist, personally presented his latest find hot from the gravels of East Africa to the lecture section of our anthropology class. Leakey called his discovery Zinjanthropus. This, he said, was the first toolmaker and the earliest known man. It was exciting hearing about this straight from the horse's mouth, but I was not all that impressed with Zinjanthropus. His skull didn't even look near-human to me. There was no dome to his cranium at all, and his forehead went straight back from the top of his eyebrows. I've seen cocker spaniels who looked about as human as this. Still, if Zinjanthropus actually made stone tools, that seemed to settle the matter. Unfortunately, it did not occur to me at the time to ask Leakey how he could be positive that this creature had made tools.

I was vaguely aware that other discoveries of ancient creatures supposedly ancestral to man had been made since the finding of Zinjanthropus. I didn't know if they were more convincing or not, but whatever difficulties pertained to them, I knew that there was at least one great unassailable fact behind all the evolutionary scenarios concerning the emergence of man: the striking similarity of the human skeleton to those of the present-day apes and earlier "near-men" such as Neanderthal, Peking man, Java man, and others. I was not under the impression that anyone had been able to explain exactly how modern man came about, but however it happened, the evidence of our skeleton suggests that man's origin is in some way connected with these other creatures.

While predisposed to acknowledge this connection, I did not see this as the total or even the most important aspect of man's emergence. I knew from my other studies that the advent of human consciousness on this planet appears to be an altogether deeper problem than can be satisfactorily explained by the postulated slow rise from a stock of killer apes. Many of the oldest records of man show no diminution of consciousness whatever. Human consciousness seems to spring into existence full blown and is so different in degree and kind from other manifestations of intelligence that I could see how there was possibly some truth in both religious and evolutionary interpretations of man's emergence.

I was also still influenced by the professor under whom I had studied anthropology in the early 1960s, the man who had hosted Louis Leakey. For this professor, evolution was an important and useful concept for elucidating certain relationships between various forms of life. But this man lived in a very large conceptual universe, most of which was still unknown. Evolution was a good explanation for certain aspects of the natural order, but it was not necessarily the explanation for everything.

As a result of these attitudes and interpretations, I found myself square in the middle of the road. I was encouraged to maintain this position by further experience in academe. One of the tools that have made me an historian of science is a master's degree in behavioral science. The popular view of behavioral science seems to be that of a man in a white coat electrocuting one-half of a rat's brain to see what that does to the other half or to determine which way the rat will jump next. Regrettably, I am not in a position to deny that such amusements are not somewhere perpetrated in the name of science. However, the behavioral science I studied was of an altogether different kind. It was not that it was more theoretical, rather that it was less mired in nerves and twitches and more concerned with concepts and interactions.

My chief professor in this field was fond of emphasizing the transactional nature of behavior and perception. For example, if the natives are complaining that foreigners are coming in and buying up the country, one must ask who is selling it to them. There cannot be a buyer without a seller. This approach has wide application. It highlights the importance of the context in which we place a problem and illustrates the determining role of the perspective and perceptions we bring to a situation.

The simplest way of stating the relevance of this stance to scientific endeavors is to say that evidence is only evidence when it is perceived as evidence. To illustrate: In the late eighteenth century the foremost scientific body in the world was the Académie française. The Académie was a 1790s equivalent of the AAAS, and the Académie was also involved in a great public debate, just as the AAAS is today. This earlier debate concerned the reality and nature of meteorites. There were meteor showers in the eighteenth century, just as there are in the twentieth, but while members of the Académie had witnessed the streaks of light produced by meteorites, they had never seen one of these bits of rock or iron from interplanetary space survive its passage through the earth's atmosphere. Peasants and countryfolk affirmed that rocks did occasionally fall from the sky; they had seen them. However, this was not an everyday event in Paris, and the scientists simply did not believe the witnesses. The more they thought about it, the more illogical and absurd the notion of rocks falling from the sky became. They supposed that the streaks of light associated with meteorites were atmospheric phenomena like lightning.

Once this explanation had been arrived at, the Académie was impervious to further testimony. It simply didn't matter what evidence was produced or how well it was attested. On July 24, 1790, a widely witnessed shower of meteorites fell in southwest France. Samples of these meteorites and three hundred statements by witnesses were sent to the Académie. But the scientists "knew" rocks could not fall from the sky. It was "a physically impossible phenomenon," and they, after all, were the most respected authorities of the time. Accordingly, the Academicians ridiculed the rock samples and the statements by witnesses and sent them back.

The greatest impediment to the advancement of science is not lack of evidence but lack of perspective. Like the rest of us, scientists are emotional beings. They can become so committed to a particular stance that they forfeit their detachment. At one time or another, respected authorities have declared that it was impossible that the earth could be a sphere, impossible that it could turn on its axis, impossible that matter could spontaneously decompose (which we now know happens with radioactive elements), impossible that man could fly, impossible that man could break free of the earth's gravitational field.

Indeed, it is fascinating how the perspectives of science keep changing. Repeatedly entire patterns of evidence have been overlooked or misinterpreted, and then when such patterns are properly taken into account, a completely different interpretation emerges. But new interpretations are rarely hatched without controversy, and the more important the question, the greater and more extreme the controversy is likely to be. The idea of rocks falling from the sky was profoundly upsetting for many eighteenth-century scientists because it challenged their belief in the stability of nature. Agreed among themselves that this thing could not be, and encouraged by the sound of their own voices, they went out on a limb and fell off. Their example is a pertinent reminder that just because most of the authorities in a field are shouting in unison that they know the truth, it ain't necessarily so. The more emotive the issue, the more likely is shouting in unison to be heard. And of course there are few subjects more emotive than the origin of man.

All of which made me wonder, How good *was* the evolutionary evidence? Perhaps in addition to those 100 million facts that proved evolution, there were another 100 million facts they had chosen to ignore that proved something else.

I was no longer an innocent bystander. I loaded my briefcase with notepaper and moved into the library.

II.

My deepening entanglement in this mad affair was ensured when, a few weeks later, news of further skirmishes on the same turf bubbled up through the media. This time the combatants were Kelly Segraves and the State of California. Segraves, director of the Creation-Science Research Center in San Diego, sued the State of California for violating the religious freedom of his children. Segraves maintained that as taught in state schools, evolution amounts to a secular religion. Since California school board policy does not allow the "divine origin theory" to be presented in biology classes, Segraves claimed a violation of principle.

Judge Irving Perluss heard the case in early March 1981 and dismissed the claim, ruling that since evolution was not taught as dogma, the rights of Segraves' children had not been violated. But Segraves did not come away empty-handed. Judge Perluss ordered statewide distribution of an earlier school board statement cautioning that textbooks should indeed avoid dogmatism on the question of man's origin. Having scored this point, Segraves' cause was also assisted by the enormous media coverage the case received, with Time (March 16, 1981) headlining it as DARWIN GOES ON TRIAL AGAIN.

The Time article acquainted me with the fact, of which I had previously been ignorant, that in some sections of the country state and local school board policy decisions over the last few years have already effected significant changes in biology textbooks. In one standard text, discussion of the origins of life had been cut from over 2,000 words in the 1974 edition to only 332 in the 1977 edition. In Texas, high school biology texts are now required to present evolution as a theory, not as a fact.

Time also gave a slightly fuller version than CBS had of Reagan's campaign statement to which the AAAS had reacted so shrilly. Apparently Reagan had indicated that if evolution is taught in public schools, then he thought "the biblical story of creation should also be taught." *Time* also noted the opinion of educators who saw the present situation as a consequence of their own failure to teach evolution effectively. One teacher said he felt the creationists had already "won," because they *had* changed the textbooks. Others felt they were clearly on the defensive and were shocked and dismayed at the upsurge of creationist sentiment.

On the one hand I could now better appreciate some of the pressures that had provoked the AAAS response. On the other, I wondered why they found the prospect of competing with the biblical creation story so threatening—especially if the evidence for evolution were as overwhelming as they claimed. My perplexity was confounded by *Time*'s emphasizing that many creationists actually believe that the world and all in it was *literally* created in six days and that this had taken place only about five thousand or ten thousand years ago—a view more appropriate to the seventeenth century than to the twentieth. How had the situation in the United States reached such a pass that apparently millions of people were turning their backs to the evidence of geology? While not inclined to believe that every word proceeding out of the mouths of geologists was infallible truth, I felt that of all the straw men science has ever had to knock over, the belief in a recent creation of the earth should be among the easiest.

However, *Time* also provided another instance of a scientific spokesman employing peculiarly dogmatic language. The same article quotes paleontologist Stephen Jay Gould: "That evolution occurred is a fact. People evolved from ape ancestors even though we can argue about how it happened. Scientists are debating mechanism, not fact."

Now, it so happened that among the first couple dozen books I brought home from the library was one bearing the title *Not from the Apes*. The author is paleontologist Bjorn Kurten, who is described on the dust jacket as follows:

. . . a professor at the University of Helsinki, [who] has worked extensively in Europe, Africa, and North America. He has published about eighty scientific articles, several volumes in English on mammals and the ice ages, and a number of novels in Swedish. He has held a lectureship at Harvard's Museum of Comparative Zoology and has been awarded a Rockefeller Foundation research grant, a University of Florida fellowship, and the Finnish State Prize for popular science writing.

In short, Kurten is a respected scientist of international reputation. He is also a thoroughgoing evolutionist. But contrary to Gould's flat statement that people evolved from apes, Kurten thinks the human line has been separate from that of the apes for more than 35 million years. In fact, according to Kurten, it would be more accurate to say that the apes descended from man! So Gould also comes across dogmatically; and though he may not have heard of it, it seems that some scientists, every bit as reputable as he, are still debating the facts. It is one thing to express an opinion that is in some measure still indeterminate. It is quite another to declare that the answer has been found and that there is no uncertainty about the matter, merely because it is one's opinion.

I had now encountered the second glaring instance in only a couple of months where spokesmen for science publicly failed to make this elementary distinction. Certainly neither the AAAS nor Gould seem to have much respect for the diversity of opinion in their own ranks. People with as much valid evidence as paleontologists and geologists have needn't fear comparison with competing ideas. Nor need they engage in gross oversimplifications.

Were these simply a couple of clumsy press releases, or were they signs of a spreading intellectual disease? What had happened to that traditional confidence in the scientific process?

III.

The early months of 1981 were a propitious time to find out. The April issue of *Science Digest* featured an article by one Boyce Rensberger, "Ancestors: A Family Album." Rensberger is senior editor of *Science 82*, a popular science magazine published by the AAAS. Of course, *Science Digest* is also a popular, not a professional, magazine. But for that very reason it was likely to be diagnostic of the state of public discourse. I did not have to read far before I was assaulted by the same flat-footed style encountered earlier. In his opening paragraph Rensberger says,

Except for those who believe in miracles of special creation (events that, by definition, can neither be proved nor disproved), no one doubts that our heritage can be traced back nearly four million years to little creatures that, as adults, stood only about as tall as a five-year-old today.

No one doubts? What an extraordinary statement. Even having surveyed only a dozen texts by that time, I knew that among leading paleoanthropologists themselves there were many doubts, many opinions as to what the human lineage was four million years ago. Surely Rensberger knew that. Surely large sections of the public knew it. Why employ such language? It seems almost calculated to discredit the subject.

Further examples of contemporary evolutionary discourse did not prove any more felicitous. Early 1981 saw the publication of *Lucy: The Beginnings of Humankind* by Donald Johanson and Maitland Edey. An account of Johanson's discoveries of primate fossils in Ethiopia—the first significant discoveries by an American paleoanthropologist in quite some time—*Lucy* seemed to be more of a promotion to convince the public that Johanson's fossils were more important than Richard Leakey's, rather than an attempt to present an evenhanded assessment of current paleoanthropology—but more of that later.

Though its formal publication date was 1980, early '81 also saw the appearance on the best-seller lists of Carl Sagan's beautifully illustrated *Cosmos*. An astronomer with interdisciplinary interests and a bent for popularization, Sagan sketches the possible workings of evolution over the life of the universe and where we stand today. At first *Cosmos* seemed a welcome attempt at a wider perspective in an era of too much specialization and compartmentalization. I was only slightly disappointed to find that much of what Sagan says about ancient science is superficial. Few writers handle the subject well. I found it somewhat more disturbing that Sagan plays heavily upon classical Darwinism, as if zoologists, biologists, and paleontologists hadn't moved an inch from Darwin's ideas in the last century. But in comparison with many of the recent examples of evolutionary discourse put out for public consumption, *Cosmos* went down like a drink of cool water—until I got to page 30, where, after a fashion, Sagan suddenly decides to play theologian. Speaking of the evolutionary process in general, Sagan says,

The secrets of evolution are death and time—the deaths of enormous numbers of life-forms that were imperfectly adapted to the environment; and time for a long succession of small mutations that were *by accident* adaptive, time for the slow accumulation of patterns of favorable mutations.

Sagan emphasizes the words *by accident* by italicizing them and makes it clear that accident is the fundamental factor in the emergence of life-forms, including the appearance of life in the beginning. Indeed, Sagan invokes accidents the way others invoke God. His position implies that not only man but the entire universe is, in the final analysis, merely the result of a series of billions of accidents over billions of years.

On the face of it, this is not satisfying scientifically or philosophically. Scientifically, this position is no more capable of proof or disproof than miracles of special creation, and all the laws of probability are dead against it. Philosophically, even a child can see there is too much order and pattern in nature for this to be credible. It used to be said that God geometrizes. Do accidents geometrize? In Sagan's accidental cosmos, consciousness becomes an excretion of matter, and the divisions between the earth's life-forms are so arbitrary that he finds no incongruity in telling us that oak trees are our relatives—a rather tremendous leap in the dark when we consider that no one on earth really knows how life began.

I was amazed that Sagan would put this utterly simplistic presentation before the public. After years of reading scientific and quasi-scientific literature, it was suddenly clearer to me than ever why society has developed the cultural stereotype of the mad scientist. One is never more apt to get carried away with his ideas than when he extrapolates, and no one extrapolates like an astronomer. Astronomers are brought up believing they can calculate stellar distances and the rate the universe is expanding from the red shift on their photographic plates. When this style of extrapolation is applied to biology, slime molds begin to look like cousins and potato bugs are practically next of kin.

Whatever happened to concepts such as intelligence, design, and purpose? There *are* ways of discussing the origin of life without falling back on literal fundamentalism or crassly mechanical explanations; but Sagan insists on playing the high priest of materialism and does it badly. If this opinion about accidents is perceived as the reigning scientific wisdom, it is not surprising that many people have forsaken the counsels of science entirely and harken to different drummers. Many parents, even those who are not overtly religious, could well conclude that it would be better for their children to distrust the pronouncements of science than to be taught that they and life were mere accidents. If millions are ignoring the evidence of geology, for example, it may not be that the dulcet tones of Jerry Falwell and other prime-time preachers are utterly irresistible, but that the scientists themselves are driving them away in the first place with vacuous absurdities.

When Sagan excludes even the possibility that a spiritual dimension has any place in his cosmos—not even at the unknown, mysterious moment when life began—he makes accidental evolution the explanation for everything. Presented in this way, evolution does indeed look like an inverted religion, a conceptual golden calf, which manages to reek of sterile atheism. It is little wonder that many parents find their deeper emotions stirred if they discover this to be the import of Johnny's education. Having surveyed the reigning wisdom according to Sagan, my own emotions were sufficiently agitated that I no longer doubted that the exchange between Reagan and the AAAS was indeed symptomatic of a much larger and deeper problem. Once one has seen the inside of the accident factory, he hopes it will collapse before it devours the innocent; but that this contraption is actually on sale as a model of the universe is a sure sign that evolutionary discourse in the United States is now working to discredit science, rather than enhance it.

IV.

I began my deeper researches into the question of evolution in a position I described as "middle of the road." I was generally inclined to believe there might be some truth in both creationism and evolution, and so do I now. But my position is not unaltered. So far as the evolution of man is concerned, the direct evidence from the fossil record is even weaker than I had thought, and what there is is much distorted by wishful thinking and, again, by wild extrapolation. The indirect evidence (such as evolution in species other than man) is in certain instances stronger than I had expected.

All in all, I found far more of a story than I had anticipated, much of it quite entertaining and completely unknown to the public. I found respected anthropologists talking about a modern-type human skull that is as much as 700,000 years old. Most anthropologists say as little as possible about this skull, and among those who mention it at all, not a few misrepresent it, because it contradicts their theories that modern man did not exist until about 50,000 or 100,000 years ago.

I found that in recently proposing "Lucy" or Australopithecus afarensis as man's animal ancestor, Donald Johanson and Timothy White abbreviated their analysis of the fossils rather severely and either overlooked or ignored several important features indicating that these fossils represent two species, not one, and that neither is a likely human ancestor.

I next discovered the amazing fact, which I will document in detail, that almost every ancestor of man ever proposed suffers from disqualifying liabilities that are not widely publicized. I gradually came to realize that the presentation of fossil evidence for human evolution has long been and still is more of a market phenomenon than a disinterested scientific exercise. For nearly a century the search for the fossils of man's antecedents has excited the imagination of the world. Virtually everyone is curious about how we got to be what we are. Finding truly definitive evidence of man's evolution from animal ancestors would be about as sensational as capturing a flying saucer complete with occupants from outer space. In terms of fame, funding for further excavations, professional advancement, and literary royalties from published accounts of their discoveries, many fossils portrayed as ancestral to man have proved to be worth far more than their weight in gold for the discoverers.

Again and again these proposed ancestors have been discredited by subsequent discoveries. For instance, dear old Zinjanthropus, sold to my college class as the earliest known man by Louis Leakey, had, I discovered, been evicted from our family tree long ago. In fact, it was just after Leakey left the States on his Zinjanthropus trip, only about two years after the discovery.

A review of the international literature shows that this market phenomenon is particularly inflamed in the United States because of the desire to outpoint the fundamentalists, and it is especially the remarks of scholars from other countries that cast doubt upon most candidates that still appear in American models of man's descent. It is not correct to say there is no evidence for man's evolution, but this evidence is very much slighter and more enigmatic than many people imagine.

If we are to consider human evolution seriously, we must first talk about bones, most of them so old they have turned to stone. After we have toured the boneroom, we should examine evolution and man's origin in a much wider context. Not only should we survey the evidence for evolution in species other than man, but we should also note the wider human and behavioral context as well. For most writers on this subject, this includes diaries of chimpanzee-watchers and studies of reproductive success among the Wuli Wilu tribe. In my admittedly unorthodox opinion, however, the creation stories of the world's ancient and archaic peoples are of more relevance to the issue than how many ways a chimpanzee can grab a banana, and I have emphasized these instead. I have also described recent developments in parapsychology that appear to verify certain elements in the old creation stories.

My general thesis is that much of the current hyperbole about man's origins is being emitted by people who have specialized in such tiny cracks of the Grand Canyon of life that they have lost all perspective. As Goethe said, in studying the parts the spirit has been lost.

There is one conclusion I would emphasize. To give schoolchildren or anyone else the impression that the only scientific way to explain man is by slow evolution from the animal kingdom is totally unwarranted by the positive facts and a serious abuse of the public trust. It is also a disservice to the scientific enterprise. I hasten to add, if it is not already clear, that I am not promoting a literal reading of the first chapters of Genesis. Indeed, I am convinced that the emergence of man is a far deeper mystery than either creationists or evolutionists contend. Whether the alternate possibilities I point out are any more satisfying, I leave the reader to judge. But it is safe to say that when the problem of man's origin is considered holistically, it is thoroughly possible to doubt the man-from-animal theory without being either misinformed or a rock-bottom fundamentalist. And in view of the ridiculous rhetoric currently stultifying the American public, some of which I have already quoted, it seems high time that someone explained why.

PART 1

A Tour of the Boneroom

If this book were to catalogue all the mistaken claims about
hominid fossils made by layman and expert alike, it would
have to be far longer than it is.

—MAITLAND EDEY
The Missing Link

1: A Catalogue of Fiascoes

I.

IN 1864 BENJAMIN DISRAELI (1804–81), prime minister of England and a man of letters, posed the argument about the origin of man at its most elegant and most extreme:

> Is man an ape or an angel?
> Now I am on the side of the angels.

However, Disraeli also said,

> What we anticipate seldom occurs;
> what we least expect generally happens.

It certainly would have amazed Disraeli and most other people of the time to find that what has endured of Victorian England to the present day has not been the steam engine and the British Empire, but the flush toilet and the theory of evolution. Each displays severe and continuing problems. And of the two it is the unflagging scientific respectability of the theory that is the most astonishing. One can only doubt that the relevant facts of paleoanthropology are really reaching that many people. If they were, the idea that the human body evolved from something like an ape would probably have been laughed off stage by the general public long ago, and new ideas and different concepts would have been demanded. Yet the theory thrives despite the track record of paleoanthropology over the last century. Given the extent to which this notion is intellectually fashionable, one would have thought that the history of this field was an unbroken string of triumphant verifications; instead it is mostly a catalogue of fiascoes.

II.

Of course, there are many claims that at least some evidence connecting man with simian forebears has been found. But to a very considerable extent, this evidence is merely in the eye of the beholder and, seen in another perspective, is not nearly as persuasive or clear as many people imagine.

Unfortunately, fossils do not come with labels reading, "I am an ancestor of man," "I am the ancestor of the chimpanzee," or "My line became extinct." If someone finds a skull with some humanlike and some apelike features, how can we tell whether it indeed belonged to an ancestor of man, to one of the apes, or is merely another of the millions of species who vanished without transmitting their genes to creatures alive today? In many specific cases it is now quite impossible to answer these questions with any kind of certainty, but there are useful criteria that can tell us quite a bit. The most important criteria employed in paleoanthropology may be summarized under six headings: morphology, bipedalism, tools, fire, dating, and context. These are the basic tools of the trade. Each has its value and its limitations, and it is helpful to have some idea what these are.

Morphology is defined as "the science of the form and configuration of animals." In other words, if someone finds the skull of a possible ancestor, we can ask questions like, How large was its brain? Are its teeth human or apelike? Does it have peculiar features that are specific to man, to apes, or to some other creature? Morphology is the very heart of paleoanthropology, but it creates almost as many arguments as it solves. In many of the most important fossils there is a mixture of humanlike and apelike traits, and the overall significance of each type is ultimately nothing more than a subjective judgment. One expert may emphasize the human characteristics; another may declare that in its overall features the creature was clearly an ape.

Bipedalism simply means "walking on two feet." As might be expected, bones from the foot, leg, knee, and pelvis are, as they say in the trade, "diagnostic" of bipedalism. For example, in man an angle is found between the femur (thighbone) and tibia (large bone in the calf) when these are viewed from the front or rear. In man the femur angles outward to connect with the pelvis; in apes the femur is in a straight line with the tibia.

Sometimes even if we have nothing but the skull, we can tell from the position of the foramen magnum whether or not the creature to whom it belonged was bipedal. The foramen magnum is the hole on the bottom of the skull through which the spinal cord passes. In man this hole is far forward, reflecting the way the skull is balanced upon the spine in an upright posture. In four-legged animals this hole is more to the rear of the skull.

These criteria are valid and useful as far as they go, but in practice there are two major limitations upon how much they can tell us. The first limitation is due to the character of primate fossils. Since much of the heaviest bone in the body is in the skull, it is this part that is most apt to be fossilized, and often little of the rest of the skeleton is preserved. Especially with fossils of great age, however, not even all of the skull is present, but only fragments forming an incomplete puzzle. And since the bone around the foramen magnum is some of the thinnest in the cranium, it is often missing. So even the discovery of three-fourths of a 2-million-year-old skull may raise as many questions as it answers—if not more. In short, the evidence is very often so fragmentary as to be highly ambiguous.

This well-known impediment has not discouraged fossil hunters because for many years it has been assumed that there was only one lineage of bipedal creatures—the lineage that resulted in man. And so paleoanthropologists needed only the slightest evidence of bipedalism to come up winners, since by definition such evidence implied that the ultimate prize, the ancestor of man, was at hand.

Perversely enough, the second major limitation to the significance of bipedalism arises because occasionally paleoanthropologists have had the perseverance and luck to overcome the tremendous odds against them and actually find such evidence. The trouble is that a good case can now be made that no less than four or five different prehuman or subhuman species were to some degree bipedal, and all these do not appear to have belonged to the same lineage. This is terribly inconvenient because we can no longer automatically hang the "ancestor" label on any creature that stood on two feet—unless we adopt the unpopular theory that man has descended from not one but several different lineages. Although anthropologists do not like to dramatize this development, it is a simple fact that bipedalism is no longer the open sesame it once was. We shall look more closely at this problem when we come to the particular species involved.

A somewhat more secure attribute of man is his ability to make tools. Anthropologists often define man as the toolmaking animal. While simple tools may be made of various organic materials, such as bone, shell, and wood, easily the most enduring and anthropologically significant are those made of stone. Because it takes special conditions to fossilize a skeleton, stone tools are found far more often than the remains of those who made them. Ancient stone tools range from the most crudely shaped rocks from which a few pieces have been chipped to produce a sharp edge or point to beautifully worked blades, axheads, spear points, and arrowheads that may rival the craftsmanship required for accomplished sculpture. Where the fossil evidence itself is ambiguous or missing, we can sometimes estimate the kind of beings who once inhabited a site by the character of the tools found there.

In the early days of paleoanthropology it was generally assumed that any toolmaking creature by this ability alone proclaimed himself to be a man or on the road to man. This is still the position of the majority of anthropologists, and certainly with the more finely wrought stone tools there is no question that they are of human manufacture. But with the intensive study of animal behavior in the last couple of decades, there are now reasons to doubt if "made by man" is an invariably safe conclusion when it comes to the crudest stone tools. It has now been amply documented that even chimpanzees make simple tools of various kinds. They trim shoots, branches, and twigs into prods or "fishing poles" for extracting termites from rotting logs. They also make sponges from chewed-up leaves for use in dipping water from cracks and crevices, and they use stones to smash nuts. Without instruction captive chimps have put together two-part poles to reach bananas hung beyond their grasp.

It is even more interesting to hear what orangutans can do with a little instruction. They have been taught in an hour or two to make crude stone-cutting tools like those attributed to man's "ancestors." Although apes have never been observed making stonecutters by themselves in the wild, the experience does show that a specialized primate of their limited cranial capacity (350–400 cubic centimeters) can manage this task. And it raises the distinct possibility that over the last few million years there could well have been slightly brainier apes not ancestral to man who had learned to chip a few flakes off a stone without human instruction. Toolmaking remains an important indicator of man, but with the simplest stone and bone implements it is well not to assume too much.

The least ambiguous sign of man is the ability to make fire. Man is known as "the maker of ashes." Occasionally (but not very often) paleontologists find ashes or hearth sites in strata containing fossils and/or tools. If the evidence of fire can be clearly associated with a particular type of ancient or "near-man," we have a solid indication that the creature in question was on our side of the divide between the animals and humankind.

The limitations to the significance of man-made ashes are simply that they occur so rarely at the relevant sites; and even when they do, there are often additional factors that make it impossible to attribute them with certainty to the creatures represented by the fossils at the site. The fossils around an ancient hearth may be merely the remains of a victim, even a dinner, of the man that made the fire—a man who was under no obligation to deposit his skeleton in the same place.

Next we come to dating, which alone can do much to elevate a fossil species to contention as a possible ancestor of man, or to rule it out. For example, if fossils of a previously unknown primate are found in deposits that are reliably dated to, say, 100,000 years in age, the sample may have to be put on a back shelf as a mere curiosity regardless of its other characteristics unless and until a much older example of the same species is found. There is now good evidence that modern-type men were already in existence at least 100,000 years ago, so there would be little point in looking at a species of that age as our possible ancestor. On the other hand, if the same species were dated to 3 million years old, there might have been sufficient time for it to have been transformed into man.

There are various methods whereby the age of a fossil may be estimated, but none are foolproof. The method of widest application is contextual dating. The age of fossils may be estimated by the presence of other fossil species in the same strata whose age has been broadly established by their occurrence elsewhere in the fossil record. Of course, the actual geology of a site may not lend itself to this kind of dating, and even if it does, we do not get hard, absolute dates, but broad temporal ranges, such as "between 1 and 2 million years old."

In recent decades scientists have developed sophisticated technical procedures to analyze chemical or atomic traces that gradually build up or diminish in fossils and associated materials. One of the earliest techniques was fluorine dating. Fresh bone has little or no fluorine content, but fluorine occurs as a trace element in the earth's surface, and buried bones gradually absorb fluorine from their surroundings. Thus, if a laboratory could demonstrate that a fossil had a relatively high fluorine content, this was a confirmation of its antiquity. Since the amount of fluorine in the earth's surface varies from place to place, this kind of dating yielded only rough estimates at best. And even when we speak of a relatively high fluorine content, we are still talking about chemical traces so minute that the best experts and equipment produce highly variable results. In one famous case, an expert dated part of the Piltdown skull at roughly 50,000 years old, and then a few years later the same expert concluded it was only 500 years old.

Today the most widely talked-about dating technique in paleoanthropology is the potassium-argon method. An isotope of potassium (potassium 40) decays into an isotope of argon (argon 40) at a known rate over millions of years. Potassium 40 occurs in its pristine form (before it begins to decay) in certain types of fresh volcanic ash. The age of fossils found beneath a layer of volcanic ash can be estimated by dating the ash. Using special air pumps, a mass spectrometer, and strict laboratory procedures, the amounts of the isotopes in a sample of ash can be directly measured and the time required to produce that amount of argon 40 from the potassium can then be calculated. In theory, the age of the ash can be determined with great precision. And if, as occasionally happens, fossils are found sandwiched between layers of volcanic ash, their age may be theoretically pinpointed by dating both layers.

The potassium-argon method is ingenious and scientifically exciting, but again, it has its limitations. In the first place, only a minor fraction of fossils are found beneath datable ash layers. In the second, as with the fluorine method, the traces of potassium and argon are so tiny that even the best technicians and equipment give varying results. In a recent important case, one laboratory dated an ash layer at 1.8 million years, while another dated the same layer at as much as 2.9 million years. With results like these, the age of the fossil can hardly be said to have been pinpointed, but we nevertheless have a probable range for its age. Fundamentalists arguing for a recent creation of the earth see this variability as total unreliability, while some paleoanthropologists tend to give complete credence to a particular figure from a particular laboratory that supports their own version of evolutionary theory. As usual, the truth is somewhere in the middle: These dating methods are better indicators than creationists claim, but not nearly as trustworthy as some scientists would like to believe.

Finally, after a fossil has been evaluated with respect to general morphology, bipedalism, associated tools and ashes, and its age estimated, it must be seen in light of the context of similar criteria of all other fossils relevant to the theory that the human body evolved from that of an ape or similar creature. This is the most crucial step of all, and, unfortunately, by and large it is also the most inadequately performed. Quite a few relevant fossils are now known, and if one chooses to look at only part of the collection, lineages suggestive of the ape-to-man theory can indeed be constructed. But there are a couple of very old human skulls that so embarrass these lineages that some anthropologists completely ignore them, and a good many others skip over them lightly with little more than a mention of their name and a glib generality.

Of course, in the early days of paleoanthropology this larger fossil context was mostly nonexistent. When a slope-browed Neanderthal skull, found in a German valley in 1856, was first brought before a scientific congress in that country in the 1860s, the scientists present didn't know what to make of it. Some thought it was the skull of an idiot. Others put forward the suggestion that it belonged to a Cossack who had fought in the Napoleonic wars a half century earlier. These opinions may seem silly or humorous today, but what they really represent is not stupidity but the lack of a context in which to place the discovery. There was simply nothing with which to compare it. Nor was much help to be had from the theoreticians. Darwin's *Origin of Species* had only been out a few years. But then, the book never has had the impact in Europe that it has in Britain and America, and it certainly had not converted the scientists at the congress. In any case, Darwin did not deal with the origin of man in that work, except by implication. It was not until 1871 that he published the inferior and rambling work called *The Descent of Man*, in which he wrote that man is descended from some lowly organized form, "a hairy, tailed quadruped, probably arboreal in its habits."

Although many relevant fossils have been unearthed since the 1860s, even today the total context has huge and gaping holes in it. Among them is the complete lack of ancestors for the modern apes *after* 8 million B.C. One might think that older fossils would always be scarcer than more recent ones, but this is not always so. Louis Leakey found huge deposits of Miocene apes on islands in Lake Victoria. The Miocene is a geological period extending from roughly 5 to 25 million years ago. These Miocene apes appear to have been far more numerous both in species and in absolute numbers than modern apes. That part of the world seems to have been thoroughly infested with them. Some scientists who have studied these fossils think they can discern an ancestral gibbon here and there, but for the most part there are no clear connections between these Miocene apes and modern species. No one has been able to demonstrate the fossil antecedents of the chimpanzee, for example, and until someone does so, we cannot eliminate the possibility that some of the older species now proposed as part of the human lineage actually turned in other directions and became gorillas, orangutans, or chimps. As it is, fossils of previously unknown primates up to 4 million years old are still being found rather regularly, and when this happens, often entire lineages have to be—or should be—reconsidered.

One might think that this situation would provide ample reasons for caution in interpreting new finds of fossil primates. But just the opposite has happened. When it finally sank in that the theory of evolution requires actual physical links between man and some apelike progenitor, many people sensed that this was the most sensational prospect science had yet arrived at. The fame and ancillary benefits awaiting the men who find and announce the crucial links are tremendous, and the lack of a more complete fossil context works in practice so that virtually all contenders can apply.

Even the most farfetched claims extrapolated from the most meager evidence—sometimes no more than a single tooth—have been presented as evidence of man's evolution. If further evidence supporting the ancestral affinities of the species to which the tooth belonged is later found, the tooth expert will be congratulated on his wisdom and keenness of vision. But such extrapolations, which are not at all uncommon in paleoanthropology, are also extremely hazardous, because more often than not, later evidence has embarrassed the expert and his ancestral candidate.

Possibly the most singular such case involved a creature that had been named Hesperopithecus by the discoverers of a solitary molar tooth found in Nebraska in 1922. The tooth, these experts decided, was close enough to man's to signal the presence of one of the legendary missing links. As usual, scientists and artists conspired to reconstruct the full creature, and portraits of the new species, male and female, brutish and slope-browed, were published in the Illustrated London News. With this favorable publicity heightening his significance, Hesperopithecus' tooth was introduced as evolutionary evidence in the Scopes "monkey trial" in Dayton, Tennessee, in 1925. But Hesperopithecus' career as a missing link was short-lived. In 1927 other parts of his skeleton were uncovered, a discovery paleoanthropologists are reluctant to celebrate: The molar had come from an extinct pig.

It has not been just an occasional opportunistic radical who has behaved in this way, but broad reaches of the profession. I am joined in this assessment by Sir Solly Zuckerman, a leading British scientist. Sir Solly complained that with the discovery of almost every new primate fossil the discoverer has attempted to present it as the chief ancestral link between the animals and man. Applying as much sarcasm as is possible in a technical paper, Sir Solly remarked, "It is . . . unlikely that they could all enjoy this distinction. . . ."

There are at least a few other paleoanthropologists who seem sensitive to Zuckerman's point. In recent decades several fossil candidates have been rather quickly shot down or disqualified before they infected too many books or theories and made the profession look even sillier than it did when conjuring man out of a pig's tooth. But it is not unprecedented for many in the profession to lose sight of the distinction between solid science and mere speculation and for years at a time and in millions of copies of books to endorse pivotal interpretations that later turn out to be built upon sand.

III.

Almost everyone interested in anthropology knows the story of Piltdown man. In 1912 a human skull was found by Mr. Charles Dawson in a gravel pit near Piltdown in County Kent, England. The skull, formally named Eoanthropus dawsoni (Dawson's dawn man), looked like that of a modern human being, but its jaw, found nearby, was extremely apelike. These two pieces were estimated to be half a million years old, thus fulfilling the predictions of some scientists who postulated this kind of missing link. They had argued that man's large brain was among the first distinctively human elements to appear and that the brain itself had then led to toolmaking, bipedalism, and the other changes that transformed an ape into a man. In 1915 Dr. A. S. Woodward and Arthur Keith, the two most eminent paleoanthropologists in England, declared that Eoanthropus "represents more closely than any human form yet discovered the common ancestor from which both the Neanderthal and modern types have been derived."

For over forty years the Piltdown skull served as one of the most important evidences of man's evolution from lower primates. For many, it was the most important evidence of this evolution. Then in November 1953 the scientific world was rocked by the news that recently developed dating techniques and other analyses definitely showed that the Piltdown specimen was a hoax.

Some scientists had long been skeptical that the skull and jaw really belonged together. In 1948 a fluorine test was applied to the remains. According to Kenneth P. Oakley, who performed the test, it showed that the skull and jaw were the same age; but he reduced the dating from a previously estimated 500,000 to about 50,000 years. This still did not allay the critics who said that the two parts were incompatible, and in 1953 the entire matter was reinvestigated. This time the fluorine test as well as the recently developed carbon 14 test were employed, and each indicated that the jaw and the rest of the skull were both relatively young. It is now thought that each is about 500 years old. Closer investigation showed that the jaw had belonged to an orangutan. Its teeth had been filed, its joint broken and the whole piece stained to make it appear ancient. Only someone with a knowledge of the issues at stake and considerable expertise in paleontology could have staged this hoax. The discoverer, Dawson, and Teilhard de Chardin, who was assisting in the excavations, have both been suggested as the culprit.

What was especially embarrassing for the profession is not that one of its crazier members should have stooped to manufacturing the evidence, but that so many made so much out of so little. Anthropologist Loren Eiseley's summation of the situation is still relevant:

The amount of subjective speculation indulged in for years over the Piltdown "fossil," and to which many leading authorities contributed, can now be viewed historically as a remarkable case history in self-deception. It should serve as an everlasting warning to science that it is not the theologian alone who may exhibit irrational bias or give allegiance to theories with only the most tenuous basis in fact. That scientists in the early years of a new discipline should have been easily deceived is not nearly so embarrassing as the rapidity with which they embraced the specimen solely because it fell in with preconceived wishes and could be used to support all manner of convenient hypotheses. The enormous bibliography in several languages which grew up around the skull is an ample indication, also, of how much breath can be expended fruitlessly upon ambiguous or dubious materials.

Of course, the Piltdown case is old and oft-repeated news. The author of practically every general book on human evolution still feels compelled to mention it if for no other reason than that Piltdown was so important to evolutionary theory for so long. Many writers also use the incident to illustrate the greater certainty that pertains to contemporary paleoanthropology. Piltdown, they tell us, could never happen again. Modern dating methods and other techniques make it impossible for anyone to replay the Piltdown hoax. From the point of view of faking the fossil evidence, this is probably true. But when it comes to the more important consideration of endorsing and promoting a questionable ancestor on the basis of fossil evidence that, for whatever reason, later turns out to be inadequate, the Piltdown fiasco has happened repeatedly and is being reenacted again today. Piltdown is the most famous instance of "premature conclusions," but it is not the most recent, nor, arguably, even the most important such "case history in self-deception." Consider the following list of species that were all at one time advanced as ancestors of man:

> Hesperopithecus, 1922–27, new evidence
> Gigantopithecus, 1946–50, reconsideration
> Piltdown man, 1912–53, reconsideration
> Zinjanthropus, 1959–64, new evidence
> Australopithecus robustus, 1938–64, new evidence
> Australopithecus africanus, 1924–72, new evidence
> Lothagam man, 1967–77, reconsideration
> Ramapithecus, 1964–79, new evidence

The first date after each species is the year when someone first advanced it as an ancestor to man. In all cases except Ramapithecus this is also the year of its discovery. The second date after each name is the year when its "stage career" as a missing link fizzled. The primary reason for the termination of its career is given as "new evidence" or "reconsideration." In some cases, it was a bit of both. Even now not all paleoanthropologists are willing to give up entirely on all these candidates. The new evidence against Ramapithecus has emerged so recently that it has not yet been fully digested. And some advocates are still hanging onto Australopithecus africanus with both hands—although this is now becoming a minority position. During his forty-eight-year career, some professors became so committed to africanus that it is simply too embarrassing to give him up, despite the new evidence.

Since 1960, no fewer than five ancestral candidates have bitten the dust. Of these, africanus was easily the most important. Judging by the number of professionals who declared that africanus was indeed our animal ancestor, it would seem that this character had become more important to human evolution than Piltdown had ever been. Yet the fact that much of the profession *has* replayed the Piltdown fiasco *without* being hoaxed by fake fossils seems to have gone almost completely unnoticed. And, as I say, this is not the only case.

Examining what was said by way of advertising these failed candidates when they were fashionable and noting the circumstances that brought them down is an interesting story in itself. It also shows the extent to which speculative salesmanship has displaced solid science in this field and provides an invaluable perspective for judging those ancestral candidates that are still on the stage. This is a much shorter list:

> Neanderthal, 1848 and 1856
> Homo erectus, formerly "Java man," "Peking man," 1891
> Homo habilis, 1960
> Australopithecus afarensis and "Lucy," 1974

The year following each species is the first discovery. We will see how very shaky the evidence for these remaining candidates is. Homo habilis is probably the strongest. Australopithecus afarensis, the most recently proposed, is also the weakest and may be said to strike a new low in scientific credibility. None are without problems.

The general plan of the following chapters is to work from those candidates and questions that are most peripheral to those that are most central. In this way we will gradually develop a context clarifying just how mysterious the origin of man actually is—or, to put it more provocatively, why the Texas state school board was quite correct when it required biology textbook publishers to include a statement that evolution is still a theory, and not, as is so widely claimed, an all-embracing fact.

2: Ramapithecus and the Tooth Fairy

I.

HAVING SURVEYED THE TOOLS of the trade and discussed the problem of the larger context, it is now appropriate to say a few words about what it is, exactly, that paleoanthropologists are looking for. Even today scientists speak so loosely about man descending from the apes that it is worth pointing out they do not mean any presently existing apes, but only some theoretical apes who lived long ago. No reputable scientist suggests that the gorillas and chimpanzees of Africa or the orangutans and gibbons of Asia were our ancestors. Louis Leakey stated the common position with respect to the apes in *Adam's Ancestors* (1960):

None of them could ever be regarded as representing a close cousin of man, nor could any of them qualify as representatives of a stage of evolution through which man had passed in his gradual rise to his present position.

The reason the living apes must be ruled out is that they are far too "specialized." Scientists now recognize that the general pattern of change in species is from nonspecialized to specialized forms that have peculiar anatomical and behavioral traits enabling them to enjoy a particular mode of life. The most obvious specialized features of the modern apes are their long arms and the "simian shelf," a bridge of bone joining the two sides of the lower jaw directly behind the front teeth. The simian shelf strengthens the lower jaw, a function performed in modern man by the chin. The long arms, of course, are great for swinging through the trees.

These specializations are not primitive features but relatively recent developments. The Miocene apes discovered by Louis Leakey had short arms and still had not developed a simian shelf, indicating that with respect to these features the apes have been getting progressively less manlike over millions of years.

What most anthropologists do believe is that, somewhere along the way, present-day apes and man shared a common ancestor—a creature who lived millions of years ago, who was different from both man and the present-day apes but from whom both groups descended. While this common ancestor may at first seem slightly less objectionable as parental stock than chimpanzees or gorillas, according to Harvard professor G. G. Simpson, a leading evolutionist, it was still an ape:

Apologists emphasize that man cannot be a descendant of any living ape—a statement that is obvious to the verge of imbecility—and go on to state or imply that man is not really descended from an ape or monkey at all, but from an earlier common ancestor. In fact that common ancestor would certainly be called an ape or monkey in common speech by anyone who saw it.

The same general point is neatly expressed in recent titles such as The Ape Within Us, The Human Animal, and The Naked Ape. And when Stephen Jay Gould, the paleontologist quoted earlier, says that man descended from the apes, he is talking about the same common ancestor as Simpson, not about any living ape.

In demonstrating the descent of man from this ancient ape we need more than a single missing link. As Louis Leakey, perhaps the most quotable authority on such questions, expressed it,

Instead of the popular conception of scientists being engaged in the search for "the missing link" the truth is that whole lengths of the chain are still missing, and often when we do discover one of the many missing links we find it hard to decide just whereabouts in the chain it properly belongs.

We need, then, not only a common ancestor but a chain of forms connecting man and that ancestor. Some scientists think this common ancestor lived as little as 4 or 5 million years ago; others have reason to think he lived in the very remote past—as much as 35 million years ago, or more. The very fact that there is such enormous diversity of opinion on this question indicates how extremely inadequate our knowledge of the overall picture actually is.

II.

The earliest known creature that seems to be a kind of proto-ape is Propliopithecus, an animal who lived 30 or 35 million years ago and was about the size of a domestic cat. Its fossils were found in the desert badlands of the Faiyüm, Egypt. At about 28 million years ago, we have fossils of Aegyptopithecus, a larger creature, about the size of a modern gibbon (15 to 25 pounds), also found in the Faiyüm. Present opinion is that Propliopithecus and Aegyptopithecus were probably ancestors of a large genus known as Dryopithecus (or as the Dryopithecids), consisting of perhaps twenty species varying in size from small chimps to large gorillas. Fossils of these creatures span an era of roughly 20 to 10 million years ago. The usual guess (without secure connecting links, it is no more than a guess) has been that the ancestors of today's apes are to be found somewhere among the Dryopithecids.

Another collection of Miocene apes consisting of species with names like Ramapithecus, Rudapithecus, Sivapithecus, Ouranopithecus, and Gigantopithecus have been lumped in a group called the Ramapithecids. Their fossils cover a period from 18 to 8.5 million years ago.

As might be expected, when we are talking about fossils of this age, we are usually dealing with the merest bits and shards of ancient bone and not with anything even approaching a complete skeleton. The evidence is frequently so fragmentary that people without psychic powers cannot even reliably reconstruct a complete jaw, much less say anything about a general skeletal outline. Surveying this paleontological mash, it is often quite impossible to tell if the species grouped under the Dryopithecid and Ramapithecid labels are really related to each other, much less if there is anything there that could be the hypothetical common ancestor. And even if the fossils were more complete, one might think it would be hazardous in the extreme to put one of these old species in the human lineage when there is a 5-million-year gap between the Ramapithecids and the next proposed ancestor down the line.

But science does not lack its daring young men. As astronomers make mammoth extrapolations from the red shift on their photographic plates to tell us that the universe is expanding at the rate of 660 million miles an hour, attentive paleontologists, after staring for hours at three or four teeth in a row on a couple of pieces of broken jaw, can form in their imaginations the complete lower jaw with the right shape and all the right teeth for the precursor of man.

One can go quite some way with this kind of imagination. An 8-, 10-, or 15-million-year-old precursor of man provides the kernel for a wonderful story that, if scientifically sanctified with enough Latin names and repeated by enough professors, begins to sound as if there were no question who or what man was even in the mists of the Miocene. Paleontologists are as susceptible to a good story as anyone else, and it was by gazing at the denture fragments of Ramapithecus, flashiest member of the Ramapithecids, that Elwyn Simons and David Pilbeam—with a little help from the Tooth Fairy—descried the precursor of man.

Fossils attributed to Ramapithecus have been found in India, China, Europe, and East Africa. Assuming these attributions are correct, it would seem Ramapithecus was widespread. Until recently, all that had been recovered of this creature were bone fragments of its face and jaw. We have no idea if it walked on two or on four legs, or whether it was hairless, sported a sleek black pelt, or was covered with a light purple fuzz.

The jaw fragments had been described as early as 1934 but aroused no real excitement until three decades later, when Simons and Pilbeam concluded that the *assumed* shape of the whole jaw (based on their reconstruction of it from two rather small pieces) and the shape of the known teeth were definitely tending toward those of man. Ramapithecus was then pronounced a hominid and "the oldest probable forerunner of man" (*Anthropology*, vol. 54, 1964). A hominid is an erect, bipedal primate. Modern man is a hominid, and most anthropologists assume that all previous hominids have been either ancestral to man or collateral relatives to man. In his 1964 *Anthropology* paper, "On the Mandible of Ramapithecus," Elwyn Simons wrote,

Ramàpithecus punjabicus is almost certainly man's forerunner of 15 million years ago. This determination increases tenfold the approximate time period during which human origins can now be traced with some confidence.

Since Simons is one of the acknowledged experts on Ramapithecus, this assessment quickly became fashionable and was repeated by many writing anthropologists until very recently. Bjorn Kurten, *The Age of Mammals*, 1972:

The human line itself seems to be represented in Miocene and Pliocene times by the genus Ramapithecus.

J. B. Birdsell, *Human Evolution*, 1975:

There is general agreement that these [Ramapithecus] finds represent a very early type of hominid, primarily based on the dental evidence.

Richard Leakey and Roger Lewin, *Origins*, 1977:

Ramapithecus . . . as far as one can say at the moment . . . is the first representative of the human family—the hominids.

Brace, Nelson, Korn, and Brace, *Atlas of Human Evolution*, 1979:

There is general agreement that Ramapithecus, a derivative of the Dryopithecine complex, is ancestral to *later* ground-dwelling, bipedal, and tool-using creatures; in other words, ancestral to all true hominids including modern humans.

While these and other statements of this tenor were the dominant note struck by most writers on the subject, a few expressed a more cautionary stance. Maitland A. Edey, who in various publications has shown that he is not otherwise remarkable for his caution, wrote in *The Missing Link*, 1972,

On grounds of pure logic, it is tempting to regard Ramapithecus as a sort of proto-Australopithecine [a form long considered by most anthropologists at the time Edey wrote as ancestral to man]; after all, the Australopithecines had to start somewhere. But, however tempting such an idea may be, it is premature. We have no knowledge whatsoever of the nature of the rest of Ramapithecus' body. We do not know what its skull was shaped like or how large its brain was. We know nothing about its hand or foot. We do not know if it stood upright. All we know is that it was a widespread, and therefore presumably successful animal.

And in *From Ape to Adam*, 1972, Herbert Wendt wrote, "Whether Ramapithecus, which some experts think does not really belong to the race of hominids in the narrow sense of the term, was already a tool-maker, we do not know."

This reluctance to claim definitive significance for Ramapithecus has recently been vindicated. The supposedly parabolic and thus human shape imputed to the Ramapithecus jaw was based on a reconstruction from two pieces of upper jaw. Even though these pieces of upper jaw had some hard palate attached, there was no midline indicating the center of the palate. Thus the reconstructed shape, although arrived at by experts and widely accepted by most anthropologists, was in fact purely conjectural.

As described by A. L. Zihlman and J. M. Lowenstein in "False Start of the Human Parade" (*Natural History*, August 1979), the speculative nature of the reconstruction, and everything that had been derived from it, became painfully obvious when the first complete Ramapithecus lower jaw was recently found. This jaw is rather V-shaped, making it unlike either the parabolic-shaped human jaw, or most ape jaws, which have parallel sides. Thus what Pilbeam has given, Pilbeam must now take away:

As I now realize, extinct hominids were not particularly modern. They were not like either living apes or human beings, but instead were unique, distinct animal species. . . . Consequently, Ramapithecus is still important in the story, but it is not the star. (*Natural History*, August 1979)

For a time, Pilbeam believed that Ramapithecus was an ancestor neither of modern humans nor of modern apes. Instead, he suggested, it represented a third lineage that has no living descendants. Then the February 6, 1982, issue of *Science News* added a new twist to the Ramapithecus story. Compiling information from an article in *Nature* (January 21, 1982) and a telephone interview with Pilbeam, *Science News* now has Ramapithecus

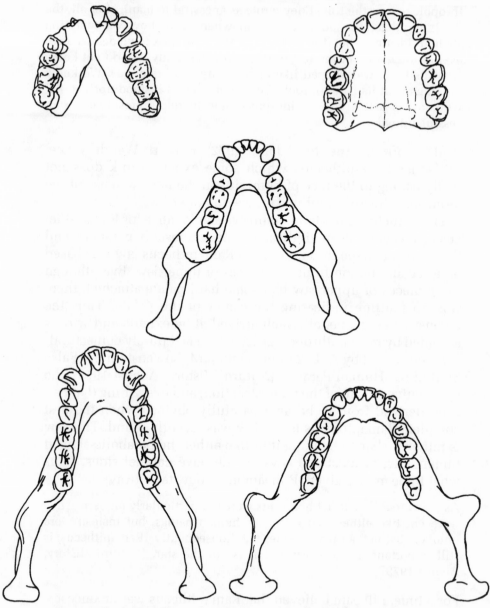

Upper left is the standard reconstruction of the Ramapithecus upper jaw as it appeared in millions of copies of books. Upper right is an upper jaw of Homo sapiens, which the Ramapithecus fragments were made to resemble. Center is the first complete Ramapithecus lower jaw that has been found, which proved to be V-shaped, contrasting with the parallel-sided lower jaw of the chimpanzee (*lower left*) and the parabolic curve of the lower human jaw (*lower right*).

D.E.F. after Zihlman and Lowenstein.

as "part of the orangutan lineage." It seems Pilbeam recently discovered a good portion of an 8-million-year-old Sivapithecus skull in Pakistan. The Sivapithecus specimen turns out to be "nearly identical" to Ramapithecus and has specialized features "identical to those the orangutan has derived from its ape ancestors." The suggestion made in the previous chapter, which was written before this latest development, that some proposed ancestors of man might turn out to be ancestors of apes, is not, then, an idle cavil.

III.

It is no slight matter that Ramapithecus was in the books as our Miocene ancestor for fifteen years before the Tooth Fairy struck on the rebound and transformed him back into a quaint old ape. When respected professionals wrote, as many did, that "there is general agreement" on the relevance of Ramapithecus to man's origin, it naturally affects the opinions of other professionals and of the general public, contributing to the sentiment that human evolution is a proven fact with only certain stages and details to be filled in. As with Hesperopithecus, anthropologists were not victims of fake fossils as they were in the Piltdown case; they were victims of their own imaginations, their willingness to extrapolate sensational conclusions from minimal data and to publish these in the name of science.

Defenders of the tribe will no doubt protest that no one is infallible and that every profession has its share of embarrassments. But we are dealing here with more than an unfortunate minority who imbibe too deeply this heady mixture of enthusiasm and one-sided imagination. If we include not only those who produce the extrapolation but those who swallow it, then it would seem that most of the profession is similarly addicted. At least this is what we must conclude unless anthropology boasts a silent majority, because it is a matter of record that not a few, but *most*, of the ancestors of man endorsed by eminent students over the years have later had to be recalled.

Paleoanthropologists are particularly apt to be mesmerized by teeth and jaw fragments, and it is with respect to such mesmerizations that some of the most blatant infractions of sanity have occurred. Hesperopithecus and Ramapithecus are not the only examples. Around 1946 Franz Weidenreich played the same old tune, this time as a variation on the molars of Gigantopithecus. Before the Second World War the Dutch geologist G. H. R. von Koenigswald bought some giant fossilized molar teeth from apothecary shops in China, thereby saving them from the customary fate in those days of being pulverized and ingested by senior citizens seeking to preserve or enhance their sexual powers. The molars seemed clearly to belong to a primate, but were much larger than those of a gorilla, the largest living ape.

Like some ring imbued with magical powers in the stories of J. R. R. Tolkien, these teeth found their way into the hands of the man who could see the most in them. Weidenreich's earlier promotional campaign on behalf of Peking man bloomed into full success shortly after the war. His stories and articles on the significance of the Peking fossils made him a figure of international recognition. When Weidenreich gazed at the ossified enamel preserved by von Koenigswald, he perceived another missing link, announcing this in *Apes, Giants and Man* (1946). This link presumably stood more than 8 feet tall and weighed over 400 pounds.

The announcement of Gigantopithecus, it must be said, did not provide one of those occasions when most of the profession piled on with hearty support. On the contrary, even among the heaviest extrapolators, the reaction may be summed up as gulping astonishment. Especially in America, Weidenreich's colleagues were still fighting for acceptance of Peking man, a far more humanlike candidate, and soberer things were expected of the man who had done so much to introduce the Peking fossils to the world. Weidenreich's philosophy seemed to be that if one problematic ancestor was selling well, another one would be even better. It didn't matter if the proposed ancestor was two or three times too big or if there were no connections at all between it and anything else: That ossified enamel seemed too enticing to pass over.

But Weidenreich also had been ambushed by the Tooth Fairy. In terms of larger market forces, it was the wrong move at the wrong time: This ancestral model had a shorter run than the Edsel. Of course there are a few lonely souls who still sing the virtues of Gigantopithecus, or Giganthropus as they call him, since they consider the owner of the molars a giant man instead of a giant ape. But most anthropologists regarded the Gigantopithecus proposition as an eccentric afterthought by a great man, and with more recent finds of Gigantopithecus fragments in India and reappraisal by other experts, this creature is now generally ruled out as having anything to do with human evolution and is seen as a giant ground-ape of the later Miocene who left no recognizable descendants.

Yet another example of the Tooth Fairy in action occurred in 1967 on Lothagam Hill in Kenya when Bryan Patterson of Harvard found a piece of lower jaw immured in that eminence. The fragment was dated at 5.5 million years old and was widely presented as "the oldest hominid fossil yet known apart from Ramapithecus." In The Missing Link, Edey wrote,

The Lothagam jaw is . . . a piece of lower jaw with one molar attached. Definitely hominid, it more closely resembles the human jaw . . . than it does any ape jaw.

How Edey could have been so circumspect with Ramapithecus where two pieces of jaw were involved, and so uninhibited with his "definitely hominid" for the Lothagam fossil when only a single small piece was in hand, only he can explain. In any case, ten years after the discovery the Tooth Fairy called in the debt. In June 1977, Current Anthropology announced that new measurements showed the jaw could not have come from an early type of man after all.

These Tooth Fairy episodes not only illustrate an aspect of the profession that is not as well known as it should be, but by noting the cases of Ramapithecus and Lothagam "man" in particular, we have already narrowed our proposed ancestors down to creatures who lived in the last 3.75 million years. There is simply nothing earlier known at present that deserves serious discussion.

IV.

It is appropriate to emphasize, before we move on to the meatier, more recent candidates, that while there are numerous instances when much of the profession has abandoned caution and scientific discipline and become thoroughly beguiled with inadequate or ambiguous evidence, usually one can find at least a few critical voices who are not swept away with premature sensationalism. Harkening back to the Piltdown bones for a moment, we find a singular instance of critical intelligence at work in Louis

Leakey's assessment of them. This is the same Louis Leakey who was none too critical when hawking his own discovery, Zinjan-thropus, but he was a perfect bulwark against Piltdown. Before Piltdown man was exposed as a fraud, Leakey wrote in earlier editions of *Adam's Ancestors* that had the skull been found without the lower jaw it "undoubtedly" would have been con-sidered a form of Homo sapiens itself, not an earlier ancestor. Leakey acknowledged that the bones of the skull were "very thick," but otherwise the skull seemed comparable to the re-mains from Fontechevade and Swanscombe.

Leakey simply couldn't put the skull and the fake lower jaw together. What upset him was that the jaw had a well-developed simian shelf and a large canine tooth. If the jaw and skull really belonged to the same individual, "then Piltdown was unique in all humanity," he wrote. Leakey declared that no other known form of living or extinct human or "near-man" has ever had a simian shelf or such large canines. He also noted that "a number of anatomists" saw the jaw as that of a modern ape and felt that it could not belong to the skull.

Leakey had hoped that when Kenneth Oakley carried out his fluorine tests in 1948 they would show that the skull was a different age from the jaw and canine. But for the moment, it was a vain hope:

His results, however, leave no doubt that not only the skull, but also the jaw and canine tooth are of the same age and belong with the younger fossil fauna of the Piltdown gravels.

Leakey, then, clearly had his doubts. But the second thing to notice is that even he was drawn by Oakley's fluorine test to say that it left "no doubt" that the skull and jaw were real fossils of the same age. Of course, Leakey is not responsible for Oakley's results; and we now know through long experience that dating techniques based on fluorine content or radioactive elements are not 100 percent trustworthy. But Leakey did not know that at the time, and given the test results, it is quite remarkable that he still would not say these pieces belonged to the same creature, nor was he willing to use Piltdown man as evidence for human evolution. Even with those results, he insisted that it was still possible that the jaw and canine tooth did *not* belong to the skull. He said it was easier to believe in the million-to-one chance that the only known ape jaw from the Pleistocene of

Europe just happened to be found with the Piltdown skull, rather than to believe that one type of man—alone in all known human or near-human types—independently evolved "such modern ape-like characters as the simian shelf and a large canine." Later in the same book Leakey wrote,

The Piltdown skull is a problem. The question of whether the jaw and skull belong to the same creature is still an open one, and personally I feel that they do not.

Thus we also see that while many anthropologists are willing to draw tremendous conclusions from the most uncertain materials, and are sometimes able to carry most of their colleagues along with them, the profession also displays a history of producing a few skeptics who may be long neglected and even derided, but who do establish that there are scientific objections to such claims. As it is, these skeptics are really the saviors of the profession. If it were not for them, we would be beleaguered with so many ancestors that man's evolutionary lineage would look like a New Year's crowd at Times Square.

3: Advertisements for an Animal Ancestor

I.

WE NOW COME to the heart of the subject: the chain of proposed links connecting modern man with earlier "near-men" and "ape-men." Moving from the archaic forms toward the present, the standard chain of ancestors now commonly proposed is as follows:

	Usual Estimated Time Range in Years before Present	Cranial Capacity in Cubic Centimeters
Australopithecus	3.75 to 1 million	380–550 cc.
Homo habilis	3 to 1.5 million	600–850 cc.
Homo erectus	1.7 to .1 million	700–1,250 cc.
Neanderthal	100,000 to 30,000	1,100–1,700 cc.
Modern man	100,000 to present	1,000–2,000 cc.

Without this chain, claims made for such creatures as Ramapithecus before his recent return to apehood can be little more
than groundless speculations. It is to this proposed lineage that
the great majority of fossils relevant to man's possible evolution
apply. But even here in the heart of the subject, with far more
evidence available, evolutionists have shown themselves just as
prone to "premature conclusions" as they have when dealing
with scraps of jaws and isolated teeth. Not all paleoanthropologists now propose all these entries as ancestral forms, but most
of the literature on the subject in the last fifteen years mentions
all these, and any comprehensive discussion should deal with
all of them.

In general, the foregoing list displays just the kind of pattern
that many feel argues strongly in favor of human evolution: a
gradual increase in cranial capacity over time as seen in several
grades of creatures. All authorities are agreed that the earliest
appearance of a species in the fossil record is the most crucial of
its dates. No matter how well qualified a proposed missing link
may otherwise be, it obviously cannot be considered a definite
ancestor of another species so long as there is a single genuine
fossil of the second species that is older than the oldest example
of the first. There also has to be sufficient time for one type to
develop from another. To take an extreme example, the discovery of just one well-authenticated 2-million-year-old skull of
modern man would completely demolish the evolutionary significance of all the previous links in the chain. At 2 million
years, such a skull would still not be as old as the oldest Australopithecines, but the morphological gap between them and
man is so great that without a chain of intermediate forms, no
serious person could propose them as direct ancestors.

Even without such a discovery, there are fundamental problems with this proposed evolutionary progression. The great
question is, Are these forms really ancestral to modern man? In
order to consider this question properly, we shall examine each
of these candidates in detail, beginning with Australopithecus.

II.

If Australopithecus is the weakest link in the chain, it is also the
most complex, at least on the surface. Under the genus name

Australopithecus the reader may find as many as five different species listed in contemporary literature. These species are:

> A. africanus
> A. robustus
> A. boisei
> A. africanus/habilis
> A. afarensis

The first example of A. africanus was found by South African anatomist Raymond A. Dart at Taung, South Africa, in 1924. Dart acquired some fossils from workers in a limestone quarry, among them the skull of a five- or six-year-old primate that looked half human and half ape. Indeed, its teeth were quite humanlike, at least as compared with those of apes, and the position of the foramen magnum—the hole on the bottom of the skull through which the spinal cord passes—indicated that the "Taung baby" was possibly bipedal. Yet the skull was clearly not that of a human being. Dart announced that he had found a creature "intermediate between living anthropoids and man," a missing link.

Since it is well known among anatomists that the skulls of juvenile apes are all much more human-looking than those of adults, since Dart then had little other evidence to support his claim (such as an adult of the same species), and since the scientific world was then distracted by Piltdown man and Hesperopithecus, his claim received little attention. But Dart found an ally in Robert Broom, another South African anatomist turned paleontologist. In 1936 Broom found a skull, most of a pelvis, and arm and leg bones of an adult creature of similar type. This find at Sterkfontein, however, seemed dissimilar enough that Broom invented a new species, calling it first Australopithecus transvaalensis, and then changed the genus, so that it became Plesianthropus transvaalensis. Between 1947 and 1962 Dart found more specimens at Makapansgat and named these Australopithecus prometheus, in the mistaken belief that these creatures used fire.

Meanwhile, Broom, and after his death J. T. Robinson, found skulls, teeth, jaws, arm and leg bones, and a pelvis of yet other, heavier creatures at Swartkrans and Kroomdraai. The Swartkrans type was named Paranthropus crassidens, and those at Kroomdraai Paranthropus robustus.

Today, with the perspective that time and further finds have afforded, these five species have been reduced to just two. Australopithecus africanus, Plesianthropus transvaalensis, and Australopithecus prometheus are now all called Australopithecus africanus. The two Paranthropus types are known as Australopithecus robustus.

Africanus has a cranial capacity between 425 and 480 cc. Robustus' is slightly larger, usually around 500 to 525 cc. These figures are not much larger than those for chimpanzees, and while the evidence for bipedalism was interesting, the Australopithecines long suffered from a great disability: Because of the situation in which they were found, they could not be accurately dated. Broom guessed that they might be 2 million years old, but at the time this seemed incredible to most anthropologists.

It was not until 1959 when Mary and Louis Leakey found a very similar creature at Olduvai Gorge in East Africa under layers of volcanic ash that *could* be dated, that paleoanthropologists began to look at the Australopithecines in a new light. The Leakeys found a skull that they christened Zinjanthropus boisei. It had a cranial capacity of 530 cc. and dated to 1.75 million years. The Leakeys had been working in East Africa since 1935 and, in the same strata that yielded Zinjanthropus, had found many chipped stones that could conceivably have been used as simple tools. It was thus presumed that these were made by Zinjanthropus, and since anthropological custom at the time extended the title of man to any hominid capable of making tools, Louis Leakey presented this fossil as not only a "true" man, but "the earliest known stone-tool-making man."

As with Hesperopithecus and others, this initial glow of great significance quickly evaporated. It is interesting that in *Olduvai Gorge* (1979), Mary Leakey describes her husband's immediate reaction of extreme disappointment when the Zinjanthropus skull first came to light. He recognized it as another variety of Australopithecus, she says, a creature he had earlier concluded was already too specialized to be an ancestor of man. Yet somehow Zinjanthropus was presented to the world as the oldest known "true" man.

Twenty years later virtually no one believes this, not even the Leakeys. It seems the attribution of "toolmaking" to Zinjanthropus was premature. The simple pebble tools are now attributed to higher forms that have since been discovered in the same deposits. Today Zinjanthropus has been reclassified as Australopithecus boisei, just the sort of classification appropriate to Louis' initial judgment of this creature. Boisei is a heavier and somewhat more specialized type of robustus, and some doubt that it even deserves its own species label, concluding that boisei and robustus are basically the same creature. Not surprisingly, robustus has received much the same evaluation as boisei. Both had a sagittal crest—a ridge of bone running front to back across the top of the skull—a highly specialized feature now found in male gorillas and some male chimpanzees that serves to anchor massive jaw muscles. This feature is never found in man. Today there is a very broad consensus among anthropologists that both boisei and robustus were dead ends that became extinct about a million years ago.

But even though Zinjanthropus (or Australopithecus boisei) proved a washout as a missing link, his discovery and relatively firm dating did have the effect of focusing anthropological attention on the long-neglected Australopithecines from South Africa. Suddenly it was apparent they could be as much as 2 million years old, and when 1.7-million-year-old specimens of A. africanus were subsequently discovered in datable deposits in East Africa's Great Rift Valley, africanus became the rage as the oldest missing link.

Before we examine the history of the controversy over africanus, it remains to say something about A. africanus/habilis and A. afarensis. The designation africanus/habilis is not significantly different from africanus except that those who use it mean to indicate that they consider those specimens that are called Homo habilis to be simply larger forms of africanus and undeserving of the appellation Homo. Since I shall discuss Homo habilis on its own merits, africanus/habilis need not detain us here.

A. afarensis, found by Donald C. Johanson in 1974, is so named because many fossils of this creature were discovered in the Afar region of Ethiopia. Others have been found at Laetoli in Tanzania. The pelvic and leg bones of afarensis indicate he probably walked erect. His brain capacity was only about 400 cc., but given his stature of about 4 feet, it was fairly large for his body size. Afarensis' chief claim to fame is that he is currently dated at 3.75 million years old, the oldest hominid known. Afarensis is said by Johanson to be the ancestor of two distinct lineages, giving rise to africanus and robustus in one direction, and to Homo habilis, Homo erectus, and modern man in another—a highly dubious proposition. Afarensis' relevance to the origin of man is best discussed after we have examined the illuminating story of africanus.

III.

It is easy to see why africanus became widely acclaimed as an important missing link—once it was realized that he dated to at least 1.7 million years. The shape of his jaw, the size and shape of his teeth, even the pattern of tooth wear were all said by various experts to be closer to human characteristics than those of apes. Not only the way his skull sat on his backbone but his pelvic and leg bones indicated to some paleoanthropologists that he probably walked erect. And although there is still controversy on this point, several investigators were convinced that africanus made tools, while others suggested he may have at least used stones, sticks, and bones as tools, even if there was no certainty he "made" implements by altering natural forms.

As we saw with Ramapithecus, the opinions and announcements of "experts," especially those favorable to the general evolutionary hypothesis, quickly became fashionable throughout the profession. As a result, africanus reigned for over a decade as our animal ancestor. Recently, he has been displaced by the discovery of an older, more developed being, with the result that there is now a major revolution taking place in paleoanthropology. In order to appreciate the scale and depth of this revolution, let us note some representative opinions about Australopithecus africanus that were written before 1973. (When writers speak loosely of "Australopithecus" in the following quotes, it is basically africanus they are referring to.)

Ernst Mayr, "Darwin and the Evolutionary Theory in Biology," 1959:

... it is not necessary to consider a form like Australopithecus with its mosaic of human and anthropoid [ape] characteristics as an aberrant sidebranch. A mixture of primitive and advanced characters may occur in any phyletic line. Australopithecus could be directly in the line of human ancestry or at least near it.

Four different "artistic reconstructions" of Australopithecus africanus derived from the literature. Their incredible variety, ranging from practically human to thoroughly apelike, demonstrates the arbitrary and unscientific nature of such images.   *W.R.F.*

S. L. Washburn, "Tools and Human Evolution," 1960:

From the evolutionary point of view, behavior and structure form an interacting complex, with each change in one affecting the other. Man began when populations of apes, about a million years ago, started the bipedal, tool-using way of life that gave rise to the man-apes of the genus Australopithecus.

Kenneth P. Oakley, "Dating the Emergence of Man," 1961:

There no longer seems any reasonable doubt that the African australo-pithecines were hominids, that some of them made tools according to a definite tradition, and, therefore, although small-brained, were "men" in the sense of regular tool-makers.

The evolving hominids were distinguished from the pongids or typical apes by their dentition and by their ability to walk habitually on two feet, but there must have been some threshold at which their mental attributes became "human" as generally understood.

Oakley then explained that this threshold used to be thought of as simply the average brain-size expanding to a certain volume, such as 750 cc. or 900 cc. But Oakley favored tool-making itself as the threshold at which apes became men, and since he did not question the suggestions that Australopithecus made tools he had no difficulty concluding that this was man's ancestor.

F. Clark Howell, *Early Man*, 1965:

Between 1961 and 1963 further finds had permitted a view of the over-all picture that shapes up something like this: Paranthropus [now called A. robustus] did not change. Australopithecus did. Furthermore, he evolved quite rapidly. He started off small, but in half a million or a million years he was appreciably larger and more man-like. In still another half-million years, according to the latest evidence from a series of remains found at various levels in Olduvai, he had become a man. He apparently is our ancestor.

Indeed, in Howell's "chain of ascent" he shows Australopithecus as a direct ancestor of Homo sapiens.

Ashley Montagu, in *Man: His First Two Million Years* (1969), is slightly uncertain whether the Australopithecines should be considered "the first men" or directly ancestral to Homo sapiens, but suggests, in effect, that they probably were. Over the section in his book dealing with the Australopithecines, Montagu puts a question: "The Earliest Men—The Australopithecines?" Montagu acknowledges that

they are in most respects apelike, except that their brain capacity is larger and that their hipbones and the bones of the thigh (femur), leg (tibia and fibula), and foot are manlike.

He points out that "the skull form of all australopithecines is extremely apelike."

But the fact is that the australopithecines do exhibit many manlike traits, which without doubt place them within the genus of man. The teeth, for example, are more like those of human beings than those of any other known creature. So are the bones of the lower extremity and the hip.

Montagu states categorically, "the australopithecines also used the limb bones of antelopes as implements," but indicates that some authorities do not agree with this conclusion. Despite his reservations, according to Montagu the Australopithecines are directly relevant to the evolution of man.

Thus now, for the first time, we have clear evidence of the order of the functional evolution of some of the parts of the human body. The erect posture was attained before the brain evolved to a large size. Some authorities used to think that it was the other way around. Now we know with certainty that man's ancestors stood erect first, before their brains increased in size.

Clifford D. Simak, *Prehistoric Man*, 1971:

The australopithecines made and used tools. It is doubtful that they had fire. Claims have been made that they did, but the evidence is shaky. They ran in hunting packs and were a noisy lot. . . .

We do know that two different types of australopithecines evolved. One of them, Australopithecus robustus, a larger primate than Australopithecus africanus, took a wrong turning of an evolutionary path and wound up extinct. His smaller cousins, according to present evidence, evolved into men.

The record, of course, is far from clear. In addition to Australopithecus, there may have been many other groups of men or creatures that were very close to men. And while there even now may be some controversy as to whether the australopithecines were or were not men, there came a time, perhaps a million years ago or so, when one, or several branches of australopithecines finally evolved into creatures that undeniably were men. We call this new creature Homo erectus.

Bjorn Kurten, *The Age of Mammals*, 1972:

. . . Australopithecus was still quite primitive. The average braincase volume was about 450 c.c., which is nearly the same as in the gorilla, and one-third of that in modern man (about 1350 c.c.).

In spite of his shortcomings as regards brain volume (and, perhaps, manual dexterity) Australopithecus fashioned various kinds of stone and bone tools; it is only at the oldest site (Omo) that the artifacts are definitely missing. His so-called pebble culture, of which the Oldowan is a good example, features pebbles from which one or a few flakes have been chipped off to produce a working edge—very likely used to cut up the game animals that he killed for food. At Olduvai he also erected small circular stone shelters. . . .

At Olduvai . . . both [africanus and robustus] have been found at early levels dated at about 1.75 million years. In the middle Pleistocene, however, only A. robustus survived. It is thought that A. africanus had vanished at that time because it had already given rise to more advanced forms of man, present in the middle Pleistocene both at Olduvai and Swartkrans.

Maitland A. Edey, *The Missing Link*, 1972. On the front of the dustjacket, this book is advertised as "The Fascinating Story of Australopithecus, Man's Animal Ancestor." After some introductory remarks, Edey asks,

Does Australopithecus qualify as the missing link? In the sense that it appears to lie in the shadow land between man and ape, yes, it does. But Australopithecus comes in more than one model, and the names that scientists give those models have changed in the past and may change again—reflecting the confusing ways that one model dissolves gradually into another over a period of time.

So for the moment it will be prudent to defer the pinning of a final missing-link label on anything. Instead, now that we have Australopithecus roughly located in space (Africa) and in time (about two million years ago), let us take a look at this creature, bearing in mind that the following description is highly tentative. Some conclusions about its habits and appearance are better than others; none are undisputed.

Edey then speculates on Australopithecus' life-style. Toward the end of these descriptions he says, "Where Australopithecines went at night is not known." He discusses possibilities and then says, "Whatever they did, they survived, because I am here to talk about them. My ancestors." Becoming prudent again, he then qualifies these remarks:

This preceding thumbnail sketch of Australopithecus is concise and clear enough. But is it true? That is a very large question that cannot be answered satisfactorily by simply lining out a confident description. There must be some proof in the form of arguments to back up that description, particularly since parts of it are given with more assurance than others. Awkward questions arise.

For Edey these questions include problems with dating the fossils, how we can tell manlike from apelike characteristics when we have nothing but teeth to work with, why anthropologists posit an ape-to-man evolution in the first place, and what influences propelled some apes in the direction of man. Edey offers the usual fabric of evidence and reasoning to answer these questions, and then concludes that hominids

had evolved into two or three different kinds by about five million years ago. One kind continued to evolve, producing a better brain and a primitive culture. These developments enabled him to exterminate his relative about a million years ago. He has lived in solitary supremacy on earth ever since.

The hominid that continued to evolve was, of course, A. africanus. This is made clear by an illustration Edey offers, showing the evolution of man from ape. We should note that Edey does not separate africanus from the larger but similar form that had been first discovered in the early '60s and which some had labeled Homo habilis. When constructing the line of descent connecting ape and man, Edey uses the designation Australopithecus africanus/habilis, which leads to Homo erectus, Neanderthal, and modern man. But by virtue of the fossil evidence Edey cites in defining africanus/habilis, it is clear that he is basically talking about africanus. He uses the skull of "Mrs. Ples," a well-known africanus skull discovered by Robert Broom in South Africa, as his example of this species. And so, despite occasional reservations, Edey offers a conclusion that is more or less as advertised: Australopithecus africanus is man's animal ancestor.

Finally, let us briefly note B. J. Williams' assessment in *Evolution and Human Origins*, published in 1973, but written earlier:

Whatever the interpretation attached to the gracile (africanus) versus robust forms, it appears certain that the genus Australopithecus is hominid and ancestral to modern man.

It is also noteworthy that in Jacob Bronowski's *The Ascent of Man* (1973), one of those works that attempts to apply evolutionary principles supposedly illustrated by paleontology to the wider stage of man's culture and science, it is Australopithecus that is cited as man's proven link with the animal kingdom.

The authors of these opinions range from a popularizer (Simak) to some of the most respected authorities in the field (Mayr, Oakley, Washburn). It is obvious from these quotations that africanus was taken very seriously, and again we see how prone many writers on man's origin are to tell us there is no reasonable doubt about matters that are thoroughly questionable. Similar assessments could be quoted at great length, and rather than just one school of thought among many, it is fair to say that for a considerable time the consensus among the great majority of paleoanthropologists—especially in the U.S.A.—

was that Australopithecus africanus was indeed a crucial link in man's ancestry.

Certainly, had one studied anthropology at an American university in the late '60s or early '70s, he would have been handed that conclusion on a platter. By then africanus was more secure and more important than Piltdown ever was. The rotund affirmations that africanus used primitive tools and the consequent assumption that this made him a fledgling man are particularly interesting. In *African Genesis* (1961) it was from this assumption that dramatist Robert Ardrey conflated africanus into the Killer Ape, the First Murderer, an image that achieved sufficient publicity to be incorporated into the opening scene of that epic of the silver screen, *2001: A Space Odyssey.*

But was the attribution of toolmaking really secure, or did it rest largely on the same kind of assumption Louis Leakey fell prey to with Zinjanthropus? Was the ancestral status of africanus really demonstrated knowledge, or merely science by assertion?

4: Sir Solly's Reservations

I.

NOT ALL PALEOANTHROPOLOGISTS rushed to embrace Australopithecus africanus as man's ancestor. The great French scientist Marcellin Boule, one of the world's foremost experts on fossil men, fully acknowledged the importance of africanus to the general problem of how man may have evolved, but, in characteristic fashion, distanced himself from hard-and-fast conclusions.

It cannot be denied that the fundamental human characteristic, that is the great development of the brain, the basis of all our psychological evolution, was never fulfilled in them. Human as they are in their dentition and posture, the Australopithecinae are none the less apes in terms of their brain. (*Fossil Men*, 1957)

It was clear to Boule that whatever the connection between man and these creatures, it was not a case of the Australopithecines evolving en masse into a higher species: "It seems, in any case, that the last of the Australopithecinae were contemporary with man." Rather than man's animal progenitor, Boule thought it equally likely that "Far from being our ancestors, these primates may only have been . . . 'Man's less evolved cousins.' "

As mentioned earlier, Louis Leakey was another who contested Australopithecus as an ancestor of man. In the 1953 edition of *Adam's Ancestors*—well before the later discoveries that disqualified the Australopithecines—Leakey indicated that there were signs in the bones themselves that pointed to the same conclusion. Leakey noted the interpretation that what the Australopithecine fossils represented was the persistence of a side branch of a stage through which man passed. In other words, in this interpretation man did not come directly from the South African Australopithecines discovered by Dart, Broom, and others, but rather came from an earlier generation of the same stock. Millions of years earlier, the stock supposedly divided, with one stem evolving further into man, while the other remained mostly unchanged. It continued to survive, however, and eventually produced the South African fossils.

Even this generous interpretation, which gives africanus much more time to become human, did not prove credible for Leakey. He felt it took too little account of the fact that africanus (as he is now called) and the other Australopithecines have a number of peculiar characteristics very strongly suggesting "overspecialization" in directions not leading to man. Among such specializations he included the strange flattening of the face, the height of the eye-sockets above the level of the root of the nose, the shape of the "external, orbital angles," and the forward position of the root of the cheek-bone process. Like Boule, Leakey chose the term "cousins," rather than "ancestors," to describe the Australopithecines' relation to man.

II.

In 1954, in a rather technical paper entitled "Correlation of Change in the Evolution of Higher Primates," Sir Solly Zuckerman subjected the Australopithecine fossils to the most critical and detailed examination I have yet found in print. Australopithecus supporters claimed that this candidate had thought like a man, chewed like a man, stood like a man, and walked like a man. On all these points Zuckerman came to conclusions that were quite opposite to those that became so widely repeated among American anthropologists. I quote Zuckerman at length because his criticisms represent not merely a conservative opinion but the results of detailed studies based on the actual evidence. His analysis is especially interesting because, like the comments of Boule and Leakey, it was made well before those numerous affirmations cited earlier. Any professional worthy of the name should have been well acquainted with these criticisms before the Australopithecus fad bloomed in the '60s. The reader will see that there were many scientifically sound reasons to doubt africanus' connection with man.

In his introduction Zuckerman made a general observation that is as true now as it was on the day it was written:

... the number of fragments of fossil hominoid bones that have been described, although relatively small, has increased fairly rapidly in the past thirty years. Against this we have to reckon that the evaluation of most of these remains has been embroiled in much controversy. Here the fundamental difficulty has been that in the great majority of cases the descriptions of the specimens that have been provided by their discoverers have been so turned as to indicate that the fossils in question have some special place or significance in the line of direct human descent, as opposed to that of the family of apes. It is so unlikely that they could all enjoy this distinction that, in the circumstances, an outside observer might well imagine that an enterprising anatomist would find little difficulty in substantiating a claim that an artificially fossilized skeletal fragment of any one of the living great apes had a greater relevance to the story of man's evolution than to that of the skeleton of which it was a part.

Zuckerman emphasized that, "from the point of view of scientific method and logic," claims for the evolutionary significance of Australopithecus had, in general, been overstated:

Views on phylogeny [the evolutionary lineage of organisms] are never more than inferences, drawn in the light of the geological timescale. . . . The inferences are sometimes very insecurely based because of inadequacies of the evidence. . . . But whatever the inferences, in the final analysis it is the anatomical evidence which counts. . . . No single part of it is given greater factual substance, merely by the frequent repetition of some phylogenetic idea which it is held to support.

The lack of accepted criteria by which to judge the hominid nature, or otherwise, of "borderline" features in bones makes the whole position very difficult. For this reason it is every bit as justifiable for Wood Jones to emphasize the lack of a premaxillary suture in man, and its presence in the Australopithecinae, as implying the absence of a close evolutionary connection between the two, as it is for others to illustrate an opposite view by reference to certain Australopithecine dental features. . . . It is almost always possible to derive from the same anatomical material patterns pointing to different conclusions—for example, one set of characters in a fossil bone suggestive of a hominid, and another of a pongid [ape] affinity.

Zuckerman then analyzed the Australopithecine fossils to see if they showed

(1) the development of a brain of human shape and proportions; (2) a decrease in the size of the teeth and of the face, with the associated changes in the curvature of the dental arcade; (3) evidence of an upright posture, with the appropriate dimensional relations of limb and trunk.

These points were crucial because

This three-fold pattern of physical change is necessarily presupposed by the belief that man is descended from a non-human primate—however many other specifically hominid features of a less obvious kind may also have evolved in the process.

Investigators proposing Australopithecus as a link between ape and man had made casts of the inside of Australopithecine skulls, in an attempt to study the fissures and convolutions of its brain. (Such casts are called endocranial casts.) They claimed that Australopithecus' brain was virtually human, but Zuckerman strongly challenged this conclusion:

In their general shape the endocranial casts of the Australopithecinae . . . do not appear to diverge in any material way from existing apes, nor do their surface markings provide any reason for supposing that there were any differences from the apes in the fissural pattern of the brains of these creatures—regardless of claims to the contrary by Broom and Schepers (1946) and by Broom, Robinson and Schepers (1950). This view is securely based on the results of several studies, all of which have shown that there is very little correlation between the fissures and gyri of the brain and the markings on related endocranial casts.

Zuckerman then cites seven different studies that show that there is no such correlation:

Weidenreich (1948) has underlined the tenuous nature of these claims (as also has Connolly). He quotes Schepers' statement that the area around the sylvian fissure, which in man forms "the neural basis for vocal and manual dexterity alike," is well developed in Australopithecus. From this Schepers infers that the Australopithecines "must have been virtually true human beings, no matter how simian their external appearance may have remained." Here, as Weidenreich indicates, we have the complete *reductio ad absurdum*. The Australopithecinae must have been hominids even if their morphology reveals them as apes.

Even Weidenreich, we see, could be quite critical of fossils in which he did not have a personal interest. Zuckerman continues:

Once we leave the field of speculation . . . there is no reason to believe that the Australopithecinae did possess human brains. . . . As scientists, therefore, we have to dismiss as groundless such arguments about the hominid status of these creatures as have been based upon the internal conformation of the cranial cavity.

Zuckerman knew, of course, that there was more to Australopithecus than his brain, and he was not averse to the idea that in his other features this creature may indeed have been a missing link.

The fact that the Australopithecinae had the brains of apes, which is the safest inference we can make from the facts now available, does not, however, preclude the possibility that they are "missing links" in our own evolutionary lineage, or, as Le Gros Clark (1949) has suggested, the "little modified survivors of such an ancestral stock." For as students of human evolution have always realized—even if only as speculation—man may not have evolved in an orderly way, all bodily features becoming less monkey- or ape-like, and more human, in a regular gradation. The big brain may have come after the upright attitude.

Zuckerman then examined the creature's other features, beginning with the jaws and face:

It is unnecessary here to enter into any detail about the relative size of the teeth and face of the Australopithecinae. For whatever qualitative differences there may be between certain of their dental features and the corresponding ones of existing apes, it is a fact that with the exception of their incisors and canines, the size and general shape of the jaws and teeth of these animals were very much more like those of the living apes than like acknowledged members of the Hominidae, either living or extinct (Ashton and Zuckerman, 1952a; Zuckerman, 1952). There is, indeed, no question which the Australopithecine skull resembles when placed side by side with specimens of human and living ape skulls. It is the ape—so much so that only detailed and close scrutiny can reveal any differences between them. In saying this, no more is being stated here than has been admitted by Le Gros Clark (1950) and Gregory (1949), both staunch adherents of the view that the Australopithecinae are phylogenetically more closely related to man than the apes, and both of whom describe the jaws of these animals as massive and projecting. . . .

The jaws and face of the Australopithecinae, like the brain, thus provide no obvious sign of the major changes in the evolutionary transformation of some monkey-like creature to manhood.

III.

What, then, about the oft-repeated claims that africanus had an upright posture? Zuckerman went over the evidence piece by piece. It was the position of the foramen magnum that first led Dart to claim that the Australopithecines were erect, because he believed it was further forward than in the apes. Here Zuckerman simply noted an earlier study by Keith:

Keith (1931) pointed out, however, that Dart was comparing the position of the foramen magnum in the Taung skull—that of an infant in which only the first molar of the permanent dentition had as yet appeared—with that in adult apes and adult man. When the comparison is properly made between skulls in the same stage of growth, the Taung skull, according to Keith, "takes its place in the anthropoid, not in the human series. . . ."

Next there was a fragment of a femur (thighbone) attributed to Plesianthropus (now A. africanus) that Broom, Schepers, and Le Gros Clark said "shows a resemblance to the femur of Homo which is so close as to amount to practical identity." Again, Zuckerman could point to the studies of other researchers:

Against this we have the findings of Straus (1948) and Kern and Straus (1949), who submitted the data to a somewhat more detailed analysis than was published either by Broom or Le Gros Clark. . . . The fragment of femur was found to be "definitely not great-ape," in its morphology. "At the same time it is not peculiarly or exclusively hominid, for it resembles man and the cercopithecid monkey in about equal degree. . . . Its characters in *toto*, therefore, no more betoken an erect, bipedal posture than they do a pronograde quadrupedal posture."

When it came to the pelvis, the evidence for an upright posture was so ambiguous that even Broom, Robinson, and Schepers did not claim otherwise:

The main feature in which the Australopithecine ilium [the uppermost of the three sections of the hipbone] resembles the human rather than the ape is in its breadth and shortness. This is taken to imply a significantly different gluteal musculature [buttocks] than is found in apes, which in turn is taken to mean that the animals walked upright. Robinson (1950) however points to two features in which the Australopithecine innominate [hipbone] differs from the human innominate bone. . . . In these characters, he observes, the Australopithecine innominate resembles that of the ape, but he suggests that these features "may simply indicate incomplete adaption to an erect gait." Other features in which the human and Australopithecine innominate differ are described by Broom, Robinson and Schepers (1950) who, in concluding their account of the orientation of the Plesianthropus bone, wrote that in this respect the ilium is "almost that of man, but that the pubis and ischium [lowermost of the three sections of the hipbone] resemble more those of the chimpanzee."

It has become customary to treat the different kinds of evidence that have been adduced in support of the view that the Australopithecines walked upright as interdependent, and to counter-balance any deficiencies in one by reference to the indications provided by another. So it is that [though] Robinson (1950) can suggest that the innominate bone of the Australopithecines is ape-like, reference to the structure of the base of the skull . . . indicates that we are nevertheless dealing with a creature that walked upright.

Zuckerman questioned whether this was a legitimate practice and turned his attention to indices based on detailed measurements in order to determine how the Australopithecine skull was balanced on the spinal column. Two indices showed the skull was within the human range in this respect, but the third and most important "is very much closer to the range for the sub-human primates than for the three human types studied." "The obvious conclusion from all the evidence is that if Plesianthropus did stand upright, its head was balanced as in apes rather than as in man." This conclusion, Zuckerman said, "cannot . . . stand on the basis of this evidence alone," because the total body of evidence had to be considered; but it "hardly supports the inferences about posture that have been drawn from the nature of the innominate bones."

On the contrary ... they actually suggest that the Australopithecine head was carried as it is in a quasi-quadrupedal animal, such as the gorilla and chimpanzee.

IV.

Zuckerman was particularly interested in the claim by Le Gros Clark and Robinson that in the Australopithecines the crowns of the molar teeth "became quickly ground down to an almost flat surface as they are in man, indicating that the movements of the jaws in chewing were similar to those of the human jaw." This was an area in which Zuckerman himself had special expertise. This claim, he said, was based on the belief "that man is able to grind his teeth by rotary movements of the jaw, whereas in the ape, movement is practically restricted to the vertical plane [up and down], and to antero-posterior [back and forth] movement, because of the locking action of the large canines." But this belief rested upon a fragile theoretical basis:

Almost all statements that contrast the manner of dental attrition in man and apes have been based upon theoretical appreciations of the movements of which the mandibles [jaws] are capable in dried skulls (e.g. Marston, 1952). In order to see whether there are any differences in the order and way the teeth wear an analysis . . . has been made of the order of appearance of the facets of wear on all the teeth in the skulls of about 500 gorillas, chimpanzees and human skulls.

Tooth by tooth, Zuckerman takes the reader through the results of this exhaustive study. The result is that the pattern of tooth wear in man and apes is found to be virtually identical:

The remarkable similarity in the order of appearance and coalescence of facets of wear in the teeth of apes and men, and in the final results of the process of attrition, can only mean that if wear in man is due to a capacity to "grind" the premolar and molar teeth, then the ape is able to do the same. This conclusion will not be surprising to those who have studied living apes, for it is a matter of simple observation that chimpanzees, gorillas and orangutans chew their food in the same way that we do. . . .

It follows from all this that if the teeth of . . . any . . . member of the Australopithecinae became worn in the human fashion, they, *ipso facto*, also became worn in the same way as an ape's teeth.

With these other claims for Australopithecus' human features disposed of, Zuckerman returned to further consideration of the hipbones, since these then carried the whole weight of the argument that this creature walked erect. He describes a detailed study by "Mr. J. Williams, working in my Department" based on "thirty-three main dimensions" of the hipbones:

They showed clearly that in the bulk of their biometric characters, the Australopithecine bones resemble those of the ape, and particularly the orang, far more than they do the human. . . .

In short, the evidence for an erect posture, as derived from a study of the innominate bones, seems anything but certain.

Finally, he concludes,

The answer to the question . . . whether the characteristics of the Australopithecinae conform either with the whole or a large part of the pattern of change that must have occurred during the transformation to manhood of a nonhuman primate is thus, in general, negative.

V.

Zuckerman and Leakey wrote before the discovery of Australopithecine remains in East Africa and their relatively firm dating of africanus to 1.7 million years, but none of these subsequent discoveries offered secure evidence that overruled their studies. The wave of enthusiasm for africanus as a missing link that followed the East African discoveries seems to be attributable to the notion that it is easier to make an old ape into a missing link than a more recent one, because we have more time to allow him to assume the human shape. The assumption that africanus was responsible for the extremely primitive chipped pebbles sometimes found "in association" with his fossils also played a part. This almost invariably led to another assumption, namely that any creature who could so much as smash two stones together to remove a flake or two was by definition on the road to becoming man. Of course, both assumptions are highly questionable, and were so at the time. But given the peculiar atmosphere in the scientific community where American academics in particular seem to regard it as an intellectual duty to endorse human evolution, and given the volatile and trendy nature of the literary marketplace, it only takes one or two well-published "authorities" to jump to an unwarranted conclusion, and soon it is repeated everywhere, and a new "orthodoxy" has arisen.

The nature of this problem is considerably illuminated by the realization that it is nowhere more acute than in the United States, where, of course, evolutionists are reacting—or over-reacting—to the pressure exerted by the creationists. The reader will notice, for example, that the three substantial dissenting voices I have quoted are all non-American, belonging to a Frenchman, a Kenyan, and a Briton.

If it is a fair comment, as Zuckerman himself acknowledged, that some of the evidence regarding africanus could be argued either way, it is also a fair comment that the vast majority of writing paleoanthropologists who influence professional and public opinion in the U.S. chose the most speculative of these options. And then, forgetting that these speculations were pro-visional at best, they often went on to pronounce the ancestral status of africanus in the most declarative terms. Typically, this conclusion then served as a foundation for yet more specula-tions, which, in service of the ape-to-man hypothesis, painted imaginary scenarios of africanus' life-style based on inferences drawn from the behavior of chimpanzees and the hunting and gathering peoples of Africa.

What the testimony of Leakey and Zuckerman in particular indicates is that there was nothing so overwhelmingly persua-sive in the total body of evidence concerning africanus as to compel paleoanthropologists to endorse this creature as our ancestor. Whatever compulsion they felt to head in this direc-tion derived more from that same uncritical and unscientific "enthusiasm" that gave us Hesperopithecus, Zinjanthropus, and Ramapithecus than from anything that was actually known. And as it turned out, it was only a matter of time before this doubtful ancestor was also exposed as yet another embarrassing case, in which the specimen had been embraced "solely because it fell in with preconceived wishes and could be used to support all manner of convenient hypotheses."

5: Showdown at Koobi Fora

I.

THE PRESENTATION of Australopithecus africanus as our animal ancestor would probably have continued unabated to the present day were it not for two major discoveries made in East Africa in 1972 and 1975. Both were made by Richard Leakey's team headquartered at Koobi Fora on the eastern shore of Lake Turkana in Kenya. Of the two, the 1972 find is the more important —one of the most important discoveries, in fact, in the history of paleoanthropology.

In ancient sedimentary deposits east of Lake Turkana (formerly Lake Rudolf), Bernard Ngeneo of the Leakey team found a shattered skull in August 1972 that took weeks to reconstruct. The reconstructed skull was highly remarkable in several respects. It has a large cranial capacity of about 800 cc., far above the range of Australopithecine skulls. Even more surprising is its shape—the cranium is high-domed, with nearly vertical sides as in modern man, and the forehead is not nearly as receding as most other ancient "near-men." Nor, like Homo erectus and Neanderthal, usually presented as man's closest evolutionary forerunners, does it have massive browridges above its eyes. Instead its browridges are moderate and much closer to those of modern man.

These attributes are especially significant in light of its age. The lake sediments in which this skull was found were interspersed with layers of volcanic tuff (ash and dust), which could be dated by the potassium-argon method. Jack Miller, of England's University of Cambridge, and Frank J. Fitch, of Birkbeck College in London, dated a critical ash layer known as the KBS tuff at about 2.6 million years. Since the skull was found beneath the KBS tuff, it had to be even older, probably 2.8 or 2.9 million, over a million years older than the oldest Australopithecine skull then known.

Richard Leakey's immediate assessment of this skull appeared in *National Geographic* in June 1973: "Either we toss out this skull or we toss out our theories of early man. . . . It simply fits no previous models of human beginnings." Leakey said the skull "leaves in ruins the notion that all early fossils can be arranged in an orderly sequence of evolutionary change. It appears that there were several different kinds of early man, some of whom developed larger brains earlier than had been supposed." The skull is indeed so unusual that Leakey did not at first designate a species name for it, but simply assigned it to the genus Homo (man). In *Origins* (1977), however, he tells us that there is every reason to classify it as Homo habilis. The skull is usually known as "1470," its registration number in the National Museums of Kenya.

The dating of 1470 at 2.8 million years not only wrecked the proposed ancestral status of africanus, but, as Leakey indicated, seriously upset the rest of evolutionary theory applied to man. Even the status of Homo erectus, the most secure and important link in the evolutionary chain, was seriously jeopardized, because the oldest erectus skull then known was only about one million years old, and 1470 looks more advanced than Homo erectus.

Not surprisingly, some evolutionists complained that 1470 could not possibly be 2.8 million years old. When challenged, Miller and Fitch reran their potassium-argon test and this time arrived at 2.4 million years for the KBS tuff. However, this still did not allay certain critics of the dating, among them Basil Cooke, an expert on biostratigraphy—the art of dating strata by the type of fossils found in them. Cooke had studied numerous remains of fossil pigs that have been found at all the major East African paleontological sites, such as Omo, Olduvai, Laetoli, and Hadar. These pigs showed definite changes between 3 and 2 million years ago, and according to the pig fossils beneath the KBS tuff at Koobi Fora, Cooke and others felt that 1470 could not be more than 2 million years old. Associates of Richard Leakey who support the idea that 1470 might be nearly 3 million years old argue that these pigs need not have developed at a uniform pace over all East Africa.

The debate on the dating was taken a step further when Thure Cerling, a University of California graduate student, brought samples of the KBS tuff to Garniss Curtis, of Berkeley, one of the deans of potassium-argon dating. Curtis ran two series of tests. The first showed that the tuff was 1.8 million; the second gave a 1.6-million-year reading. Some commentators attribute the discrepancy between the Miller-Fitch dating and that of Curtis to the purity of the samples used. If Miller and Fitch used samples containing much weathered material, this could have caused a falsely high reading. Of course, the fossil pig experts think that Curtis' dating is correct.

On the other hand, another independent dating system suggests that the Miller-Fitch figures may be closer to the truth. This other dating technique is called fission-track dating. It depends upon the presence of tiny zircon crystals in volcanic ash and upon traces of uranium in the zircon. Naturally occurring uranium contains a radioactive isotope, uranium 238, which, atom by atom, decays into lead at an extremely slow and steady pace. (It has a half-life of billions of years.) Every time a U-238 atom decays, it actually "explodes" and leaves a small track in the zircon crystal. By determining the percentage of uranium in the zircon and then counting the number of tracks in a sample of crystals, it is possible to estimate the time at which the crystals were formed—in this case the time of a particular volcanic eruption.

In "The Hominids of East Turkana" (*Scientific American*, August 1978), Alan Walker and Richard Leakey discuss 1470 and the disparity of the potassium-argon dates. They also report that "fission-track studies of zircons from the KBS tuff indicate that the older dates are correct." Thus 1470 may be nearly 3 million years old after all, but this would still leave a problem in biostratigraphy with the fossil pigs. For the present it seems best to work with a minimum date of 1.8 million years for 1470, mindful of the possibility that it may be considerably older. As it is, 1470 is still thoroughly revolutionary at this younger date.

Even at 1.8 million years, 1470 still destroys the ancestral status of africanus. Even if 1470 and africanus were of the same age, most of the simple pebble tools attributed to africanus are much more likely to have been the work of 1470's species. And if one is intent on having an evolutionary sequence, it is obvious that in terms of brain size and the shape of the skull, 1470 is far more human-looking than africanus.

A second blow was dealt africanus' ancestral prospects in 1975 when Bernard Ngeneo, working for Richard Leakey, again hit pay dirt east of Lake Turkana. This time he found a skull—KNM-ER 3733—of Homo erectus, a much larger-brained and more humanlike creature than africanus, which dated to 1.7 million years, the oldest skull of this type so far discovered. In the conventional theory, africanus evolved into Homo habilis, which in turn evolved into Homo erectus. Yet this 1975 discovery establishes that erectus was contemporary with the earliest known, firmly dated africanus. (KNM-ER stands for Kenya National Museums—East Rudolf.)

With 1470 and 3733 both on stage around 2 million years ago, the case for africanus as a missing link is revealed as the piece of imaginative speculation it always was. Again, we are reminded of Piltdown. The greatest difference between Piltdown and the africanus affair is that the africanus fossils are genuine. As in other cases, the deception the profession suffered with africanus was again self-inflicted through its overeagerness to read into the fossils "some special place or significance in the line of direct human descent, as opposed to that of the family of apes." In fact, africanus was more likely ancestral to the chimpanzee than to man. But the American end of the profession in particular seems to be laboring under the assumptions that an animal ancestor is good for us and that the truth about this ancestor may be arrived at by majority vote within the profession.

If anything, the case of africanus should be even more troubling to the profession than was Piltdown. As we have seen,

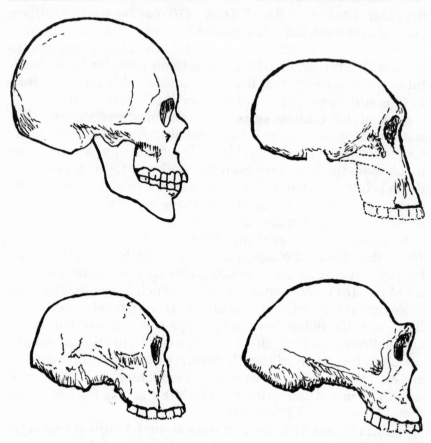

Skull of modern man (upper left) for comparison with profiles of skull 1470 (upper right), Australopithecus africanus from Koobi Fora (lower left), and Homo erectus skull 3733 (lower right). Scale not exact.

W.R.F. after Leakey and Walker for 1470, africanus, and 3733.

paleoanthropologists have not been backward in attaching great significance to exceedingly fragmentary remains (for example, Hesperopithecus, Gigantopithecus, Ramapithecus, Lothagam), but these never became keystones in the proposed human lineage, nor were they so broadly endorsed by the profession in numerous popular and academic publications. Although the fossils of africanus amount to far less than a complete skeleton, there is much more than the various pieces of Piltdown and very much more than the mere scraps of jaws and individual teeth from other species that have so occupied the Tooth Fairy. And yet most of the profession managed to read africanus wrong, dreadfully wrong. If Loren Eiseley were still with us, he could thunder more righteously than ever about "subjective speculation," another "remarkable case history in self-deception," "irrational bias," and those who "give allegiance to theories with only the most tenuous basis in fact."

The truth—and this will become even more evident as we examine the remaining ancestral candidates—is that Piltdown was not an unfortunate lapse of scientific poise in the infancy of this discipline, but was symptomatic of its standard operating procedure. Much anthropological literature written before 1973 is now as obsolete as that endorsing Piltdown man as an ancestral form. But there has been little righteous thunder over the africanus affair by those concerned with the integrity and credibility of science. The generation of Eiseley, Zuckerman, Boule, and Louis Leakey has passed, and most of those who have replaced them are not inclined to rock the boat, especially since the external threat from the fundamentalists has become more acute. Consequently, there is very little public awareness that paleoanthropology has replayed Piltdown with a vengeance.

II.

The africanus fiasco would be less alarming scientifically if the profession showed a more uniform tendency to be self-correcting. But surveying how anthropologists have dealt with africanus, 1470, and 3733 since the discoveries of the latter two, we find that some in the profession prefer to keep their eyes closed and to walk on in the darkness.

Naturally, Richard Leakey disowns africanus as an ancestor. Influenced by his father's opposition to Australopithecus, and with 1470 and 3733 in his hand, Leakey writes in *Origins* (1977):

This remarkable skull [1470] confirmed two things. First, that the human ancestral line, Homo, originated much earlier than most people suspected. . . . Second, because the history of Homo goes back that far, it means that these individuals were living at the same time as some of the earliest australopithecines, making it unlikely that our direct ancestors are evolutionary descendants of the australopithecines— cousins, yes, but descendants, no. Up to that time [when 1470 was discovered] workers in this field believed that . . . Australopithecus af-

ricanus was certainly marching along the main route, eventually to
give rise to the Homo line.

Otherwise, reactions in anthropological literature to these finds
have ranged from confusion and petulance to more or less ignoring 1470 and refusing to let africanus go. Gertrude and Pertti
Pelto, authors of a college text, *The Human Adventure: An Introduction to Anthropology* (1976), indicate that they are aware of
the discovery of 1470, but seem unable to adjust their theories
accordingly. In one place they are cautious enough to remark,

There is always the possibility that both forms [robustus and africanus]
are side branches rather than direct human ancestors.

But in others, they seem to cancel all doubt:

The evidence of both Ramapithecus and Gigantopithecus is frustrat-
ingly incomplete, and more definite interpretation of these fossils will
have to wait. Fortunately the physical remains of a later fossil hominid
—Australopithecus—are relatively extensive, and anthropologists are
beginning to put together a fairly extensive picture of this early ancestor of ours.

They also refer to Homo erectus as the "grandchild" of Australopithecus, and of course Homo erectus is supposed to be in
"direct relationship to us." The reason why Australopithecus is
retained, even with 1470 now onstage, is not far to seek.

Of course, we must be very cautious and skeptical when trying to
reconstruct aspects of the social life of our early ancestors. We have to
put together the scraps of evidence from fossils and stone tools, plus
careful inferences from the behavior of our nearest kin like the chimpanzees and gorillas. In addition data from historically recent hunting
societies are also helpful. Part of the logic of all this depends, of course,
on the evidence of continuities from Australopithecus down to modern
man.

It is an interesting fact that almost all general books on human
evolution, including the Peltos', devote many times more pages
to "the social life of our early ancestors . . . inferences from the
behavior of chimpanzees and gorillas . . . (and) . . . data from recent hunting societies" than they do to the fossil remains themselves. This is because the fossil species which hold any direct
significance for the question of man's origin are still very few,
and if one accepts the standard interpretations, there is really

not that much that can be said about the fossils themselves. Without "continuities from Australopithecus down to modern man," the theoretical underpinning for this standard elaboration into "the social life of our early ancestors" is threatened. In other words, without Australopithecus in the inventory of ancestors, an entire literary industry based on that "ancestor" begins to look silly. So the logic seems to be that we must keep Australopithecus—otherwise we won't know what to write about.

Finally, the Peltos publish a few lines that I think provide a wonderful commentary on the rigor with which scientific logic is applied in certain quarters of this field:

Of course, all reconstructions of cultural behavior and social organization of the Australopithecus specimens are based on a series of assumptions and inferences. None the less, these projections are valuable because they serve as guidelines for assumptions about human origins. They are more reliable than pure speculation.

This, I repeat, was written three years *after* the discovery of 1470 and a year after 3733. We get assumptions based on other assumptions about the cultural life of a species that the evidence now clearly indicates was not ancestral to man, and this is "more reliable than pure speculation"!

III.

Next, it is interesting to note the treatment given to these two revolutionary finds in *Atlas of Human Evolution*, second edition, 1979, by Brace, Nelson, Korn, and Brace. The senior editor, C. Loring Brace, of the University of Michigan, has long been an advocate of africanus as man's ancestor.

Brace does everything he can to downgrade the significance of 1470 and the threat to africanus. He gives 1470 the 1.8-million-year dating without even mentioning the possibility that it may be older. He says 1470's cranial capacity was 750 cc., even though the lowest estimate I have otherwise found in professional literature is 775 cc. And he puts 1470 in the section of the *Atlas* dealing with Australopithecines, suggesting that "1470 represented a stage intermediate between the Australopithecines and full Homo erectus status." The 1470 skull fits "between" the Australopithecines and Homo erectus about the way the skull of a chimpanzee fits between that of a rabbit and a Saint Bernard. This is a nonsensical progression, which we shall examine more fully later. Even Brace is forced to admit that 1470 "does not fully fit in either category," but he is not going to call it Homo habilis, because habilis was named by Louis Leakey, and Brace does not agree with Leakey's conception of human ancestors.

When it comes to Richard Leakey's 1975 discovery of 3733, a 1.7-million-year-old Homo erectus who was also contemporary with africanus—and further evidence that africanus was not ancestral to the Homo line—Brace becomes petulant but still refuses to let africanus go. When Brace refers, in the following quote, to fossils proposed by Louis Leakey as ancient true man that "turned out either not to be ancient, or not to be true man," he is referring in the first case to several discoveries Leakey made at Olduvai and Lake Victoria early in his career. At Olduvai Leakey had misread the geology; at Lake Victoria he could not substantiate the antiquity of his find because rainstorms had washed out the site. In the second case (the fossil that turned out not to be "true man"), Brace is referring to Zinjanthropus. Here are Brace's comments on 3733:

For years, the late Louis S. B. Leakey had been offering now one find now another as evidence for the existence of "true man" back at a time when Australopithecus was in existence. Presumably this would deny Australopithecus place in the ancestry of Homo. For years, each specimen offered as ancient "true man" turned out either not to be ancient, or not to be "true man," and many anthropologists put Dr. Leakey in the category with the "little boy who cried wolf." But just as the little boy eventually did encounter a genuine wolf, so the efforts of the Leakey family eventually did lead to the discovery of a genuine representative of the genus Homo that *was* a contemporary of a representative of the genus Australopithecus. Both had evidently descended in diverging lines that can be traced back to an earlier form identifiable as Australopithecus africanus.

But there simply is no evidence for this earlier africanus. Such is the depth of Brace's commitment to this extinct ape. Aside from the matter of taste, one also wonders if the comparison of L. S. B. Leakey to "the little boy who cried wolf" is appropriate. In the original story, the "little boy" came to regret sounding a false alarm; Leakey's beliefs have been doubly vindicated. The loser in this case is not Leakey, but Brace and others of the same school.

All in all, Brace's performance brings to mind some words of the distinguished philosopher of science, Sir Karl Popper: "The wrong view of science betrays itself in the craving to be right."

IV.

Thus far in this brief survey of reactions to the new situation in paleoanthropology following the finds at Koobi Fora we have seen how they are dealt with in an average textbook (Pelto) and by an influential and well-published member of the profession. (As a supplement to general texts, Brace's *Atlas* is more widely read than most general works.) It is refreshing to find, however, that certainly not all writing anthropologists are afflicted with the kind of bias we have thus far seen displayed. In *Man Before History* (1976) author John Waechter takes account of 1470 and knows a revolution when he sees one:

... the finding of 1470 man in particular has thrown the whole subject of the patterns of human development back into the melting pot.

One of the most forthright and extensive treatments of 1470 is provided by J. B. Birdsell in *Human Evolution* (second edition, 1975). Birdsell addressed the situation in the belief that 1470 was 2.8 million years old, but as indicated, even if it is only 1.8 million years old, its revolutionary impact is little diminished. Birdsell refers to "the problem of ER 1470"—a major problem at the very heart of evolutionary theory.

Birdsell outlines the problem by pointing out that there is a tendency in paleoanthropology, as in other natural sciences, to build systematic interpretations of data. While this data has been "spotty in both time and space," prior to 1470's discovery there was general agreement on a three-tiered scheme for the evolution of man. The earliest grade consisted of the Australopithecines, particularly Australopithecus africanus. The second grade was Homo erectus; and the third Homo sapiens.

The way Birdsell sees it, 1470 thoroughly upsets this generalized scheme, making "a different game of the interpretation of fossil man." He says that it is "surprisingly modern-looking" to have come from the Lower Pleistocene, and, as I say, it is still surprisingly modern-looking even if it comes from the Middle Pleistocene. Birdsell notes that the revised estimate of its cranial

capacity, which is 780 cc., is well outside the range of the Australopithecines and that the form of the skull is more like that of
modern people than that of the Australopithecines. Another
very significant difference as contrasted with the Australopithecines, Birdsell indicates, is that 1470's foramen magnum, the
place where the spinal cord enters the skull, is farther toward
the front. Consequently, 1470's head was better balanced on the
vertebral column.

Taking all these features together, Birdsell says it is now evident that neither Australopithecus africanus nor robustus was
an ancestor of modern man. "From the very nature of its characteristics," Birdsell writes, "cranium 1470 does not seem to fit
the standard scheme of the three grades of human evolution."
As far as he is concerned, the story of human evolution has been
revolutionized by 1470, and no satisfactory synthesis replacing
the old scheme has yet been achieved.

Far from being intimidated by 1470, Birdsell is willing to entertain the possibility that 1470 might be even more revolutionary than it appears at first glance. This possibility arises if we
take into account the effect that sexual differences have on the
problem. The skull is so modern in form that it is "very tempting" to think that it belonged to a female—an interpretation that
Richard Leakey has also suggested. Birdsell says:

In this case it can be estimated that an average male from the same
population would be about 55 centimeters larger, or have a cranial
capacity of 835 cc. This places the population from which we have
this interesting sample even higher on the evolutionary scale and so
creates a greater problem because of the very early date at which it
lived.

Birdsell emphasizes that skull 1470 simply cannot be made to
disappear within the normal range of any other known group of
early fossils.

So we have an interesting contrast between Brace, whose theory is threatened by 1470, understating the cranial capacity at
750 cc., and Birdsell, who is willing to take the data as it comes,
suggesting that a male of the same kind carried 835 cc., creating
an even "greater problem."

Later in his text Birdsell shows how the three grades of human
evolution appear on a graph. He says that 1470 is a "flyer" in
this pattern, calling it both "too early and too big" to fit with the

other clusters of data. This is significant, he says, because "by ignoring 1470" we could show statistically that human capacities, as reflected by other fossils, have increased consistently through time. This, however, is not Birdsell's style, and he ends with a comment from which a great many people in anthropology today could profit:

... data which do not fit the general trends in evolution sometimes are the most revealing, and must not be ignored for mere economy of hypothesis.

If Birdsell demonstrates that the scientific spirit is still alive in some quarters of paleoanthropology, by contrast his performance also helps show that in other quarters that same spirit is indeed seriously compromised for the sake of "mere economy of hypothesis." And while it is laudable that some in the profession are self-correcting, this process would not be repeatedly necessary if more anthropologists exercised appropriate caution in evaluating their material in the first place. Certainly, anyone who bought Australopithecus africanus as man's animal ancestor a few years ago must wonder how the salesmen could have been so positive about a model that is now being recalled.

6: THE LUCY CAPER

I.

FOLLOWING THE CAREERS of Hesperopithecus, Gigantopithecus, Piltdown, Zinjanthropus, Lothagam, Ramapithecus, and Australopithecus africanus, the behavior of paleoanthropology itself becomes suspect. We see a regular pattern of poorly qualified, inadequately considered ancestral candidates attain a temporary academic respectability until the evidence catches up with them. This pattern of behavior is the more suspect in that while they are in vogue, these bones usually bestow fame and fortune upon their discoverers and promoters. The pattern is so well established that one can predict it will be only a matter of time before the performance is repeated.

Indeed, the ink was hardly dry on africanus' pink slip when Donald Johanson, Timothy White, and Maitland Edey placed Australopithecus afarensis before the public as his replacement. Afarensis, who goes under the stage name of Lucy, is an even older, less manlike creature than africanus. Lucy was discovered by Johanson in Ethiopia in 1974, only two years after the discovery that disqualified africanus. When it comes to finding a new trooper to star as our animal ancestor, there's no business like bone business.

Even without the skepticism that must be engendered in the breast of anyone sensible of the history of paleoanthropology, afarensis is a weak and extremely questionable candidate. After we review the history and problems of afarensis, this candidate may well appear to strike a new low in scientific credibility. But there is a positive aspect to Johanson's proposal that, in view of all its negative features, deserves emphasis at the outset.

The positive aspect is that Johanson knows that what he is offering is only an hypothesis. He holds Lucy up as our ancestor with a light hand. He does this because Lucy is dated at 3 to 4 million years old, and there is a million-year gap between her and 1470, the form into which afarensis supposedly evolved. Johanson is convinced 1470 is no more than 2 million years old, and so if another 1470 type were found that did clearly date as old as Lucy, he would have to drop Lucy immediately.

In his public lectures Johanson has pointed out this million-year interval in which there are at present no connecting forms between Lucy and 1470 and emphasizes that, in proposing afarensis, he is in effect predicting that appropriate forms will be found. Johanson cultivates the hypothetical nature of his stance more in person than in his book, Lucy: The Beginnings of Humankind (1981). One could wish that this consciously tentative pose were more pronounced in the book, but to find it expressed in any manner is a real improvement over the all-too-positive anthropological declarations that have so frequently been placed before the public in the past only to be later discredited.

Perhaps because of the very uncertainties surrounding his proposal, Johanson has in fact struck the proper scientific stance. For anyone who cares about the integrity and role of science at a time when these are being abused by extremist tendencies outside and within the scientific community, the stance is at least as important as the merits of the proposal.

II.

The story of how the Lucy proposal came together begins with Johanson, a trained field paleontologist, on the banks of the

Awash River at a place called Hadar in the Afar Triangle of Ethiopia in the fall of 1973. There he found the lower end of a thighbone and the upper part of a shinbone forming the knee joint of a very small creature that was apparently bipedal. The two parts did not connect in a straight line, as they do in apes, but at an angle, as they do in man. Johanson had found remains of a previously unknown creature who lived an estimated 3 to 4 million years ago. While not spectacular, this discovery was more than enough to encourage Johanson to return for another season of exploration. About a year later, on November 30, 1974, Johanson did find something spectacular—about 40 percent of the skeleton of the kind of creature to whom the knee belonged. A Beatles' song, "Lucy in the Sky with Diamonds," was repeatedly played on a tape recorder in Johanson's camp as a kind of celebration the night of the discovery. Since Johanson had deduced from the pelvis of this creature that it had been a female, she became nicknamed Lucy. Her technical designation is AL 288-1, or Afar Locality 288, specimen 1.

Lucy is perhaps most remarkable in that never before has so much of such an old hominid skeleton been recovered. In order to find a more complete fossil hominid, one must move to Neanderthal man, who lived about 50,000 years ago. Lucy, by contrast, is now estimated to be about 3.2 million years old. In *People of the Lake* (1978) Richard Leakey described Lucy's importance and her peculiar features as follows:

For the first time it was possible to compare proportions of different parts of the body in a single individual. This was very important. For one thing, the arms are unusually long in relation to the legs in this individual, a clue that suggests that whatever else it did, the ancient hominid was probably adept at climbing trees.

Equally important though was the nature of the hominid. It was distinctively "advanced" in that it had clearly walked upright. But the jaw had some persuasively primitive features, somewhat reminiscent of Ramapithecus. The jaw is distinctively V-shaped; the relatively large molars are flat; and the first premolar has a single cusp, a very primitive apelike feature.

Lucy's unusually long arms, her archaic V-shaped jaw, and the single-cusped first premolar are features we shall hear more about. Lucy was only 3 to 3½ feet tall. She was neither an Australopithecus africanus nor a robustus.

All this made Lucy a unique and interesting find. But if 1470 really was 2.8 million years old, as it seemed at the time of her discovery, Lucy was peripheral to the mainstream of human evolution. And there were other discoveries just over the hill that also pushed Lucy from center stage.

The most dramatic of these was made by Johanson himself just one year later in the same region that yielded Lucy. Even before the discovery of Lucy, an Ethiopian member of Johanson's team had found fossil jaws that were U-shaped and much larger than Lucy's jaw. These jaws—sometimes called Alemayehu's jaws, after their discoverer—are now dated to about 4 million years old. Johanson, as well as Mary and Richard Leakey, who visited Hadar in 1974, shortly before Lucy came to light, all inclined to the belief that these jaws were closer to very early human types than anything else. But they were only enigmatic jaws, and not too much could be deduced from them.

Then in November 1975, Johanson's team found numerous remains from as many as thirteen individuals, including parts of femurs (thighbones), many hand bones, and more teeth and U-shaped jaws like those found a year earlier. Although these all

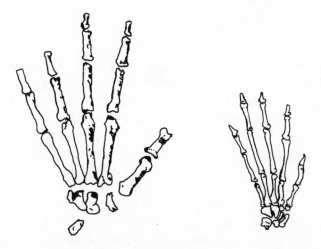

Left: A nearly complete hand assembled from various members of "the first family." (*After Johanson*) *Right:* The hand, or forepaw, of Notharctus, a lemur that lived about fifty million years ago. Illustrated in isolation, as it usually is, the "first family" hand looks compellingly human. The comparison with Notharctus, however, shows that vertebrate hands, or forepaws, are extremely conservative in their skeletal morphology. Were Notharctus known only from its hand, it too could be called "compellingly human."   W.R.F.

had the same shape, there was considerable variation in size among jaws that were deemed adult. There are sufficient hand bones from different individuals to make up a nearly complete set of hands. In *National Geographic* for December 1976, Johanson said these "bear an uncanny resemblance to our own—in size, shape, and function." This 1975 discovery was made at Afar Locality 333 and has been dubbed "the first family." Initially estimated at 3 million years old, the first family is now thought to be about 3.5 million years old.

Of course, if the first family were human or in the Homo line, as Johanson maintained in articles for *Nature* (March 1976) and *National Geographic* (December 1976), then in terms of the development of man, Lucy herself would be nothing more than an evolutionary sideline. Further news to this effect had also come from Mary Leakey in 1975. She had been working a site called Laetoli, about twenty miles south of Tanzania's Olduvai Gorge, where she had found jaws very similar to those from Hadar. These, she declared, were early human types. Of equal interest was their dating, which had been determined, via the potassium-argon method by Garniss Curtis of Berkeley, to be 3.35 to 3.75 million years old, or as much as half a million years older than Lucy.

III.

The next chapter in the Lucy story would not have been possible without the involvement of Timothy D. White, paleontologist, working at Richard Leakey's camp at Koobi Fora. White, described as having a highly critical and skeptical mentality, early became suspicious of the dating of 1470. Together with another paleontologist, John Harris, a specialist on fossil giraffes, White wrote a paper on fossil pigs and the correlation—or lack of it—of Koobi Fora with other East African hominid sites. As described by Johanson and Edey, White is not the world's most accomplished diplomat, and apparently he went further afield in this paper than Richard Leakey, for whom he was working, thought appropriate. Harris toned down the paper, which was eventually published in *Science* (October 1977), but White's differences of opinion and manner of expressing them were such that he was not invited back to Lake Turkana.

Next he went to work for Mary Leakey at Laetoli. He there became thoroughly familiar with the jaws she had found and made casts of them for further study. He also played a part in uncovering a famous set of footprints at Laetoli. These very small, humanlike prints were recorded in a thin layer of volcanic ash when just the right sequences of rain and further ash falls cemented the impressions made by a pair of hominids as they passed through the area an estimated 3.7 million years ago. The footprints were made by feet about the size of a five-year-old's. Many writers assume that these footprints were made by the beings whose jaws have been found nearby, but there is as yet no definite proof of this. To assume so would be about like Louis Leakey's assumption that Zinjanthropus made the tools at Olduvai, only to find more advanced forms later. There is also a problem in that the jaws seem too large for the creatures who made the prints. In any case, White claimed these footprints were made by creatures who were as fully bipedal as we are, while others, Mary Leakey among them at one point, have thought the prints indicate the gait of a creature who shuffled and was not perfectly bipedal. White's arguments seem to have made him unwelcome at Laetoli also.

Johanson and White had met several times, once in Nairobi when Johanson, Hadar fossils in hand, had visited Richard Leakey. In Africa, White had already suggested to Johanson that his U-shaped jaws from Hadar and Mary Leakey's Laetoli specimens were the same species. By the summer of 1977 Johanson and White were back in the United States. It was an appropriate moment for reassessments. The dating of 1470 was becoming more questionable, with Garniss Curtis getting dates of 1.8 and 1.6 million from his potassium-argon readouts. At the time, White had just finished his Ph.D. dissertation, and Johanson was in the Cleveland Museum of Natural History staring at his fossils, wondering just what it was he really had. White still had casts of those Laetoli specimens, and it was hardly surprising that Johanson wanted to have further discussions with White.

The discussions became extensive. It wasn't long before White convinced Johanson that, excluding Lucy, the Hadar and Laetoli fossils represented the same species. Next he convinced Johanson that, contrary to what the Leakeys had suggested and what Johanson himself had already written, this species did not belong to the genus Homo. Then, after more discussion, White persuaded Johanson that the distinctive differences in jaw shape and size between Lucy and the other Hadar and Laetoli creatures

were not critical and that Lucy belonged to the same species
they did. Realizing that they had a new species—which they
called Australopithecus afarensis—Johanson and White finally
convinced each other that it was nothing less than the common
ancestor to the later Australopithecines *and* to man—a crucial
missing link in the chain of ancestors!

In other words, Johanson and White see afarensis splitting into
two groups. One of these became africanus, which in turn gave
rise to robustus, which then went extinct about a million years
ago. The other group, they hypothesize, became the earliest
Homo habilis types, from which Homo erectus and all later humanity then supposedly evolved.

Australopithecine line:	Lineage of man:
	Homo sapiens
	Neanderthal
	Homo erectus
A. robustus	
A. africanus	Homo habilis
A. afarensis	

The formal announcement of this new species and their place-
ment of it in man's lineage appeared in *Science,* January 26,
1979, under the title "A Systematic Assessment of Early African
Hominids." The reader will notice how similar this arrangement
is to that which preceded the discoveries of 1470 and afarensis:

Australopithecine line:	Lineage of man:
	Homo sapiens
	Neanderthal
	Homo erectus
A. robustus	
A. africanus	

In other words, afarensis has simply replaced africanus as man's
animal ancestor. Between the discovery of 1470 and the proposal
of afarensis as occupying this pivotal position, it seemed that
there was no connection between man's lineage and that of the
Australopithecines. Except for a brief lapse during the Zinjanthropus episode, this has always been the interpretation of the
Leakey family. Louis in particular believed that man's lineage
was distinct and did not connect with either that of the apes or
the Australopithecines, at least in the known material from the

fossil record. This is the major difference between Johanson's theories and those of the Leakeys today.

Johanson's preference in this matter is also symptomatic of most American anthropologists. They have become so accustomed to thinking in terms of a direct animal-human connection that most were reluctant to accept the displacement of africanus by 1470 until afarensis came along to take africanus' place. The inclination for U.S. anthropologists to support Johanson is further abetted by a "nationalistic" factor. The Leakey family completely dominated paleoanthropology for so long that, by comparison, the American end of the profession began to look like a collection of armchair philosophers. Johanson is the first American anthropologist who has ever made really major discoveries, so there is a tendency to back the local boy for reasons of professional and national pride.

IV.

What, then, are the strengths and weakness of Johanson's position? In defense of his interpretation one can see an obvious mix of human and nonhuman characteristics in the material under review. Lucy's bipedal pelvis, the Laetoli footprints, and the small, humanlike Hadar knee all point to man. Lucy's long arms and single-cusped first premolar; the heavy, apelike Hadar and Laetoli jaws; and the reconstructed, chimpanzeelike afarensis skull all point to something other than man. With this mixture of features, it is not difficult to see why one might propose afarensis as an intersection of lineages.

However, it is precisely the matter of mixing all these materials together as if they belonged to a single species that is one of the most debatable aspects of the proposal. There may in fact be two, three, or even four different species represented by these materials, which are more varied and difficult to interpret than the remains of africanus ever were. We recall the words of Sir Solly Zuckerman: "The lack of accepted criteria by which to judge the hominid nature, or otherwise, of 'borderline' features in bones makes the whole position very difficult."

The inherently ambiguous nature of these remains and of the degree to which they lend themselves to subjective interpretation is illustrated by the story of the jaws, There are three main categories of jaws: Lucy's V-shaped jaw, which is in a class by

itself; U-shaped jaws from Hadar; and U-shaped jaws from Laetoli. These jaws came to light during the mid '70s, when 1470
was at the height of his powers. For almost everyone interested
in the subject, 1470 was the superstar among fossils. With "Old
Homo," as 1470 has been called, visible at 2 million years ago or
more, the hottest game in East Africa was to find even older
Homos. Both Mary and Richard Leakey tended this way, attaching the Homo label to the Laetoli jaws without any convincing
evidence that these creatures were, in any meaningful sense of
the word, "men." Johanson followed this same tack at Hadar. In
1976 the Hadar U-shaped jaws were represented in National
Geographic in terms that make them qualify as Old Homo:

The mandible is U-shaped, like those of humans today, not V-shaped,
like those of australopithecines. One evening for a lark, members
of the research expedition made clay casts of their own teeth; one
woman's jaw bore a startling resemblance to a three-million-year-old
specimen.

And at that time Johanson saw Lucy's V-shaped jaw as highly
diagnostic of something other than Homo and distinct from the
U-shaped specimens. The December 1976 National Geographic
article has a large photograph of Lucy's skeleton showing her V-
shaped jaw, of which it is said, "The lower jaw's V shape and its
narrow incisors resemble those of Australopithecus."

By 1979—after 1470's age slipped—the U-shaped jaws were
no longer reminiscent of Old Homo but of Australopithecus (or
so they have named it), and the differences between Lucy's jaw
and the rest are said to be attributable to sexual dimorphism
(sex-related variations). In the process, Lucy is transformed into
the most complete example of man's oldest ancestor—"the beginnings of humankind."

And so we see how these assessments can slip around in service of the most convenient hypothesis. This plasticity of view
has not increased the general credibility of the Lucy proposal.
Nor was credibility served with the choice of Maitland Edey as
co-author of Lucy, despite that work's winning the 1981 National Book Award for Science. This is the same Maitland Edey
who sold us Australopithecus africanus as man's animal ancestor in The Missing Link back in 1972. For Edey now to market
Lucy in the same role is a bit like selling two different stones as
the Hope diamond.

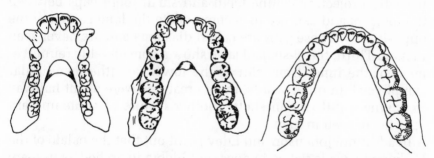

The lower jaw of a chimpanzee is on the left, clearly showing a massive simian shelf. Center is jaw AL-400 from Hadar, showing a simian shelf almost as developed as that of the chimp and contrasting strongly with a human jaw on the right.   *D.E.F. after Johanson and Edey.*

Regardless of what Richard and Mary Leakey may say, however, Johanson was wise to abandon the "Homo" classification of the U-shaped jaws. Despite what was said in the December 1976 *National Geographic* about a cast of a modern woman's jaw resembling the U-shaped Hadar jaws, closer scrutiny has revealed very significant differences—another example of why it is best to take these ancestor advertisements with a grain of salt. In their total morphology, the U-shaped jaws are more like a chimpanzee's than man's. Johanson has it about right when he says that instead of the jaws being human with apish tendencies, they are more apish with human tendencies.

While the afarensis jaw is roughly U-shaped, the tooth pattern does not display the true parabolic curve seen in human jaws. Instead, the dental arcade is closer to that of the apes, where the cheek teeth form parallel rows. Second, the afarensis jaws have

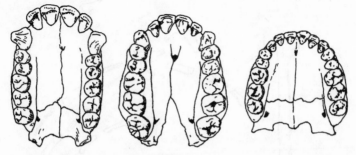

Upper jaws of a chimpanzee (*left*), Afar specimen AL-200 (*center*), and Homo sapiens (*right*). Note the tooth gaps in the chimp and AL-200 and the distinctive tooth alignments.   *D.E.F. after Johanson and Edey.*

partially projecting canine teeth and small tooth gaps between the incisors and canines to accommodate the long canine of the opposite jaw. These gaps are called diastema and are never seen in man. Third, the U-shaped jaws show a considerable reinforcement of the inner front part of the lower jaw (the mandibular symphysis). In other words, these creatures were about halfway to having a full simian shelf, another feature of contemporary apes never seen in man.

In addition, Johanson and Edey point out that the palate of the U-shaped jaws is flat as in apes, not high and arched as in man; the face of these creatures was prognathous and convex in the snout, like the apes; the canine tooth roots were the large, bulging ape type, not the small human type. All of which fits well with the estimated cranial capacity, an apelike 380 to 450 cc., slightly larger than that of a chimpanzee.

So whatever else one may think of the new assessment of the Hadar-Laetoli material, it is not difficult to agree that the U-

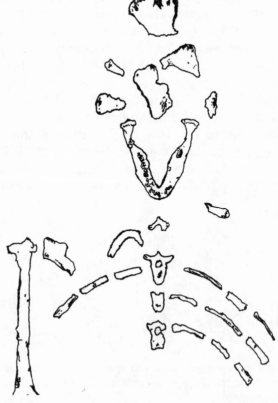

Lucy's V-shaped jaw amid fragments of her skeleton.   W.R.F. *after Johanson.*

shaped jaws are not close to anything human. Nor is it difficult to side with Johanson, White, and Edey against the Leakeys on the question of whether the U-shaped jaws from Hadar and those from Laetoli belong to the same species. Mary Leakey has opted for two species, complaining that the fossils come from separate sites a thousand miles apart and that—as it seemed at first—they are different in age; but this was before the dating of the Afar remains was moved back half a million years to the 3.2- to 4-million-year-old range. Even if the Afar fossils were not later dated closer to those from Laetoli, these criticisms are not convincing. Homo erectus specimens date from 1.7 million B.C. down to about 100,000 B.C. and were distributed from East Africa to China and Java. Thus with Homo erectus there are far greater temporal and spatial ranges than those Mary Leakey has mentioned in her public lectures regarding afarensis. And in any case, Johanson and White do clearly demonstrate that—exclusive of Lucy—some of the best-preserved Laetoli and Hadar jaws are virtually identical in size, shape, and dentition.

V.

What, then, of the further and more contentious claim by Johanson and White that Lucy is also a member of the afarensis species —the smallest adult female of that species yet discovered?

There are two factors to support this interpretation: sexual dimorphism and allometry. *Sexual dimorphism* refers to characteristic differences between the sexes of particular species. One example is the difference in size between males and females in many species, including the primates. In modern human populations adult males are about 20 percent heavier on average than adult females. In other primates, such as the gorilla, the average male weighs as much as twice what the female weighs. A similar degree of sexual dimorphism has been suggested for Australopithecus robustus, and somewhat less for Homo erectus. In the case of Lucy versus the larger afarensis males, the difference would be still somewhat more extreme. Lucy is estimated to have stood between 3 and 3½ feet tall and to have weighed 50 to 60 pounds. An adult afarensis male stood about 5 feet tall and weighed as much as 150 pounds.

In order to find this degree of sexual dimorphism among the primates, we have to go to its most extreme example, namely as it is found in certain varieties of baboon. Paleoanthropologists generally believe that sexual dimorphism became less extreme in ancestral hominids as they approached more closely the form of Homo sapiens. If we take Johanson's theory seriously, we must assume that afarensis was more closely related to Homo sapiens than the baboon is. Thus, while sexual dimorphism might just possibly explain the size difference between Lucy and the rest, it is not a particularly strong or convincing argument.

The second factor by which Lucy might be explained as a member of the afarensis population is *allometry*—the variations among different-sized individuals of the *relative* size of certain bones and teeth. A male, of course, is not merely a larger version of a female. Beyond the well-known differences in the pelvis, and so on, there are other significant variations in skeletal structure between male and female in many primates. For example, the male gorilla has a well-developed sagittal crest (a ridge of bone running front to back on top of the skull that anchors huge jaw muscles), which the female lacks. And in chimpanzees and other primates the male has proportionally much larger canine teeth than the female. Even if the female were ballooned out to the same size as the male, her canines would not be as large as his.

Johanson, White, and Edey claim that by taking allometry into account, Lucy's V-shaped jaw can be made to fit within a species where the rest of the presently known jaws are U-shaped. The manner in which they pose this "solution" is worth noting in some detail. They begin by suggesting that the difference between Lucy's small front teeth and the large front teeth of the U-shaped jaws found by Alemayehu reflect the same kind of allometric differences seen in the canines of baboons. Male baboons have very large canines, far larger in proportion to the rest of their teeth than the canines in females. They argue that if a paleontologist had a collection of jaws and teeth consisting of only female baboon specimens, "he could be excused" for supposing that a canine from a male baboon belonged to a different species. It would seem to the paleontologist, they say, that the jaw itself would have to be shaped differently in order to accommodate the male canine.

Similarly, they argue, Lucy's small front teeth account at least in part for her V-shaped jaw. Even if Lucy's jaw were modeled

on the same scale as those found by Alemayehu, the jaw would
have to become wider and rounder in front in order to accommodate the large front teeth of the U-shaped jaws. Johanson and
Edey then treat us to the following piece of reconstructed shoptalk.

Johanson: "You claim allometry."

White: "I don't claim it. I'm just suggesting it."

Johanson: "Well, it's a dumb suggestion."

White replies that if this is "the only significant difference"
between Lucy and the others, then it's worth thinking about.
Johanson then thinks about it for the next seventeen pages. He
discusses the biases he had brought to the situation, regales us
with more shoptalk, remembers the owls in Ethiopia, notices
that the Hadar-Laetoli jaws seem markedly more apelike than
human, and decides to do an analysis of the teeth of the type Le
Gros Clark performed on Australopithecus specimens back in
1950. Le Gros Clark made his study in response to criticisms by
Solly Zuckerman to the effect that the Australopithecines were
so close to the apes that they could not be considered in the line
of human evolution. Le Gros Clark's study showed that the Australopithecines' teeth were closer to the hominids' than they
were to apes'. This study of a single set of features was substantially superceded by Zuckerman's more broadly based 1954
paper, which we reviewed earlier, but Johanson and Edey do
not tell us that, nor even indicate that they are aware of that
paper.

At any rate, Johanson takes us through the study of the teeth.
As a result of this study, they satisfied themselves that they
indeed had a new species that "by Le Gros Clark's yardstick . . .
stood somewhere between humans and apes," and as they themselves make clear, closer to the apes. But there was still the
question of Lucy.

In the meantime, Johanson and Bill Kimbel, another colleague,
had become convinced that Lucy's smallness in itself did not
exclude her from the species represented by the U-shaped jaws.
There was sufficient variation in size among the other fossils,
they say, so that size alone no longer appeared to be a problem.
But they were still stuck on the distinctive shape of Lucy's jaw.
Timothy White met this objection by laying a graduated row of
jaws on the table, running from the largest to the smallest in the
collection. Then they tell us:

When Lucy's jaw was placed at the end of the series, it became plain that she belonged there. There was a compelling shrinkage of features down to her. She differed *only* in the narrowness of her jaw. Otherwise she had the same set of primitive teeth that all three of us, after months of mulling them over, could now recognize instantly as being representative of our fossil collection—and no other.

Even after this exercise, Johanson professes to have been stubborn, still maintaining that Lucy's V-shaped jaw was nevertheless different. White then insisted that they arithmetically reduce all the other jaws to Lucy-size. When this was done, we are told that the difference in width at the front of the jaws "nearly disappeared." The remaining difference, White suggested again, must be due to allometry. More from weariness than conviction, it seems, Johanson finally conceded the argument. "Okay," he says. "They're all one kind."

This analysis, I submit, does not really solve the problem.

First, Johanson suggests that a paleontologist who knew baboons only through a collection of female jaws would, upon finding a single male canine, be excused for supposing that in order to accommodate such a tooth "the jaws themselves would have to be differently shaped." But are there such allometric differences between the jaws of male and female baboons of the same species? Johanson does not illustrate that there are differences of this magnitude in any other hominid or primate species, living or extinct. Since Johanson himself as well as the Leakeys has published earlier assessments in which Lucy is said to be clearly a separate species, the burden of proof rests upon Johanson. But on this point he neglects to shoulder that burden.

Second, is Lucy's the only V-shaped jaw they have? Apparently it is. Are other, presumably female jaws U-shaped, or are we to suppose that all the other specimens from Laetoli and Hadar are male? How many jaws do they have that are complete enough for them to diagnose the shape? If they have six or eight or ten or twelve, what is the probability that they would find only one female in such a random population? Questions along these lines have rightly been asked where sexual dimorphism and allometry have been suggested to explain other fossil populations such as those of South Africa, which some felt were better explained by two different species—namely, africanus and robustus. Johanson, White, and Edey must be aware of the literature on this matter, but they do not address a single one of these questions.

Third and most important, aside from size, Johanson tells us (on page 273) that Lucy "differed *only* in the narrowness of her jaw." (His italics.) But what about Lucy's strange first premolar? Back on page 180 he was still mindful of that very apelike first premolar with a single cusp that Richard Leakey noticed immediately. And at that point it seems to have differed plainly from the two-cusped premolars of the larger jaws.

. . . its first premolar had only a single cusp. The larger jaws had two-cusped premolars. Since the one-cusp condition is the more primitive and the two-cusp condition the more human, I came to the tentative conclusion that Lucy was different from the larger-jawed type.

In their tooth-by-tooth analysis they show an illustration of a single-cusped first premolar—from a chimpanzee rather than from Lucy, the partially bicusped premolar of Afar jaw AL-400, and the fully bicusped premolar of a modern human. It is odd that they do not illustrate Lucy's single-cusped premolar to show how it compares with AL-400, since the reader was told that the purpose of this analysis was to determine if Lucy belongs to the same species as the large jaws. Following these illustrations, Johanson and Edey then summarize what was learned about the premolar as exemplified by AL-400. They say it does not have the form found in apes nor that of later hominids and man. Its crown, they tell us, is not square to the tooth row, as in Australopithecines and men, but is at a sharp angle, as in apes. However, it is a much rounder tooth than ape premolars, and yet its internal cusp is much smaller than that of the same tooth in man. They conclude that the tooth is not a true bicuspid, calling it "a tooth in transition."

It may not be a full bicuspid, but their illustration shows it is

Left is a single-cusped first premolar from a chimpanzee—the type Lucy has. Center is the partially bicuspid first premolar of Afar jaw AL-400. Right is a fully bicuspid premolar from modern man.   *D.E.F. after Johanson and Edey.*

clearly not a single-cusped tooth either, such as Lucy has. Tooth shape is one of the most stable characteristics of species. How do they address this remaining and significant difference between Lucy and the large-jawed creatures?

They say absolutely nothing about it!

I was incredulous. Just five pages after showing us the premolar of AL-400, Johanson tells us, "They're all one kind." The heart of the Johanson-White analysis of the Hadar-Laetoli specimens is the shape of the teeth and their configuration in the jaw. Yet when it comes to that particular tooth in Lucy's jaw, which is so singular and which by Johanson's own testimony differs from the corresponding teeth in the large jaws, we get no comment at all.

Nor can we accept the notion that the difference between Lucy's premolar and those in the larger jaws might be explained because this is a tooth "in transition." The latest version of the Hadar stratigraphy shows that Lucy's "more primitive" jaw is at least 500,000 and possibly as much as 800,000 years younger than some of the U-shaped jaws. If Lucy were that much older than the U-shaped specimens, the idea that her premolar was in transition would at least be arguable, but the stratigraphy points in just the opposite direction.

So in neither the 1979 Science article announcing the single-species hypothesis, nor in Lucy where they have much more space to present their arguments, do Johanson, White, and Edey convincingly demonstrate that Lucy is the same species as the others. The differences in body size, jaw shape, and the first premolar are not, in toto, satisfactorily explained. The age and ambiguity of the material is such that one cannot declare categorically that they are not a single species, but with the evidence now on the table it is highly unlikely that they are.

This, however, is only the beginning of the difficulties.

7: A Lesson from Louis

I.

THE SINGLE-SPECIES HYPOTHESIS is doubtful at best. Even if we grant it, we find ourselves with a strange animal. It has the feet, knees, and pelvis of a biped. The hand bones are close to human. Its head, though, was virtually that of a chimpanzee. Indeed, the resemblance between afarensis and chimp skulls is extraordinary, the greatest difference being that the chimpanzee's canine teeth are larger. If afarensis were known only from its skull, it would almost certainly be considered an ancient variety of chimp. But with the feet, knees, and pelvis of a biped, it is neither a chimp nor a man. It is a bipedal ape, the most provocative example yet of the "ape-man." Given the long-standing belief that man is descended from an apelike creature, superficially it is not difficult to see why afarensis could be proposed as this very ancestor.

The question that must be asked, however, is whether this ape-man was acquiring human characteristics and evolving toward man—as Johanson assumes—or whether it was acquiring simian characteristics and evolving toward the apes. The larger context of paleontological evidence indicates that both Lucy and the owners of the U-shaped jaws had already specialized in directions that did not lead to man and were moving away from the human condition, not toward it.

Johanson and Edey do not address this larger context in *Lucy*, nor do they give any indication they are aware that their proposal of afarensis as our ancestor is strongly contradicted by the patterns of specialization disclosed by this context. If Lucy's long arms and the partial simian shelf seen in the afarensis jaw were really primitive characteristics, afarensis' ancestral status would at least be arguable. But as Louis Leakey explained in *Adam's Ancestors* (1960), the larger paleontological context shows that these features are not primitive, but recent, extreme specializations within the family of apes.

Leakey made a major point of distinguishing "primitive characters" from specializations. He said it has been all too common to write or speak of the great apes of today as "primitive" members of the ape-human stock and then to conclude that physical characteristics which we find in the apes are, by definition, also primitive. If one is beguiled by this premise, one then mistakenly expects to find these same "primitive" characteristics in prehuman fossils that were in the direct line leading to man himself. Leakey maintained that this was a widespread misconception "fostered to a not inconsiderable extent, in the past, by scientists themselves."

The two most obvious features of today's great apes that have been misinterpreted in this way, Leakey said, are the "simian shelf" and the apes' long arms. All presently existing apes have a simian shelf—a ledge of bone uniting the two halves of the lower jaw on its inner aspect. Leakey wrote that for years the simian shelf in particular was regarded as a sort of absolute indicator of primitiveness in the primates, and on this basis it was assumed that man also had a simian shelf in some of the early stages through which he evolved. Similar reasoning was applied to long arms. All the great apes of today have arms that are very long in proportion to their legs. This was also regarded as a primitive feature. It was widely assumed, "and still is in some quarters," wrote Leakey, that at one time man passed through a stage in which he had very long arms that subsequently became shorter as he evolved.

Leakey pointed out that there is a considerable body of evidence clearly indicating "that scientists were wrong in regarding these characteristics as primitive just because they were found in the apes." "It now seems certain," he continued, that both the simian shelf and long arms, as well as "a good many other" characteristics, "must instead be regarded as extreme specializations in the apes." In other words, these are specializations that markedly separate apes from man, specializations "which we must expect to find less and less accentuated as we trace back the ancestors of the present great apes to the point where their branch and ours join."

The reason why we must expect to find these characters "less and less accentuated as we trace back the ancestors of the present great apes" is that it has been established for some time that the earliest Miocene apes of about 20 million years ago showed no trace of a simian shelf and had short arms.

Leakey wrote of "the great diversity of genera and species [of apes] which are found in the . . . Lower Miocene, in Kenya and elsewhere. The main evidence for the apes of the Lower Miocene comes from Kenya . . . from sites round the Kavirondo Gulf of Lake Victoria, like Koru and Songhor, and islands in the lake such as Rusinga. The quantity of fossil apes from these deposits is very great indeed." Speaking of Proconsul, one of the best known of these genera, Leakey said that in none of the large number of Proconsul jaws that have been recovered is there any sign "whatsoever" of a simian shelf. What we find instead in all the species of this genus is a condition intermediate between the simian shelf of present apes and the development of the chin as found in modern man. Therefore, given the remote date of the Lower Miocene, we may reasonably suppose "that the condition which we find in Proconsul is the truly primitive one." This seems especially probable in that the same condition is also found in the Limnopithecus genus, which was contemporary with Proconsul. It follows that the development of the chin and the simian shelf, seen in man and the apes respectively, represent "evolutionary trends in divergent directions."

Leakey also remarked of Proconsul africanus, the most numerous Proconsul species, that "there is no trace whatever of a ridge of bone over the eyes, separating the brain-case from the face. Instead, the forehead is smooth and rounded and curves evenly from the root of the nose, rather as in a baby." This is one of the reasons why Leakey thought heavy brow ridges as well as a simian shelf and long arms automatically disqualified a fossil from man's direct ancestry.

It is worth emphasizing that these features in earlier apes are well known and are not the interpretation of one man. Regarding arm length in earlier apes, for example, Bjorn Kurten says in *Not from the Apes* (1972) that "ancestral gibbons in the later Tertiary [about 30 to 5 million years ago] still had short arms and long legs, and the same is true for the ancestors of the larger apes."

What this amounts to is very bad news for afarensis' ancestral prospects in relation to man. Neither long arms nor any trace of a simian shelf have ever been found in any being in the human lineage, ancient or modern. Lucy's long arms and a burgeoning simian shelf in the U-shaped jaws clearly indicate that this creature (if we accept the single-species hypothesis) or these creatures (if we do not) were moving away from the truly primitive nonspecialized condition and had already traveled a considerable distance toward the highly specialized state of modern apes.

II.

This criticism of afarensis' ancestral candidacy is so fundamental that the reader may wonder if Johanson has really failed to take account of these developmental trends. Unfortunately, Johanson displays obvious confusion about what is primitive and what is specialized in precisely the way Louis Leakey warned about over two decades ago. In summarizing the contents of a 1975 paper he wrote describing the 1974 Hadar season, Johanson says in *Lucy*: "The gist of it was that two kinds of hominid had been found. One kind . . . represented some sort of extremely primitive Homo. Another, smaller kind [Lucy] represented something else." Johanson seems to have considered the afarensis jaws "extremely primitive" precisely because they have certain telltale apelike features: "What were we to make of features that were not like those of either Homo or Australopithecus but seemed markedly more apelike?" And in another place he says:

. . . one of the best-preserved and oldest bona fide hominid fossils in the world [1470] was a human and not an australopithecine. And yet, australopithecines [of equal age] were clearly more primitive in a number of characteristics. That just did not make sense.

Had he substituted "specialized" for "primitive" in that sentence, it would make sense.

Johanson is certainly not the only American anthropologist who has failed to assimilate the distinction between primitive and specialized features and the fact that heavy brow ridges, the simian shelf, and long arms are post-Miocene developments all leading away from man toward the apes. For instance, in his *Atlas of Human Evolution,* C. Loring Brace says of the afarensis jaws,

> . . . the robust and partially projecting canine teeth, the elongate lower first premolars, and the reinforcements on the inner side of the mandibular symphysis [the midpoint of the lower jaw] are just half way in between the hominid and the pongid [ape] condition—making these a good candidate for the legendary "missing link."

The notion that these features make afarensis a good candidate for the missing link is a complete contradiction. Of course Brace, the africanus enthusiast who disliked Louis Leakey, is unlikely to accept Leakey's opinion about anything. But at least Brace mentions these "reinforcements." For all his analyses of teeth and four hundred pages of space to work with, Johanson never discusses these "reinforcements" and their relationship to a developing simian shelf. Not until he discusses tooth alignments does he give an illustration of an afarensis lower jaw (AL-400), comparing it to a chimpanzee jaw. As noted, it shows a simian shelf almost as developed as that in the ape, but Johanson says nothing about it.

Both Johanson and Brace could well ponder L. S. B. Leakey's remarks on specialization. They are proposing a conception of the missing link that is thirty years out of date. That the afarensis hominids were already strongly specialized in the direction of the apes, and thus could not be ancestral to man, is also indicated by the other apelike features of the jaw already mentioned —the tooth alignments, the partially projecting canines and the associated tooth gaps, the flat palate, the prognathous snout, and the large, bulging canine tooth roots.

The case for Lucy herself is weaker still. Lucy had proportionally much longer arms than man has. Richard Leakey says they were "unusually" long. Since earlier apes had short arms, this indicates that Lucy was also already specialized in the direction of the modern apes. But Johanson is no more forthcoming in dealing with this problem than he was with the simian shelf. Toward the end of *Lucy,* after he has already described how he sees her as our ancestor, he adds this almost as an afterthought:

Lovejoy [C. Owen Lovejoy, a consultant on bipedalism] does not have a good explanation for the condition of Lucy's hand or arm. Compared with the human arm, hers is rather long.

Johanson does not have a good explanation for it either, and promptly drops the subject.

Given the larger context of paleontological evidence and the pattern of specialization it illustrates, the only way Lucy or afarensis could be ancestral to man would be if they somehow managed to reverse these trends. I know of no other case in the fossil record where such a reversal has been documented. It would be unscientific to say that it was impossible in the case of Lucy and afarensis, but it is unlikely in the extreme. Specialization seems to be an inexorable tendency, almost a law of nature. Once it is flowing in a certain direction, it is reversed with about the same frequency that rivers are found flowing uphill. In another important instance Johanson himself looks upon such a reversal as highly unlikely.

Johanson argues that if the relatively small molar of the Laetoli-Hadar hominids is taken as the prototype, it is possible to see the increasing size of the Australopithecine molars as a type of increasing specialization that became ever more extreme through time. He summarizes the basic data as follows:

Specimen	Approximate Age	Molar Size
Laetoli-Hadar Hominids	3.5 million	small
South African Gracile Australopithecine (africanus)	2.5 million	large
South African Robust Australopithecine	2 million	very large
East African Robust Australopithecine (Zinjanthropus)	1 million	super large
East African Homo (1470)	1.5 million	very small

In this summary Johanson assumes rather a lot in regard to the dating, and the chronology is not as clear as he suggests. (There is no firm dating for africanus earlier than 1.7 million; the robust types are as old but persisted longer; East African Homo [1470] may be much older than 1.5 million.) But let us grant the increas-

ing specialization of the Australopithecine molars. At one point
Johanson had considered the super-large molar of the East African robust type (Zinjanthropus) to be the most primitive rather
than the most specialized, since they are furthest from the
human condition. He finally sorted out his thinking in this instance and argues that if the Australopithecine's molars were
getting larger and larger, and if afarensis is ancestral to man, it is
necessary to remove africanus from our lineage:

Can molars start small, swell, and then shrink again? They can, if three
dietary adaptations to explain them can be postulated, but it is extremely unlikely. That is parsimony in reverse.

The very same logic applies to Lucy's arms and the afarensis
jaws. If afarensis and Lucy really are ancestral to man, it would
require us to imagine that the human line began with short arms
and without a simian shelf, that it developed long arms and
something close to a simian shelf, and that it then gave up these
specializations and reverted to an earlier nonspecialized condition. This also is parsimony in reverse.

I was so surprised that Johanson overlooked the difficulties
raised by these specializations that when the opportunity to
meet him arose, I used the occasion to ask him about these problems. He in turn was surprised by my questions and had no clear
answer regarding the jaws. As for Lucy's extra-long arm, he said
that bipedalism expert Owen Lovejoy was now putting out the
idea that it is not so much a case of long arms as of short femurs
(thighbones). This, however, merely restates and confirms the
problem rather than solving it. The same thing can be said of the
chimpanzee.

III.

Given the past behavior of the profession, it is, as I have said,
almost predictable that every new discovery vaguely resembling
a fossil hominid will be put forward as man's ancestor. It is
doubly unfortunate that this course was followed with the Laetoli-Hadar materials. Not only is this behavior damaging to the
credibility of the profession—one can also predict that it will be
only a matter of time before Lucy and afarensis are also discarded as ancestors—but in this case the ancestor hypothesis
obscures the true significance of what is really an important

discovery. Lucy in particular creates a monumental challenge to all standard assumptions about the significance of primate bipedalism and, accordingly, the meaning of the term *hominid*.

Here are the ingredients that create a new situation.

We now know that there were at least one and perhaps two very unmanlike bipedal species 3 to 4 million years ago. Johanson, White, and Edey claim that both Lucy and the owners of the U-shaped jaws were "well-adapted" bipeds. "She (Lucy) walked as well as you do," Johanson tells a questioner. Johanson and White also claim that the Laetoli fossil footprints were made by afarensis. "They [the footprints] confirm without a shadow of a doubt what Lucy confirmed at Hadar: that hominids were fully erect walkers at three million B.C. and earlier." " 'Make no mistake about it,' says Tim. 'They are like modern human footprints.' "

The second ingredient is that despite assurances from many quarters and hundreds of published illustrations showing africanus and robustus as fully erect walkers during their heyday as missing links, further discoveries and analyses since Sir Solly's 1954 critique have raised yet more questions as to just how erect these Australopithecines were. Comparing the femur of an Australopithecine with one thought to come from a 1470 type, Richard Leakey wrote in *National Geographic* (June 1973):

. . . a marked dissimilarity appears at the necks of the shafts, just below the ball-and-socket joints with the pelvis. The more ovoid, less robust shaft neck of Australopithecus implies that the latter, though capable of walking upright, did so only for short periods. [The] stronger neck shaft of the femur [of the 1470 type] suggests its owner probably walked upright as his normal mode of locomotion.

More recently, C. E. Oxnard, a British anatomist now at the University of Chicago, again analyzed the pelvis and ankle bones of Australopithecus and came to conclusions similar to Zuckerman's twenty years earlier. As reported in *Nature* and *Scientific American* (February 1976), Oxnard found Australopithecus "unique in some characteristics and in others closer to the orangutan than to man." The pelvis and ankle bone "indicate that Australopithecus was far from being able to walk upright in the human sense." Oxnard argued that "it is very unlikely that Australopithecus occupied a position on the evolutionary line leading to man."

The third ingredient is the Johanson-White hypothesis that afarensis gave rise to africanus, which in turn gave rise to robustus.

If we put these ingredients together, we arrive at an extraordinary proposition: We have a lineage of fully bipedal hominids, some of whom, foresaking all the advantages ascribed to bipedalism, evolved into creatures with a quasi-quadrupedal posture. This could happen if, in contrast to the common notion that man's ancestors came down from the trees, these creatures abandoned a primarily terrestrial existence in favor of an arboreal one.

I am not suggesting this is impossible. On the contrary, it seems to be the most important and likely conclusion to emerge from the discovery of afarensis. Preoccupied with the ancestor hypothesis, Johanson, White, and Edey never draw this conclusion, but it is clearly implied by the evidence now available.

It is supremely important to the question of human origins for two reasons. It provides another indication that, given Lucy's specialized, apelike arms, her "human" feet did not necessarily carry her in the direction of man. Second, on the wider scene, it implies that manlike feet and bipedalism are the truly ancient, unspecialized, and primitive condition—not a recent acquisition of a single line of creatures who became men. And this in turn casts considerable doubt on the long-standing definition of a hominid. Johanson states this as "a hominid is an erect-walking primate. That is, it is either an extinct ancestor to man, a collateral relative to man, or a true man."

This begins to seem like wishful thinking in view of such profoundly unmanlike features as Lucy's long arms, V-shaped jaw, single-cusped first premolar, and the remarkably chimpanzeelike afarensis skull. A far better case could be made for Lucy and afarensis as collateral relatives than direct ancestors, but given the craving for an ape-man ancestor there is little glory in that. Even then, too little thought is given to the possibility that there may have been literally dozens of species of bipedal primates 3 to 10 million years ago, of which we have thus far only discovered a handful. Evolutionists do not even like to consider this possibility, because it is far easier to pick an ancestor out of two or three contenders than out of a crowd. If there were dozens of species running around on two humanlike feet, it could be that some were never related to man, even collaterally. The no-

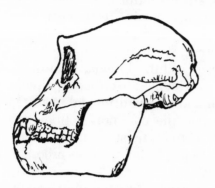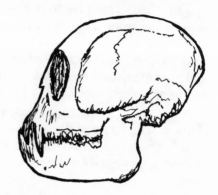

The chimpanzee-like skull of afarensis (*left*), compared with that of a present-day monkey (*right*). In some respects, such as the shape of the forehead, the monkey skull seems closer to man's than afarensis', yet no one suggests that man is descended from present-day monkeys.

W.R.F. after Johanson and White for afarensis.

tion that evolutionary lineages neatly converge in common ancestors is (as we shall hear more fully in part II) also more of an assumption than demonstrated knowledge.

Suffice it to say that Johanson's discoveries provide the best reasons to date for rethinking the whole question of primate bipedalism. This is a real and important advance in scientific knowledge, and it is a shame those discoveries were not presented in this light.

IV.

It is also a shame that in the discussion of scientific issues we must occasionally "descend," as it were, to the discussion of personalities. However, in *Lucy*, Johanson and Edey discuss certain personalities so extensively, and these have already played so great a part in forming the now fashionable interpretation of afarensis, that if we are to gauge what is happening in anthropology today, we cannot ignore the personal factor.

The first personality of special interest in this context is Richard E. Leakey. Richard's father, Louis, was not only the world's leading field paleoanthropologist for two decades, he was also a highly tutored, well-educated man. Richard, by contrast, doesn't have a scrap of university education. He learned fossil hunting in the field from his mother and father. By the time he was ready to enter university, he was thoroughly bored with the fossil business. He didn't want to go to college to study bones and theory. His father told him that he could then fend for himself. Richard did. He became a big-game hunter and safari guide. He was very good at it. Richard is a third-generation Kenyan. The alien wastes of East Africa are his backyard. He established that he was his own man and achieved a high reputation for organizational ability and much knowledge in navigating rough country. Then, at the invitation of his father, he agreed to participate in a 1967 American, French, and Kenyan expedition to the fossil beds of Omo in southern Ethiopia. These fossil beds had been known for years. International experts agreed it was one of the most promising sites on the continent.

But Richard was not impressed. It was not long before he decided that he could find his own fossil patch; and if he was to be involved in the fossil business, he might as well do it on his own terms. In typical fashion, he took off in a helicopter and set down at Koobi Fora on the eastern shore of Lake Turkana in Kenya. The experts up at Omo did eventually find fossils of scientific value, but nothing of much significance for the ancestry of man. Quickly, easily, and on his own Richard had found what is today the most important mine of hominid fossils in the world. In a few years he had 1470 and 3733 in his hand, and this by a man who probably would rather have gone hunting or fishing.

Richard's career is the perfect antithesis of that of most American anthropologists. They've spent years in classrooms studying bones and digesting literature as they inch toward their Ph.D.'s. The possibility of their doing actual field work is remote, and even to get the chance they must engage in endless correspondence and paperwork, meet the right people, secure funding, and be very lucky. If they do get to Africa, their time and funds are limited. They are outsiders subject to endless uncertainties.

This antithesis creates a strange tension in the American profession. For example, in Lucy, Richard is described as paleoanthropology's "certified supernova," because 1470 is simply undeniable, "an utterly dazzling find." "Richard Leakey was made world-famous by 1470," they tell us wistfully. And yet they also describe Richard as a "nonprofessional." How galling for the academics!

Against this background I must once again allude to paleontologist Timothy D. White, who, as described by Johanson and Edey, had very considerable difficulties getting along with the Leakeys. By his own account, Johanson would never have claimed Lucy as "the oldest human ancestor" if he hadn't listened to White—who was, to use Johanson and Edey's word, "infuriated" by certain decisions of Richard Leakey when White was at Koobi Fora, and who left that camp under a cloud. Imagine the young scholar having to take orders from the "nonprofessional" golden boy. The story as told in Lucy itself puts White under heavy suspicion of wanting nothing so much as a chance to dethrone King Richard. In the world of paleoanthropology, Richard is king only as long as he has the "oldest human ancestor," another reason why the elevation of Lucy to this position is so thoroughly questionable scientifically.

Unfortunately, there are quite a few people in American anthropology who would like to see King Richard dethroned. It is, after all, embarrassing when over decades a single family outperforms all the anthropologists in the United States. Now that the heir to the dynasty is a "nonprofessional," it seems it is time to declare independence. Having reviewed the great difficulties raised by Lucy as "the oldest human ancestor," we can appreciate how incongruously inflated Boyce Rensberger's rhetoric was when, speaking of her, he claimed, "except for those who believe in miracles of special creation . . . no one doubts that our heritage can be traced back nearly four million years to little creatures that, as adults, stood only about as tall as a five-year-old today." But this pronouncement is significant in that Rensberger is senior editor of Science 82 magazine, a publication of the American Association for the Advancement of Science. This certainly does not augur well for the American public's receiving dispassionate appraisals of Johanson's hypothesis.

In view of these factors and of the history of this profession insofar as I have laid bare its opportunistic tendencies, I suggest that no sensible person interested in human evolution can properly evaluate the American hyperbole on behalf of afarensis without at least considering that there may be less than purely scientific motives involved. I also suggest that the true advancement of science—American or any other kind—would be better served if Johanson's hypothesis were not used as a stick with which to beat the fundamentalists, but were considered with the cautious skepticism that is so obviously appropriate.

Nor, as I keep saying, should we lose sight of the fact that what we are dealing with is in no small measure a market phenomenon. Millions of people might buy a book entitled *Lucy: The Beginnings of Humankind*. But aside from a few specialists, how many people would buy a book entitled *Lucy: An Extinct Specialized Hominid of Uncertain Phylogeny from the Late Pliocene?*

I'd rather spend the money on a thriller.

8: The Twilight of Neanderthal

I.

SINCE THERE ARE clear and fundamental difficulties with the Australopithecines as ancestors to modern man, the possible evolutionary sequence of hominid forms becomes somewhat shorter:

> Modern man
> Neanderthal
> Homo erectus
> Homo habilis

Even though we have thus far been working from the oldest forms toward the present, it is particularly illuminating to take up the case of Neanderthal at this point because certain evidence relevant to him is also important for interpreting Homo erectus.

The first Neanderthal skull known to the records of modern science was found at Forbes Quarry on Gibraltar in 1848, eleven years before the publication of Darwin's *Origin of Species*. In those days it aroused little interest and was left for many years in the Garrison Library, completely unrecognized. The next Neanderthal discovery, which became the type-specimen, was found by a quarryman in a cave under limestone cliffs in Germany's Neander Valley in 1856. The find was given to J. C. Fuhlrott, a local high school teacher. Although this find was not nearly as complete as that from Gibraltar, consisting of only the top of the brain case, Fuhlrott was versed in evolutionary concepts and convinced that this relic had great significance. He found an ally in an anatomy professor from Bonn, H. Schaafhausen, who was also an evolutionist. As mentioned earlier, the skull was presented at a scientific congress a few years later, where some of Germany's highest authorities declared that, rather than a primitive form of man, it was the remains of a microcephalic idiot, or an ancient Dutchman or Celt, or a diseased specimen, or yet again, possibly a Cossack from the war of 1814.

But it was not long before Fuhlrott and Schaafhausen were vindicated. The founder of modern geology, Charles Lyell, came from England to examine the Neanderthal site and found evidence of its great antiquity. Someone remembered the Gibraltar skull and presented this at another scientific congress in 1864. Within a few years other Neanderthal-type remains were discovered at several sites in Europe. Either microcephalic idiots on this continent were especially fond of caves, or Neanderthal man was something else. As early as 1863, in *Evidence as to Man's Place in Nature*, Darwin's advocate T. H. Huxley accepted Neanderthal as an intermediate form between the apes and modern man. When further discoveries began to accumulate, it was not long before this opinion became the accepted consensus among evolutionists. Today over sixty Neanderthal sites are known in Europe alone, and others have been found in Africa, Asia, and the Middle East. By a wide margin, Neanderthal is the most abundantly documented premodern hominid.

Some of the early Neanderthal discoveries were the remains of individuals who, it is now realized, had suffered from arthritis and other crippling ailments. But this was not appreciated at the time, and for many years the scientific as well as the popular image of Neanderthal was of a being even more stooped and brutish than he in fact was. In the last few decades Neanderthal's image has been substantially rehabilitated so that we find some anthropologists telling us that if we put him in a Brooks Brothers suit, he would fit in well in a group of modern people.

Whatever truth there may be in this assertion has more to do with the extreme variability of modern man than with the modernity of Neanderthal's appearance. The classic Neanderthals of Western Europe were very robust, squat beings with bull necks; enormous browridges; long, flat skulls with receding foreheads and chins; and enormous nasal cavities, probably with noses to match. Their eye sockets were distinctively circular as opposed to the angular, more rectangular sockets of modern man. The males averaged just over 5 feet tall; the females were under 5 feet. They probably looked like trolls.

These characteristics are somewhat less extreme in the Neanderthal populations found outside Europe. The European Neanderthals are remarkably uniform in their appearance, showing less variability than most other hominids. The type of stone tools they produced, called Mousterian culture, are also amazingly uniform. There are some indications that the Neanderthals extend back 100,000 years or more, but they are only clearly documented from about 75,000 to 35,000 B.C. when they suddenly disappear.

For many years, the majority of paleoanthropologists presented Neanderthal as ancestral to modern man. The popular and enduring image of a club-toting caveman immortalized in the comic strips was derived from descriptions of Neanderthal. Actually the thickness of the Neanderthal skull indicates he probably could have sustained a knock on the head that would kill a thin-skulled modern, but whether Neanderthal man ever captured brides by clubbing them on the cranium is pure conjecture.

Despite this lingering popular conception that the Neanderthals were brutish people, there are a couple of factors suggesting they were not entirely devoid of intelligence and sensitivity. Although they were packaged differently, the brains of many European Neanderthals were actually somewhat larger than the average for modern humans. The modern average is about 1,350 cc., whereas Neanderthal skulls sometimes show cranial capacities of 1,500 to 1,700 cc. However, much of the Neanderthal brain was in the lower, rear part of the skull, which is especially wide in just this area. The point of greatest width in a modern skull is much higher than with Neanderthal, and in modern man the frontal lobes of the brain, thought to be the seat of the higher mental processes, are far more developed. So although the Neanderthal brain was large, we have no real way of knowing if his intelligence was comparable to ours. Some anthropologists even doubt Neanderthal's thumb was fully opposable and question whether he had anything except the most rudimentary language.

But there can be no doubt that Neanderthal was capable of emotions and behavior deeper and more complex than that of a mere animal. For one thing, he buried his dead with ceremony. At Teshik-Tash in Uzbekistan, a site in the Soviet Union, an eight-year-old boy was buried in a grave surrounded by goat horns; and in a cave at Shanidar in northern Iraq, an unusual concentration of flower pollen in the soil surrounding a Neanderthal burial suggests flowers were part of the interment ceremony.

With this evidence of their humanness, many anthropologists today consider Neanderthal as conspecific with modern man— that is as simply a variety or race of modern man. This is reflected in the technical terminology now often used: He used to be called Homo neanderthalensis; now he is called Homo sapiens neanderthalensis, meaning the Neanderthal type of modern man. Oddly enough, this is the same position taken by some creationists. If they can write off Neanderthal as just another variety of modern man, he has no evolutionary significance. Like politics, particular fossils sometimes make strange bedfellows.

But though Neanderthal has been much upgraded in recent years, and though it is probably safe to say that the majority of evolutionists still consider him as ancestral to us, there is a considerable body of opinion to the contrary. Of course, it is the more ardent evolutionists who see a smooth continuity between Neanderthal and us, and this is hardly surprising. If a man can visualize Ramapithecus or A. africanus as his ancestor, he has no trouble seeing Neanderthal as his neighbor. However, it has also been argued that even with Neanderthal the evidence for his ancestral status is far more ambiguous than has been widely represented.

II.

There are three major obstacles to Neanderthal's ancestral status: his highly specialized characteristics; the existence of a few skulls that are much older than Neanderthal but much more modern in appearance; and the suddenness of his disappearance.

Among Neanderthal's most conspicuous specializations are his enormous browridges, massive bars of bone above his eye sockets that with his sloping forehead, gave him a profoundly beetle-browed appearance. The Neanderthal browridges are not only much larger than modern man's, they are different in structure. In Neanderthal the browridge over each eye is made up of one solid bar. In modern man, according to Louis Leakey, the brow ridge over each eye consists of two parts. One part begins just above the nose, extending sideways and slightly upward. This overlaps the second part, which begins on each side of the skull at the extreme edges to the right and left of the eye sockets. This extends inward toward the nose and slightly downward. The two elements overlap above the center of each eye socket.

Another structural difference between Neanderthal and contemporary man is that beneath each eye we have a slight depression in the facial bone called the canine fossa. In the same place Neanderthal has instead a swelling or convexity of bone. The jaw is also different. Neanderthal had no chin. Because of his squat, low-domed skull and receding forehead, the face of Neanderthal was further in front of, rather than below the forepart of his brain, which is the modern condition. Because of this, Neanderthal's face was much larger than ours, despite his short stature.

For Louis Leakey, Neanderthal's massive browridges were the most interesting of these several features because they indicated that Neanderthal could not be an ancestor to modern man. The browridges of gorillas and chimpanzees, he pointed out, have a form quite unlike that in Homo sapiens. Those of Java man, Peking man, and Neanderthal "are outside the range of Homo sapiens," and are different from either those in chimps and gorillas or in man, but in some ways are more like the apes'. Leakey recounted how many anatomists used to make the same mistake with massive browridges of the ape type as they made with the simian shelf and long arms. They used to be thought of as a primitive feature, and when rather similar ridges were found in Neanderthal and Peking man, they were regarded as evidence of their primitiveness. In this instance, though, Leakey thought that the tide was turning and that it was increasingly being realized that massive browridges are specialized characters rather than primitive ones. As far as he was concerned, it was clear that their presence did not indicate an ancestral stage in human evolution, "but a side branch that has become more specialized, in this respect, than any Homo sapiens type."

Leakey used the term Homo sapiens in the old sense, excluding Neanderthal, whom he called Paleoanthropus neanderthalensis. He saw Neanderthal splitting off from the stock that gave rise to modern man, then becoming increasingly more specialized until he became extinct. Neanderthal had "no descendants living in the world today." Far from being simply a variety of our own species, Leakey thought that "from the zoological point of view" the differences between Neanderthal and modern man "are fully as great as the differences between the gorilla and the chimpanzee. . . ."

Leakey was not the only authority who held such views. In *Fossil Men* (1957) Marcellin Boule and Henri V. Vallois also describe Neanderthal as an archaic, separate, and extinct species. Although their appraisal was written before the recent upgrading of Neanderthal by some writers, the main points upon which they base their conclusions are still valid and unanswered.

Their first point is that Neanderthal differs much more from all types of modern skulls, even with their racial variations, than these modern types differ among themselves. In the modern group, all the transitional forms between the extreme types of human skulls can be discovered. But Neanderthal, they indicate, is "clearly separated" from this modern series "by a kind of hiatus, corresponding to a real morphological break." Boule and Vallois cite the findings of other researchers, working with the "laborious biometrical methods," who have also arrived at the conclusion that there is a "very distinct break" between Neanderthal and modern man.

Their second point is that the difference in bone structure between Neanderthal and existing men are "much more important" than the differences mammalogists conventionally appeal to for separating the various species of mammalian genera. Seen this way, Neanderthal, they say, is clearly a distinct species from Homo sapiens. There is no getting around Neanderthal's peculiar characteristics, which are not found "normally and in association" in any present race. Each of these special characteristics, they suggest, would be almost enough in itself to justify distinguishing a distinct species, "were it a question of a mammal not belonging to the genus Homo."

Boule and Vallois consider Neanderthal to be a fossil species "in a double sense." It is a fossil species in the usual sense, in that it dates from a prior geological period. It is also a fossil "because we are aware of no descendants from the Upper Pleistocene onwards." Boule and Vallois conclude that during the so-called "Mousterian period" when Neanderthal was relatively numerous, he "represented a belated type existing side by side with the direct ancestors of Homo sapiens. . . . Perhaps," they suggest, "one might go so far as to say that it was a degenerate species."

II.

The second and greatest stumbling block to seeing Neanderthal as our ancestor is the existence of well-authenticated skulls and skull fragments that are both more modern in appearance and much older than Neanderthal. Fossils from four sites in particu-

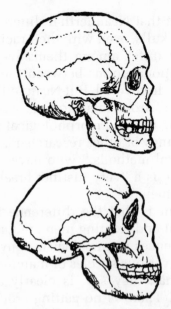

Skulls of Homo sapiens (*above*) and classic Neanderthal, showing many pronounced differences in structure.   W.R.F.

lar may be mentioned in this regard: Swanscombe, Steinheim, Fontechevade, and Vertesszollos.

The Swanscombe skull, although far from complete, is one of the most intriguing fossils in all of paleoanthropology. It consists of the rear half of a human skull, including the occipital bone and the left and right parietal bones. The occipital bone forms the lower rear part of the skull. The parietals form the sides and top. A third element in the top of the cranium, the frontal bone, is missing, as is the entire face and jaw.

The occipital bone came to light in 1935 when gravel was being extracted from a pit at Swanscombe, Kent, England. Over a year later one of the parietals emerged from the same deposit; it fit the occipital bone perfectly. It was not until 1955, during a controlled paleontological digging, that the other parietal was found. It fit the other two pieces exactly.

The sand-and-gravel deposits from which these bones came are part of a well-recognized and dated geological formation: the 100-foot terrace of the River Thames. Because of animal fossils and other indications, these deposits are dated between the Mindel and Riss glaciations, or between 200,000 and 300,000 years ago. The age of the Swanscombe skull is thus about 250,000 years.

These three pieces of bone may not seem like much to work with, but they are quite a bit more than mere jaw fragments that were sufficient to fuel endless speculations about creatures such as Ramapithecus. And in fact there is just enough of the Swanscombe skull to reveal some very interesting information. The rear of the skull is smoothly rounded, as it is in modern man, not squat and "bun-shaped" as it is in Neanderthal and Homo erectus—a creature who lived, as far as is now known, from about 1.7 million to perhaps 100,000 years ago and who is supposed to be the next earlier link in the chain of ancestors. There is also enough of the skull to estimate Swanscombe's cranial capacity closely, which works out to 1,325 or 1,350 cc. This is virtually the same as modern man's. In fact, in Fossil Men Boule declared that the Swanscombe skull shows exactly the same shape and size as that of a present-day Englishwoman. The only dissimilarity he could find was that the bones were thicker in the Swanscombe skull. But thick bones alone are apparently not necessarily an indication of primitiveness or specialization. The Piltdown skull (excluding the jaw) turned out to be that of a modern human being who lived about five centuries ago, and yet the bones of that skull were also said to be "very thick." Writing before the exposure of the Piltdown hoax, Louis Leakey found the Swanscombe skull directly comparable to the Piltdown specimen—minus the jaw. Yet there is no question that the Swanscombe skull is about a quarter of a million years old.

Almost all paleoanthropologists agree that people like ourselves have been on this planet for at least 35,000 to 40,000 years, and many find sufficient indications in the fossil record to extend our tenure to 100,000 years. What is so fascinating about the Swanscombe skull is that it is a bona fide indication that our species may have been roaming this planet a full quarter of a million years ago, thus extending our prehistoric sojourn to fifty times the length of our recorded histories. This is an extraordinary possibility, and more than a few anthropologists endorse it. In *Human Evolution* (1975) J. B. Birdsell says the Swanscombe bones are "modern in form" and that this is "a surprisingly modern type for such ancient deposits."

Of course, with the face and jaw missing, we cannot be certain that the Swanscombe man (or perhaps woman) did not have some atavistic feature, such as heavy browridges, and because a date of 250,000 B.C. for modern-type people does not fit well with much evolutionary theory, the more ardent evolutionists back away from suggesting anything of the kind. But this is not the only evidence that "modern" man is very ancient.

In 1933 a nearly complete skull, minus the lower jaw, was found in a gravel pit near Steinheim, twenty miles north of Stuttgart, West Germany, by F. Berckhemer, a professional paleontologist. It is of an age comparable to Swanscombe, but may be slightly younger. It has a cranial capacity of about 1,150 cc., which is small for modern man, but entirely within our range. It has heavy browridges, though not as heavy as those of Neanderthal. It also has some entirely un-Neanderthal features. According to J. B. Birdsell, "The vault is rounded in the back, has its maximum breadth high on the side, and is apparently both narrower and lower than the skull from Swanscombe." Neanderthal skulls have their greatest width low in the back and are not well rounded there. "One other surprising feature is that the upper third molars are much reduced in size, which is surprising for this early date. The teeth show moderately developed pulp cavities and are smaller than those of the average Australian." (The

Australian aborigines have the largest pulp cavities of contemporary races.)

There is disagreement about whether the Steinheim skull belonged to a male or a female, which affects our interpretations as to just how modern-looking this population was. But as Birdsell says, "Irrespective of these points of disagreement, the important conclusion is that another Middle Pleistocene skull from Europe proves to be of the grade Homo sapiens rather than Homo erectus."

A third prehistoric site to yield evidence of modern human beings who lived before the heyday of Neanderthal is at Fontechevade in France. Located in the southwest corner of the country, this is said to be the best example of a stratified cave in Europe. The floor of the cave yielded clear strata of several Stone Age cultures: remains of the sophisticated Magdelanian culture on top; then less sophisticated Aurignacian flints; then a layer of clay without fossils or artifacts; then fairly crude Mousterian flints—the type consistently associated with Neanderthal. Beneath this layer there was what appeared to be a limestone floor, but in 1937 the chief excavator, a certain Mlle. Henri-Martin, discovered that it was not a solid floor of bedrock but a layer that had been gradually built up by the process that forms stalagmites —dripping water with a high lime content. Beneath this layer of precipitated limestone—and thus beneath the Mousterian-Neanderthal remains—there were twenty feet of debris that contained fossils of warm-climate animals, such as rhinoceroses; stone implements; and fragments of two human skulls, eventually unearthed in 1947.

As usual J. B. Birdsell provides one of the more accurate and detailed descriptions of these remains. The largest fragment is an incomplete skullcap which reveals that the shape of the skull was relatively long, low, and broad compared with modern man. Birdsell says, however, that it belonged to a large-brained individual "whose cranial capacity was about 1,465 cc." Its bones are as thick as those of the Swanscombe fossil and, according to Birdsell, there are other technical characteristics heightening the resemblance.

The remains of the second individual consist of small fragments, not exceeding two inches in any dimension. These fragments, however, come from that critical part of the skull above the root of the nose where we find the browridges. Small as these fragments are, they thus provide important evidence because there is enough to determine that it belonged to an adult and yet its forehead had no superorbital torus or heavy browridge such as Neanderthal had. What we find, writes Birdsell, are "separate brow ridges as small as in European women of today. Except for the thickness of their cranial bones, the inhabitants of the cave at Fontechevade could pass for modern Europeans." Birdsell stresses this point because with the advent of the Wurm glaciation the whole of Europe seems to have been taken over by classic Neanderthal, a completely different type. These individuals at Fontechevade, who could pass for modern Europeans, lived somewhere between 85,000 and 130,000 years ago. It therefore seems that our race was here with Neanderthal and even before.

III.

Finally, the fourth fossil discovery that casts further doubt on the ancestral status of Neanderthal was made in the middle 1960s at a place called Vertesszollos in Hungary. Along with skull 1470 and the Swanscombe remains, this is one of the most important as well as the most controversial discoveries ever made. It comes from such an ancient horizon that it not only compromises Neanderthal, but Homo erectus as well. For this very reason the find at Vertesszollos is almost uniformly ignored or misrepresented in American texts. Fortunately, there are a few exceptions to this general posture, the most notable again that of J. B. Birdsell (*Human Evolution*, 1975) who deals with it straightforwardly. The following description of this discovery, in many ways the most important and unusual of all remains relevant to dating the tenure of our species on this planet, is largely derived from that of Birdsell.

The Vertesszollos fossil consists of a single, complete occipital bone of an adult male. Associated with it are chopping tools of a type "previously unknown in Europe." The deposit in which the occipital bone and tools were found was sealed, says Birdsell, "both above and below by unbroken beds of travertine." This means that there was no chance of intrusion of the remains from later (higher) layers and that "its date of Mindel II is undoubted." Mindel II refers to one of the well-demarcated phases of glaciation that have periodically overrun Europe. Translated into years, it means that the Vertesszollos fossil is between 400,000 and 700,000 years old, depending on whether one prefers a shorter or longer chronology for interpreting the ice ages.

Birdsell acknowledges that ordinarily single bones do not usually provide critical information about the type of individual to whom they belonged. But this is not the case with this complete occipital bone. It defines the shape of the back of the skull, "which," Birdsell emphasizes, "was totally unlike the vertically compressed occiput of the pithecanthropines," by which he means the Homo erectus types.

It has a rounded form and open angle found among modern men. It has correctly been identified as belonging to a Homo sapiens, and so it is the earliest relic of this most advanced grade of humanity.

There are two other striking features about the Vertesszollos discovery. The first is that evidence of hearth sites, and thus knowledge of fire, was also found. The second is the great size of the occipital bone. Professor Andor Thoma, the first to describe it, related its dimensions to a cranial capacity of 1,516 cc., well above the modern average of about 1,350 cc. Birdsell accepts 1,516 cc. as the "best estimate" of its capacity and points out that at a 95-percent level of reliability, the lower limit of the estimate would be 1,405 cc. while the higher limit—which is just as probable mathematically—rises to 1,600 cc.

Birdsell notes that even by modern standards this was a large-brained individual and sees this as confirming the designation as Homo sapiens. Consequently, he seems to cut off later Homo erectus types (whom he preferred to call Pithecanthropines rather than "men") from being our ancestors. "Since the rest of the world was populated by Pithecanthropines, it is likely that the man of Vertesszollos was on the direct line leading to surviving modern groups."

Birdsell is not entirely alone in his appraisal of the Vertesszollos fossil. Andor Thoma named it Homo sapiens paleohungaricus in his original description, and in Mankind in the Making (1967) William Howells also accepts this designation. Howells says that with a cranial capacity of 1,400 cc.'s we are talking about "a modern figure." He calls this a "very important fossil," describes it as an "exception" to the general pattern of Homo erectus, and asks, "Are we here at the origins of Homo sapiens?"

The Vertesszollos fossil is thus extremely unusual. When the

evidence it provides is added to that from Swanscombe, Steinheim, and Fontechevade, we arrive at a remarkable proposition.
It could be held, with much better evidence than many interpretations in this science, that modern man dates back roughly half
a million years.

Very few people are aware of this possibility. Unless one is
among the relative few who happens to have read J. B. Birdsell,
one could wander for years through the writings of American
anthropologists and never find a word suggesting that modern
man is more than 100,000 years old at most. The reason for this
"news blackout" is that a half-million-year age for modern man
is so disconcerting to long-established candidates such as Neanderthal and Homo erectus, of which Peking man is the most
famous example, that most anthropologists and popularizers
drastically deemphasize the significance of the Vertesszollos fossil and not infrequently misrepresent it completely.

The Vertesszollos specimen is dreadfully inconvenient because it is nearly twice the age of Peking man, and the profession
is heavily committed in print to the ancestral status of Peking
man. Peking man, whose brain was only half to two-thirds as
large as Vertesszollos man's, has been known for half a century.
Today's American anthropologists have been brought up believing in Peking man with the same certitude they believe the earth
is a sphere. To many scientists it is simply inconceivable that
modern man could be older than this subhuman "ancestor."
Their reasoning then takes the following form: "We know Vertesszollos cannot be a modern man because it is too old. Therefore, it must be the type of creature that we find elsewhere who
lived at this time—namely Homo erectus." Consequently we
find that the great majority of writers who mention Vertesszollos
at all classify him as Homo erectus, even though the shape of the
back of the skull is totally unlike Homo erectus and the size of
the skull is completely outside the range of Homo erectus. Usually they say nothing about these difficulties. When they do
mention the Vertesszollos cranial capacity, they almost invariably use the minimum figure of 1,400 cc. rather than the median
estimate of 1,516 cc. or the upper figure of 1,600 cc. Occasionally
a writer will explain that Vertesszollos is classified as Homo
erectus mainly for "chronological reasons," but will then back
away from the subject like a fundamentalist exiting a pornogra-
phy shop.

We shall hear more of Vertesszollos. In conjunction with Swanscombe, Steinheim, and Fontechevade, it certainly shows that there is significant evidence that modern-type humans were in existence long before Neanderthal. Accordingly, it is difficult to see how Neanderthal could have been our ancestor.

IV.

The third major indication that Neanderthal was not our ancestor has to do with the suddenness of his disappearance. The twilight of Neanderthal was not a gradual blending of one human type into another. There is no smooth continuum in the fossil record showing the transformation of Neanderthal into modern man. Some evolutionists have maintained, and a few still do maintain, that fossils from caves in Israel show this transformation. But according to Bjorn Kurten in *Not from the Apes*, a restudy of this material has not supported this interpretation. It is not difficult to find anthropologists who now describe the situation along the same lines as Kurten; and when he uses the term *Homo sapiens* in the following paragraphs, he means fully modern man, not including Neanderthal:

The appearance of modern man in Europe about 35,000 years ago is very sudden: There is no known transition from the Neanderthalers to those essentially modern-looking people who have been called Cro-Magnon men. Furthermore, these new Europeans are definitely not some kind of "generalized" Homo sapiens, but clearly belong to the Caucasoid, or white race. At this early date, then, man had already split up into distinct races. In the same way, the earliest modern men in China are recognizable as Mongoloid, those of Australasia are related to the living Australian aborigines, and early South Africans seem to be allied to the Bushmen. Where did they all come from?

The Cro-Magnon men Kurten refers to were first found in France in 1868. Their remains have since been found in many places in Europe. They were virtually identical to modern people, with two interesting differences. Not only were they taller than the squat Neanderthalers, they were even taller on average than the Europeans today. Many of the men were well over 6 feet. The second difference is that they also had larger brains than the average European of today. So did many of the Neanderthals, but their brains were packaged differently. The Cro-Magnons had brains proportioned like ours, and yet they were on average somewhat larger. If brain size is an index of human evolution, as is so often argued, then modern man has actually devolved since the appearance of the Cro-Magnons.

Whatever happened during the brief twilight of Neanderthal must have been dramatic. Kurten points out that the physical change from Neanderthal to modern Homo sapiens correlates with a striking change in culture—from so-called Mousterian tools to the much more accomplished blade cultures of the late Paleolithic. Suddenly, about 35,000 years ago, there was a dramatic increase in the quality and style of the cultural artifacts, and cave art appeared. Indeed, the art of Cro-Magnon man that is preserved on the walls and ceilings of caves in France and Spain shows a mastery of line and form rivaling that of any two-dimensional graphic art from any age and culture. It is ancient art, but it is not primitive art. We can only guess what their more perishable cultural products were like.

With refreshing candor, Kurten admits that we simply don't know where modern man came from:

At this point, we are presented with the outlines of a major problem. Almost everywhere, either Neanderthalers or late Homo erectus were replaced more or less suddenly by modern types of Homo sapiens. Moreover, these invaders show different racial traits which must have taken some time to evolve. But where did Homo sapiens originate?

One theory, says Kurten, is that modern man evolved locally from Neanderthalers. He cites C. S. Coon as a recent advocate of this position. But while Kurten grants that a theoretical case can be made for this theory, he says he cannot find it convincing. "The change is too great, the time too short, and there is nothing like it in previous times or in other evolving lineages." He notes that in evolving Cro-Magnon from Neanderthal we must contemplate an extreme change in body build within 5,000 to 10,000 years. Kurten says that this is not impossible, "but it smacks too much of coincidence and involves too much special pleading to be palatable to the evolutionist."

The possibility that Cro-Magnon evolved from Neanderthal is diminished even further by Kurten by the evidence that Homo sapiens much precedes the era of change reflected in the cultural remains:

We cannot get around the fact that Homo sapiens, at least in an early guise, was present in Europe in the Eemian interglacial, most probably in its earlier part, about 100,000 years ago.

This is enough to show that the modern type of man has been in existence for a fairly long stretch of time and probably can be derived from something pretty close to Steinheim and Swanscombe men. . . . The main question is: where was the original homeland of this stock? We simply do not know at present.

Kurten is not an isolated voice in acknowledging this mystery. J. B. Birdsell, for example, says virtually the same thing:

The homeland of living types of modern populations remains unknown. Their appearance in marginal areas such as Australia and probably North America prior to Europe poses real problems which existing data cannot solve.

This reference to North America will come as a surprise to many people, because for decades the standard teaching has been that man did not enter the New World until about 20,000 years ago, when he crossed a land-bridge that then existed across the Bering Strait between Siberia and Alaska. However, in the early 1970s a modern-type skull, which has been dated to about 50,000 years, was found at Del Mar, in southern California, and there are some indications that it may be even older.

V.

Finally, an additional ingredient in the mix of evidence surrounding Neanderthal that casts further doubt on his ancestral status is his static culture. As mentioned, Neanderthal remains are closely associated with a particular stone-tool culture called the Mousterian. The association is so uniform and well documented that often sites may be attributed to Neanderthal even when nothing else is found except tools. Neanderthal is the only "near-man" to whom sites may be reliably attributed on this basis.

The curious thing about these tools is that they show little or no development over a period of 40,000 years or more. A cultural standstill of this duration might not be unusual for a creature a million years older, but for the most recent "near-man" this complete lack of dynamism seems unusual. Homo sapiens is the most dynamic and changeable being on earth, and the static, troll-like mentality of the Neanderthals does not recommend them as the ancestors of those who have subdued the planet.

VI.

It only takes a few inconvenient facts to spoil the most beautiful theory. It is unfortunate that such evidence as we have reviewed here does not receive the publicity appropriate to its importance. The real complexities and mysteries of the human emergence have simply not reached the general public. Little attention has been given to the Del Mar skull and to the antiquity of man in the New World, or to the fact that there is solid evidence that modern man is at least 100,000 years old and may well be 250,000 or even 500,000 years old. Most people still think Neanderthal was our ancestor.

I should point out that these challenges to the ancestral status of Neanderthal are not taken from an extreme position nor are they held by authorities with extreme views. Probably a majority of evolutionists consider Neanderthal as merely a variety of Homo sapiens, and many still present him as ancestral to us, mostly for reasons of economy of theory. Neanderthal is obviously closer to the modern form than other proposed ancestors, such as Australopithecus, Homo habilis, and Homo erectus. If even Neanderthal cannot be made to fit into our evolutionary lineage, it sets a bad precedent, and the whole theoretical structure becomes more questionable. But even among professional paleoanthropologists the emerging consensus may be turning against Neanderthal's ancestral claim. In *Atlas of Human Evolution* (1979) C. L. Brace, himself an extreme evolutionist, shows four phylogenetic or family trees representing various schools of anthropological thinking. Of these four trees, only one shows Neanderthal on the road to modern man.

Reviewing the evidence surrounding the twilight of Neanderthal, we uncover a double mystery. Not only can we not explain the suddenness of Neanderthal's disappearance, but of greater importance is the fact that on the basis of the presently known evidence we cannot answer the basic question: Where did Homo sapiens originate?

This unanswered question makes a strange contrast with those assertions announced by the public voice of paleoanthropology that there is "no doubt" that we came from apes or 3-foot-tall simian creatures who lived 4 million years ago. And as we look at the evidence concerning the remaining proposed ancestors, the contrast between solid knowledge and mere assertion becomes stranger still.

9: The Hunter and the Hunted

I.

WITH SERIOUS OBSTACLES to the ancestral status of Neanderthal, the evolutionary scenario becomes even briefer. Between 3 and 2 million years ago Homo habilis supposedly begat Homo erectus, who, in turn, theoretically pedaled his way into the modern human body sometime between 700,000 years ago (if one accepts the Vertesszollos remains as those of modern man), and 50,000 years ago (if the Swanscombe and Fontechevade remains as well as those of Vertesszollos are considered too fragmentary to be diagnostic of our species).

While most anthropologists are decidedly uneasy contemplating modern man at much above 100,000 years, I am still in good professional company in saying that only habilis and erectus are worth defending as serious contestants for the honor of linking us with lower forms of life. For example, this extremely brief cast of characters is what Richard Leakey and Roger Lewin limit themselves to in *Origins*, published in 1977. The only addition they suggest is Ramapithecus as the possible antecedent of

Homo habilis, but this was before Ramapithecus was declared "a False Start of the Human Parade" in 1979.

With only two premodern forms worthy of serious consideration as our ancestors, the entire question of human evolution begins to assume a different dimension. If either or both of these creatures are in fact ancestral to our species, then of course the basic theory is still intact; but it is quite remarkable that after 120 years of fossil collecting and the invention of literally dozens of species names to identify possible ancestors, the field now consists of only two serious contenders.

Of these two, Homo erectus is in certain respects the most crucial. He has reigned as an ancestral candidate almost as long as Neanderthal, and in terms of the evolutionary sequence, his place is the most important of all. Without erectus, evolutionary theory applied to man would appear a good deal more problematic. Without erectus, there would be no evolutionary sequence; there would be only Homo habilis and modern man, with a huge temporal gap between them. The vast majority of anthropologists in the English-speaking world endorse erectus as our ancestor; but even with erectus, there are a few prominent dissenting voices, and although their reasons for dissent are usually ignored or brushed aside by the more ideological evolutionists, these reasons are most interesting to ponder.

The story of Homo erectus began in the 1880s with a wild surmise on the part of a young Dutch doctor, one Eugene Dubois. Dubois was influenced by the ideas of Ernst Haeckel, the German naturalist, who hypothesized that if man were descended from the apes, it should be possible to find fossils of a genuine ape-man, a creature exactly halfway between the two. Since modern apes live in the tropics, Dubois reasoned that the Dutch East Indies would be a likely place to look for such fossils. Having only limited personal means, Dubois sought an appointment in the Dutch Army, with the understanding that he would be sent to the East Indies. He was first stationed on Sumatra, where he excavated without luck. Then he was transferred to Java in 1890 and began excavations on the banks of the River Solo at a place called Trinil.

In September 1891 Dubois found an apelike tooth and, one month later, only about a yard away, a remarkable skullcap. It was smaller and more apelike than the top of a Neanderthal skull but larger than that of a chimpanzee. Its estimated cranial capacity is about 850 cc. It belonged to a previously unknown primate corresponding amazingly to just the type of creature Dubois had hoped to find.

The significance of these discoveries was considerably enhanced in August 1892 when Dubois uncovered a manlike femur (thighbone) about fifty feet away from the skull. Since no other remains of large primates had ever been found in Java, Dubois presumed that the femur belonged to the same creature as the skullcap. The shape of the femur indicated its owner had possibly walked erect, and so Dubois christened his discovery Pithecanthropus erectus—or erect ape-man. In a paper he published in 1894 Dubois described Pithecanthropus as the "intermediate form between the Anthropoids [apes] and Man" that was implied by the theory of evolution. It was, he said, the "precursor of Man."

This paper was very widely read by paleontologists and anthropologists, and there was much discussion of Pithecanthropus at the International Zoological Congress held at Leyden in 1896. Although Neanderthal man had been known for forty years, Pithecanthropus was so much more apelike and, at the same time, so unlike anything else that had been discovered that scientists and the public alike again did not know quite what to make of it. Even though evolutionists like T. H. Huxley and Haeckel had postulated the existence of an ape-man, Pithecanthropus provoked intense controversy because many scientists still could not quite believe it. Furthermore, with only a skullcap, a thighbone, and a couple of teeth to work with, the fossils were mockingly ambiguous. Finally, in the 1890s, little if anything was known about the geology of Java. Dubois suggested that Pithecanthropus, or Java man as he is popularly called, might have lived as early as the Pliocene—a geological period now thought to have begun about 10 million years ago and to have lasted some 7 million years. This was a mind-boggling concept in the 1890s and added yet more to the controversy. Accordingly, some scientists declared that Java man was a full-fledged ape, a giant gibbon, since gibbons have femurs much like men. Others said this was a full-fledged man. Some thought he was a real missing link, as Dubois had claimed. And there were those who ridiculed the whole business.

Dubois possessed one of those temperaments that was perfectly geared for the hardships of venturing halfway around the globe on an exotic adventure, but he could not bear the disputes and ridicule his discovery attracted. Embittered and frustrated, he finally locked his fossils away for over a quarter of a century, beyond the reach of contentious scientists.

Toward the end of his life Dubois reconsidered the evidence and concluded that he *had* probably found the remains of a giant gibbon. But once he let the erect ape-man out of the bottle, it could not be recalled. Other paleontologists went to Java, hoping to increase the documentation of Java man. In 1906, Frau Selenka, the widow of a German naturalist, dutifully sifted 10,000 cubic yards of material in the vicinity where Dubois found his fossils. She found many fossil animals, but not a single fragment of Pithecanthropus. This was disappointing, but at least the animal fossils enabled the age of the site to be estimated. Pithecanthropus is now dated at about 500,000 years old.

It was not until 1936 that G. H. R. von Koenigswald, a geologist, found another fossil of Java man on the island itself. This was only half of a lower jawbone, but it was followed in 1937, 1938, and 1939 by discoveries of important parts of several skulls. By then, however, the main focus of attention in paleoanthropology had shifted to China with the discovery of a much larger deposit containing a similar if not identical creature at a place called Choukoutien, about twenty-five miles southwest of Peking.

In 1927 Davidson Black, a Canadian anatomy professor teaching at a medical college in Peking, was shown a fossil tooth from Choukoutien, which had been mined for its fossils and limestone for many years. Black was intrigued by its size and cusp pattern and confidently announced that it belonged to an ancient type of man whom he dubbed Sinanthropus pekinensis, popularly known as Peking man.

Excavations under the direction of Dr. W. C. Pei, a Chinese paleontologist, were begun at Choukoutien that same year. Pei was to uncover the fossils, and Black was to describe and publish them. In 1928 Pei found fragments of skullcaps, two pieces of lower jaws, and many isolated teeth. In 1929 he found a well-preserved skullcap, similar to but slightly larger than that of Java man, creating a great stir in the world press. When a second skullcap turned up a little later, the Geological Survey of China acquired the site, and excavations were sustained for many years thereafter by the Rockefeller Foundation. Over the next decade remains of between thirty-eight and forty-five individuals of the same type were recovered from the deposits, which were as much as 160 feet deep. These remains consisted of fourteen partial skulls and skullcaps, fourteen lower jaws, and about 150 individual teeth. There were also a few postcranial bones, that is, bones other than those of the skull.

Black died in 1934, and his place was taken by Franz Weidenreich. The site was also described by Teilhard de Chardin, who was stationed in Peking at the time. In addition, Choukoutien was visited by two of the most notable authorities in paleoanthropology in the 1930s, the Abbé Breuil and Marcellin Boule. All these men provided assessments, and Weidenreich also produced casts, photographs, and models of the specimens, which was just as well because the entire collection of Peking man fossils disappeared during the Second World War and has never been relocated.

In the 1950s, Pithecanthropus erectus and Sinanthropus pekinensis were reclassified as Homo erectus, meaning erect man. Zoologically this name is meaningless, since it does not distinguish between the several beings that attained bipedalism, nor does it now refer to the first creature capable of walking erect, if 1470, Lucy, and/or afarensis were also indeed bipedal. What is significant is the word Homo.

The reclassification of the Peking and Java fossils as Homo erectus did not come about because of the perception of new evidence clearly proving that the creatures were men and thus our ancestors; nothing so grand as that. The reason was simply that on paper the number of ancestral candidates had become an embarrassment of riches. Practically every discoverer of a fossil possibly related to man had, in naming it, not only created a new species (for example, pekinensis) but a new genus (for example, Sinanthropus) as well. In certain instances, this was clearly unwarranted. The Java and Peking remains were obviously more closely related than that. For those fossils now covered by the term Neanderthal, about a dozen different names had been invented. This multiplicity of species and genera obscured their similarities and made it difficult to talk and write about their phylogenetic relationships.

In 1950 Prof. Ernst Mayr of Harvard proposed lumping all hominid fossils in the genus Homo in order to simplify the situation. Mayr is regarded as perhaps the most learned biologist in the United States, and his influence is considerable. His reclassification has now been widely accepted in Britain and the United States. There is little doubt that something of the sort was needed, but whether the genus in which these creatures have been lumped should have been called Homo (man) begs the very question at issue. In Britain and the United States there now seems to be a tendency for writers to reason that the Peking and Java fossils must represent ancestors to Homo sapiens because they have been classified that way. Few are willing to challenge the professional trumpetings of a Mayr.

Now, of course, the truths and laws of science are supposed to be universal. That is to say, if $E = mc^2$ on one side of the Atlantic, it is supposed to equal the same thing on the other side. However, taking an international view of the meaning of the Peking and Java fossils, we receive notice from France that Mayr's taxonomic trumpetings have not been universally agreed to. In that land of independent spirit, the creatures now called Homo erectus in most English-speaking countries are generally considered to have been generically distinct from man. That is, they are not given the ennobling epithet Homo. Instead, they are still called Pithecanthropus erectus or Pithecanthropines, and they are not considered by most French anthropologists to be ancestral to man.

It is not simply the independence of the French that accounts for this lack of uniformity. The French, in fact, have some very good reasons for their position, of which most American scientists do not now seem to be aware. Since I regard the ancestral status of fossils of the Peking and Java type as a case yet to be proved, I will refer to them as Pithecanthropus and Pithecanthropines. And in order to see why the French take such a different view of these creatures, we must look more closely at the deposits in which Peking man was found.

Skullcaps, jawbones, and teeth of Pithecanthropus were not all that was found among the compacted debris in the limestone hill at Choukoutien. The fossils of over a hundred species of vertebrates, eighty-eight of which were mammals, were also unearthed. These included deer, an ancient elephant, two species of rhinoceros, a true horse, an extinct buffalo, a wolf, several kinds of bears and hyenas closely related to our own, many cats, and rodents, including a large type of beaver. There were also worked flints, bone fragments that might have been used as tools, many pieces of quartz, which had been imported from a considerable distance (the local formation being devoid of this stone), and most important of all—ashes.

Aside from those resulting from volcanic eruptions and forest fires of natural origin, ashes are one of the clearest signs of man. Those at Choukoutien were concentrated in such a fashion as to leave no doubt that they derived from human activity. The ashes at Choukoutien were doubly important; not only did they indicate the presence of man, but for many years they were the oldest evidence of man-made fire anywhere and were the chief reason why Peking man was given a branch on the family tree.

So far this description of the Choukoutien deposit is what might be called a standard account. It contains little or nothing to constrain speculation that the Chinese Pithecanthropines were having regular picnics of rhinoceros burgers and bear puddings around the campfire in the mouth of their cave. Indeed, this is just the way in which sympathetic artists have re-created the Choukoutien milieu: Uncle Wilbur, unashamed of his naked-

The imagined scene at Choukoutien as suggested by Maurice Wilson's 1950 painting.   W.R.F.

ness, crouches cozily by the campfire as he smashes his pinky finger with a hammerstone; Hungry Jack staggers on stage dragging an antelope he felled with a high fastball on the inside corner; for a lark, Little Timmy disembowels a mountain lion with a pointed stick. Isn't science wonderful? Who can doubt the Pithecanthropines' essential humanity? They have everything except Heinz ketchup.

A picture is worth a thousand words, and if anthropologists employ artistic re-creations to convey the imagined scene (as they almost invariably do), they must take responsibility for them.

But as I have said, not everyone is happy with the foregoing script. At least some would take it a bit further and color it with a more poignant tone. It is noticeably odd, they say, that with remains of about forty individuals we should have almost nothing except their skulls, and all these smashed up in such a way that it seems someone wanted to get at the brains. In other words, Hungry Jack, depositing the antelope by the fire and Uncle Wilbur, is drawn by the excited squeals of Little Timmy and suddenly conceives the kid a damned nuisance and a good deal more appetizing than the antelope. He runs over and starts cutting off the brat's head with a hippopotamus jaw when he is interrupted by Uncle Wilbur. Wilbur, older and wiser than Jack, knows an opportunity when he sees one. He throws a perfect strike to second base with his hammerstone, catching Jack on the uttermost point of his elongated occiput, or, as they say in Texas, square in the back of the head. Then *he* works the hippopotamus jaw. Wilbur has always regarded these sometime colleagues as rank outsiders in his family nest, qualifying them for the role of nutritional supplement. He takes the heads home, cracks them open with his trusty hammerstone, and has the brains for dessert. Lest you wonder how a species this self-destructive could have evolved into anything, you must remember that Uncle Wilbur has kept all the girls for himself. They have been hiding in the back of the cave chewing bear skins into miniskirts.

Now in fairness, I must acknowledge that not all erectus supporters are happy with this scenario either. Some would have it that Pithecanthropus was not this crude; that headhunting and cannibalism may have involved "religious" motives, in which case we should include a scene where Uncle Wilbur says grace to the Great Pithecanthropine in the sky before making an omelet with Timmy's gray matter.

Still and all, these supporters do not shrink from hard-core realism and make it plain that this happy family had not read Emily Post. They suggest that the fast-food craze had to start somewhere, and this is as good a place as any. We must get used to the idea that what constitutes a nutritional supplement has varied considerably from place to place and time to time.

II.

Admittedly, a ticket full of creatures with an insatiable appetite for the brains of their own kind might not seem the ideal item to convince the general public that their great-great-grandfathers to the nine-hundredth power were bushy beasties. If we have to derive man from the animals, it is better to sell the idea in as innocuous a form as possible, and Uncle Wilbur is hardly that. So we should not be surprised to find a deal of back-pedaling and soft-peddling. For instance, in *Peking Man* (1974), Dr. Harry Shapiro offers the amiable suggestion that perhaps the skulls in the Choukoutien caves were all smashed up because the roof fell in and that their condition has nothing to do with a craving for sweetmeats. But this is lamentably weak because it fails to explain why little or none of the postcranial skeleton was attached to these skulls and deliberately ignores the fact that certain of the larger hunks of skulls showed man-made holes on the top or bottom that have no conceivable purpose except the extraction of the brain. In *The Evolution of Man* (1970) David Pilbeam prefers to march right through the anatomical evidence without ever mentioning cannibalism at Peking. In *Early Man* (1965) F. Clark Howell says nothing more than that cannibalism is "hinted at" in the remains of Peking man. In *Origins* (1977) Richard Leakey and Roger Lewin admirably do everything they can to explode the idea recently much in vogue that humans are inherently aggressive, but somehow end up arguing that the charred and battered skulls of the Peking Pithecanthropines got into this condition as "a mark of the love and respect" of their relatives.

There is really not much help for it: If the Peking Pithecanthropines are our ancestors, the implications of their fossils are grisly, ghastly, and godawful. Even prominent voices within the profession are not happy enunciating an ancestor with this kind of personality. Nevertheless, the animal-ancestor advocates who have dug deeper into what kind of deposits these were at Chou-koutien hang onto the cannibalism explanation with both hands, because there is yet a third possible scenario that is even more objectionable—at least to them.

This third perspective was elucidated by a man who was then the leading paleoanthropologist in France, and some say the world, the late Marcellin Boule. Boule's interpretation has much to do with why the French refuse to package Pithecanthropus with the label Homo.

It seems the Choukoutien deposits were even more peculiar than the standard descriptions indicate. The Pithecanthropine remains were not neatly segregated from those of the many other animals; all these remains were mixed up together with the ashes, as they might be in a garbage heap. (Not too much "love and respect" shown by tossing Timmy's fractured bean into the communal compost pile.) And worst of all, the sheer volume of these "campfire" ashes and the tens of thousands of quartz fragments beneath them have more in common with the level of industrial activity of U.S. Steel than with a creature on the edge of becoming human.

I do not exaggerate. If one looks into the story of Peking man far enough, one will find reports that these "cozy family hearths" produced piles of compacted ashes 22 to 39 feet deep, over 300 feet long, and nearly 100 feet wide! Quite a roast.

On the face of it, it seems absurd to attribute this scale of activity to a creature on the level of Pithecanthropus. There is no positive evidence from elsewhere that the Pithecanthropines even knew fire. Nothing comparable has been found at the dozens of Neanderthal sites, and Neanderthal was supposedly much advanced over Pithecanthropus.

What, then, is the explanation? Marcellin Boule, whose text *Fossil Men* (1957) is considered "the most comprehensive and authoritative general work on human paleontology," was not only one of the few top-rank experts to visit Choukoutien, he was certainly the only one who was dispassionate enough to suggest that the deposits might not be quite as significant for human evolution as others have painted them.

Boule was one of those men whose confidence in the general idea of evolution was such that he felt the facts would speak for themselves as they were developed and that significance did not need to be forced out of the fossils by slanting the evidence or conjured out of mere assumptions. As he deftly stated his position in the preface to *Fossil Men,*

I have endeavored to write this work with complete detachment of mind, confining myself exclusively to scientific ground. In my anxiety to avoid attributing conclusive value to any but positive facts, I have not hesitated to strew my text with more marks of interrogation than of affirmation; and this I have done in the belief that thus I may best advance science, and at the same time show most consideration for my readers.

This attitude, I might say, is exceedingly rare in this profession. So here is how Boule, limiting himself only to "positive facts," saw this creature that was still called Sinanthropus at the time he wrote:

Obviously, if Sinanthropus knew how to make fire, if he knew how to manufacture implements, if he was a *faber* [a maker], the question is—by definition—settled in favour of his human status. But are the facts proven? It is permissible to dispute them.

Boule then disputes them cogently and at length. He first notes that in order to give Sinanthropus human status, the anatomists lean on the archaeologists and the archaeologists on the anatomists. The two points of view must be dissociated, he says. The archaeology and morphology must be analyzed separately before we arrive at larger conclusions. Boule found the archaeology very peculiar:

The circumstances of the deposit and the unvarying nature of the bone-remains of Sinanthropus recall what we find in a purely geological bed of fossil animals, rather than the manner in which discoveries of human skeletons normally present themselves.

Boule had first-hand experience excavating such discoveries. Why was it that at Choukoutien we find a considerable selection of bony parts all belonging to the skull and almost a complete absence of bones from other parts of the skeleton? Boule agreed with Weidenreich that the skull parts did not come into the cave by natural means, but that they must have been imported by hunters who had a preference for heads or parts of heads. This was thoroughly plausible, as far as it went, "but the problem is to name the hunter." He notes that to Weidenreich's mind the hunter was Sinanthropus himself, making him a cannibal, "the first cannibal." But Boule thought this was far-fetched.

To this hypothesis, other writers preferred the following, which seemed to them more in conformity with our whole body of knowledge: the hunter was a true Man, whose stone industry has been found and who preyed upon Sinanthropus.

Boule then discusses the stone industry at Choukoutien. He says it is important to note that this industry is not primitive. He cites M. Breuil as writing that many of its features "are not found in France until the Upper Paleolithic." By the Upper Paleolithic stone tools had become highly crafted instruments. Boule remarks that Breuil's observation certainly does not enhance the credibility of seeing Sinanthropus as the author of those tools from a chronological standpoint. One would expect to find a very primitive ("eolithic") industry accompanying a being like Sinanthropus, he says, "and not true gravers and scrapers and other tools sometimes of fine workmanship."

So Boule reiterates his conception that Sinanthropus was merely the prey of a true man, and he anticipated the objection that if such a man had lived at Choukoutien, "he would be bound to have left all or part of his skeleton there." This, he said, did not necessarily follow. He pointed to the numerous, heavily filled grottoes and caverns of Western Europe "so rich in the products of the Paleolithic human industry." The proportion of these deposits that have yielded skeletal remains of the manufacturers of this industry "is infinitesimal," he wrote. "We may say that the absence of human bone-remains is the rule and their presence the exception." He then cites the example of the so-called Prince's Cave at Grimaldi. This cave was carefully excavated "precisely in the hope of finding skeletons like those of the neighboring grottoes." The cave's filling abounded in animal bones and worked stones, but its 4,000 cubic yards of material yielded not the slightest fragment of human remains. "Why should it not be the same at Choukoutien?" he asks. This question is still entirely valid, and so is his conclusion:

We may therefore ask ourselves whether it is not over-bold to consider Sinanthropus the monarch of Choukoutien, when he appears in its deposits only in the guise of a mere hunter's prey, on a par with the animals by which he is accompanied.

III.

So this is why erectus supporters hang on to the cannibalism hypothesis with both hands: The dreadful alternative is that Peking "man" had about as much relevance for human evolution as a fossilized hambone.

Indeed, this seems to be the only explanation that accounts for a grim fact that I confess to having withheld from the reader. In the second scenario of what happened in the mouth of the Choukoutien cave a quarter of a million years ago, I gave the reader the impression that the girls were all at the back of the cave awaiting the attentions of Uncle Wilbur. In the heat of the lurid description of those dire events, I could not bring myself to snatch from the reader the faint hope that at least a muted ray of sense and chivalry could be reconstructed from the evidence of the refuse pile. Unfortunately, these broken skulls belonged not only to males and young ones, but to females as well. It must be regretfully stated that the etiquette of the lifeboat did not there prevail. If one persists with the ancestor hypothesis, he must acknowledge that Uncle Wilbur was in such a rudimentary condition as to prefer brains to sex, not a good omen for the expan-

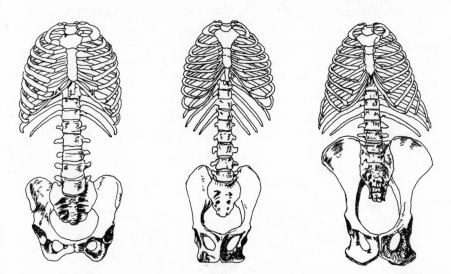

Left to right: The skeletal torsos of man, gibbon, and chimpanzee reduced to the same size. If Peking "man" was indeed a giant gibbon, it would have been easy to mistake his fossils for human ones, especially since little of the skeletal torso has been recovered.   *D.E.F.*

sion of the species or the development of a life-insurance industry.

If, on the other hand, the Pithecanthropines were merely hunted quarry, as Boule suggested, these alarming inferences do not apply. In putting this forward, Boule did not casually conjure a quarry out of the air; he had a particular genus in mind: Hyboletes, or the gibbons. Present-day gibbons are small, twenty-pound, arboreal creatures with long arms. The long arms are a recent specialization, and the gibbons' skeletal torso, if inflated to the same size as man's, is perhaps the most similar to our own of all modern apes. Add to these facts the consideration that in earlier epochs there were giant forms of mammals whose living representatives are now greatly reduced in size, and Boule's suggestion that the Pithecanthropines were "a large form, a giant ape, related to the gibbon group" seems plausible.

Whatever the group to which the Pithecanthropines belonged, Boule's reasons for interpreting them as prey hunted by a true man remain as valid as they were fifty years ago. Indeed, certain discoveries in the intervening years make his interpretation more likely than ever. Yet I have still to find an American anthropologist who even breathes a word that Boule's perspective should be entertained as a scientific possibility. On the contrary, most seem to believe in the ancestral status of the Pithecanthropines (under the name Homo erectus) with the same world-structuring intensity with which other people believe in Jesus Christ. Given the background I have related and the central importance of erectus in the scenario of man's evolution, it is appropriate to examine how and why American anthropologists were rendered so uncritical as to swallow the ancestral status of "Peking man" hook, line, and sinker.

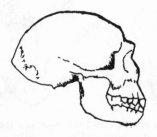

Sketch of the reconstructed skull of Peking man (*left*) compared with that of a modern gibbon. Scale not exact.   W.R.F.

10: Nettlebottom's Career

I.

THE EXPLANATION for the present unanimity of opinion among American anthropologists on a question of such arcane fascination and profound uncertainty as the ownership of those antique refuse heaps at Choukoutien seems to run along these lines.

As Boule pointed out, there were two aspects to the discovery of the Chinese Pithecanthropines: the archaeological and the anatomical. The archaeological character of the deposits suggested the Pithecanthropines were merely an item on somebody else's menu. The anatomical evidence, however, was such that in certain of their features these creatures appeared to be ideal candidates for a missing link between man and the apes—especially if one was predisposed to see this connection in the first place. As Sir Solly Zuckerman noted, there are many evolutionists who are so biased in their perception and presentation of the evidence that they would have little difficulty in making the bones of a contemporary ape seem more closely related to man than to

124 A Tour of the Boneroom

the species that they actually represent. Such enthusiasts, in this case primarily Franz Weidenreich and Fr. Pierre Teilhard de Chardin, became hypnotized by the anatomical aspect of Pithecanthropus and simply refused to confront the archaeological evidence indicating that this creature was merely a gourmet's delight—except as a form of cannibalism. They deemphasized the problematic archaeology to the point of invisibility at the same time that they took a large capital gain on the anatomical side, thus considerably inflating their version of the evolutionary ledger.

This shifty procedure probably would not have had the far-reaching consequences it did if Marcellin Boule had been better known in the United States. Had his comment that these controversial fossils appeared in the deposits in the guise of common prey been meditated upon in more faculty cafeteria, there might have been less of a tendency for elements of the intelligentsia to take a flying leap onto the Pithecanthropine bandwagon. But as it was, with the intervention of the Second World War and plenty of evolutionary copy on the American side of the water, Boule's observations about the hunter and the hunted were never adequately presented to American scientists until his book, *Fossil Men*, was translated and published in English in 1957. By that time, the enthusiasts had had the American market to themselves for twenty years. Weidenreich and Teilhard had found the necessary credulous supporters among American authorities; and from there on professional support for the ancestral status of the Pithecanthropines snowballed. We all know how this works: Prof. Braincrack, head of the department, declares his belief. Associate Prof. Speakmore can tell which way the wind is blowing. Assistant Prof. Frogmire jumps aboard. It hardly requires the perspicacity of an Hercule Poirot to predict which way graduate student Nettlebottom will run.

In short, by the time Boule's remarks appeared in English, the American profession had thoroughly convinced itself that it was already in possession of the truth. By 1957 the cautious interpretation of the only really dispassionate expert who had actually visited Choukoutien seemed nothing more than a quaint, conservative reaction. Which, more or less, is where this matter still stands up and down the American academic landscape in the 1980s.

Of course I am painfully aware that in putting the matter thus

I am stepping on some large and very delicate toes. The Nettle-bottoms of this world—now Prof. Nettlebottom—will probably declare that I am a raving fanatic. I will be accused of mere drollery and of besmirching the sacred cow. After all, had he not received the truth of this matter on the very knee of the late, great Braincrack?

Anticipating an adverse reaction from the founts of latter-day idolatry, I have assembled the following ammunition.

There is definite evidence that the American profession was laboring in a decidedly overheated atmosphere when the Chou-koutien fossils were uncovered. We recall that the first fractured skullcaps came to light in the late '20s, a decade that was a roaring success for practically everyone except American evolu-tionists. The wounds that smarted were the disheartening expe-rience with Hesperopithecus the pig-man and the Scopes Trial.

The Scopes Trial not only had a lot to do with the easy accep-tance of Peking man by American evolutionists; its conse-quences still have much to do with the continuing and now ridiculously polarized debate in the United States between cre-ationists and evolutionists.

On May 9, 1925, the science teacher of Rhea County High School in Dayton, Tennessee, one John T. Scopes, was arrested for violating the state anti-evolution law. The case ignited na-tional and international interest in evolution as nothing else ever had. Two of the most famous lawyers of the time argued the case. The liberal Clarence Darrow defended Scopes, and William Jennings Bryan, three-time candidate for president and secretary of state in Wilson's first cabinet, spoke on behalf of the state. Darrow cross-examined Bryan himself in a successful attempt to discredit a literal interpretation of the Bible. Bryan appeared bumbling and foolish defending literal interpretations of the par-ables about Jonah and the Whale and Joshua making the sun stand still. Bryan also seemed to know next to nothing about the age of the earth and the antiquity of man. Indeed, although anti-evolution laws were pending in fifteen other states and plans had been laid for a concerted fundamentalist campaign to get them enacted, Bryan's performance was so disastrous that this campaign was stopped in its tracks.

Nevertheless, the judge ordered much of Bryan's testimony stricken from the record and found Scopes guilty, fining him a hundred dollars. It rankled many scientists that the teaching of evolution had been hauled before a court of law and had been rejected. Scientifically, this had devastating consequences. As J. P. Cohane has expressed it, "The very fact that the fundamentalists were shouting so loudly, 'Man is *not* descended from monkeys and apes,' caused their opponents to shout back just as loudly, 'Man *is* descended from monkeys and apes.' " Commenting on the aftereffects of the trial some years later, the eminent British anatomist Frederic Wood Jones remarked that the Dayton episode had provoked "a return to the age of dogmatism" by evolutionary protagonists.

So the pig-man debacle and the Scopes verdict were recent memories when the Chinese Pithecanthropines were announced. The atmosphere in paleontological circles was not made any cooler by the dearth of speculative fodder at the time. Paleoanthropology had not provided much grist for the evolutionary mill since the flutter over the first Pithecanthropine, "Java man," in the 1890s. There was the enigmatic and (to some) troublesome Piltdown skull; a heavy, nonmodern jaw found near Heidelberg, Germany, in 1907; and the undatable remains of Australopithecus africanus from South Africa; but these were not as exciting as Pithecanthropus. And then Dubois became temperamental and hid his fossils away. As F. Clark Howell describes the situation, it is clear that what the profession wanted more than anything else was another Pithecanthropus:

Many anthropologists, of course, were passionately interested in what the Java man had to say about human evolution. They suspected the truth about it, and were waiting in a fever of impatience for more information to be released about it or for a breakthrough somewhere else that might throw some light on it.

If any further confirmation were needed, phrases such as "passionately interested," "suspected the truth," and "fever of impatience" should remove all doubt as to just how overheated the atmosphere had become. The evolutionary mill was geared up and ready to roll. Eager hands awaited their chance. The bright faces and best brains in the anatomy department had performed more pushing exercises than an obstetrician's wife expecting triplets. Then came the discovery of those magnificent ashes and fabulous skull fragments. The "breakthrough" had occurred!

As if this combination of ingredients was not enough to warp the judgment of all but the coolest heads, the final touch was added when Fr. Teilhard de Chardin, then resident in Peking, blessed the breakthrough and took the Pithecanthropines out of limbo as no one else could. Teilhard joined Weidenreich in attributing the ashes to Sinanthropus and emphasized the human qualities of his anatomy. Given all the other ingredients pressurizing the atmosphere in paleoanthropology at the time, one could hardly expect Father Teilhard's secular paleontological colleagues to be less enthusiastic than he—particularly those colleagues in the U.S. of A., where the atmospheric pressures were greater than anywhere else. And indeed they were not. Here was a good Catholic priest, who seemed to many a noble Seeker of Truth, not only endorsing human evolution, but pronouncing very agreeable syllables about the maker of those ashes. When a few years later his superiors in the Church forbade him to publish any more evolutionary papers during his lifetime, his fans in the faculty cafeteria saw shades of Galileo and a wonderful opportunity to relive history. If the Church was against it, it must be true. As far as they were concerned, the creature later renamed Homo erectus was given his papers and admitted to the human race. He has been with us ever since.

II.

It is not difficult to account for erectus' endurance. As noted earlier, if one ignores the peculiar character of the deposits and gazes fixedly only at certain anatomical features of the reconstructed skulls, these creatures seem ideally suited for the role of missing link. Their estimated cranial capacity falls into a range between 800 and 1,200 cc., averaging about 1,000 cc. This is just halfway between the gorilla and man. Moreover, it is significantly larger than the 850 cc. estimated for Java man, and since the Peking fossils also appear to be more recent (usually estimated at about 250,000 to 300,000 years in age as against 500,000 for Java man), it is not difficult to see these fossils forming an evolutionary sequence leading to Homo sapiens.

It is important to realize that Boule did not contest that *if viewed by themselves* certain Pithecanthropine anatomical features could be seen this way. He noted the opinion to which the enthusiasts had come, that the Pithecanthropines were "true ancestors of the genus Homo," and said,

This conclusion, drawn solely from the study of anatomical factors, is all the more admissible because it accords very well with the general idea we may form of the morphological processes by which the passage from a generalized anthropoid stage to a primitive human stage may or must have taken place.

More than this, Boule quoted Black, Pei, Weidenreich, Teilhard, and Abbé Breuil so that the reader could understand exactly why they held the positions they did. However, these "protagonists and supporters," as Boule called them, promoting the ancestral status of the Pithecanthropines did not extend the same courtesy to Boule or their readers.

What was put forward instead were the kind of statements found in Weidenreich's paper "Facts and Speculations Concerning the Origin of Homo Sapiens," published in the April–June 1947 issue of *American Anthropologist*. This, it is worth remembering, is the same Franz Weidenreich who, in one of the wildest flights of fancy ever to afflict a member of the profession, found no incongruity in proposing Gigantopithecus as an ancestor in 1946. His 1947 paper begins,

> The discovery of Sinanthropus and the more recent finds of Pithecanthropus specimens [by von Koenigswald on Java] once for all settled the question of the *morphological* character of the immediate forerunner of Neanderthal man. Both Sinanthropus and Pithecanthropus have been acknowledged by all experts as true hominids, closely related to each other. They represent a phase of human evolution which exhibits more primitive features in number and kind than any of the known types of Neanderthal man. So far as doubts have been entertained, the main reason for skepticism was the incompleteness of information due to the lack or insufficiency of communication during the years of war.

First we should note that von Koenigswald's finds on Java in the late '30s were again highly fragmentary and added nothing to Pithecanthropus' credentials. Second and more important, Weidenreich was simply not telling the truth when he said, "Both Sinanthropus and Pithecanthropus have been acknowledged by all experts as true hominids. . . ." Boule acknowledged nothing of the kind. Instead of confronting Boule's criticism, Weidenreich supports his own view by quoting (who else?) Teilhard de Chardin, which on this matter is a bit like Tweedledum quoting Tweedledee.

... Teilhard made the following statement as to the *anatomical* character of Sinanthropus. ... "On the whole, Sinanthropus decidedly stands, in his *anatomical* features, on man's side among the primates. ..."

I have emphasized the words *morphological* and *anatomical* in the preceding quotes because it is on that basis and only on that basis that Weidenreich can claim Sinanthropus represents "a phase of human evolution." Weidenreich never mentions the unusual archaeology of Choukoutien and never mentions Boule's question "whether it is not over-bold to consider Sinanthropus the monarch of Choukoutien, when he appears in its deposit only in the guise of a mere hunter's prey. ..."

Unless the American reader of 1947 had read the 1946 French edition of *Fossil Men*, he could not have guessed from Weidenreich's paper that there was anything in the total pattern of evidence concerning Peking "man" to compromise Weidenreich's conclusions based on the anatomy. Since Weidenreich was aware of "an incompleteness of information due to the ... insufficiency of communication" during the war years, one might have thought he would round out "the main reason for ... skepticism" as voiced by Boule. But he doesn't. He clearly prefers the role of protagonist for Sinanthropus' evolutionary significance to that of dispassionate reporter. And it cannot be that Weidenreich was not aware of Boule's criticism because elsewhere in his paper he quarrels with Boule for provisionally calling the group to which Sinanthropus and Pithecanthropus belong prehominids rather than hominids, but he does not mention why Boule preferred that designation.

This is quite a strange science, all in all. Too often there is not even a pretense at objectivity; not even a hint that there really is more than one possible explanation. Anyone questioning the credentials of a particular missing link is portrayed as having missed the boat—until something embarrassing happens to discredit the ancestor. Then that "ancestor" is put to one side as quietly as possible, and the profession moves on to other fossils.

Of course, the Pithecanthropines have not yet been put to one side by most anthropologists. When Boule's *Fossil Men* did finally appear in English in 1957, the cards were already thoroughly stacked against a fair hearing for his view simply by the nearly universal repetition of Weidenreich's credo. But the

profession wasn't taking any chances. In 1957 the exposure of
the Piltdown hoax was still a recent memory. If the English-
speaking public were now to hear that one of the top two or
three authorities in the history of the profession were telling a
completely different story about Choukoutien than the version
that had become canonical in their own countries, it might look
queer. The best place to forestall this possibility was in the introduction to the English edition of *Fossil Men* itself and the man
for the job was Kenneth P. Oakley. In an introduction to a book
of this type, dealing with virtually all the fossils relevant to
human evolution discovered anywhere up to that time, it would
normally have been sufficient to say a few words about the author. Instead, we find Oakley contesting that author's interpretation of one particular deposit:

Perhaps the most outstanding aspect of our knowledge of Peking man
is the archaeological one, for the Choukoutien excavations provided
unquestionable evidence that he was a tool-maker, a regular fire-user,
a meat-eater and almost certainly a cannibal. To the more conservative
students of human evolution, at first it seemed possible that "Sinanthropus" had not been responsible for any of these activities, but was
a sub-human being that had been the victim of a higher type of true
man. . . . The evidence was eventually seen to be overwhelmingly on
the side of the simpler explanation. Before the end of the nineteen-
thirties there was no longer any question that hominids of the Pithecanthropus group were capable of such essentially human cultural
activities as making tools and using fire.

Throughout much of this, Oakley is talking through his hat. Oakley manages to sound as if he is dealing with an archaic text
whose author would now agree with "the simpler explanation."
Nothing could be further from the truth. The 1957 edition was a
revised edition, vetted by Boule's collaborator Vallois; there was
no reason to change Boule's comments on Peking "man." Oakley
says that before the end of the 1930s, there was no question that
the Pithecanthropines could make fire: On the contrary, by the
end of the '30s there was no positive evidence whatever that
these creatures did anything of the kind, and there still isn't. In
an article for *L'Anthropologie* in 1937, Boule expressed himself
on this question even more vigorously than he did in *Fossil Men*:

To this fantastic hypothesis, that the owners of the monkey-like skulls
were the authors of the large-scale industry, I take the liberty of prefer-
ring an opinion more in conformity with the conclusions from my

studies, which is that the hunter was a real man and that the cut stones, etc., were his handiwork.

Oakley's hyperbole appears the more grandiloquent when we remember that Boule investigated the actual site, whereas Oakley did not. And given all the features of Choukoutien, it is mere sophistry to suggest that the Weidenreich-Teilhard hypothesis is "the simpler explanation."

However, if in saying, "The evidence was eventually *seen* to be overwhelmingly on the side of the simpler explanation," Oakley means that the majority of American and British anthropologists chose the Weidenreich-Teilhard interpretation over that of Boule, he is certainly correct. There was hardly a man among them who wanted to appear more conservative than Father Teilhard.

Not unnaturally, there is another view of Teilhard's career than to see him as a modern Galileo, and given his role in the creation of this "ancestor," it is appropriate to notice it. Few people will contest the richly ideational character of Teilhard's writings or the deeply philosophical perspective his words occasionally evoke. For his fans, his deservedly high literary reputation seems to have washed over onto his reputation as a paleontologist. In the case of Peking man in particular, however, there are some legitimate doubts as to the value of Teilhard's opinion.

These doubts spring from Teilhard's little-known involvement in the Piltdown affair. Louis Leakey was convinced that Teilhard was directly responsible for acquiring, fashioning, and planting some of the fake fossils, acting as a co-conspirator with Charles Dawson. Quite a few of Leakey's colleagues shared his suspicions. In the August 1980 issue of *Natural History* ("The Piltdown Conspiracy") Stephen Jay Gould serves up "new" evidence of Teilhard's role.

Teilhard was still alive in 1953 when Kenneth Oakley, J. S. Weiner, and W. E. Le Gros Clark proved that the Piltdown bones had been doctored. (Teilhard died in 1955.) It was well known to these men that along with the solicitor Dawson and Arthur Smith Woodward, Teilhard was the only other individual present during most of the Piltdown "discoveries," which came from two different sites from about 1911 to 1915. Smith Woodward, keeper of paleontology at the British Museum at the time, was shown the early discoveries from one site in 1912, when the discovery was announced, and thereafter was present when some of the other "finds" were made.

Teilhard had become involved fortuitously. Born in 1881, he joined the Jesuits in 1902, studied on the island of Jersey until 1905, taught physics and chemistry at a Jesuit school in Cairo until 1908, and from 1908 to 1912, when he was ordained, was a theological student at Ore Place in Hastings, next to Piltdown. He was at least as interested in natural history as in theology and bumped into Charles Dawson while hunting fossils in a stone quarry in 1909. Teilhard's correspondence indicates that they became good friends.

Kenneth Oakley, one of the debunkers of Piltdown, was keen to clarify the mystery of who had done it and why. Both Smith Woodward and Dawson were dead in 1953, and the only person directly involved with whom he could correspond was Teilhard. Gould visited Oakley in 1980 and noticed a slip Teilhard had made in some of his 1953 correspondence with Oakley. Teilhard indicates knowledge of some of the fossils before they were "discovered." This is by no means the entire case, but proved a pivotal clue for Gould, who goes on to present a convincing pattern of other circumstantial evidence, including Teilhard's strange silence and embarrassment on the subject of Piltdown in later years.

Gould is extremely charitable to Teilhard. He suggests the motive for Teilhard's involvement with Dawson in perpetrating the fraud was more or less a schoolboy prank designed to embarrass a profession they envied but had little hope of entering. But the joke went too far, duped too many people, and later, when Teilhard did get a chance to study paleontology, it became impossible to burst the bubble without scuttling his own career and those of many others.

This is possible, but when the mischief was at its height around 1911, Teilhard was thirty years old and on the verge of ordination as a priest. In light of his later writings, it seems at least as likely that Teilhard saw Piltdown as a first step in his personal campaign to save the Church. Convinced of the general veracity of evolution and of its application to man (Neanderthal and Java man were already known), Teilhard despaired that the teachings of the Church were being swamped by facts from the physical sciences. In *Science and Christ* (1968), one of the many posthumous collections of his writings, Teilhard remarks in an early lecture to the effect that the Church has abundant authorities on doctrine but no research department. The general body of his work represents a powerful and for many a successful attempt to reconcile the facts of physical science with a universe invested with spirit. In other words, Teilhard seems to have seen himself as the Church's equivalent of just such a "research department" as he thought it needed. At the time of Piltdown, he did not have the credentials to be much more than a science teacher in the Jesuit educational system. Participation in a paleontological discovery would make his name, putting him in a far stronger stance to launch his work of synthesizing science and religion. Certainly in 1911 he had little reason to anticipate the development of the fluorine test, which eventually did much to discredit the Piltdown bones.

As it happened, Teilhard received permission to do graduate work with Marcellin Boule back in France shortly after his ordination and the first official announcement of the Piltdown finds. Gould documents a consistent pattern in Teilhard's writings from 1920 on, showing that after his career was launched, he was extremely diffident about Piltdown and appears to have deeply regretted his involvement. Piltdown man rapidly assumed an importance in scientific writings of far greater proportions than Teilhard could have imagined. After his return from the First World War, in which he performed much distinguished service as a stretcher-bearer, he became professor of geology at the Institut Catholique of Paris. But due to conflicts with ecclesiastical authorities he was ordered to leave this post and was sent to China in 1926, where he was given a clerical teaching position in Peking.

Teilhard was never formally attached to the excavating team at Choukoutien. He acted as a free-lance reporter, submitting articles to French magazines, which published them readily. Consider what a godsend Sinanthropus must have seemed: At last there was a discovery taking attention away from Piltdown. How could he be anything but a protagonist and supporter of Sinanthropus, even if it meant breaking with his beloved teacher Boule? If Teilhard had followed Boule in his assessment of Peking man, it would only have heaped yet greater importance on Piltdown, which was the last thing he then wanted.

Gould's case against Teilhard is evenhanded and persuasive. He provides a fair assessment, I think, when he says that the burden of proof now rests with those who would hold Teilhard blameless. This does nothing to affect the importance or validity of the philosophical concepts through which he sought to reconcile religion and science; they deserve to be judged on their own merits. But for the reasons outlined, the value of Teilhard's support for Sinanthropus is seriously jeopardized and should not be approached with the attitude that Sinanthropus must be a missing link if even this priest accepted it. And even if Teilhard was innocent of involvement in the Piltdown fraud, it is indisputable that he was allowed to find some of the bogus fossils. He was obviously less than infallible as a paleontologist, since these instant antiques literally passed through his hands and he saw nothing wrong with them. Of course this was before he studied with Boule, but even afterward his paleontological expertise seems to have been much more limited than many now assume. According to one critic, Piltdown and Choukoutien were the only sites at which Teilhard was seriously involved, and only in a peripheral way at the latter.

III.

The point to be emphasized about the Peking man affair is not that Boule had ascertained the unblemished, copper-bottomed truth and the others had overlooked it; it is rather that the mere existence of an opinion so contrary by a man of such standing should have been sufficient to warn professionals of genuine scientific spirit from making unwarranted assumptions and extrapolations from a deposit of decidedly ambiguous value—no matter how they were prodded along by Teilhard. There is not now, and certainly was not in 1957 when Oakley wrote that introduction, a bit of new evidence or a single "positive fact" to dissolve this ambiguity. It was merely the willingness of anthropologists to believe in the evolutionary significance of the Pithecanthropines, and the necessity of defending that belief, that motivated empty assertions like Oakley's. And this willingness to believe, coupled with a concern for one's career, is all that sustains the case for the Pithecanthropines today. The Nettlebottoms of this world have been delivering the canonical version of those ash heaps all their working lives. Their psychological commitment to defending the verisimilitude of this position is now so tremendous that we cannot expect them to be swayed by mere evidence.

Unfortunately for Nettlebottom's place in history, however, fossil hunters have collected quite a few interesting specimens in recent years, and several of these make it more evident than ever that Boule's caution should have been heeded. In the wake of the discovery of the Vertesszollos individual in Hungary and skulls 3733 and 1470 in Kenya, Boule's remarks regarding Choukoutien have taken on new importance.

The Vertesszollos remains are older than those at Choukoutien and appear to be those of Homo sapiens, seriously compromising the significance of Peking man. The Richard Leakey discoveries don't help either. The first, 3733, is the oldest and best preserved Pithecanthropine skull ever found. It is dated at about 1.6 or 1.7 million years and thus creates a problem for the Homo erectus group itself. The problem is this: 3733 has a cranial capacity of about 900 cc. Java man, who lived about 1.2 million years later, had a cranial capacity of only about 850 cc. Moreover, the forehead of Java man was much more retreating than that of 3733. We have to go to Peking man, about a quarter of a million years ago, before we find a comparable form. There the average adult skull size is around 1,000 cc., but the forehead is not more developed, and if anything was less developed than that of 3733. In other words, viewed from the criteria of 3733, Homo erectus shows no evolutionary progress over a period of 1.4 million years!

Now, as I say, the profession has been committed to Homo erectus for so long that this development has hardly raised an eyebrow. Nevertheless, the evidence we *have*, the positive facts, now show an evolutionary standstill in this species of well over a million years at just the time it should have been evolving most rapidly if it was indeed on the road to Homo sapiens.

The other remarkable Leakey discovery, skull 1470, also creates a problem for Homo erectus. Here the problem is even more obvious. Although it is slightly smaller, at 780 to 835 cc., this skull (which is a minimum of 1.8 million years old) is in most of its features far more modern looking than 3733 or any other Pithecanthropine specimen. The sides of the 1470 skull are nearly parallel (as in modern man); the cranium is well domed; the forehead far closer to modern than in the Pithecanthropines; and the browridge is much more moderate and nothing like the heavy visor from which 3733 peered. It is a very strained theory that posits that we moved from 1470 to 3733 and then back again to lighter brows, fuller foreheads, higher domes, and straighter sides to our skulls.

IV.

Those who worry that I refer to the English-speaking section of "the profession" as if they are uniformly a pack of self-deluded rascals may take some solace in hearing that even on this question of the Pithecanthropines—where there is more uniformity and absurdity than on any other—there are a few stalwart individuals who have not bought the party line. For example, even before the discovery of the Vertesszollos man, 1470, and 3733, Louis Leakey declined to endorse the Pithecanthropines as leading to man. The size of the Pithecanthropine skull did not weigh as heavily with Leakey as other anatomical features, such as the creature's enormous browridges, which are so massive as to make even Neanderthal seem delicate by comparison. To be sure, the most widely reproduced pictures of the skull of Peking man do not show the browridges as dramatically as this, but these pictures are of Weidenreich's *reconstructed* version of the skull, which happens to be based on adolescent and probably female fragments. Thus it is far more human in appearance than an adult, male skull of the same species would be, since these show specializations more clearly than do crania of females and juveniles. Louis Leakey demonstrated this in 1960 with the discovery of a Pithecanthropine skullcap at Olduvai Gorge with browridges so tremendous that it strains even the most credulous imagination to see in it the precursor of man.

For Leakey, the same general problems that beset Neanderthal also disqualified the Pithecanthropines as ancestors: overspecialization away from the human condition. As he put it in *Adam's Ancestors* (1960), "Peking man was an over-specialized offshoot of the human stem." But this is not the only problem he saw. Perhaps unaware how committed most of the American profession had become, he continued blithely,

The late Professor Weidenreich, however, maintained that Peking man was ancestral to Homo sapiens, and some scientists still hold this view. It cannot, however, be accepted, for the skulls show many marked specializations and also have now been proved to be of Middle Pleistocene age, a date which is far too recent for them to be regarded as ancestral to Homo sapiens.

Then there is at least one American anthropologist who recently questioned the ancestral status of the Pithecanthropines. Writing in *Human Evolution* (second edition, 1975) J. B. Birdsell was not yet ready to abandon the Pithecanthropines altogether, but at least he had the open-mindedness to point out that with 1470 on the scene there were now certain obvious problems. "It is an interesting point that they [the Pithecanthropines] are not as advanced-looking as ER-1470," Birdsell observed and, like a lonely pilgrim at Reason's throne, carried this theme further. The cranial capacity of the Javanese Pithecanthropines (750 to 975 cc.), he notes, is not really much greater than that of 1470, who lived at a much earlier date. If we combine this observation with the fact that 1470 is much more modern in appearance than the Pithecanthropines, "an evolutionary problem is posed but not solved."

The problem, of course, is that if both 1470 and the Pithecanthropines are ancestral to man, then given the chronology it means Pithecanthropus descended from 1470, but as Birdsell says, "Anatomically in some ways such an evolutionary stage would seem retrogressive, for in a real sense it postulates that more archaic kinds of men evolved out of a surprisingly advanced form, ER-1470."

At least Birdsell can hear the gears grinding and is not afraid to say so. Richard Leakey could also hear them grinding when he described the significance of 1470 for *National Geographic* in June 1973. "Either we toss out this skull or we toss out our theories of early man," he asserted. It seemed obvious then that "It simply fits no previous models of human beginnings," meaning that erectus and 1470 made a strange pair of ancestral bedfellows. Apparently someone got to Richard with dire forecasts of how silly the profession would look after thirty years of unstinting affirmations of erectus' importance if the world's leading paleoanthropologist were now to jettison this creature. Only four years later in *Origins*, Leakey and Lewin plugged erectus back into our lineage and are thus compelled to say rather comical things. Erectus' massive browridges, for example, are now described as a "more advanced feature" than the moderate brows of 1470. Well, as Richard's father, Louis, explained, they are a "more advanced feature" for Pithecanthropines specializing in a particular direction, but this "advance" is *away from* the modern human condition. However, this is not what Richard and Lewin are trying to tell us. If we accept their meaning, then we have sadly declined since the days of Neanderthal.

V.

One could prattle on merrily for considerable additional length as to what's wrong with the Pithecanthropines as ancestors— such as Java man's enormous canine teeth and large tooth-gaps, features never encountered in any kind of true man, living or extinct; or the fact that his forehead was more receding than that of a chimpanzee; etc., etc., etc. But this is small beer compared with the prospect that Peking man was the equivalent of a ham sandwich, and rather than recite all the other objections to elevating the Pithecanthropines to Homo status, it is more interesting to see what has been made of this "ancestor."

If one accepts the Weidenreich-Teilhard view that the Choukoutien fossils represent primitive human beings who made fire, stone tools, and were efficient hunters, it is possible to work up a story not only about the scene in that part of China but about the rest of the world as well. The Chinese Pithecanthropines become industrious, upstanding citizens, Homo erectus for short, and of course the same courtesy must then be extended to Java man and to all fossils of similar type wherever they are found. Pretty soon we have this kind of "man" distributed throughout the Far and Middle East, Africa, and parts of Europe, occupying a time niche of over a million years. This is enormously convenient for the storyteller because he can now attribute practically everything to Homo erectus that falls within this time range. If someone finds skeletons of giant elephants slaughtered in Spain 400,000 years ago, we "know" who did it—even if there is no direct evidence.

Lest the reader doubt that anthropologists actually engage in reasoning this specious, here is an instance. There is such a site in Spain, or rather a pair of sites, Torralba and Ambrona, about a mile from each other near the center of the country. They were excavated by F. Clark Howell in the 1960s, who found remains of slaughtered elephants some of which had stood 13 feet tall at the shoulder. Almost all contemporary American anthropologists I have read attribute these sites to Home erectus. In *Lucy*, Johanson and Edey state the case in an interesting manner:

Howell's work at Torralba and Ambrona is regarded by professionals as a model of site development. Not only did it prove that bands of Homo erectus lived in Spain about four hundred thousand years ago— something that had not been demonstrated previously for Western Europe—but it showed in considerable detail what they had been doing; all this without his finding a single hominid fossil.

That's right, folks. Not a single hominid fossil was found at either of these sites—no bones of Homo erectus—not a single tooth or toenail. Yet Johanson and Edey tell us that Howell's excavation *proved* the elephant butchering had been done by Homo erectus! Do Johanson and Edey possess clairvoyant powers they have not told us about? No. This assertion is "proved" the same way so much else in this profession is "proved" or "beyond doubt." In terms of hard, positive evidence, it rests upon nothing but mere assumptions and considerable extrapolations. There is not a jury in the world that would convict Homo erectus of this instance of elephant rustling—unless that jury were made up of American anthropologists.

But it is, then, a fair question: Who else could have done it? Perhaps early Cro-Magnon man did; we still don't know where he came from. Most anthropologists will say 400,000 years ago is far too early for Cro-Magnon man and that we have no evidence for him at this date.

But what about the Vertesszollos man discovered in the 1960s? There we have a good part of a large-capacity skull— about 1,500 cc.—with a rounded occiput like Homo sapiens, as well as evidence of fire 400,000 to 700,000 years old, long before Peking man. This could well be the type of true man Boule thought responsible for the Choukoutien industry. Vertesszollos provides hard evidence that beings of requisite size, shape, and abilities did then exist.

Well, as I said, most erectus supporters have reached the point of commitment where they are not swayed by mere evidence. Vertesszollos presents yet another inconvenience for their theory, but they have found a tidy way of dealing with it: They simply tell themselves and the public that Vertesszollos was Homo erectus too—even if the skull is the wrong shape and has a capacity entirely outside the erectus' range. They can't possibly allow a Homo sapiens that far back. It would destroy the significance of Peking man, erectus in general, and much of contemporary anthropological theory.

The reader will notice that when aspects of a fossil's anatomy suit the theory, as with Peking man, great stress is laid upon them. But when the anatomy doesn't suit the theory, as with Vertesszollos man, it is ignored.

I should mention that Ambrona and Torralba are not the only sites attributed to Homo erectus without any direct evidence whatsoever. Remains at Terra Amata in southern France and Latamne in Syria have also been interpreted in this way. With this technique, it is not difficult to create something of a population explosion of Homo erectus in the Middle Pleistocene. Jaws, teeth, and other fragments have been found at a few additional sites, but it is not necessary to discuss every scrap of bone. The crucial site for establishing the significance of this species remains Choukoutien, and we have seen how problematic that is. Vertesszollos, 1470, and 3733, combined with Boule's original testimony should be enough to tip off the profession that the erectus story doesn't add up. But evidence, logic, and the integrity of science only play a limited role in determining what the public is told. The operative factor in this case is Nettlebottom's career. He has been telling the same story for a quarter of a century, and he will continue to tell it—if there is anyone to listen—until the day he dies.

11: The Lonely Lineage

EVEN IF WE PROVISIONALLY REJECT Homo erectus as an ancestor, we have still not oversimplified the situation beyond what Louis Leakey himself advocated: The path to modern man proceeded directly from Homo habilis without passing through Homo erectus or Neanderthal. Since we have seen the difficulties with all the other fossil species that have been proposed, this obviously makes Homo habilis a being of considerable interest.

The story of Homo habilis is short and recent. Until the announcement of Australopithecus afarensis by Johanson and White in 1979, habilis was the newest hominid species, having been announced in 1964 by Louis Leakey, John Napier of England, and Phillip Tobias from South Africa. The bases of this announcement were the remains of four extremely fragmentary skulls found by Leakey in the two lower beds of Olduvai Gorge in the early 1960s. Following the discovery of Zinjanthropus in 1959, Leakey finally received funding from major foundations such as the National Geographic Society. Those four partial skulls were the fruits of the accelerated activity that funding had permitted.

These skulls were all between 1.3 and 1.7 million years old, no older than Zinj. What made them special was their size and shape. They were definitely not Zinjanthropus types, to whom the chipped pebbles in these deposits had previously been attributed; they were rather more like the "gracile" Australopithecine, africanus. But Leakey insisted that they were not africanus either. They were too large. The normal range of cranial capacity for africanus was about 430 to 530 cc. These skulls averaged around 640 cc. and held the possibility of being something distinct. They also happened to be what Louis Leakey had been looking for all his life.

II.

Before the discoveries of the early '60s, Leakey had long believed that there were two strains of ancient men and "near-men": Those he called Paleoanthropus and Neoanthropus. The specialized line of Paleoanthropus had passed through Homo erectus and Neanderthal, which went extinct. The nonspecialized line of Neoanthropus had passed through individuals like those from Swanscombe and Fontechevade and resulted in modern man.

In this view Leakey was not entirely alone. Boule sympathized with it, as did others. But most American students of paleoanthropology thought otherwise, favoring a single evolutionary strain that had passed through Australopithecus and Homo erectus. Moreover, they could point to the fossils of Java man, who at roughly half a million years old was significantly earlier than the Swanscombe fossil, as well as to the Australopithecine fossils, which were older still. Where were the fossils representing the strain of Neoanthropus at the time of Java man and Australopithecus? Having searched for them for most of his life without luck, Leakey certainly had ample reasons for discouragement, but he never gave up. Then he found those four fragmentary skulls at Olduvai Gorge. This, he said, was the ancestral strain. This was the earliest "man" yet discovered. He called it Homo habilis, meaning "handy man," because of the simple stone tools in the deposits in which he was found.

As soon as he was christened, Handy Man ran into a bog of

controversy. There were many valid points for criticizing this new species. The skulls were so extremely fragmentary; how could Leakey be sure they were nothing but large gracile Australopithecines? Even his son thought that might be true of a couple of the four skulls. Others said these skulls were small and early examples of Homo erectus. In addition, at around 1.5 million years old they were three times as old as the oldest "man" then accepted, Java man. Even within a profession not noted for its sobriety, many thought that Louis was hamming it up a bit much. Not a few felt that Leakey should reverse himself and withdraw his new species. Wilfred Le Gros Clark said,

"Homo habilis" has received a good deal of publicity since his sudden appearance was announced, and it is particularly unfortunate that he should have been announced long before a full and detailed study of all the relevant fossils can be completed. . . . From the brief accounts that have been published, one is led to hope that he will disappear as rapidly as he came.

C. Loring Brace, dogged defender of Australopithecus, sensed a threat to his pet species. "Homo habilis is an empty taxon [classification] inadequately proposed and should be formally sunk." Leakey had as much propensity to retreat as a Sherman tank in high gear.

The howling went on until 1972. Shortly before Louis Leakey's death, his son Richard presented him with 1470, the skull that shocked the world. But it didn't shock Louis. Far more dramatically than his own discoveries, it triumphantly vindicated his belief that there were very old creatures distinctly less specialized and more humanlike than their contemporaries, africanus, robustus, and erectus.

If we didn't have skull 1470, Homo habilis would indeed be hardly worth taking seriously. However, Richard Leakey did not immediately give 1470 the species label habilis. It is interesting that to many anthropologists it was not at all clear that 1470 was the same species as that represented by the four skulls from Olduvai Gorge. At about 800 cc., 1470's skull is significantly larger. As recently as 1976, John Waechter, author of Man Before History, clearly thought that 1470 was completely distinct from what Louis had been proposing with habilis:

The appearance of 1470 has tended to produce an argument similar to that of Zinj versus habilis at Olduvai, the morphologically superior creature being credited with the toolmaking. Does the finding of 1470, apparently more advanced than habilis and clearly earlier, imply that the industry from Bed I [the lowest bed] belonged to neither Zinj nor habilis, but to some relative of 1470?

However, in *Origins* (1977) Richard Leakey and Roger Lewin say that "there is every reason to classify it [1470] as a Homo habilis." From the standpoint of evolutionary theory, it is certainly not very satisfactory to be told that 1470 was the ancestor of creatures who lived between 300,000 and 1.3 million years *later* (depending on which age for 1470 one accepts) and yet had only 80 percent of his cranial capacity. The human brain is supposed to be getting larger, not smaller.

But that takes nothing away from 1470. Even if we choose to reject the Olduvai specimens as too small, too fragmentary, and too ambiguous to be meaningful, we are still faced with 1470; and whether we choose to call him Homo habilis or simply by his number, this is one fossil candidate for the ancestor of modern man that at first sight at least looks the part.

The skull seems remarkably modern if viewed from the front or side. The sides of the skull are nearly parallel, as in modern man. It is well domed. The browridges are moderate, and it has a reasonably good forehead. At around 800 cc., the cranial capacity is near the very lower limit of Homo sapiens itself. Skull size is highly variable in modern man. It averages around 1,350 cc., but ranges from 1,000 to 2,000 cc., and within this "normal" range there is no correlation between size and intelligence. However, even this range is arbitrary, and modern Europeans of "good intelligence" have been reported who had only 800 to 900 cc.'s. Even 1470's eye sockets are the more rectangular style of modern man's.

All of which makes 1470 very provocative. If we limited ourselves to photos of the front and side—which are virtually the only views seen in popular books—we might think we were looking at a slightly misshaped, small modern skull. Viewed from the top and rear, however, a couple of features leap out to dispel this notion. Seen from the top, there is a very marked and deep constriction behind the eyes in the area of the temples indicating 1470 had massive jaw muscles and, therefore, massive jaws. This postorbital constriction, as it is called, is so much more pronounced than in modern man that it alone is enough to raise the question whether this should be considered a man (Homo) of any kind. Seen from the rear, the skull also seems to bulge out around the base in a manner reminiscent of the Australopithecines. This bulge is another nonmodern feature and implies heavy neck muscles of the sort necessary to hold the head in a creature who was not fully erect. This indication, though, is contradicted by what is said of the foramen magnum, which is described as well forward, thus implying erect posture. A very human-looking thighbone was found in nearby deposits, and if this belonged to 1470 types, it is another indication of erect posture. But then, as we saw with Lucy, bipedalism is not necessarily the certain passport to man it was once thought to be.

At 1.8 million years old, 1470 may be modern enough to disqualify the Australopithecines and Homo erectus, but it is still so far from Homo sapiens that without firm evidence of associated culture and connecting links to something like Vertesszollos we cannot be sure what it was. Evolutionists can suspect the truth in one direction; creationists can suspect it in another. If we take the evidence from Fontechevade, Swanscombe, and Vertesszollos as indicating that modern man is roughly half a million years old, we still have an enormous gap between 1470 and

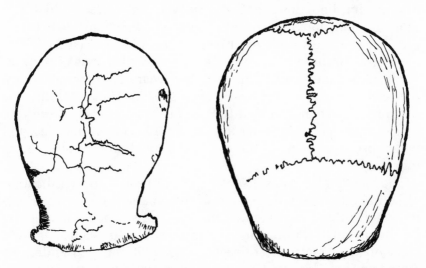

The top of skull 1470 (*left*, after Leakey and Walker) showing its pronounced post-orbital constriction. For comparison, the top of a modern human skull is shown on the right. Scale not exact.   W.R.F.

the oldest of these specimens. Whether 1470 is really our ancestor or something else will simply remain indeterminant until
more fossils dating between 100,000 and 2 million are found. It
is an important point that as diagnostic as the Fontechevade,
Swanscombe, and Vertesszollos evidence is, none of these specimens is as complete as 1470 itself. This points up that the present fad for scouting around on 3- and 4-million-year-old
paleontological horizons is not anywhere as relevant as obtaining firmer knowledge of the last million years.

III.

There are problems with 1470, but if one is not inclined to dismiss the possibility of human evolution on principle, this is
about as good an evolutionary candidate as one could hope for.
The general shape, size, and nonspecialized browridges are very
strong points. And with all the discredited ancestral candidates,
numerous instances of science by assertion, and a bumper crop
of hyperbole in this field, it is important not to overlook the
instance of at least one conspicuous success. One of the hall-
marks of a truly scientific theory is the power of prediction.
Louis Leakey's theory that the human lineage is very old and
distinct implied the eventual discovery of a much older and
more modern-looking ancestor than any that had been found
during paleoanthropology's first century. While Leakey fell into
a certain disrepute with American scientists because of the Zinjanthropus caper and then, only five years later, with the announcement of another questionable species, Homo habilis, it is
clearer today than ever that L. S. B. Leakey understood the process of specialization better than any of his contemporaries, and
better also than many of the younger generation who are writing
today.

The fact that his son's discovery of 1470 was also a vindication
of Louis' rather singular vision of the emergence of man is perhaps not duly appreciated. Louis was not swept off his feet by
Piltdown, Australopithecus africanus, or Homo erectus, as were
most of his American colleagues. When it came to endorsing
ancestors, he advocated the least, and his model has fared the
best. Not only is it somewhat galling for many American scientists to acknowledge that the evidence now does seem to corrob-

orate Louis' position, but his personal triumph is perhaps made more difficult to swallow because in so many ways he stood apart from the American academic network. L. S. B. Leakey was self-reliant, self-made, and supremely independent in a profession where practically everyone else is heavily dependent upon academic institutions and the endless machinations of departmental politics. It is now fashionable to talk about "Leakey's Luck," as if this were all that separated him from his colleagues. He may indeed have been lucky, but this would have done him little good had he not also comprehended the pattern of specialization and displayed herculean perseverance in the field under conditions that would have withered less determined men. He was really very different from the armchair theoreticians, and many of them have never forgiven him for it.

Considering the Zinjanthropus caper and my personal exposure to that instance of bone peddling, it may strike the reader as curious that I end up defending Louis as the hero of the profession. But in the final analysis, it is results that count, and the Zinjanthropus episode is rather different from the games played with Ramapithecus, africanus, Peking man, and afarensis. Leakey had been pounding around in the heat and dust of Olduvai Gorge for twenty-five years, stringing along on one meager grant after another and on what he could make on the side. Then he found Zinjanthropus in tool-bearing deposits. In retrospect it is hard to blame him for presenting Zinj as the earliest known man—even if he knew in his heart it was nothing but an Australopithecine. It was a major discovery in an area where there had been none previously. It could be dated to a remote age. And it did allow the previously undetermined age of the South African Australopithecines to be at least estimated. Moreover, the funding that followed Zinj enabled the Leakeys to open up East African paleontology for the later discoveries at Olduvai, Omo, Koobi Fora, Laetoli, and Hadar. Paleoanthropology would be a much poorer field today without the work of Louis Leakey.

It is difficult to avoid the conclusion that the current American enthusiasm for Lucy is not a case of sour grapes. The simple and staggering fact is that the Leakey family—Louis, Mary, and Richard—have produced more important discoveries than all American anthropologists put together since the beginnings of this discipline.

IV.

As important and intriguing as 1470 is, it would certainly be a mistake to proceed as if the ancestral enigma has at last been solved. It is worth emphasizing that as relatively human as 1470 looks, even his ancestral credentials could evaporate tomorrow. This could happen in several ways. A still more modern skull of similar or greater age might be discovered. And then, we have no teeth from 1470, and if these were found, they might show that he possessed enormous canines, or other unknown parts might disclose some other totally nonhuman specialization. If 1470 was a female, a male, for example, might be found to have a sagittal crest.

Or something much more exotic might turn up. One thinks for instance of the famous "giant's footprints" supposedly found in the Paluxy River bed near Glen Rose, Texas. Long beloved by all creationists, these apparently human footprints were first described by Roland T. Bird in the May 1939 issue of *Natural History*. The prints are about 15 inches long and half as wide. The most extraordinary feature of these footprints is that supposedly 70-million-year-old dinosaur prints have been found in the same strata, including tracks from a large three-toed carnivorous variety and those of a gigantic sauropod. The oval sauropod impressions measure 24 by 38 inches. They are about 12 feet apart and are sunk deeply into the limestone, which was once mud. *National Geographic* carried a photo-essay on these prints in May 1954.

These prints, both human and reptile, are one of the standard salvos in the creationist arsenal. They remind us immediately of the biblical statement "There were giants in the earth in those days" (Genesis 6:4). Even more devastating for evolutionists is the implication that any kind of man or manlike creature was contemporaneous with dinosaurs. If this were actually demonstrated in indisputable fashion, it would completely scuttle all presently held orthodox theories of geological chronology.

Despite the wide currency given these prints by the creationists during the last twenty years, geologists and paleontologists are so convinced that the contemporaneity of man (giant or otherwise) and dinosaurs is impossible that until very recently, it seems, no recognized professional has bothered to visit the site and examine the documentation. *Scientific American* for June 1983 carries a letter from William D. Stansfield, a professor of biological sciences, indicating that physical anthropologist Laurie Godfrey and some colleagues have now done this. Godfrey found the "human" trackways to have many inconsistencies, such as prints changing size and direction with every step. Stansfield says that Godfrey's documentation will soon be published. Stansfield also reports that some of the so-called human footprints have distinct claw marks protruding from the heel. Godfrey, he says, also analyzed a film, Footprints in Stone, produced some ten years ago by the Films for Christ Association, which, I hardly need add, presents them in their most provocative light. It seems the filmmakers "highlighted" the outlines of the footprints very extensively with oil or shellac and that when these outlines are removed, the tracks all but disappear.

Stansfield does not indicate whether Godfrey's investigation of the documentation extends to the remarkable photos found in Henry Morris' and John Whitcomb's creationist epic, The Genesis Flood (1961). These latter authors have photos of one set of clear, giant-man prints deeply sunk in stone no longer in situ. They also have photos of a clear dinosaur print supposedly from the same strata. Even if it is true, as Stansfield states, that during the Depression residents of the area excavated some tracks and fabricated others to sell to tourists, this alone does not permit us to dismiss the samples presented by Morris and Whitcomb.

As it is, geologists generally accept the Paluxy dinosaur prints as genuine but believe someone must have carved the human ones. I am inclined to think so myself, but unless and until we have better reasons to conclude that Morris and Whitcomb do not have photos of something genuine, there is still room for other possibilities. I certainly do not believe that any kind of human lived on this planet 70 million years ago, or that the earth is only ten thousand years old. But as Boule remarked, there were giant forms of many animals including the primates in earlier eras, and this could also apply to man. It is also conceivable that some of these forms appeared much earlier than now believed and that some dinosaurs persisted in local pockets much beyond their general extinction about 70 million years ago. After all, there are those who are convinced that some sort of dinosaur still lives in Loch Ness, and the coelacanth, an ancient armored fish thought to have been extinct for 70 million years, was discovered alive and well in waters off South Africa in 1938.

Our ignorance of the past is still far greater than our knowledge of it. For all we really know, it is not impossible that more such prints, human and dinosaur, could be found tomorrow in such a situation as to preclude all possibility that they were carved. Or the future may bring other tremendous surprises. At a stroke, evolutionary theories could come tumbling down, and meditations on the meaning of 1470 would be a waste of time.

So even with 1470 it is best to be cautious. Maybe this is an ancestor; and maybe it isn't. Scientifically, it is folly to pronounce anything more definite. We may not be able to gauge 1470's significance for another twenty years. The fossil record pertaining to man is still so sparsely known that those who insist on positive declarations can do nothing more than jump from one hazardous surmise to another and hope that the next dramatic discovery does not make them utter fools. Historically, every time someone finds a new type of skull, or simply a previously unknown part of some fragmentarily sampled species, half the profession falls over itself adjusting their models of how man evolved while the other half starts emitting a new batch of unproven certitudes. Clearly, some people refuse to learn from this. As we have seen, there are numerous scientists and popularizers today who have the temerity to tell us that there is "no doubt" how man originated. If only they had the evidence.

V.

The question of man's origin is among the most emotional of all issues. I do not expect to convince those already committed to a particular position. But if one cultivates a degree of detachment, I hope he can see that a thorough review of the presently known evidence shows that human evolution is still only a theory. The validity of this conclusion is unaffected by those who announce it. One may be otherwise implacably opposed to the political, intellectual, and moral positions of, say, President Reagan, the Texas State school board, or fundamentalist preachers. That they have been the most prominent voices enunciating this position in the recent past has no proper scientific bearing on the issue.

Figuring out the emergence of man is not a popularity contest. It is a matter of evidence and of interpreting that evidence. It has long been apparent in other fields, such as Egyptology, that those who make a discovery are not necessarily those most competent in its assessment. In view of the opportunism that has become almost traditional in paleoanthropology, this is also obviously true in this discipline. This is a good reason why a certain number of "armchair theoreticians" also have their place. But especially in the United States, all too often they do not live up to fulfilling a valuable critical function. Instead they are pulled one way and another by every changing tide of fashion and encourage the opportunism instead of providing the corrective. Polarized by the fundamentalists, they are now part of the problem rather than the source of its solution.

Regardless of how robustly dogmatic assertions to the contrary may be, even if they are made by the American Association for the Advancement of Science and endorsed by fifty thousand scientists, human evolution is simply *not* proven. Anatole France is reputed to have said: "If 50 million Frenchmen say a foolish thing; it is still a foolish thing." And if fifty thousand scientists jump to an unwarranted conclusion; it is still an unwarranted conclusion. Let us remember the Académie française in 1790.

Like it or not, a committed creationist can still maintain that he or she is under no compulsion from logic or evidence to abandon the theory of the special creation of man. Doubtless, if this were a tract designed to appeal to the Rev. Jo Jo Thumpwell of the Hallelujan Heights Reformed Fundamentalist Church of Rockyblowtop Flats, Virginia, this would be the place to stop. As we all know, Reverend Jo Jo's following is considerable. His endorsement would carry news of the foibles I have described even so far as the depths of Tennessee. When I first realized how rickety the evolutionary structure is, I was severely tempted to write something solely for Jo Jo's gratification, since he is such a fine, outspoken fellow and his audience is so tremendous. But I have been unable to follow this admirable course. It was probably the devil that made me do it, but I have decided to stick strictly to the middle of the road and to look at the question holistically. If one is in this position and does pretend to a degree of scientific detachment, then it is not sufficient to pronounce human evolution not proven and the question closed.

The horribly ambiguous truth is that human evolution is still a reasonable possibility. We should do everything we can to find out the truth of the matter. We should have ten or twenty times the number of excavations we have at present. Among other places, there should certainly be major, professional excavations along the Paluxy River. Whoever does it best goes with an open mind. It really is not impossible that giant human footprints and dinosaur prints in the same strata could be genuine. This discovery would not mean that the earth is only ten thousand years old, but that is the conclusion some will draw if scientists take the a priori position that it is impossible and creationists assert the contrary.

VI.

To say that human evolution is impossible would be just as absurd as to claim it is a fact. And even without the fossils, there is still a major reason why the argument that man is a special creation is not convincing to many people: man's skeleton. Man indeed has the same basic skeletal structure as the rest of the primates—the apes, monkeys, marmosets, and lemurs. This basic fact is what convinced Darwin, T. H. Huxley, and other early advocates of human evolution that man is related to these creatures. It is ironic that after 120 years of paleoanthropology this fact, drawn from anatomy, not paleontology, is perhaps still the strongest single item of evidence supporting human evolution.

Of course, one can argue about the significance of skeletal similarity, as about so much else. Resemblance does not necessarily imply descent. The skeletal torsos of man and the gibbons are remarkably similar, but no one suggests that one descended from the other, and a common ancestor remains undemonstrated. And then, over the last century science has also disclosed that the soft, fleshy parts of animals vary far more greatly than do their hard parts. This is especially evident in marine life, where animals of great diversity inhabit shells of unusual similarity. Thus even a skull as close to ours as 1470 could have carried a most unhuman face.

Furthermore, one may quite appropriately suggest that to look at only the skeletons of apes and men is to view similarities in design too narrowly. Snails and galaxies both have spiral patterns, and there is no question of descent in that case. It is not just with apes, but with all vertebrate life that man shares basic patterns. If one entertains the possibility that the universe is the product of intelligence and design, it is perfectly logical to suggest that basic patterns and ideas could have served as models upon which intelligent, guiding forces have played countless variations in expressing the life and substance of the cosmos. And there is no logical necessity to suppose that these myriad variations all followed one another in lineages of physical descent—a conclusion that we will find emphasized when we survey the discoveries of microbiology and the genetic relatedness of homologous organs in part II.

The fact remains, however, that in many of our basic anatomical features we are part of an earthly continuity. That is why even those paleoanthropologists who admit that they do not know where modern man came from still continue to believe in the evolution of man. Anatomically, we simply have too much in common with other terrestrial life to airily dismiss some kind of intimate connection. It would be far more convenient for the theory of the special creation if man possessed six or seven fingers on each hand or had some other skeletal peculiarity setting him apart from the animal kingdom in addition to his unusually architectural skull.

VII.

Having concluded our tour of the boneroom, it seems that the origin of man is more mysterious than either evolutionists or creationists contend. The "positive facts" are much rarer than most scientists admit, and half the time—with Fontechevade, Swanscombe, and Vertesszollos—those very facts embarrass evolutionary theory rather than support it. On the other hand, the structural kinship of the human skeleton with that of other terrestrial creatures is also a positive fact, a fact whose overtones few fundamentalists adequately acknowledge.

It is thought-provoking to discover that modern man may be as much as half a million years old, but of course we need more evidence before we rush out to carve this conclusion in stone. I have gone to some trouble to show that there are formidable objections to all the subhuman and near-human species that have been proposed as ancestors. But it is also thought-provoking to notice how much better candidates several of these would be were it not for a single overriding factor: the process of specialization. That process now appears to be inexorably one-way. But if further discoveries or the perception of additional factors enabled us to explain how specialization can be reversed, we might have a very different situation.

But now it is time to leave the boneroom. The trail does not end here. There is much else to consider. If human evolution is still a possibility, it is also possible that man's appearance on earth may be due to factors in addition to or instead of an evolutionary process. In order to develop a more informed opinion as to what man is and where he came from, we have to enter a much larger universe of discourse—a universe so large that I am afraid neither Nettlebottom nor Thumpwell will feel comfortable in it.

PART 2
A WidER PERSPECTiVE

Most zoologists in America believe that evolution has come
about by natural selection of mutations. Unfortunately, while
mutations do occur in nature they are very rare, and there is
the strongest evidence from paleontology that evolution has
been by extremely minute changes—changes so minute that it
is inconceivable that they could have had any survival
value. . . .

Whatever it is, there is reason to believe there is something in
life which is not governed by the laws of physics and
chemistry.

—ROBERT BROOM
The Coming of Man: Was It Accident or Design?

1: The Archaeopteryx and the Whale

I.

In a wider perspective on the origin of man, the first subject that naturally invites our attention is the evidence for evolution in other species. We hardly need to go over the technical literature with a fine-toothed comb to find that it is often assumed, inferred, or asserted that there is "no doubt" evolution is the total explanation for all other species. And those who so assume, infer, or assert almost invariably conclude that man must be a product of the same biological process.

Of course, anyone concerned with a scientific use of logic can maintain that even if evolution were conclusively demonstrated as the sole explanation for the origin and development of all other species, this still would not in and of itself necessarily imply that man had also come about by the same process. We share a basic skeletal structure with many other creatures, but

157

once we get beyond the bare bones, the uniqueness of man is obvious and staggering. Written language, religion, music, art, science, technology, tremendous organizational ability, a capacity for great enterprises both constructive and destructive, a supersensitive skin, and heightened sexuality are a few of the attributes accompanying the one indisputably dominant lifeform on the planet.

But as it is, evolution is very far from demonstrated as the sole explanation for all other species. This is not to say there is no evidence whatever for evolution; there is a great deal of it as a matter of fact, but almost entirely of a certain kind, and this is not of a sort to encourage speculation that man evolved from an ape.

II.

It is well to point out that the word *evolution* has different meanings in different contexts. It has first of all an historical meaning. People sometimes use the word simply to indicate that there has been a succession of varying life-forms on this planet, without offering or implying an explanation as to their origins and extinctions. In this sense, evolution is beyond dispute. The dinosaurs, mammoths, and saber-toothed tigers are no longer extant. Virtually no one still defends the notion, formerly advanced by clerical apologists, that the fossils of these and other creatures were created with the earth and are thus not the remains of once-living animals.

Evolution in the sense in dispute implies that the earth's life-forms are biologically related by physical descent. For most scientists, historical evolution implies biological evolution. It is important to realize that there are two distinct aspects to biological evolution: microevolution and macroevolution. The prefix *micro* means "small," and *microevolution* refers to the relatedness of basically similar species, subspecies, and varieties. There is a great deal of rather persuasive evidence not only that microevolution takes place but how it takes place.

A classic example of microevolution is seen among the finches of the Galapagos Islands off the west coast of South America. These finches were studied by Charles Darwin during the voyage of the *Beagle* in the 1830s and provided one of the prime inspirations leading him to formulate his theory of the origin of species.

There are several species of Galapagos finches; their chief distinguishing characteristic is the form and function of their beaks. A couple of species have large, blunt beaks, enabling them to crack open and feed on seeds. A couple of others have small, sharp beaks, equipping them to attack and devour insects. These birds might be compared to a line of General Motors cars all built on the same basic chassis but with differences in the grille and trim identifying them as Chevrolets, Pontiacs, or Oldsmobiles.

Although no one saw it happen, it is not difficult to believe that thousands of years ago a parental species of finches took flight from the South American mainland, were perhaps caught up in a storm, but one way or another found themselves on the Galapagos, where they remained and diversified into several species as individuals and groups gradually became more and more specialized in relation to particular food supplies.

The Galapagos finches are but one example among hundreds of this kind of diversification. Darwin thought such diversification could be explained by competition, survival of the fittest, and adaptation. As we shall hear shortly, these concepts have not proven to have much explanatory power, but genetics and population studies, two modern fields Darwin knew little or nothing about, have provided data enabling us to understand how such diversification apparently takes place.

Mathematical studies have shown that (other things being equal) the gene pool of a large interbreeding population is more stable than the gene pool of a small, isolated population. This is another way of saying that genetic variation or novelty has far greater consequences in small, isolated populations than it does in large ones, where it would likely be "swallowed up." The mathematical studies are directly corroborated by field studies of species reminiscent of the Galapagos finches. In a 1954 paper, "Change of Genetic Environment and Evolution," Harvard biologist Ernst Mayr described this pattern of variation with the kingfishers of Papua (New Guinea) in southeast Asia:

Let us look, for instance, at the range of the Papuan kingfishers of the Tanysiptera hydrocharis-galatea group. It is typical for hundreds of similar cases. On the mainland of New Guinea three sub-species occur which are very similar to each other. But whenever we find a representative of this group on [a small outlying] island, it is so different that five of the six Papuan [outlying] island forms were described as separate species and four are still so regarded.

Thus there is a direct relationship between the variability of the various species or subspecies and their genetic isolation from other kingfishers. When novelties produced by latent genes, mutations, or by an occasional immigrant from other groups enter the gene flow of the smaller, isolated populations, they have a greater chance of being passed to succeeding generations than they would in a larger group. It seems fairly straightforward that over time, the relative genetic isolation of small populations does account for the origin of quite a few species. As Mayr says, hundreds of similar cases exist, and the convergence of the conclusions from genetics with observations from the field is certainly powerful.

This is fine as far as it goes, but how far does it take us? The variations in those kingfishers and in the Galapagos finches are mostly differences in beaks and feathers. The birds may be "dressed" differently; they may be recognized as separate species; but they are still kingfishers and finches.

III.

The evidence for microevolution is persuasive; macroevolution is another kettle of fish. *Macro* means "large." With macroevolution we have the idea that all life on earth gradually evolved from one or a few primitive life-forms quivering spasmodically in the primeval sea. Macroevolution implies very great transformations indeed. In theory, we are supposed to be able to trace bats and whales back to a common ancestor; turtles, eagles, oak trees, horses, and polar bears are supposed to share a protean grandmother.

It is not correct to say there is no evidence for macroevolution. Perhaps the strongest example is provided by the horse. Fossil forms connect the large, modern, one-toed horse having specialized teeth with small, ancient three- and four-toed varieties with unspecialized teeth. The earliest type, which lived about 65 million years ago, is known as Hyracotherium, sometimes also called Eohippus.

In earlier decades the custom among museum keepers and textbook illustrators was to represent these horses as a series of gradually ascending forms, getting larger and more specialized step by step. This straight line of ancestry has now been discarded for something called a phylogenetic net, which, as its name implies, shows multiple intersecting strands. The extent to which these many strains actually interbred is unknown. The phylogenetic net simply allows us to cover a multitude of possibilities and is a better reflection of the fact that during certain geological epochs many of the forms that could be arranged in a straight line were alive in all sizes at the same time. The progression from four to three to one toe on the foot also seems to be erratic, with many retrogressive stages. The complexity of the situation is increased because the fossils in Africa, Eurasia, and South America are all offshoots; pivotal intermediate forms are found only in North America. Consequently, there are now many versions of the horse's ancestry, and it is unlikely that they are all correct.

In the past, evolutionists have waxed lyrical about the horse's lineage, claiming it shows just what Darwin suggested: the gradual transition from one genus to another over 60 or 70 million years. Prof. N. Heribert-Nilsson, of Lund University in Sweden, has commented, however, that "the family tree of the horse is beautiful and continuous only in textbooks."

It may well be that the evidence has been oversimplified and exaggerated. Still, in its general architecture the skull of the modern horse so closely resembles Hyracotherium that any reasonable person would grant their possible relatedness. Someone will have to produce striking contrary evidence if we are not to conclude that the horse and his ancestors have been around a long time and have evolved considerably. And whether it took place once or several times, the transition from three toes to one is biologically more significant than the variations in beaks and feathers in the Galapagos finches.

Hyracotherium also provides an example of a creature that can be seen as a true missing link. Hyracotherium appears to be about midway between ancestral horses, asses, and zebras on the one side and rhinoceroses and tapirs on the other. But as dissimilar as the horse and rhinoceros might seem, they are both herbivores and classed as ungulates.

The most significant example of a missing link has long been Archaeopteryx lithographica, a small creature weighing less than a pound who lived about 150 million years ago. Archaeopteryx is usually considered to be the earliest known bird and is usually described as resembling reptiles in having a long bony tail, three clawed fingers on the wing, teeth in its jaws, and solid bones. If Archaeopteryx is truly a transitional form between cold-blooded reptiles and warm-blooded birds, then at least in some instances evolution has produced very large macro changes. As George Gaylord Simpson remarked in *Tempo and Mode in Evolution* (1944), Archaeopteryx is "one of the most perfect of all interclass discoveries. . . ." In fact, it has probably assumed a significance greater than any other species outside the primates, having become the standard example of transitional forms.

But is Archaeopteryx as advertised? After a century of vacillating fortunes, the significance of Archaeopteryx is now more questionable than ever.

A remarkably well-preserved fossil of Archaeopteryx, including impressions from its feathers, was first found in a Bavarian limestone quarry in 1860, fortuitously for Darwin less than a year after the first publication of the *Origin*. Because of its supposed reptilian features, it was seized upon by T. H. Huxley and most other nineteenth-century paleontologists as a missing link between dinosaurs and birds. But this view went into abeyance when it seemed impossible to find dinosaurs with collarbones (clavicles). In birds, such as Archaeopteryx, the clavicles are fused to produce the furcula, or wishbone. If dinosaurs had lost their clavicles, they could not have been direct ancestors of birds. So, for much of the twentieth century, it was supposed that dinosaurs and birds shared a common ancestor (still unfound) and then went their separate ways.

But eventually two coelurosaurian dinosaurs were found that did have clavicles after all. And then other new information came to light strongly suggesting that dinosaurs were warm-blooded, not cold-blooded creatures, thus bringing birds and dinosaurs more closely together. S. J. Gould has neatly recounted the warm-blooded dinosaur theory in "The Telltale Wishbone," an essay in *The Panda's Thumb* (1980). He points to the work of paleontologist R. T. Bakker who with others has been persuasively arguing for nearly a decade now that we have misread dinosaurs as cold-blooded reptiles. The two strongest elements of evidence supporting this conclusion are analyses of bone structure and the ratio of predators to prey.

As Bakker has pointed out, bones of cold-blooded animals show growth rings, like trees, and for much the same reasons. Since neither trees nor cold-blooded animals are able to control their body temperature, their growth rates slow dramatically or stop entirely during winter, and this hiatus is reflected in the familiar pattern of rings found in tree stems, and in the bones of cold-blooded animals. The bones of warm-blooded animals do not show growth rings because of their ability to maintain a relatively constant body temperature throughout the year. It now eventuates that even dinosaur fossils found in latitudes with intense winters show no growth rings.

Second, cold-blooded animals eat less than warm-blooded varieties, simply closing up shop, metabolically speaking, during the off-season, hibernating the time away. Warm-blooded animals, of course, have to consume more or less consistently throughout the year to keep their internal fires burning. In cold-blooded populations, predators may be as much as 40 percent of the total; in warm-blooded groups predators never exceed 3 percent of the population—since each predator requires so much more prey than his cold-blooded counterpart. Fossil dinosaur populations are now known to display the ratio of predators-to-prey found in warm-blooded groups.

Thus the whole relation of birds and dinosaurs is again being rethought. Several leading investigators are advocating a radical restructuring of vertebrate classification; removing dinosaurs from Reptilia, abolishing the standard class of Aves (birds), and bringing the two together in a new class to be called Dinosauria. If it seems a long way from brontosaurus to the hummingbird, advocates of the new class can respond that it is no greater than between the whale and the bat. If dinosaurs were warm-blooded, then the transition to birds is less macro than previously supposed, but the relation between them seems to be more closely established than ever.

However, in *The Neck of the Giraffe* (1982) Francis Hitching presents a very strong case that the intermediate status of Archaeopteryx has been misinterpreted. Hitching takes Archaeopteryx's alleged reptilian features (the long bony tail, claws on the wings, teeth in the jaws, and solid instead of hollow bones such as birds have) and dismisses them one by one. Some living birds have more tail vertebrae in embryo than Archaeopteryx. Instead of fusing to become a bone called the pygostyle as in birds, in Archaeopteryx the caudal vertebrae are greatly elongated. Hitching cites one authority who says that there is no difference in principle in these cases and that the elongated vertebrae do not make a reptile. The claws on its wings are not unique but are found on living birds such as the hoatzin, the touraco, and the ostrich, which no one supposes to be transitional forms.

Hitching acknowledges that modern birds do not have teeth in their jaws, but says that many ancient varieties did. "There is no suggestion that these are intermediates," he comments. "It is just as convincing to argue that Archaeopteryx was an early bird with teeth." As for having solid bones, Hitching writes that they are now known to have been both thin and hollow, just like modern birds.

Hitching's strongest point, however, is a new discovery. Until 1977, Archaeopteryx appeared to predate the general arrival of birds by 60 million years. But in that year Brigham Young University archaeologists discovered the fossil of "an unequivocal bird" in western Colorado in rocks of the same period as Archaeopteryx. He quotes Prof. John H. Ostrom, of Yale, who identified the specimen: "It is now obvious we must now look for the ancestors of flying birds in a period of time much earlier than that in which Archaeopteryx lived."

If this is true, then much of Archaeopteryx's evolutionary significance has evaporated, a sobering outcome when one considers how much play it has received in the literature. Of course neo-Darwinists can insist that this changes little; we must still expect to find the ancestors of birds among the dinosaurs. What has changed, however, is that this expectation is now based largely on faith and hope rather than on dramatic fossil evidence such as Archaeopteryx was formerly thought to be.

Archaeopteryx has become such a set example for evolutionists that it may take them some time to adjust their thinking to the 1977 discovery of an unequivocal bird of equal age. It is curious, for example, that in "The Telltale Wishbone" (last published in 1980), Stephen Jay Gould paints the significance of Archaeopteryx in the broadest and brightest evolutionary colors and several times refers to the same John Ostrom quoted by Hitching; but Gould says nothing about the 1977 discovery.

It might be convenient to dismiss macroevolution altogether, but even if we put Archaeopteryx aside for the time being, we still have the evidence pertaining to the horse. Many writers have pointed out that domestic dogs of today display variations in size and shape on the same order as ancient and modern horses. Some have suggested that if fossils of Saint Bernards,

Chihuahuas, and breeds in between were found in a series of rock strata, they would almost certainly be arranged as an evolutionary sequence.

The future may yet disclose that some supposed evolutionary lineages are nothing more than the imposition of an idea upon a population something like that of the dog; but on the evidence we have at present the ancestry of the horse cannot be so dismissed. The transition from three toes to one and the development of specialized teeth represent changes in form that are more fundamental than any variations seen in dogs. Furthermore, despite their tremendous variations in size, domestic dogs can all interbreed and are grouped as one species. Species are real units. The horse and the ass might seem less dissimilar than a Great Dane and a dachshund, but they are separate species, and if they mate they produce a mule, a sterile hybrid.

So the horse is a good example of macroevolution by any commonsense meaning of the term. Dedicated creationists can argue that fossils can never disclose whether they actually were ancestors of anything else, a point that even many evolutionists acknowledge. But if the theory suggests the existence of ancient forms intermediate between Hyracotherium and the modern horse, and fossils of such creatures are actually discovered, then a detached observer can hardly help see this as evidence supporting the theory.

So there is evidence for macroevolution—in some strains and species. But there is also a great deal of evidence that this is *not* the sole explanation for all organic life.

The same fossil record that gives us Eohippus and Archaeopteryx also shows us that whole groups of species have appeared suddenly without any indication of their supposed ancestors and that many species have persisted over immense periods of time (hundreds of millions of years in some cases) virtually without any change whatever.

IV.

Of course, people have been talking about gaps and spurts in the fossil record for well over a hundred years. One of the first to do so was Charles Darwin himself. The outlines of the fossil record were already known by the latter half of the nineteenth century, and the information then available posed several major problems for Darwin's theory. He discussed these rather candidly in *The Origin of Species*. Possibly the best known of these problems is the "Cambrian explosion"—the sudden appearance of many life-forms in the Cambrian period, about 600 million years ago. Darwin did not minimize the difficulty posed by this explosion. Having discussed some other problems, he said,

There is another and allied difficulty which is much more serious. I allude to the manner in which species belonging to the main divisions of the animal kingdom suddenly appear in the lowest known fossiliferous rocks. . . .

Darwin went on to acknowledge that some of these most ancient animals do not differ much from living species. But it is not only in the Cambrian period, as Darwin and many others have noticed, that whole groups of species, some of them of the same genus, seem to appear out of nowhere. Darwin wrote,

The abrupt manner in which whole groups of species appear in certain formations has been urged by several paleontologists . . . as a fatal objection to the belief of the transmutation of species. If numerous species, belonging to the same genera or families, have really started into life at once, that fact would be fatal to the theory of evolution through natural selection. For the development by this means of a group of forms, all of which are [according to the theory] descended from some one progenitor, must have been an extremely slow process; and the progenitors must have lived long before their modified descendants.

Attempting to mitigate these difficulties, Darwin pleaded the imperfection of the fossil record and hoped these apparent contradictions would evaporate with the further progress of paleontology. "In all cases," he wrote, "positive paleontological evidence may be implicitly trusted; negative evidence is worthless, as experience has so often shown."

Paleontologists have, of course, greatly expanded their researches since Darwin's day, and as it happens, these fundamental difficulties have not evaporated but if anything now appear more acute. Naturally, most evolutionists prefer to emphasize examples like the horse and the numerous instances of micro-evolution and skate over the difficulties as lightly as possible. They seem to be sustained in this procedure by a kind of faith that even if these difficulties have not evaporated over the last century, they still will sometime in the future.

But a few scientists have looked at the returns from the field and decided that such faith is no longer reasonable. One of these was Douglas Dewar, a British biologist and ornithologist, who as early as 1947 concluded that the evidence was running rather strongly in the other direction. Dewar and H. S. Shelton published a debate in that year entitled *Is Evolution Proved?* Shelton argued that it was; Dewar that it wasn't. "The fossil record is far more complete than Darwin supposed it to be, and than his followers admit," Dewar contended. Since Darwin's time, he said, research has shown that practically every presently known genus of animal having a skeleton or hard parts has left a fossil remains.

Dewar was not an ideologue inclined toward an overly simple dismissal of evolution. He acknowledged that the fossil record indicates that some species *have* changed into others. But nature is too variable and inconsistent to generalize from these instances to all organic life. For every example of evolution, there are many others displaying no evolution whatever. Dewar could point, as Darwin himself did, to some of the most ancient animals, such as the Nautilus and Lingula, which are virtually unchanged over half a billion years. More importantly, the contradictory implications for his theory that Darwin saw in the Cambrian explosion and in the sudden appearance of related groups of species at other times now appear more formidable than ever. Dewar described the Cambrian explosion thus:

A great and abundant marine fauna appears on the scene with startling abruptness at the beginning of the Cambrian period. Many of the pre-Cambrian rocks which immediately precede the Cambrian rocks and underlie them are rocks in which fossils could equally well have been deposited, but not a single undisputed fossil has been found in them. Suddenly in the Cambrian period we find the sea full of highly organized types. We find nothing which suggests slow evolution. We find no experiments in the production of new types, no experiments, for instance, in shell making. The first shells are fully developed. We find these earliest animals as sharply differentiated into species, genera, families, orders and phyla as they are today.

Since Dewar wrote the above, geologists have found pre-Cambrian fossils, but these do nothing to lessen the mystery of the Cambrian explosion. Rocks that are 3.8 billion years old contain what may be fossilized bacteria, six times as old as the Cambrian period and nearly as old as the earth itself. Rather than providing answers, this has raised the question of how it is possible for any kind of life to have arisen so early.

As for groups of related animals starting into existence at once, Dewar had this to say:

While it is open to doubt whether or not the geological record furnishes good evidence of one genus having been converted into another, it certainly shows that a large number of genera have persisted unchanged during long periods; in the cases where the record enables us to trace back into the past two or more genera of a family, their lines, instead of converging until they meet in a common ancestor, seem to follow a parallel course.

Dewar argued that still larger transformations, from one family, order, class, or phylum to another are simply nonexistent. Rather than an even balance between species which have evolved and those which haven't, Dewar saw the evidence as overwhelmingly against general macroevolution. Almost every type of new animal appears suddenly in the geological record, he maintained, "endowed with all the attributes by which it is characterized. The changes it undergoes afterward are comparatively insignificant."

Perhaps Dewar's most basic criticism, noted by almost every critic of the theory, is that there are far too many missing links.

One of the most formidable objections to the evolution theory is the fact that no fossil has been discovered of an animal intermediate between creatures having a very peculiar skeleton, such as bats, whales, dugongs, seals, frogs, turtles, pterodactyles, ichthyosauruses, etc., and the supposed ordinary quadrupedal animals, from which, according to the theory, they have been evolved. If this theory is true, these intermediate forms must have existed in immense numbers in the past.

But we find no trace of their existence.

V.

These criticisms are so fundamental, so well founded, and have been made so frequently that even some of the most committed American evolutionists are in effect finally acknowledging that in many cases evidence for macro changes is not likely to be found. Paleontologists Steven Jay Gould, Niles Eldredge, and S. M. Stanley are now abandoning Darwin's slow-and-regular process as the major mode of species formation. They hypothesize instead that with many species evolution proceeds in sudden fits and starts and that then the species stabilize for long periods, perhaps until extinction. Gould calls this model "punctuated equilibrium." The transition between species happens quickly (even a thousand years is a mere moment geologically) and in such small populations that there is virtually no chance of finding fossil evidence to fill those notorious gaps.

Although Gould, Eldredge, and Stanley still consider themselves loyal Darwinians, their position is one of the clearest public repudiations of classical Darwinism yet made by professional paleontologists. Of course, for reasons of sentiment, they deny this, claiming Charlie D. was still correct in principle. But the fact remains that the mode and tempo of the evolutionary process advocated by Darwin is substantially different than that of the punctuationalists. Their willingness to take the fossil record as it exists is novel and laudable, but their proposed solution has peculiar implications. In agreeing that many species did appear (relatively) suddenly, Gould and company seem to have granted about half of the creationist position. Whether they care to acknowledge it or not, they have certainly granted the major point that critics like Dewar have been grumbling about for over a century.

Another thing to be noticed is that if punctuated equilibrium operates in such a way as to leave no fossils, then in terms of paleontology the hypothesis rests largely upon negative evidence, which, according to Darwin and many other scientists, is worthless. Into the gaps in which they insert sudden fits of accidental evolution, one can with equal logic insert acts of creation, intervention by conscious beings, or any other hypothetical process.

There is simply no easy, graceful, or satisfying way around it: The geological record did not support universal macroevolution in Darwin's time and it does not do so today. For every horse there are too many cases like the whale, which, despite vestigial pelvic bones, cannot be convincingly connected with anything. There is very little that is new about all this, but it seems to need repeating. Harkening back to that remarkable assertion by the AAAS spokesman claiming that 100 million fossils in the world's museums prove evolution beyond any doubt whatever, the reader may now more readily appreciate how unbalanced that statement actually was.

2: The Lawyer's Whistle

I.

THE ABANDONMENT of Darwin's agonizingly slow-and-regular process for many species is not the only element of classical Darwinism that has been jettisoned in recent decades. In fact, when they are not overreacting to the creationists, contemporary biologists are often found occupying positions so far away from Darwin on so many points that for all practical purposes classical Darwinism is dead. Because of the public posturing in the opposite direction provoked by the creationist challenge, this fact is not widely appreciated, but it is another important indication that the theory of universal macroevolution is really on the skids. And universal macroevolution is ultimately what is at stake. It is this application of evolution that is required to make an ape into a man. Without this concept, a creationist or anyone else can still maintain that man was created as man. Perhaps his skull has become a little more rounded and his bones thinner. Perhaps his stature has increased or diminished. But these small changes hardly matter. If we look at the death of classical Darwinism in more detail, we can see from yet another direction how fragmentary and inadequate contemporary evolutionary theory actually is.

II.

The nature of science is that it inches along from one position or concept to another as it methodically develops, tests, and digests data. Occasionally a Newton or an Einstein arises who notes the course of the inching and testing and crystallizes a new perception; but there would be little science and little to crystallize without the context provided by the inchers and testers.

Although we are sometimes given the impression that paleontologists, biologists, and zoologists have done little since 1859 except issue footnotes to *The Origin of Species*, the reality is rather different. In fact, most of the leading lights in these professions have methodically inched their way some considerable distance from the concepts of Darwin, and, somewhat embarrassingly, from the positions that are still defended by many popularizers and public spokesmen for science.

As yet, not too many people seem to have noticed this. Certainly the editors of *Time* haven't. In the issue covering the Segraves trial, their headlines read, DARWIN GOES ON TRIAL AGAIN, and PUTTING DARWIN BACK IN THE DOCK. The leading professionals have had Darwin in the dock for the last 125 years. They still believe in evolution, but they no longer argue that the explanations Darwin offered account for how or why evolution happens. In fact, by *evolution* they no longer mean quite what Darwin meant.

It is perhaps unfortunate that as yet another Newton hasn't dropped in to crystallize the new perception. But a very sharp-witted Yankee lawyer has noticed just how far the theoreticians have inched away from Darwin, and noticed as well that this news has not reached the public. The lawyer decided it was time to blow the whistle. The lawyer is Harvard-trained Norman Macbeth; the whistle has been issued as *Darwin Retried: An Appeal to Reason* (1971). Sir Karl Popper, professor emeritus of Logic and Scientific Method at the London School of Economics and probably the world's leading philosopher of science, described the book as "excellent and fair" and "truly valuable." Other important reviewers have called it "brilliant" and a service to the intellectual community. The biologists and paleontologists have (of course) ignored it.

In order to understand Macbeth's work correctly, it is again well to emphasize, as Macbeth does himself, that evolution has different aspects. As Macbeth expresses it, one is "large and relatively easy, the other smaller and much more difficult." The large-and-easy aspect is simply that the fossil record shows that plants and animals did not come into existence all at once. Many species have disappeared and others have been added since the beginning of life on earth. This observation was not the discovery of Charles Darwin. It was quite well known by 1800, even before Darwin's birth in 1809. Macbeth is not challenging the evidence for this large-and-easy aspect.

The small-and-difficult aspect of evolution is to explain how and why these changes of species took place. Darwin's major work, The Origin, was an attempt to provide the explanation. Darwin was far from the first to make such an attempt. His grandfather, Erasmus, among others, wrote extensively on the subject before his death in 1802. Darwin's chief glory was that he gave a more comprehensive and seemingly organic explanation than anyone before him.

Macbeth defines classical Darwinism as the assertion that the progression from early species to later ones, as observed in the fossils in the rocks, was a process of actual physical descent. The progression of fossil forms seemed to Darwin to be elucidated by data from comparative anatomy, embryology, and the experience of breeders. Classical Darwinism posits that the process of physical descent is governed by natural selection through such agencies as the struggle for existence, the survival of the fittest, sexual selection, and adaptation. In the classical conception, all these worked in small cumulative steps over vast periods of time.

This conception, says Macbeth, has two logical corollaries. The first is that in the evolution of any structure or function, every intermediate stage must be of advantage to the species. The second corollary is that natural selection tends to make each creature or plant only "as perfect as, or slightly more perfect than," the other inhabitants of the same area. Natural selection does not produce "absolute perfection."

Macbeth's major thesis is simply that the most highly regarded paleontologists, biologists, and other specialists no longer see the fossil pattern quite the way Darwin did and certainly no longer read the data he relied upon as elucidating that pattern. Additionally, Darwin's explanations of the forces behind natural selection have not stood up to closer scrutiny. Classical Darwinism is dead.

All too well aware of the continuing influence of the fundamentalists, the biologists have not chosen to blazon this conclusion across the sky; but it is expressed clearly enough in the professional literature. In even the most conservative field there are a few mavericks; but Macbeth is not relying on the testimony of the renegades. He cites primarily the words of Ernst Mayr and G. G. Simpson, both of Harvard. Mayr is probably the most learned biologist in the United States; Simpson is sometimes spoken of as the dean of American evolutionists.

Mayr, a convinced evolutionist and an eminent member of the synthetic school, says that Darwin was "bewildered," that he was "hopelessly confused," and that he had a "lack of understanding of the nature of species." He adds that Darwin was unable to discover the origin of species: "Darwin failed to solve the problem indicated by the title of his work. Although he demonstrated the modification of species in the time dimension, he never seriously attempted a rigorous analysis of the problem of the multiplication of species." Professor Simpson, Mayr's colleague at Harvard and an equally convinced evolutionist, caps Mayr by saying that Darwin's "book called *The Origin of Species* is not really on that subject."

One gets very little sense that anything this drastic has happened from popular summaries or accounts such as *Time*'s article on the Segraves trial. In England and the U.S.A. Darwin is usually presented as the discoverer of established truths, like Newton or Einstein. But internationally Darwin has never enjoyed this kind of status. Most German, French, and Russian scientists are not now and never have been convinced that Darwin explained the origin of species. It is chiefly in the United States, because of the contest with the creationists, that Darwinism has been offered as a panacea.

Naturally, there are variations of opinion within American biology, as everywhere else, and Mayr and Simpson do not speak for the entire profession. But it would indeed by difficult to find men of more distinguished reputations. The "synthetic school" to which Macbeth refers is the amalgam of knowledge, theory, and speculation that has replaced classical Darwinism. I shall discuss this shortly, but to get an idea of the overall condition of evolutionary theory at the present time, it will be useful to note what has driven these leading theoreticians closer to their German, French, and Russian counterparts.

III.

Putting it simply, the agencies of natural selection—the struggle for existence, survival of the fittest, sexual selection, and adaptation—have been scrutinized and found wanting.

For most biologists the struggle for existence has been out of fashion for a long time. Darwin saw this struggle as essentially benevolent, positive, and developmental:

... each generation ... has to struggle for life, and to suffer great destruction. When we reflect on this struggle, we may console ourselves with the full belief, that the war of nature is not incessant, that no fear is felt, that death is generally prompt, and that the vigorous, the healthy, and the happy survive and multiply.

Early enthusiasts for Darwin's ideas, such as T. H. Huxley, carried the struggle for existence to ridiculous lengths. Huxley claimed that all the molecules within each organism were competing with each other. Others said that the major organs within the body were fighting each other for nourishment. The struggle for existence also infected much social and political theory in a way that George Bernard Shaw, among others, found thoroughly objectionable:

Never in history, as far as we know, had there been such a determined, richly subsidized, politically organized attempt to persuade the human race that all progress, all prosperity, all salvation, individual and social, depend on an unrestricted conflict for food and money, on the suppression and elimination of the weak by the strong, on Free Trade, Free Contract, Free Competition, Natural Liberty, Laisser-faire: in short, on "doing the other fellow down" with impunity.

As Macbeth says, "When the first enthusiasm wore off and the bill for the damages came in, the biologists realized that things had gone too far." Now the struggle for existence has been deemphasized to the point of invisibility. A few politically conservative biologists still emphasize the competitive aspect of existence, but most now point out that cooperation and ecological balance are far more common in nature than "war." Moreover, there is important though little noticed evidence from the fossil record that not only gives the lie to the struggle for existence but confounds the idea of a sequence of forms arising from that struggle.

This is the evidence for a phenomenon called deferred replacement. The "adaptive zone" of the ichthyosaurs, for example, is now inhabited by dolphins and porpoises, but the dolphins and porpoises did not take over from the ichthyosaurs through struggle or competition. The ichthyosaurs were extinct long before the dolphins and porpoises appeared. During the interval the adaptive zone was simply empty.

Macbeth is one of the few who is willing to talk about deferred replacement. He credits G. G. Simpson with reporting this several times and notes that according to Simpson such cases are numerous. Macbeth says that Simpson's colleagues also know about deferred replacement but rarely raise the issue. Consequently, he adds, the general public is completely unaware of it. The phenomenon of deferred replacement, as Macbeth says, "is a truly biological fact," cutting across many classical Darwinian explanations and contradicting the popular belief that the history of the earth "has been one long bloody fight."

Yet, as with so much data that confounds conventional evolutionary theory, the fact of deferred replacement is mostly neglected by the professionals and ignored by the popularizers who prefer their own fiction. An example offered by Macbeth is this line: "At night and in winter, as the great reptiles lay torpid, the mammals took over and the reptiles were driven into oblivion." He notes that even some professionals indulge the theory that mammals became egg-feeders and ate many reptile eggs. "Inevitably," says Macbeth, "I sometimes doubt that the implications of deferred replacement, especially in its bearing on the struggle for existence, have been fully digested."

The "survival of the fittest" has had an even more ignominious fate than the imaginary struggle. This once highly prized concept turns out to be meaningless, a mere tautology. This is apparent as soon as we ask, How do we determine who are the fittest? The answer is, those who survive. The concept then becomes "the survivors survive," which explains nothing. When they feel compelled to say something about survival of the fittest, contemporary evolutionists such as Mayr define the fittest as those who leave the most offspring. Simpson says much the same thing, pointing out that, used in this sense, *fitness* doesn't correspond to the common understanding of the word. "To a geneticist fitness has nothing to do with health, strength, good looks, or anything but effectiveness in breeding." But if the fittest are simply those who leave most offspring, this doesn't explain very much either. It is well known that members of a species can become too numerous, and then the species suffers a population collapse. Those left after the collapse are not necessarily fitter than their ancestors.

The concept of sexual selection has also gone down in flames. The idea that males competing for territory and females, and that females choosing the victors, engage in a selective process favoring the best qualified mates is not, as Macbeth acknowledges, entirely without examples. Indeed there are behavior patterns in some species where sexual selection is an obvious fact. He cites the account of Robert Ardrey in *African Genesis* (1961) concerning a study of the breeding habits of some eight hundred Wyoming sage grouse:

After the males had sorted themselves out on the strutting-ground, the hens gathered at five mating spots each the size of a room. Dominance established 1% of the males as what Allee terms master-cocks, 2% as sub-cocks. Copulation occurred only at the invitation of the hen; in other words, female prerogative of choice was the next step in natural selection. And the result of that selection was that 74% of all matings were with master-cocks, 1% of the total male population; and 13% with sub-cocks, representing 2% of the males. Rank order of dominance had insured that 87% of that season's crop of young sage grouse be fathered by only 3% of the male population.

But as Macbeth says, the whims and caprices of nature frustrate all efforts to generalize. For every case like the sage grouse, there are dozens of others that make a mockery of the concept: Males perform elaborate dances for females who are not watching; beautifully colored feathers are displayed for females who are color-blind; after strenuous combat among the males, the females mate with the losers just as frequently as with the victors.

The investigation of sexual selection, Macbeth claims, has been more than a disappointment. "What it has really brought forth is a monumental challenge to natural selection, the key-stone of the whole Darwinian theory." Observing behavior and structures for evidence of sexual selection has called attention to birds like the Argus pheasant and the peacock, "conspicuous and appetizing animals" that are pretty weak at running, flying, fighting, or hiding. From the late 1930s to the early '60s, Julian Huxley believed in sexual selection so strongly that he supposed the obvious disadvantages concomitant with huge and spectac-ular plumage were overcome by the reproductive advantages bequeathed by these "display-characters."

Macbeth's reply to this is that natural selection should never have allowed such birds to come into existence in the first place. But they have not only come into existence, they have stayed in existence and not become extinct. Sexual selection "has not only failed to solve the problems to which Darwin applied it," Mac-beth says, "it has called attention to a glaring weakness in natu-ral selection. It has emphasized the existence of things which, under a reasonable view of that theory, simply cannot be." So, like many other explanations, sexual selection is slowly fading. It still lingers in the popular imagination, but the younger gen-eration of biologists leave it alone.

The last concept behind Darwin's theory of natural selection, adaptation, has also created more problems than it has solved. The works of nature are replete with marvelous, mysterious, and intricate complexities of behavior and structure. One example among thousands is a small wasplike insect of southern Europe and northern Africa called Eumenes amedei. After mating, the females build small, hollow, domelike structures about the size of a cherry in which they deposit their eggs, one egg to each house. The houses are made of tiny pieces of rock held together by a mortar of dust and saliva. The houses are also stocked with food for the newly hatched grubs. This food is small pale-green caterpillars, which must be stored live, otherwise they would rot by the time the grub emerged. But they cannot be deposited in the house fully alive, otherwise they might damage the egg or break out. The Eumenes stings them in such a way as only to partially paralyze them. After the caterpillars are deposited, the Eumenes lays an egg, suspending it from the roof of the house by a tiny silken thread. This keeps the egg off the floor of the house and out of reach of the still-writhing caterpillars, which thus cannot injure it. Then the Eumenes seals the remaining small hole on the top of the dome with a cement plug. This elaborate sequence is only half the story:

When the grub emerges from the egg, it devours its eggshell, then spins for itself a tiny silken ribbon-sheath in which it is enfolded tail-uppermost and with head hanging down. In this retreat it is suspended above the pile of living food. It can lower itself far enough to nibble at the caterpillars. If they stir too violently, it can withdraw into its silken sheath, wait until the commotion has subsided, then descend again to its meal. As the grub grows in size and strength, it becomes bolder, the silken retreat is no longer required; it can venture down and live at its ease among the remains of its food.

The stone cells are not all stored with the same wealth of caterpillars. Some contain five and some ten. The young females, larger than the males, need twice as much food. But note that the cells are stocked before the eggs are laid, and that biologists generally believe that the sex is already determined when an egg is laid. How does the Eumenes know the future sex of her eggs? How is it that she never makes a mistake?

Such are the exquisite adaptations of the Eumenes. Before Darwin, marvels like this were often adduced as examples of God's handiwork. Dr. William Paley (1743–1805), archdeacon of Carlisle, published a book in 1802 called *Natural Theology, or Evidence of the Existence and Attributes of the Deity Collected from the Appearances of Nature*. The book made a deep impression on the young Darwin, who said of it, "I do not think I hardly ever admired a book more than Paley's *Natural Theology*. I could almost formerly have said it by heart."

In effect, Darwin's lifework was to rewrite Paley's book as science rather than theology, substituting for God the grand, gradual, and mechanical process of evolution. Adaptations, Darwin maintained, could be explained through the accumulation of small additional features over vast periods of time. Well, this may have been true of the diversification of the Galapagos finches, but how could this be true in a case like the Eumenes? How could a life cycle this intricate, involving many interdependent actions and structures, possibly result from a gradual, cumulative step-by-step process? Each step in the whole marvelous procedure seems as integral and necessary as every other.

The Eumenes is not an isolated example. Literally thousands of similar cases exist. For the most part, professional biologists no longer even attempt to explain how and why adaptations of such complexity came about. It was not always thus. Shortly after Darwinism first caught on in Britain and the United States in the latter half of the nineteenth century, it became the rage for biologists to explain why adaptations took the form they did. Everything was seen as a beneficial adaptation and as a confirmation of the theory. Naturally, this led to absurdities, and for a while Darwinism became discredited. This phase was long remembered, and the explainers kept their heads down. Today, however, we can still find the occasional professional indulging the old form. Macbeth singles out Professor Tinbergen, of Oxford, a leading ethologist (the science of animal behavior), for "arrant nonsense" when he said, ". . . the brightly colored patches of skin seen around the genital aperture of female baboons and chimpanzees probably guide the male to the female's copulatory organs." Macbeth remarks, "This kind of childish 'explanation' which offhandedly assumes that baboons and chimpanzees need more guidance than other primates, is precisely what brought Darwinism into contempt around the turn of the century."

Truly, the diversity and complexity of nature frustrate all attempts to generalize. It is easy enough to say that the peacock's magnificent feathers attract his mate or that the grasshopper's coloration provides camouflage, but the peacock's feathers also attract predators and the grasshopper betrays his location by chirping. In 1932 W. L. McAtee published a paper, "Effectiveness in nature of so-called protective adaptations in the animal kingdom, chiefly as illustrated by the food-habits of nearctic birds." McAtee analyzed reports on the contents of eighty thousand bird stomachs. He concluded that birds consumed species of prey pretty much in proportion to their availability and that "protective adaptations" were of no advantage. "Undeniably," McAtee wrote, "selectionists [promoters of natural selection] have been absurd in their disquisitions on adaptations."

Thus like the other Darwinian concepts, the natural selection of favorable adaptations has not proven to have pervasive explanatory power either. It is not that supportive examples cannot be found, but that an equal or greater number of contradictory instances can also be cited. Scientists at the forefront of inquiry have put the knife to classical Darwinism. They have not gone public with this news but have kept it in their technical papers and inner counsels. Many second-rank evolutionists, on the other hand, continue to repeat that minor miracles like the Eumenes life cycle were accomplished by natural selection working in a step-by-step manner; but the steps are never shown. They do this largely because they feel compelled to say something—anything is better than admitting ignorance—and they don't know what else to say.

Somewhat more alarming are the popularizers. I offer the immortal words of George Gamow and Martynas Ycas in Mr. *Tompkins Inside Himself* (1968):

The animals changed too. Some of the reptiles in the colder regions began to develop a method of keeping their bodies warm. Their heat output increased when it was cold and their heat loss was cut down when scales became smaller and more pointed, and evolved into fur. Sweating was also an adaptation to regulate the body temperature, a device to cool the body when necessary by evaporation of water. But incidently the young of these reptiles began to lick the sweat of the mother for nourishment. Certain sweat glands began to secrete a richer and richer secretion, which eventually became milk. Thus the young of these early mammals had a better start in life.

This is pure speculation. There is no positive evidence for it whatever. Unfortunately, it is but one example among thousands in the literature of "pop-evolution." Of course, much of the public does not distinguish between the professionals and popularizers and naïvely assumes that descriptions of this sort are based on demonstrated fact.

We simply do not know how or why the marvels of nature were produced, and the best scientists say so. Richard B. Goldschmidt, a leading geneticist, pointed to seventeen famous cases, including the human eye, which remain unexplained by the accumulation and selection of small mutations. Yet as Macbeth points out, Darwin himself "was willing to stake everything on meeting the challenge of the marvels. He actually said: 'If it could be demonstrated that any complex organ existed, which could not possibly have been formed by numerous, successive, slight modifications, my theory would absolutely break down.' " Macbeth says: "This fact seems to have been demonstrated, if only by default."

These are not the only problems with the concept of adaptation in classical Darwinism. The problems are so numerous and detailed that an entire book could be written on this subject alone. Here I will allude to only one more problem. If Darwin did not really explain the origin of species, neither does classical Darwinism explain extinction. In theory, organisms become extinct when they are no longer well adapted to their environment. Common examples are the mammoth and the Irish elk, which developed such huge tusks and antlers as to seem liabilities rather than assets. Yet Simpson notes that before they went extinct, the animals thrived in great numbers for tens of thousands of years, despite their anatomical excesses. Simpson admits he cannot tell why these species vanished and adds that it is also puzzling why some living species do *not* die out. There are many living creatures that are as bizarre as any that ever became extinct. He mentions elephants, whales, the narwhal, and certain insects, such as the dynasties beetle and some of the mantids.

IV.

Beyond all these difficulties with the specific mechanisms said to effect natural selection, there is a more general point concerning the image of evolution Darwin bequeathed us which Macbeth elucidates as well and as briefly as anyone:

... if a paleontologist portrays known fossil forms such as sharks, fishes, and amphibians in man's family tree, we soon perceive that many examples of these forms are still present, practically unchanged, although their former siblings are said to have worked up to human status. Thus one and the same ancient stock split into a group with astonishing plasticity and another group with almost total rigidity. This is very hard to swallow.

V.

With authorities like Mayr and Simpson declaring that Darwin did not solve the origin of species, the reader may wonder how it is that in *Origins* (1977) Richard Leakey and Roger Lewin can propose "the Darwinian revolution" as more fundamental than that of Copernicus (who noticed that the sun, rather than the earth, was at the center of the solar system), or how in *Cosmos* (1980) Carl Sagan can invoke natural selection as if this were an uncontested and immutable law of nature.

More than one responsible person has voiced concern that the real facts about Darwinism and evolution are simply not reaching the public.

3: The Synthetic Theory

I.

IF THE LEADING BIOLOGISTS do not believe that Darwin found the answer to the origin of species, what do they believe? Well, they certainly still believe in evolution; that much *is* beyond doubt. Despite the numerous difficulties and contradictions presented by the fossil record, most scientists simply see no reasonable alternative to evolution. As far as they are concerned, creationism not only lacks scientific credentials but is objectionable on other grounds, amounting in their view to a return to the Dark Ages. So, when it comes to the fossil record, or any other body of evidence, for the sake of the good cause they accentuate the supportive data and ignore or minimize as far as possible the contrary indications.

They also derive no little succor from other concepts and areas of inquiry that have opened up even as the Darwinian explanations were collapsing. Contemporary evolutionists are concerned with population studies, genetics, mutations, DNA and protein analysis, and the application of mathematics to these fields. Taken together these areas of inquiry constitute what has been called the synthetic theory. Most scientists still also employ natural selection as a kind of umbrella concept, but no one knowledgeable maintains that this selection process proceeds for the reasons advanced by Darwin, and there are frequently admissions to the effect that it cannot be seen or proved, that in specific cases we do not know how or why it operates, and that we do not know what it is doing at the present time. Some scientists are candid enough to say that it amounts to no more than speculation.

II.

The knowledge gained from population studies combined with genetics and mathematical analysis is probably the most substantial of all contributions relevant to evolution. The diversification of the New Guinea kingfishers described by Mayr, which we noted earlier, is a good example of how certain instances of microevolution can be scientifically explained. This is a real achievement, and of course most evolutionists maintain that such small changes simply must accumulate to produce major transformations. But there are even more problems with this position than those we have already surveyed.

Not only does this belief find scant support in the fossil record; there is another major body of evidence directly to the contrary produced by the profession from which modern genetics itself was derived: the breeding of plants and animals. Ironically, Darwin considered the experience of plant and animal breeders one of the keystones of his argument. He was thoroughly familiar with the great improvements breeders had been able to effect in many species. He was a crony of pigeon fanciers and raised them himself. He knew well what changes in beaks and feathers could be produced in a few years through the judicious selection of mates. Then he extrapolated. If breeders could produce these changes in three or four years, what could nature do, operating over many millions of years?

It is a familiar argument. Many popularizers still employ it. (Sagan presents it in the early pages of *Cosmos* in almost the exact form Darwin used 120 years earlier.) But there is a difficulty with it: The changes Darwin saw the breeders producing were all micro. Moreover, all the changes produced by all the breeders around the world in all the years since have also been micro. No one has ever produced a macro change—a major transformation.

It is now clear that Darwin's optimism about explaining the origin of species was based on a completely misinformed conception as to their mutability. He believed there was no limit to how much plants and animals could vary. In the first edition of *The Origin of Species* he wrote, "I can see no difficulty in a race of bears being rendered, by natural selection, more and more aquatic in their habits, with larger and larger mouths, till a creature was produced as monstrous as a whale." Few evolutionists nowadays are brave enough to mention this.

Over the years, breeders have discovered that there are clear limits to how much variation can be produced. Everyone knows we do not get carrots the size of elms or pigs with wings. But more than this, species seem to possess an inherent stability, an average or ideal size and pattern that cannot be pushed beyond a certain point. The range of variation was discussed by Luther Burbank, probably the most competent breeder of all time:

There is a law . . . of the Reversion to the Average. I know from my own experience that I can develop a plum half an inch long or one 2½ inches long, with every possible length in between, but . . . it is hopeless to try to get a plum the size of a pea, or one as big as a grapefruit. I have daisies on my farms little larger than my fingernail and some that measure six inches across, but I have none as big as a sunflower, and never expect to have. . . . In short, there are limits to the development possible, and these limits follow a law. But what law, and why?

It is the law that I have referred to above. Experiments carried on extensively have given us scientific proof of what we had already guessed by observation; namely, that plants and animals all tend to revert, in successive generations, toward a given mean or average. Men grow to be seven feet tall, and over, but never to ten; there are dwarfs not higher than 24 inches, but none that you can carry in your hand. . . . In short, there is undoubtedly a pull toward the mean which keeps all living things within some more or less fixed limitations.

On the face of it, this is not a good prescription for getting an oak from a conifer or a man from an ape. All competent biologists acknowledge the limited nature of the variation breeders can produce, although they do not like to discuss it much when grinding the evolutionary ax. But a few reputable scientists, such as Loren Eiseley, are candid enough to discuss the problem:

It would appear that careful domestic breeding, whatever it may do to improve the quality of race horses or cabbages, is not in itself the road to the endless biological deviation which is evolution. There is great irony in this situation, for more than almost any other single factor, domestic breeding has been used as an argument for the reality of evolution. (*The Immense Journey*, 1958)

III.

This brings us to mutations and the extensive laboratory work with fruit flies. Mutations are almost invariably mentioned in the mix of factors said to produce evolution. Mutations do occur in nature, and although only something on the order of one in a thousand is neither deleterious nor fatal, the remaining tiny fraction can in principle produce beneficial changes that are inheritable. While the mutation rate in the direction of evolutionary transformation is thus exceedingly low, this is again compensated for in theory by extrapolating this activity over the age of the earth. If there is an eons-long process of mutation, it is difficult to account for the persistence of numerous creatures that have not changed at all in hundreds of millions of years, but this is far from the greatest problem for those putting their faith in these random, accidental events.

The greatest problem is the conclusion drawn from observing the results of inflicting mutations induced by radiation and chemicals upon thousands of generations of laboratory fruit flies. The fruit fly watchers found the same "law" as Luther Burbank: Even the variations produced by mutations could only be pushed so far. Beyond a certain point they proved lethal or the flies became sterile. If left alone for a few generations, even the most severely mutated flies that retained their fertility returned to normal or something close to it.

These points could be documented at great length, but no testimony is more telling than the saga of Richard B. Goldschmidt (1878–1958), an important geneticist who wrote *The Material Basis of Evolution* (1940). Goldschmidt spent much of his career observing mutations in fruit flies, and then broke with orthodox theory. He saw plenty of mutations, but they were all so incredibly micro that even if a thousand were combined in one specimen, it would still not amount to a new species. He then hatched one of the most fanciful ideas in the history of evolutionary science: the hypothesis of "the hopeful monster." He suggested that perhaps somehow a huge, sudden, dramatic change could occur all at once and thereafter be preserved by a favorable environment.

At the time, Goldschmidt was strongly derided for displaying this degree of magical thinking, but lately the hypothesis of the hopeful monster is making a quiet comeback in the setting provided by punctuated equilibrium. Whatever happens with the hopeful monster this time around, Goldschmidt's experience watching fruit flies has had lasting effects. Led by Ernst Mayr, many biologists now discount the role of environmental mutations and instead see the major source of genetic variation to come from the "gene flow" of the parents in sexual reproduction. The experience of breeders, however, demonstrates that this merely transfers the problem without solving it.

IV.

Analyses of DNA and various human and animal proteins are among the most recent additions to the evolutionist arsenal. DNA or deoxyribonucleic acid is the coded component of chromosomes determining—some believe—the heredity of all living things. It was not clear how DNA could carry the genetic code until its double-spiral (or double-helix) structure was unraveled by James Watson and Francis Crick in 1953. This accomplishment is one of the scientific triumphs of the century, for which Watson and Crick shared the Nobel Prize for medicine in 1962.

The long spiral side chains of the DNA molecule are composed of sugars and phosphates. Linking these side chains are threads formed by four bases paired in two ways. These base pairs may occur in any sequence and may be oriented either way around. The basic molecular structure appears to be uniform in all living things, but the differing sequences of the threads—the genetic code—produce enormous variation. In living organisms, the DNA molecule replicates itself by "unzipping." Each side chain retains one of the paired bases; and it will only bond with another base of the kind it has lost. Thus each side of the zipper acts as a template to produce its missing side chain and bases.

DNA molecules can now also be unzipped in the laboratory,

and it has now become possible to combine half of a human DNA molecule with half from a chimpanzee or other primate. Because the threads between the side chains are sequenced differently in different species, not all threads between man and chimp match up. But many do, and by measuring the degree of bonding between the chains from man and chimp, researchers believe it is possible to estimate their genetic difference. In this kind of DNA analysis, man is said to differ from the chimpanzee by only 1 to 2.5 percent, depending on the source. There is a slightly greater difference between man and the gorilla, and yet greater differences between man and orangutans and gibbons. The genetic distance between man and monkeys is greater still.

Very similar results have been attained by matching various protein molecules of these species. Man has several different types of hemoglobin; two of these are actually identical to those of chimpanzees. The amino acid sequence of cytochrome c, a respiratory protein, is also identical. Many other protein molecules in chimps and men differ by only a few "mutation points." The degree of similarity between man and apes and monkeys suggested by this method broadly follows the same pattern found by comparing DNA. A third type of protein analysis, the immunology method measuring degrees of protein-antibody reactions, also broadly confirms the results of the other methods.

Perhaps the most impressive aspect of DNA and protein analysis is that it strikingly corroborates long-held suppositions (arrived at via anatomy, and so on) that man is most closely related to chimps and gorillas, then to orangs and gibbons, and less closely to monkeys. The various indicators all point in the same direction. This has emboldened some biologists, noting the degree of relatedness between man and chimpanzee, for example, to estimate how recently they shared a common ancestor. The answer arrived at is about 4 million years ago.

Most paleoanthropologists regard this as virtually impossible. It seems far too recent and suggests something is still lacking in our overall understanding of genetic relatedness. Thus, although the decoding of DNA really is a triumph and the genetic distance between man and chimp is, on these criteria, provocatively small, most paleoanthropologists display remarkable caution (for once) in assessing the significance of these analyses. In *Origins* Leakey and Lewin voice a typical response: "The confirmation by biochemical techniques of the stages in the evolutionary path is reassuring, but so gross a discrepancy in the apparent timing is more than a little disconcerting. The question still remains to be resolved."

Regardless of the question of timing, many scientists can and do see these tests as evidence lending powerful support to the general evolutionary hypothesis. But as ever, it is possible to bring considerable objections to this view. It is all very well for writers to claim that 99 percent of the protein structure is the same in chimpanzees and men, but this does not seem to take into account that when it comes to chromosomes, the parent body of the DNA molecule, chimps have 48 and men 46. In fact, those stressing DNA affinities seem to overlook chromosome numbers entirely. These vary widely, and larger numbers of chromosomes do not necessarily indicate higher life-forms. Fruit flies have 6 to 12, horses 64, trout about 80. Nor does the 99 percent estimate reflect other obvious differences, such as that in intelligence. According to these biochemical tests, the chimpanzee is more closely related to man than it is to Asian apes, the orangutan, and the gibbon. Yet, taking man, chimp, and orang, there is no question which two most resemble each other on the basis of virtually all other criteria.

Indeed, in a larger perspective, the close resemblance of human and chimp DNA really represents another evolutionary problem, rather than a solution. Comparisons of DNA in frogs show that there is much greater DNA variation among them than there is between the bat and the blue whale; yet the world's three thousand species of frogs are all much more similar to each other than man is to any of the other primates, to say nothing about comparing bats and whales.

If we are drawing conclusions about man's evolution using DNA comparisons, we then have to do a lot of explaining about those variations found in nearly identical frogs.

These anomalous results are but one indication that the so-called "point mutations" do not themselves produce changes in form. There seems to be something else controlling the organism. Microbiologists believe this is the "regulator genes"—a subject that occasions amusement among some paleontologists and geologists of the stone-throwing variety, since the biologists must ascribe so much to these regulators without having identified a single one, despite very long and diligent search. And even if these regulator genes are ever found, we will then have to explain how they function so intelligently.

All in all, there is little doubt that evolutionary protagonists have made far more of human-chimp DNA similarities than the situation warrants. Again and again we find that positive evolutionary aspects are emphasized and repeated endlessly while evidence from the same field contradicting evolution or carrying negative implications is ignored. The author of virtually every contemporary book supporting evolution trots out the human-chimp DNA comparison, but very few mention the frogs or another discovery of microbiology that has been known for some time.

This concerns the genetic relatedness of homologous organs, such as the similar skeletal structures in the wing of a bat and the foreleg of a mouse. The supposed common origin of these organs, says biologist Sir Alister Hardy, is "absolutely fundamental to what we are talking about when we speak of evolution." This being so, it is appropriate to let a biologist describe what has been discovered about these organs. John Randall has done it as succinctly as anyone:

The older text-books on evolution make much of the idea of homology, pointing out the obvious resemblances between the skeletons of the limbs of different animals. Thus the "pentadactyl" limb pattern is found in the arm of a man, the wing of a bird, and the flipper of a whale, and this is held to indicate their common origin. Now if these various structures were transmitted by the same gene-complex, varied from time to time by mutations and acted upon by environmental selection, the theory would make good sense. Unfortunately this is not the case. Homologous organs are now known to be produced by totally different gene complexes in the different species. *The concept of homology in terms of similar genes handed on from a common ancestor has broken down.* . . . . (*Parapsychology and the Nature of Life*, 1975)

This is not an isolated opinion. In *Homology, An Unsolved Problem* (1971), the distinguished embryologist Sir Gavin de Beer wrote,

It is now clear that the pride with which it was assumed that the inheritance of homologous structures from a common ancestor explained homology was misplaced; for such inheritance cannot be ascribed to identity of genes. . . .

But if it is true that through the genetic code, genes code for enzymes that synthesise proteins which are responsible (in a manner still unknown in embryology) for the differentiation of the various parts in their normal manner, what mechanism can it be that results in the production of homologous organs, the same "patterns", in spite of their *not* being controlled by the same genes? I asked this question in 1938, and it has not been answered.

Far from microbiology "proving" that we are only one percent away from being chimpanzees, it seems rather that this field has come around to undermining the fundamental basis of macro-evolution. Randall points to Thomas Hunt Morgan's experiments with fruit flies for some of the "most striking evidence" that there must be something controlling development beyond the level of the gene. (Morgan is one of the most important biologists of this century. His work was the greatest single factor in reconfirming and resurrecting Mendelian genetics. He was the man who introduced the fruit fly to geneticists in the first place and during the early decades of this century estalished the relationships of chromosomes to inheritance and of genes to chromosomes.) Morgan, who had produced endless mutations in color and form in fruit flies, developed a pure strain of flies bearing an "eyeless" form of the gene. But when Morgan carried the experiment further, inbreeding this new eyeless strain, he found that within a short time, perfectly formed eyes appeared! In *The Ghost in the Machine* (1967) Arthur Koestler, a strong critic of the mechanistic biology underlying neo-Darwinism, commented,

The traditional explanation of this remarkable phenomenon is that the other members of the gene-complex have been "reshuffled and re-combined in such a way that they deputise for the missing normal eye-forming gene." Now re-shuffling, as every poker player knows, is a randomizing process. No biologist would be so perverse as to suggest that the new insect-eye evolved by pure chance, thus repeating within a few generations an evolutionary process which took hundreds of millions of years. Nor does the concept of natural selection provide the slightest help in this case. The recombination of genes to deputise for the missing gene must have been co-ordinated according to some over-all plan. . . .

If homologous organs cannot be securely attributed to genetic inheritance, and if the regeneration of eyes by an eyeless strain of fruit flies implies the existence of some overall plan, it can easily be seen why DNA and protein similarities do not necessarily imply descent from common ancestors. The major groups of the earth's life-forms could have been generated in some other fashion, rather than evolving from a few primeval types, and still display fundamental biochemical affinities. However species originated, a degree of biochemical similarity may be imposed by sharing the same food, atmosphere, minerals, gravity, and so on. Furthermore, those biologists who are concerned to maintain a reasonable perspective on the significance of DNA and protein analyses point out that there is still a great deal that is unknown, including how the DNA is packed or arranged in the chromosomes, what all the DNA is doing (only the function of a fraction is understood), or whether some small pieces of chromosomes (genes) indeed function on a hierarchical basis.

These caveats do not minimize the accomplishment of decoding DNA, and so forth, and it is important to realize how and why evolutionists draw support from some aspects of the biochemical tests we have reviewed, but the implications many have drawn are inadmissible when seen in the context of those things about which we are still ignorant.

Very recently new information about similarities in genetic material has come to light that throws the whole issue into more doubt and confusion than ever. At a symposium on March 3 and 4, 1982, at the M. D. Anderson Hospital and Tumor Institute in Houston, Texas, Max Birnstiel of the University of Zurich in Switzerland announced that he has found nearly identical bits of genetic material in two distantly related species of sea urchin. According to present understanding, the two animals shared a common ancestor no less than 65 million years ago and should by now have completely different genes. Birnstiel said that at first he had a hard time believing it. The genetic material from the two species is so nearly identical one would think they had separated less than half a million years ago. He spent three years checking and rechecking his results before reporting them. He has also aired the findings in the *EMBO Journal*, published in London. Groping for an explanation for this totally unexpected discovery, Birnstiel said that the only "plausible" explanation is that genetic material was "transferred" from one animal to another in relatively recent evolutionary times, which, if it actually happened, would constitute an "astonishing" shortcut in evolution. Unfortunately, no one has any idea how such a "transfer" could take place.

V.

No review of developments in biochemistry and microbiology would be complete without mention of the efforts to replicate the initial creation of life by reconvening the hypothetical elements and conditions in the earth's primeval atmosphere.

In 1953, Stanley Miller of the University of Chicago passed an electric discharge (simulating lightning) through a mixture of gases (hydrogen, methane, ammonia, and water vapor) thought to have been present when life first arose. Miller obtained traces of fifteen amino acids, the building blocks of proteins.

Subsequently there have been many replications and elaborations of Miller's experiment. Melvin Calvin used the same gases but exposed them instead to gamma radiation, obtaining in addition to amino acids, sugars and the purine and pyrimidine bases that enter into the composition of DNA and RNA. Even more complex substances, such as polypeptides and nucleic acids, can be obtained by heating and cooling some of these substances under certain pressures and in particular concentrations. Thus it is assumed that the mystery of life's origin has been solved. As the title of an article by S. Fox in *New Scientist* magazine (February 27, 1969) proclaimed, "In the beginning . . . life assembled itself."

But did it? None of these biochemical substances produced in Miller-type experiments, we note, was of the self-replicating variety. There are two other fundamental criticisms of Fox's thesis. The first of these has been voiced by John Randall. In *Parapsychology and the Nature of Life,* Randall points to the often-overlooked fact that the synthesis of amino acids and other organic substances by Miller and his successors did *not* occur at random. Rather, they were the product of carefully arranged circumstances controlled by conscious, intelligent beings—the experimenters themselves. The undisputed role of directive intelligence in these experiments hardly allows them to be seen as positive evidence for the spontaneous origin of life. (As we shall hear later, physicists are now highly aware of the experimenter's influence as it affects the interpretation of results.)

The second fundamental criticism of the "primitive soup" theory has been made by J. Shaw and G. Brooks in their book *Origin and Development of Living Systems* (1973). This criticism concerns the basic assumptions of Miller and his followers in postulating the conditions and substances involved. If life arose in the way that Miller and Fox suggest, it is necessary to suppose that there were large concentrations of highly nitrogenous matter (amino acids, purines, pyramidines, etc.) involved over long periods of time. Since such compounds are readily absorbed on a variety of clay and rock particles, the Miller-Fox thesis implies that we should be able to find huge deposits of certain kinds of substances. As Brooks and Shaw point out:

If there ever was a primitive soup, then we would expect to find at least somewhere on this planet either massive sediments containing enormous amounts of the various nitrogenous organic compounds . . . or alternatively in much metamorphosed sediments we should find vast amounts of nitrogenous cokes. In fact no such materials have been found anywhere on earth. Indeed, to the contrary, the very oldest of sediments . . . contain organic matter very much of the sporopollenin type and degradation products of such materials, especially a variety of alkanes and fatty acids and derivatives. Sediments of this type are extremely short of nitrogen.

Not only is there this evidence that the basic assumptions of Miller and his followers are mistaken, but even if they were correct, they would still be a long way from generating even the most elementary *living* organism. In *Science, Man and Morals* (1965) Cambridge zoologist W. H. Thorp produced calculations showing that the likelihood of this event happening by chance was "fantastically improbable." Various physicists have said that the spontaneous formation of life violates the Second Law of Thermodynamics, which states that all closed physical systems tend toward a state of maximum *disorder*. Prof. Ludwig von Bertalanffy, of the State University of New York, has remarked that given the Second Law and the probability problem, the initial formation of even the simplest living organisms "would only be possible in the presence of 'organizing forces.' "

As Randall suggests, these conclusions by a variety of biologists who find grave difficulties with the primitive soup theory may come as a surprise to those who have been educated to believe that this theory is almost an established fact. Randall points out that the theory has been cited for years in most biology texts, including biology primers for quite young children, as if it were on as sound a basis as the atomic theory in chemistry. Randall says there is actually no *factual* support for it at all. It is, rather, a purely speculative theory "made to seem plausible by the avoidance of detailed analysis, and repeated confident assertion." In a similar vein, Brooks and Shaw conclude:

The acceptance of this theory and its promulgation by many workers who have certainly not always considered all the facts in great detail has in our opinion reached proportions which could be regarded as dangerous.

VI.

Thus we see that the wider state-of-the-art body of evidence relevant to evolutionary theory is very much a mixed bag. Microevolutionary speciation of the type seen in the Galapagos finches and thousands of other instances is today well documented and fairly well understood. But on the macroevolutionary level fundamental problems—such as those raised by the missing "regulator genes," the lack of genetic relatedness of homologous organs, and the genesis of life in the beginning—remain unsolved. The combined weight of population studies, genetics, the theory of mutations, protein analyses, etc., amounts to a very considerable body of scientific accomplishment, but this is very far from enough to elevate evolution to a universal law of nature by which everything in the biosphere may be explained. Yet many scientists speak as if this elevation had already taken place, as if universal macroevolution were as securely documented as instances of microevolution. In accounting for this aberration we have to look beyond the evidence and sheer enthusiasm into the deeper recesses of the evolutionist mentality.

The move from caution to certitude is lubricated by what Norman Macbeth has called "the best-in-field fallacy." This is the fallacy of assuming that the best currently proposed explanation is by the mere fact of being better than the others also necessarily the correct explanation. To illustrate the distinction, let us use a prosaic example outside biology. A backyard mechanic is trying to diagnose why the engine of an old car is firing irregularly. He considers the possibilities that he is using poor gasoline, that the fuel pump is faulty, and that the spark plugs need changing. But perhaps his brother has also bought the same gasoline and is not having problems. The mechanic has also removed the air filter and seen that fuel is being delivered to the carburetor, indicating that the pump is functioning. The best theory in the field is that he needs new spark plugs. But in the humility born of experience, most backyard mechanics would not be willing to wager everything that changing the spark plugs will infallibly solve the problem. The problem may be caused by a number of other things: a broken wire, burned contact points, or a crack in the distributor cap.

Yet many scientists jump where the mechanic pauses and are willing to wager everything that their current explanations are nothing short of the truth simply because they can see no better alternative at the moment. This, for example, is the reasoning of Sir Julian Huxley in *Evolution, the Modern Synthesis* (1942):

. . . if we repudiate creationism, divine or vitalistic guidance, and the extremer forms of orthogenesis [according to which evolving lineages are working toward a predetermined goal], as originators of adaptation, we must (unless we confess total ignorance and abandon for the time any attempts at explanation) invoke natural selection.

Given all the difficulties and objections to evolutionary theory we have reviewed, why not confess ignorance even as we search for better explanations? Is it appropriate to dismiss the possibility of any additional factor so casually? It is easy enough to set up a straw man, to point to the whale's vestigial pelvic bones, for example, and to say that if God had created the whale, directly and from nothing, he wouldn't have included these useless parts. Typically, neo-Darwinists then argue that it simply does not make sense to attribute the whale to divine creation— as if there were nothing in heaven and earth except an omnipotent deity acting as his own agent or natural selection of chance variations.

Reasoning of this sort amounts to a tremendous oversimplification. Yet the best-in-field fallacy is more than a quirk in one or two campaigners. Macbeth points out that Simpson's mind is operating in much the same vein when he says in *This View of Life* (1964): "The origin of such an organ as the eye, for example, entirely at random seems almost infinitely improbable," and then adds that there must have been "some additional factor or process" which, of course, could only have been natural selection. As Macbeth says, Simpson "creates a vacuum, offers natural selection as the only remaining possibility, and regards this as proof that natural selection can do anything. It is unnecessary for him to show what natural selection actually can do."

Huxley and Simpson, both important leaders, are typical of much of the profession in this regard. Evolutionists take real comfort in this fallacy, even if it has led to inversions of logic as strained as any in the history of science. I have mentioned the role of mathematics in the synthetic theory. It has proven useful, for example, in estimating the probability of genetic novelties surviving in various sized populations, and indeed such calculations have been borne out by observations in the field. What, then, is the probability that beneficial random mutations accumulating via natural selection could produce any of the species which have been subjected to close scrutiny? This, too, can be calculated. The result is described by Gertrude Himmelfarb in *Darwin and the Darwinian Revolution* (1959):

It is now discovered that favorable mutations are not only small but exceedingly rare, and the fortuitous combination of favorable mutations such as would be required for the production of even a fruit fly, let alone a man, is so much rarer still that the odds against it would be expressed by a number containing as many noughts as there are letters in the average novel, "a number greater than that of all the electrons and protons in the visible universe"—an improbability as great as that a monkey provided with a typewriter would by chance peck out the works of Shakespeare.

N. C. Wickramasinghe, a Buddhist astrophysicist who is head of the applied mathematics and astronomy department at Wales University and a collaborator with the noted scientist Fred Hoyle on the theory of "cosmic microbiology," has expressed the same conclusion with a different image. He has described the fortuitous accumulation of beneficial mutations via natural selection as about as plausible as "a tornado blowing through a junkyard and assembling a 747."

Whether one looks to mutations or gene flow for the source of the variations needed to fuel evolution, there is an enormous probability problem at the core of Darwinist and neo-Darwinist theory, which has been cited by hundreds of scientists and professionals. Engineers, physicists, astronomers, and biologists who have looked without prejudice at the notion of such variations producing ever more complex organisms have come to the same conclusion: The evolutionists are assuming the impossible.

Even if we take the simplest large protein molecule that can reproduce itself if immersed in a bath of nutrients, the odds against this developing by chance range from one in 10^{450} (engineer Marcel Goulay in *Analytical Chemistry*) to one in 10^{600} (Frank Salisbury in *American Biology Teacher*). (10^{450} is a way of writing the number 10 followed by 449 zeroes; thus one chance in a thousand would be one in 10^3 and one in a million would be one in 10^6.)

According to Francis Hitching in *The Neck of the Giraffe* (1982), scientists generally rule out of consideration any event having less than one chance in 10^{50} of occurring. Yet what we are contemplating in the case of this self-replicating molecule is millions of times less complicated than a tiny bacterium and billions of times less than a tiny paramecium. According to biologist Jean S. Morton, the odds against producing the 25,000 enzymes in the human body by chance is one in $10^{2,825,000}$.

An alternative way of viewing the problem is provided by information theory. Information theory begins with the concept that in constructing a building, a machine, a life-form, or any patterned system, it is not sufficient merely to have the necessary raw materials. A quantity of *information* is also required so that the materials may be correctly assembled in a certain order. This quantity of information is expressed in terms of "bits" or binary units. Several biologists, W. H. Thorp among them, have estimated that the information content of a bacterial cell—one of the simplest known—is about 10^{12} or 1,000,000,000,000 bits. Thorp remarks that even the information content of an amoeba must be "several orders that of the information content of the most advanced computer."

The source of increases in structural complexity, reflected in tremendous increases in information content, is the heart of the macroevolutionary problem, as many biologists have stated. In *A Century of Darwin* (1958, S. A. Barnett, Editor), British biologist C. H. Waddington wrote,

. . . a new gene mutation can cause an alteration only to a character which the organism had had in previous generations. It could not produce a lobster's claw on a cat; it could only alter the cat in some way, leaving it essentially a cat.

In *Darwin: Before and After* (1950) Dr. R. E. D. Clark put the matter thus:

. . . it is easy to imagine that occasionally, mutations might help individuals to adapt themselves to their surroundings, after which the mutants may replace their fellows as a result of natural selection. But to go further and to imagine that a series of changes, however long continued, would in the end create new and highly complex mechanisms, so making organisms more complex than they were before, would seem to be highly ridiculous.

Against this background John Randall paints the problem in its largest contours. In the cosmology of the modern, scientific world-view, it is usually supposed that our solar system developed by condensation from a huge blob of gas called a primordial nebula. Yet a gas is the most *random* system known to science. There is virtually no information content in the chaotic movements of gas molecules. So Randall wants to know, "whence came the tremendous amount of information which we find in living creatures?" It is in answering this question that the mechanistic theory of life signally fails. Randall, himself a biologist, finds it utterly incredible that the entire living world with all its complexities, including man and all that man builds and does, could have arisen "from purely chance events occurring in a slowly cooling gaseous system."

With the odds against the generation of even a fruit fly as indicated, the reader may understand why I am slightly impatient with Mr. Sagan (and others) for proposing, as if it were perfectly reasonable, that everything in the entire universe has arisen through pure chance and accident. Whether one is an astronomer or a biologist, he should be aware that probability studies are worth taking seriously. Virtually all the events and transactions studied in quantum physics are expressed as a series of probabilities, and these probabilities have repeatedly been verified.

So how do evolutionists reply to these calculations? It's no problem at all if you are armed with the best-in-field fallacy. They have an answer that has become famous, at least in biological circles. Natural selection, they say, generates an exceedingly high degree of improbability. That's right. Sir Julian Huxley argues that the very improbability of species arising in this way proves the immense power of natural selection. A logician would say that Huxley is begging the question. (This inversion of logic reminds me of a medieval witch trial where the defendant is immersed in water and presumed guilty if she floats, innocent if she sinks. There is no way the defendant can win; either way she dies.) If tremendous improbability is made an argument for rather than against natural selection, then there is no way to prove natural selection wrong. I cannot help but point

out that when powered by the best-in-field fallacy, natural selection becomes no less wonderful, mystical, or unfathomable than
God Almighty.

The best-in-field fallacy produces other noisome quirks. In
most other fields of science and with most other scientific questions, a valid objection to a theory or interpretation—if properly
made so as to reach the ears of the authorities—will be taken on
its merits regardless of whether a better theory or interpretation
is offered. Not so with many biologists, paleoanthropologists,
and evolution. Ernst Mayr of Harvard rules out "admittedly
valid objections" simply because the objector does not offer a
better interpretation as well. Macbeth says he thought at first
that this was a personal foible of Mayr's, but later realized it is a
widespread attitude. This is a serious departure from standard
scientific practice and works to insulate the profession from the
world of ongoing ideas and criticisms. Macbeth's excellent and
fair-minded book, *Darwin Retried,* is a case in point. It contains
many thought-provoking objections and criticisms and was endorsed by Karl Popper, the expert on logic and scientific method,
as "a really important contribution to the debate." But Macbeth
does not suggest an alternative theory; he is willing to confess
his ignorance. So in spite of Popper's endorsement, *Darwin
Retried* has been almost totally ignored by the professional
journals, and the few reviews it has received were mostly
unfavorable.

One likes to believe that highly trained professional scientists
are well-read, open-minded people, but it is apparent that those
who imagine that the synthetic theory allows us to conclude
anything very definite about the origin of man or many other
species are sustained more by insularity and a narrowly focused
faith than by real knowledge.

VII.

As mentioned earlier, the latest twist in the synthetic theory is
—finally—to take the episodic fossil record seriously. The gaps
in hypothetical lineages and the sudden appearance of many
species is no longer attributed to the accidents of geological history. Rather than arguing that species change gradually over
eons, the latest pilgrims to Darwin's shrine now suggest that the

style and tempo of evolutionary change is such that those notorious gaps are actually to be expected.

The "punctuated equilibrium" of Steven Jay Gould (*The Panda's Thumb*, 1980) and the "punctuational evolution" of S. M.
Stanley (*The New Evolutionary Timetable*, 1981) are basically
the same concept, positing that most species evolve during relatively brief periods of change (sudden emergence from parental
stocks) and thereafter remain stable for long periods. It is worth
looking at punctuated equilibrium and at Gould's work in particular because this concept is a significant advance, giving for the
first time a reasonable explanation for the fossil record as it is,
and it is therefore likely to become increasingly popular. While
punctuated equilibrium is clearly superior to tired excuses about
the imperfection of the fossil record, we do not have to look too
closely, however, to notice that this latest variation in theory
still has a tremendous hole in it.

Let us first look at the sources and strengths of this concept. It
is no accident that both Gould and Stanley are well rooted in
paleontology and geology. Arguing gradualistic evolution out
of a fossil record they know to be episodic is not a task with
which either would feel comfortable, and because of the slow
percolation of ideas, it is no longer necessary. It has taken about
twenty-five years for the implications of Mayr's work underlin-
ing species radiation in small isolated populations finally to sink
in. If divergence happens in small isolated populations, these
events would naturally be far less likely to be recorded as fossils
(and later discovered) than would samples of flora and fauna of
wide geographic distribution. If the divergent species is a successful one and circumstances later allow it to become widely
distributed, it is then that it may become part of the fossil record,
where it may appear as a new type without a neat sequence of
forms back to its ancestral stock.

Moreover, in addition to the Galapagos finches and Mayr's
work with birds in New Guinea, massive relatively recent radia-
tions can now be reasonably postulated for many other living
species. For example, Stanley relates that there are 170 species
of cichlid fishes found in Africa's 750,000-year-old Lake Victoria
that are found nowhere else. "Victoria is enormous," Stanley
points out, "having an average diameter of more than 200 miles.
The surrounding streams and rivers support only a few cichlid
species. Interestingly, these are generally types that seem to rep-

resent the ancestral condition of the Victoria species flock, which in contrast to the sparse faunas of the streams and rivers includes a spectacular variety of adaptive types." Some lake species feed on insects, some on other fish, some on fish larvae and embryos, others on mollusks or plants, and one mostly on other fishes' scales. Snails in the geologically recent Mekong River system display similar radiation. And many other examples are now known.

These observations and reasoning are fine up to a point. Divergence in small isolated populations may explain at least some of the gaps in the fossil record, and there is plenty of evidence suggesting that species radiation is taking place all around us— if only at the microevolutionary level. We are still getting cichlid fishes from cichlid fishes. It is when we ask punctuated equilibrium to explain macroevolutionary changes, the origin of the major distinct types of life, and the development of some of nature's more peculiar or perfected adaptations that the concept runs into trouble.

We first note that the pace of evolutionary change is much more rapid with punctuated equilibrium. Instead of being able to posit small, gradual changes more or less over the life of the species, according to Gould and Stanley we must now imagine that a species does most of its evolving before its gene pool expands and becomes stable. Stanley suggests that instead of millions of years, we may need only a few thousand for species radiation to take place, which is still a geological "instant." This is not implausible if we are talking about enlarging the mouth of a cichlid fish, but in more difficult cases the punctuational model creates more problems than it solves.

A more difficult case, which Gould himself takes on (in an essay called "Double Trouble," in *The Panda's Thumb*), is that of a Philippine anglerfish. In anglerfish generally, a fin spine has been elongated to project forward in front of the fish's head. At the end of this spine is a "bait," which the angler uses to attract its prey. In a Philippine variety the bait has developed into a remarkably fishlike lure, which the angler wiggles near its mouth while sitting on the sea floor pretending to be an algae-encrusted rock. In form and coloring, this lure is an extraordinarily good representation for an actual fish. It has spots of pigment to simulate eyes, compressed filaments and extensions representing all the standard fish fins and even a rear projection perfectly mimicking a tail. The Philippine angler even moves its bait so as to simulate the lateral undulations of a swimming fish.

How did this anglerfish's lure come into existence? Gould himself acknowledges the inconsistency of ascribing this "adaptation" to small, cumulative, partial modifications. If we suppose the development of this lure required 500 separate steps, of what value, Gould asks, is the first step? "Is a five-hundredth of a fake enough to inspire the curiosity of any real item?" And if we believe in small, cumulative modifications, we have to explain how the process began. We are driven to postulate some "non-Darwinian" force establishing a goal and directing the life-force of the fish to accomplish that end. And Gould, of course, is dead set against any such "non-Darwinian" force. Moreover, in the punctuational model of evolution, Gould doesn't have time for five hundred successive modifications. He has to explain how this anglerfish's lure arose relatively quickly.

In constructing his explanation, Gould harks back to the work of D'Arcy Wentworth Thompson, employs several extrapolations, and elevates natural selection to a godlike force.

Thompson, a zoologist, mathematician, and classical scholar, produced On Growth and Form, one of the great works of scientific literature. In the rapidly changing world of science, most books are largely out of date within a decade or two, but Thompson's treatise, first published in 1917 with a second edition in 1942, is still in print and still relevant.

Thompson analyzed organic forms, such as leaves, snail shells, and vertebrate skeletons, to disclose their mathematical properties. As Gould says, "He took Pythagoras seriously and worked as a Greek geometrician. He took special delight in finding the abstract forms of an idealized world embodied again and again in the products of nature." Thompson came to believe that, in the final analysis, life could only be fully explained by causes outside the Darwinist world view.

His work is of interest to Gould and some other biologists because he found more than thought-provoking geometry embodied in organic forms on a case-by-case basis. As biologist John Randall has aptly expressed it, "Thompson found that the shapes of animals belonging to the same zoological group are often related to one another in a simple mathematical way: the shape of one species can be obtained from the shape of another by a simple distortion of the spatial coordinates."

This insight would seem to have an obvious relevance to the origin of many species, and while many biologists prefer to steer clear of Thompson's work because of his metaphysical tendencies, some have risen to the bait. One of these is David Raup, of Chicago's Field Museum of Natural History, who used a computer to analyze the geometric relations among coiled shells. Gould waxes eloquent over the result:

> ... the basic forms of coiled shells—from nautaloid to clam to snail— can all be generated by varying only three simple gradients of growth. Using Raup's program, I can change [the shell of] a garden-variety snail into a common clam by modifying just two or three gradients. And, believe it or not, a peculiar genus of modern snails does carry a bivalved shell so like a conventional clam's that I gasped when I saw a snail's head poking out between the valves in a striking close-up movie.

Gould seems to be asking us to believe that this snail acquired a clam's shell through haphazard chance, as if for some reason (environmental, chemical, hormonal) the cells producing the coil grew more slowly or rapidly, governed, perhaps, by something like disturbed regulator genes. This is possible, although one wonders why, if it is so simple to affect one of these gradients of growth, there hasn't been more dramatic luck in transforming fruit flies and how a devotee of natural selection would explain the evolutionary advantage to a snail to be encumbered with the shell of a clam.

In any case, Thompson's geometry and modified gradients of growth applied to coiled shells is Gould's first step in explaining the anglerfish's lure. The next and considerably less plausible step is to apply the same kind of explanation to that peculiar adaptation known as the panda's "thumb." This strange appendage provides a major theme for Gould because as he says, perfection of form and adaptation works as well for the creationist as the evolutionist. He makes the interesting point that most textbooks like to illustrate evolution with examples of optimal design. But as he realizes, this is a poor argument for evolution because it is indistinguishable from the postulated action of an omnipotent creator. "Odd arrangements and funny solutions are the proof of evolution," he suggests, "paths that a sensible God would never tread but that a natural process, constrained by history, follows perforce." Although Gould has jettisoned Darwin's small, cumulative steps, he is a perfect Darwinian on the matter of emphasizing "odd arrangements and funny solutions," for so did Darwin himself.

The panda's thumb is an odd arrangement. It is not a true thumb, not even a true digit, and because of its peculiarities the panda (Ailuropoda) is not even considered a true bear (Ursus). Like bears, the panda has five true digits pointing forward. The thumb is an extra, sixth member, used for peeling leaves off bamboo shoots, its primary and almost exclusive food. This is an occupation true bears, who tend to be omnivorous, do not share. The thumb is built upon an extended nub of bone on an enlarged radial sesamoid bone in the panda's wrist. Explaining how this came about, Gould recapitulates the work of Dwight Davis, another biologist who wrote extensively on the panda and had also read Thompson.

Davis, he says, showed how the whole apparatus of the thumb with all its nerves and muscles might arise as a series of "automatic" consequences following a simple enlargement of the radial sesamoid bone. Davis similarly argues that only one or two underlying modifications might trigger the "complex changes" required to transform the skull of an omnivorous bear into one of suitable form and function for chewing on almost nothing except bamboo—like the panda's. Davis thought that perhaps no more than half a dozen genetic changes were required to accomplish the "primary adaptive shift."

This may be still within the realm of theoretical possibility, but one might ask in this case, just as in the small-cumulative-steps scenario, how the process began in the first place. What caused the initial "simple enlargement" of the radial sesamoid bone and the one or two underlying modifications of the skull? Was it due to a pure chance variation of the sort that seems so rare in fruit flies? Supposing that happened, how much advantage is acquired by a one-sixth enlargement of the radial sesamoid bone—or are we to suppose that half a dozen genetic mechanisms were triggered by accident all at once? Given the rarity of mutations and that only something like one in a thousand is beneficial, it seems we still have a major probability problem—even if we assume that these half-dozen mechanisms were a series accumulated over thousands of years.

The probability problem does not evaporate if we attribute these half-dozen altered genetic mechanisms to the "gene flow" produced in sexual reproduction: Breeders have never produced a form changed to the extent that a panda's is compared with a bear. And even if regulator genes were actually found capable of effecting the panda's transformation, one would still want to know why those regulators behaved so intelligently in providing those variations in form that happened to be just what the panda needed.

Gould does not see the probability problem involved in his explanation and with boundless optimism and little discussion merrily asserts that the same kind of analysis of generating factors will also account for the yet more complicated case of the Philippine anglerfish's lure. He presents his argument very skillfully, interweaving the more plausible instance of coiled shells with the panda's thumb and the fish. But does this satisfactorily meet the problem he has raised? Are we to suppose that the anglerfish's lure really arose by chance alone in one stupendous jump or in two or three explosive bursts?

Gould does speak to the probability problem—after a fashion. How he deals with it is seen in his rejoinder (in the same essay, "Double Trouble") to Arthur Koestler, a critic of mechanistic biology, who argued that there was often an additional factor at work, "some ordering force," as Gould says, "overriding the influence of natural selection." "Throughout his last half-dozen books," Gould writes, ". . . Koestler has been conducting a campaign against his own misunderstanding of Darwinism." Later he says,

. . . Darwinism is not the theory of capricious change that Koestler imagines. Random variation may be the raw material of change, but natural selection builds good design by rejecting most variants while accepting and accumulating the few that improve adaptation to local environments.

Following in the footsteps of Julian Huxley, Gould has in fact once again merely begged the question. The probability problem applies to there being sufficient variety of changes, or "raw material," available in the first place. It is Gould, rather than Koestler, who is wrestling with a misconception. Natural selection may have a good eye for engineering excellence, but this process cannot generate genetic variation. To suppose that it can is to imbue it with mind and purpose and to transform it into Ms. Natural Selection, Queen of the Forces of Nature. Something like this transformation seems to have occurred in the psyches of many evolutionists. Throughout his otherwise enjoyable and informative essays, Gould, as thorough a Darwinian as it is now possible for an educated person to be, invokes natural selection at all crossroads, in dark alleys, and whenever the absence of evidence or logic leaves a chasm at his feet—as in his foregoing reply to Koestler. He has repeated that phrase so often as an explanation that it seems to have acquired magical powers and thus can solve all problems.

But if Gould doesn't have all the answers, he has made a major contribution in espousing punctuated equilibrium, which is a better biological reading of the fossil record than we have had previously. He is also to be commended for meeting D'Arcy Thompson halfway. The metaphysical implications of Thompson's work are awesome. The geometry, simple equations, and other mathematical values Thompson found structuring species and the relations between them look powerfully like the products of mind, an unnerving prospect for those like Gould who hope to explain everything through physical mechanisms. Gould eschews metaphysics, but admits that he is floored by the degree of order Thompson disclosed:

I can identify the abstract Thompsonian forms as optimal adaptations, but to the larger metaphysical issue of why "good" form often exhibits such simple, numerical regularity, I plead only ignorance and wonder.

We suspect Gould will defend natural selection with his heart's blood. But could it be that in his innermost recesses even he knows that he has a probability problem?

VIII.

We see, then, that the synthetic theory and its latest variation has had its successes. Microevolutionary radiation of species is not only demonstrated; in some measure its mechanisms are known. But there is much that remains mysterious—all the big questions in fact, how life began, how the major groups of plants and animals originated, how and when man emerged. If anything, the mysterious element in biology seems to be increasing, not decreasing. We are still looking for those regulator genes. If they exist, how do they behave so intelligently? If they do not exist, what can it be that controls development and form? If homologous organs were not inherited from a common ancestor, how can we explain their existence in so many different groups? What is that source of increase in information content we find in living systems? We still cannot plausibly account for peculiar adaptations such as the panda's thumb, and the advent of punctuated equilibrium, with its rapid spurts of speciation, makes the explanation of macroevolutionary transformations more difficult than ever. The way is open for the return of the hopeful monster.

What we really have is a mélange of mostly unsynthesized problems and inadequate concepts from which a singular theme manages to emerge: the repeated insistence by many people of good intelligence that in explaining vestigial organs, odd adaptations, and much else, we are limited in this universe of infinite variety to only two conceivable hypotheses—either God Almighty functioning as his own agent or the latest version of evolutionary theory, however deficient. It is quite as if they felt a moral obligation to put the matter in these simplistic terms. This kind of behavior is a signal that, for many writers, what is ultimately at issue is not a matter of science at all, but something else.

4: An Object of Genuinely Religious Devotion

I.

WHEN KELLY SEGRAVES CLAIMED in the California court that evolution was a secular religion, there was more to the charge than courtroom rhetoric. Indeed, he may have touched upon the central issue of the debate. In a detached, wider perspective it is almost impossible not to conclude that what we are witnessing is a conflict between competing systems of religious belief.

Most proponents of evolution will insist that there are clear distinctions between science and religion. Certainly, there are obvious differences in style and content between a laboratory experiment and a Sunday morning service. But if we go a little deeper and ask what is the belief structure of the man conducting the experiments, we are immediately back in a universe of discourse concerning the how, what, and why of ultimate questions for which the folks at the Sunday service have supplied their own, probably different answers. Of course, it is possible that the experimenter is a Presbyterian or Catholic, one of those individuals who sees no contradiction between what he regards as the truths of science and the truths of religion. But it is somewhat more likely, especially in the United States, that the experimenter subscribes to that variety of evolutionary theory so widely taught today that is based on exclusively materialistic or mechanistic hypotheses (such as the natural selection of chance variations) and thus sees evolution and its implications contradicting and supplanting traditional religious concepts.

Such a person is apt to distinguish science from religion by saying that the former is concerned with knowledge of the proven and visible, whereas the latter is concerned with mere faith in the unprovable and invisible. Needless to say, a geologist identifying a stratum of fossils is on firmer ground than a theologian delivering a disquisition on the Trinity. But this is not where the comparison should be made. It is of much greater relevance to take natural selection as we have seen Huxley, Simpson, Sagan, and Gould employ it and ask, Is the process of selection really a proven fact based on demonstrated knowledge, or is it an unproven hypothesis to which there are so many contraindications that belief in it is also, in the final analysis, only a matter of faith?

Natural selection is surely no more visible than the Deity. And it is also relevant to ask not merely whether natural selection has been proved, but whether it can be proved. Evolutionists are fond of taunting the creationists that their miracles of special creation can, by definition, be neither proved nor disproved. Yet we frequently find evolutionists arriving at propositions that are in the same category. When Julian Huxley attempts to convert the stupendous improbability against natural selection into evidence for this wily, incalculable force, he has left terra firma as certainly as any other true believer. If there is no way to prove a theory wrong, by the same token we can never prove it valid, because there is no way to test it. In *Conjectures and Refutations* (1963) Sir Karl R. Popper, professor of logic and scientific method at the London School of Economics, remarked of such theories: "A theory which is not refutable by any conceivable event is non-scientific. Irrefutability is not a virtue of a theory (as people often think) but a vice." Popper also saw clearly that the mere guise of science does not ensure a qualitative difference in behavior: "A theory, even a scientific theory, may become an intellectual fashion, a substitute for religion, an entrenched dogma." Instead of miracles of special creation, the evolutionists have left us with undocumented hopeful monsters and accidents of special potency—hardly an electrifying advance in concept and understanding.

There is still a difference, however, between believers in miracles of special creation and believers in accidental variations: The former group has God pulling the strings; the latter has only atoms and molecules as its ultimate reality. If a proponent of evolution does not like the "secular religion" label, he might argue that the absence of God is precisely what makes evolution something other than a religion. But this objection also falls to the ground. The ultimate function of a religion is to explain the origin and meaning of life and the world, in a word, to supply a creation myth. Classical studies and cultural anthropology demonstrate that the need for a creation myth is among the most deep-seated and persistent characteristics of man. Whether the creation myth derives man and the world from a supreme being or from hydrogen atoms and a series of accidents is irrelevant to the function of the myth. Whatever else it does, the theory of evolution certainly fulfills this mythic function.

II.

Before I began to research more deeply into the substance and motives behind the rhetoric, I knew from experience in the academic world that evolution does function as a secular religion for some people. I was frankly surprised, though, at the extent to which this conclusion is corroborated in the critical literature and in many cases by evolutionists themselves. For example, the English writer John Michell reports,

Of all the subjects I have ever written about, the one that always brings the most lively response from readers is that of evolution and Darwinism. Some people seem quite upset that one should doubt Darwin's theory, and the tone of their letters is often that of people who feel their deepest religious convictions are being challenged.

Another symptom is the repeated use of the phrase *no one doubts*. "No one doubts that our heritage can be traced back nearly 4 million years to little creatures. . . ." The phrase seems to crop up again and again in the journals when evolutionists are regaling their critics or the public-at-large. It is an interesting phrase. It implies that some ultimate verity has been received. One can easily imagine its use in other contexts, such as "No one doubts that Jesus is the son of God"; "no one doubts the inevitable triumph of the working class"; "no one doubts that there is no God but Allah."

Gertrude Himmelfarb states that not long after its introduction, "Darwinism had emerged as an agreeable religious myth," and says that the desire for some such hypothesis is as powerful a factor in its perpetuation as it had been in its original acceptance. Macbeth was also surprised at the depth of the religious motive, and pointed to the words of Edwin G. Conklin (1863–1952), late professor of biology at Princeton:

The concept of organic evolution is very highly prized by biologists, for many of whom it is an object of genuinely religious devotion, because they regard it as a supreme integrative principle. This is probably the reason why severe methodological criticism employed in other departments of biology has not yet been brought to bear on evolutionary speculation.

Few evolutionists admit the situation this openly, but Macbeth found so many similar indications among his hundred-odd sources that he wrote, *"Darwinism itself has become a religion,"* the only italicized sentence in his entire book and one that would be significant in any case from a critic not given to overstatements or easy generalizations.

III.

Historically, it is not difficult to explain what has happened. For long centuries there has been an antithesis between the freedom of inquiry and expression that make science possible and the rigidly authoritarian teachings of the Roman Catholic Church in particular. In earlier times, the Church had the power to prevent the publication of opinions it considered heretical or indulged itself in the alarming practice of burning the heretic. Even today the famous case of Galileo, who was twice condemned by the Congregation of the Holy Office, in 1616 and 1633, casts a shadow across the interface between science and religion. While the power of the Church has declined, it could be argued that its authoritarianism has not. As recently as 1959, the Rev. Patrick O'Connell, a conservative Catholic creationist, made it clear in *Science of Today and the Problems of Genesis* that he would *still* condemn Galileo! "It is a fact to be noted," says the good Father, "that the condemnation of Galileo was never withdrawn." He then develops quite an argument why it should not be. Moreover, it was fairly recently that the Church forbade Teilhard de Chardin to publish his evolutionary speculations during his lifetime, and only in 1980 that it ousted theologian Hans Kung from his teaching position for questioning Church doctrine. If anything, many American fundamentalist sects are even more rigidly self-righteous than the Catholic Church. If they enjoyed the same veto power over evolutionists that the Church once had over Galileo, there is little doubt they would put a lot of people out of business.

The antithesis between narrow Christian doctrine and the facts being revealed by geology and other sciences also existed in Darwin's day, although not in such an exacerbated form as it does now. But by and large, there was no obvious alternative to the old God-centered creation myth, and it is very difficult to displace a creation myth with anything less than another system of at least equal explanatory power. Then along came Mr. Darwin with his theory of evolution by natural selection, a naturalistic, mechanistic, objective, and economical system. Himmelfarb says, "A maximum number of phenomena are accounted for in the simplest and most congenial way," and for many people one of the most congenial features of the theory is that God is not necessary to the hypothesis.

Although Darwin wisely did not emphasize the absence of God in either *The Origin of Species* or *The Descent of Man*, it was precisely his intention to short-circuit theological intrusions by keeping God out of the picture. This is clearly illustrated in correspondence between Darwin and Alfred Russell Wallace, an English naturalist who had done research in Malaya and arrived at the concept of natural selection independently. Eventually Wallace concluded, however, that natural selection could not account for man himself. He wrote that "nature never over-endows a species beyond the demands of everyday existence," in which case there is a major problem accounting for many aspects of man—from the sheer size of his brain to all his higher cultural traits such as music, literature, art, architecture, technology, science, and the power of moral discrimination. Wallace met this problem by insisting that in the final analysis the origin of man could not be separated from Divine Will.

Wallace communicated his ideas to Darwin and, according to Loren Eiseley, when Darwin read this part about Divine Will, "he wrote in anguish across the paper 'NO!' and underlined the 'NO!' three times heavily in a rising fervor of objection." Darwin wrote to Wallace, "I differ grievously from you and I am very sorry for it. I hope you have not murdered too completely your own and my child."

Back in the nineteenth century, many people were able to adjust their religious beliefs to the concept of evolution because Darwin himself, more moderate than many of his followers, had not publicly and directly addressed the question of the soul nor denied the existence of God. As long as the spiritual dimension was not threatened and a Master Designer could still be held responsible for the larger process of creation, evolution was easily accommodated, and in some cases actively welcomed, by theologians.

But increasingly in the twentieth century, evolutionists see the virtue of the theory to be precisely the exclusion of the spiritual dimension. Take, for example, Sir Julian Huxley, among the most ardent supporters of evolution, who, with many of his colleagues, met in Chicago in 1959 to celebrate the centenary of the *Origin*'s publication. Macbeth reports,

Rather to the surprise of some of his colleagues . . . Huxley declared in Chicago that he was an atheist and that Darwin's real achievement was to remove the whole idea of God as the creator of organisms from the sphere of rational discussion.

Huxley was not remaking Darwinism to his own liking. In one of his notebooks Darwin wrote,

. . . Oh you materialist! . . .
Why is thought being a secretion of brain,
more wonderful than gravity a property of matter?

For Darwin, this was the end of the hierarchic, soul-infested Platonic universe:

Plato says in Phaedo that our "imaginary ideas" arise from the pre-existence of the soul, are not derivable from experience—read monkeys for preexistence.

This thoroughgoing materialism is what distinguished Darwinism from all other evolutionary theories of the time. With all the
changes in thinking that have taken place regarding the pace,
mode, and agencies of evolutionary change since Darwin's era,
this stance of uncompromising mid-Victorian materialism remains remarkably unaltered. When it comes to these ultimate
philosophical issues, Stephen Jay Gould, possibly Darwin's
most eloquent contemporary advocate, does little more than par-
aphrase Darwin himself:

If mind has no real existence beyond the brain, can God be anything
more than an illusion invented by an illusion? (*Ever Since Darwin*,
1977)

Later, in the same volume, Gould again echoes Darwin:

The only honest alternative is to admit the strict continuity in kind
between ourselves and chimpanzees. And what do we lose thereby?
Only an antiquated concept of soul. . . .

In his essay "Darwin's Delay," Gould expresses the core of Darwin's philosophical materialism as "the postulate that matter is
the stuff of all existence and that all mental and spiritual phenomena are its by-products." This stance, which Gould is here
careful enough to call a postulate, is the central pivot of the
entire debate. Were it not for the widespread proselytization of
this "postulate," directly and by implication, there would be
very much less concern as to what children are being taught in
school. Nor is this reduction of all mental and spiritual phenomena to mere "by-products" of matter now limited to biology and
anthropology; it infects most of modern philosophy, the psychological sciences, and much else. Yet it is particularly in anthropology and the biological sciences that advocates of materialism
seem to feel required to proclaim their creed and to limit research in such a way as to confirm the basic "postulate."

Macbeth found this attitude typical, especially among the
inner circle of highly respected professors at first-class universities, of whom G. G. Simpson of Harvard is a prime example.
Macbeth notes that Simpson is frankly contemptuous of Christianity and explains that he quotes him because he is among the
most thorough and extensive writers on evolution. It is therefore
important to note that Simpson excludes design as a matter of

scientific principle. As Simpson put it in *Tempo and Mode in Evolution* (1944):

... the progress of knowledge rigidly requires that no non-physical postulate ever be admitted in connection with the study of physical phenomena. We do not know what is and what is not explicable in physical terms, and the researcher who is seeking explanations must seek physical explanations only. . . .

Among such nonphysical postulates are mind, consciousness, spiritual agencies, and of course God. Simpson's prohibition also covers much of the substance of Platonic philosophy, which holds that ideas, forms, patterns, types, and archetypes have an existence and reality of their own, and if so would seem to have an obvious relevance to the problem of the origin of species. Not surprisingly, then, Plato and Platonism are also enemies of the new revelation. Macbeth says that "Professor Mayr of Harvard . . . rejoices in eliminating the last remnants of Platonism, by refusing to admit the *eidos* (idea, type essence) in any guise whatsoever. Eiseley shuns Plato as he would the plague."

Since Plato is the most influential philosopher in the Western tradition, and for many a still-formidable voice against materialism, some evolutionists find it necessary to attack him in any way they can. To find true ideological fervor against the enemy, one should turn to Weston La Barre, professor of anthropology at Duke University and author of *The Human Animal* and more recently *The Ghost Dance* (1970). In *The Ghost Dance* La Barre attempts to show that all religions (other than evolution) are maladaptive retreats from reality. For La Barre, Plato is the greatest deceiver of all time, and he indulges in pages of defamation against him. "Platonism is not the summit of Greek philosophy, but its final catastrophe. . . ." "We must see the functioning of Platonism as a desperate historic crisis cult. . . ." "An absolute fanatic, Plato made violent and repeated attacks upon . . . the Sophists." "The conscious Big Lie of Hitler is the same contrived Noble Lie of Plato. . . ." "Politically, Plato's shamanism was quite conscious jiggery pokery, and deceptive jugglery or sleight of hand." He more than once compares Plato to Hitler. Speaking of the intellectual tradition Plato founded, he says, "his Reich stood for a thousand years and more." He neglects to mention that Hitler was an extreme Darwinist, believing that man evolved from monkeys, a proposition that Plato would have considered a joke. And he goes on and on with such language: ". . . Plato had 'plagiarized' from Pythagoreanism." "Plato's sickened hatred of reality is . . . pathological. . . ." Plato had a "neurosis." "In all areas of his thought, Plato is an inhumanist, a perverse Greek."

If Plato is correct that there are immaterial realities such as souls, archetypes, and conscious minds independent of physical brains, then the advocates of Darwinian materialism are laboring under one of history's greater misconceptions.

Aside from helping to create a milieu that encourages La Barre's style of vituperation and certainly discourages workers investigating alternate possibilities, Simpson's attitude toward "nonphysical" postulates—typical of much of the profession— is scientifically out of date. The subject matter of biology is not somehow exempt from the laws and phenomena of physics. In terms of the history of science, possibly the most remarkable thing about even latter-day synthetic neo-Darwinism of the 1980s is that it is still grounded in outmoded mid-nineteenth-century physics. When Simpson says that we must consider "physical" postulates only, many physicists might ask, How can you tell, Professor Simpson, where the physical ends and the nonphysical begins?

For some decades now, physicists have been contemplating subatomic "particles" of such minuscule dimensions that they seem more like incredibly tiny, pointlike clouds of wave energy than old-fashioned, billiard-ball matter. Not only does "matter" seem to dissolve into patterned vibrations at the most fundamental level of observation, but it has become impossible to exclude the structuring role of consciousness in assessing their significance.

A subatomic "particle" is defined by its momentum and position, but at the subatomic level the very procedures and instruments involved in its measurement mean that we must necessarily interfere with one of these. We cannot be certain of momentum without altering the "particle's" position, and vice versa. This is known as Heisenberg's Uncertainty Principle. In plain language, this means that the experimenter or observer has become part of the experiment.

As Gary Zukav says in his thoroughly readable overview of the new physics, *The Dancing Wu Li Masters* (1979), "the implications of quantum mechanics are psychedelic." Heisenberg's

Uncertainty Principle means that *we must choose* whether we want to determine momentum *or* position. Since we choose which aspect of this reality we wish to measure, to some extent *we* actualize or create this reality. As Zukav expresses it, "It is possible that we create something that has position, for example, like a particle, because we are intent on determining position and it is impossible to determine position without having some *thing* occupying the position that we want to determine."

Because of this kind of situation, quantum physicists have been led more and more to consider models of consciousness and theories of perception as part of the "stuff" that the new physics is about. Instead of a universe composed of separate parts and local causes (the universe of Darwin and Gould), many physicists are now considering the prospect of a deeper unity in nature, a universe where there are no separate parts, where non-local causes can and do operate without signals at speeds faster than light.

As Zukav points out, some quantum physicists now describe "reality" in terms that are often restatements of Buddhist metaphysics. Even some of Plato's concepts are now (again) seen as relevant to the "reality" problem.

Similar implications arise from numerous recent experiments and investigations in parapsychology. There is now much accumulated evidence, which we will survey later, that mind does exist separate from the physical brain and that phenomena like the telepathic transfer of information are not only demonstrable but that they seem to conform to the emerging new model of a universe with nonlocal causes. As the American physicists Russell Targ and Harold Puthoff have remarked, ". . . many contemporary physicists are now of the opinion that these phenomena are not at all inconsistent with the framework of modern physics: the often-held view that observations of this type are incompatible with known laws is not only outdated but false, being based on the naïve realism prevalent before the development of modern physics."

In short, the world has changed under the materialists' feet. There is a great deal in both modern physics and parapsychology well beyond the traditional boundaries of the naïve realism upon which neo-Darwinism is based, and much of it is directly relevant to evolution and the emergence of man. How peculiar it is that these phenomena can only be seriously investigated if one adopts precisely the kind of postulates Simpson and many others would prohibit.

The developments in physics and parapsychology to which I allude are not news. Extensive research is not necessary to become aware of them, nor is special training required to understand their general import. The very fact that most contemporary evolutionists still cling to old-fashioned, crudely mechanistic theories in spite of these well-known developments in related fields is a further indication of the ideological character of their thinking.

IV.

The difficulty for believers in purely mechanistic evolution is that any cosmology—old-fashioned or otherwise—has its own deeper dynamics. Once one has bought a particular world view, it organizes his perceptions, experiences, and priorities. Simpson seems driven to impose untenable restrictions upon inquiry for reasons of "religion in reverse," as Macbeth says. Even a highly trained biologist may be philosophically unsophisticated and thus unaware of his own "religiosity." Presented with the proper stimulus, he may be so filled with proselytizing missionary zeal that he is quite unable to control it. As George C. Williams said in *Adaptation and Natural Selection* (1966),

It is mainly when biologists become self-consciously philosophical, as they often do when they address non-technical audiences, that they begin to stress such concepts as evolutionary progress. This is unfortunate, because it implies that biology is not being accurately represented to the public.

Or as Henshaw Ward expressed the impulse rather crudely some years ago in a primer called *Evolution for John* (1926),

Every reputable modern scientist believes in evolution as a matter of course. It is now an integral part of all general education and culture. To suppose that it may one day be abandoned is to live in intellectual barbarism.

No one, of course, is asking scientists to deliver lectures on God's role in the universe. What is objectionable is not that anyone should seek or organize evidence to explain as much as possible of the physical world without invoking the Deity or other nonphysical agents. What is objectionable, rather, is that, increasingly of late, scientists are extending their "explanations" far beyond the areas actually covered by evidence so as deliberately to exclude the possibility of any nonphysical agent and are then capping hyperbole with arrogance by presenting these speculations as verified realities.

... chance *alone* is at the source of every innovation, of all creation in the biosphere. Pure chance, absolutely free but blind, at the root of the stupendous edifice of evolution: this central concept of modern biology is no longer one among other possible or even conceivable hypotheses. It is today the *sole* conceivable hypothesis, the only one compatible with observed and tested fact. And nothing warrants the supposition (or the hope) that conceptions about this should, or ever could, be revised.

Thus, for example, writes geneticist Jacques Monod in *Chance and Necessity* (1974). It is easy enough to dismiss Monod as holding an unbalanced view. Unbalanced or not, what is thoroughly unscientific is the implication, as with Simpson, that *only* the hypothesis of mechanistic materialism belongs within science and that other investigations are by definition nonscientific. The notion that science is somehow restricted so as to apply only to certain possibilities in certain fields is totally fallacious. In *Parapsychology and the Nature of Life* John Randall reiterates a classic principle:

There is nothing whatever about the scientific method that restricts it to any particular set of assumptions or to any particular kind of phenomenon. Scientific procedures can be applied to the investigation of an apparition no less than to the study of a spiral nebula or a bacillus. Nor need science be committed in advance, as Monod would have it, to the exclusion of concepts such as mind and purpose. Scientists proceed by making careful observations and setting up and testing hypotheses. It is this empirical-inductive approach which characterizes a particular piece of work as "scientific," not the subject-matter with which it deals.

It is ironic how widely misunderstood this point is among scientists themselves. Those with Ph.D.'s, "Doctors of Philosophy," now often have minimal training in the actual philosophy and history of science. For example, S. M. Stanley imagines he has found an amiable solution to the conflict between "science" and "religion" over man's origin by writing,

Interestingly, the Roman Catholic Church, unbound by literal interpretation of scripture, does not oppose the concept of evolution. God
created man, is its position, and to most interpreters this has implied
the injection of a soul into a seminal population of our species.

Science does not traffic in souls, but it does treat questions of cultural attitudes toward them. (*The New Evolutionary Timetable*, 1981)

Perhaps the science of which Stanley is himself aware "does not
traffic in souls," but one is quite mistaken if one thinks it is
somehow impossible or inappropriate to develop disciplined
inquiries about the soul. The ancient Egyptians, Greeks, and
Tibetans certainly had "a science of the soul" and, preliminary
as they are, several areas in modern parapsychology also amount
to such a science.

The long, dismal, and continuing story of clerical authoritarianism has ensured that many people are quite as emotionally
attached to their "liberated" evolutionary view of the world as
others are to their interpretations of Christ. This is why many
neo-Darwinists like Julian Huxley, Gould, Simpson, Monod,
and Sagan, to name but a few of the mechanist school, are unable to restrict themselves to describing the secure but limited
accomplishments of their branch of science and instead attempt to make purely mechanistic evolution the explanation for
everything.

The impulse is understandable, but it makes for bad science
and worse cosmology. To take this concept about which so many
valid, unanswered questions have been raised and make of it the
mainspring of all creation would be a difficult job for even the
most imaginative and well-read man. It would be useful to have
some knowledge of philosophy, ancient history, and other cosmologies, if one is to do this well. No modern evolutionist I have
read even comes close to bringing it off convincingly. It would
be so much better if they limited themselves to their areas of
expertise and left the rest alone, at least publicly.

More and more people are noticing the ideological character
of today's evolutionary rhetoric, but the proselytizers of a God-
less universe seem unable to stop, and this is hurting the professions involved. The descent of science to ideology will in
the long run discredit evolution and science in general far
more completely than any courtroom contests initiated by the
creationists.

Certainly the mechanists need and are entitled to a cosmology as much as other people. Certainly they have the right to investigate theories supporting that cosmology. But it is also certain that their students, colleagues, and the general public have the right to expect that their missionary zeal does not outstrip their ability to acquit themselves of a dispassionate appraisal of the facts. Otherwise, scientists risk destroying the very respect and support they still command.

Today's evangelical popularizers of evolution would do well to ponder the words of Thomas Henry Huxley, grandfather of Sir Julian, who was himself among Darwin's earliest and most effective champions. Speaking of men of science, he remarked, ". . . there is not a single belief that it is not a bounden duty with them to hold with a light hand and to part with cheerfully, the moment it is really proved to be contrary to any fact, great or small." I submit that many evolutionists no longer hold the theory "with a light hand" and that many are now so deeply committed that they can no longer distinguish their science from their religion.

5: Thumpwell's Enthusiasm

I.

IF PALEOANTHROPOLOGISTS and other evolutionists have exaggerated the implications of their evidence beyond all bounds, the situation has certainly not been helped by the character of the creationist challenge. It is one thing to blow the whistle when evolutionists parade a mere, weak, crippled theory as an undoubtable, proven fact of universal application; it is quite another to attempt to enforce the teaching of a version of creation and history based on a particular interpretation of Genesis that is at least as questionable as any of the wild extrapolations of the bonemen and biologists.

If some of the least applaudable aspects of paleoanthropology are personified by Professor Nettlebottom, we have his creationist counterpart in the Rev. Jo Jo Thumpwell. Thumpwell has been roaring about the Revealed Truth from the pulpit of the Hallelujah Heights Reformed Fundamentalist Church of Rocky-blowtop Flats, Virginia, for twenty-five years. He is in love with the Bible, God bless 'im. He has found the answer to the Universal Mystery. He has the veritable Word of God in his hand, in English, and he can read.

But does he know what he is reading? In his enthusiasm for the overall message, Thumpwell signally fails to distinguish the differing genres of the many books and sections of books that make up the large and ancient collection constituting the Bible. He mistakes parables and cosmogonic synopses for historical chronologies. He takes Jonah and the Whale and the Six Days of Creation as literal gospel.

I've always wanted to ask, Why six days? What's the Lord's hurry? High labor costs?

We cannot derive the history of the world from a literal reading of Genesis because Genesis is simply not a literal history. Nevertheless, we should not simply skip over the claims of those who advocate a literal interpretation. This position is still put forward with such urgency and frequency that it deserves some attention.

In terms of the history of biblical scholarship, the literal interpretation is essentially an uncritical, prenineteenth-century position. Just as the mid-nineteenth century saw the birth of modern geology, paleontology, botany, and other sciences, this was also the era that saw the rise of a critical, analytical approach to the Bible itself. Previously, the traditional interpretation of Genesis, and for that matter of the first five books of the Bible (collectively known as the Pentateuch), was that these were the product of a single inspired author, namely Moses. Moses was the human instrument through which the "word of God" was recorded.

There were a few isolated writers before the 1850s who had raised questions indicating that the origins of the Pentateuch were more complex than this, but these questions had no lasting influence. Gradually, however, more men were inclined to explore the implications of certain obvious problems, such as why there should be two different accounts of the creation (Genesis 1:1–2:4 and 2:4–2:24). In the first account there are eight major works spread over six days:

Day		Work
1	I	Light and Darkness
2	II	Upper and Lower Waters
3	III	Land and Sea
3	IV	Vegetation
4	V	Sun, Moon, and Stars

5	VI	Birds and Fish
6	VII	Animals
6	VIII	Man

As we see, in this account man is created on the sixth day, after everything else. But in the second account the text reads,

. . . when no plant of the field was yet in the earth and no herb of the field had yet sprung up . . . then the Lord God formed man of dust from the ground, and breathed into his nostrils the breath of life; and man became a living being. (Genesis 2:5–7)

So in the first two chapters of Genesis itself we have an embarrassing contradiction. How can a text, supposed to be the literal, infallible word of God, have man created *after* the vegetation in one place, and then a few lines later declare that man was created *before* the plants and herbs? It cannot be that these plants and herbs were of a different kind than those created in the first account, because Genesis 1:29 explicitly states that that creation refers to "every plant yielding seed which is upon the face of the earth." Which of these two conflicting versions is the literal, infallible truth? How can anyone have faith in a literal six-day creation when the chronology of the text itself is muddled and inconsistent?

The reader may be alarmed to hear that I have not set up a straw man, a theoretical opponent holding impossible views. On the contrary, Henry M. Morris and John C. Whitcomb, Jr., authors of *The Genesis Flood* (1961), make it clear that it is precisely their position that the first chapters of Genesis (along with everything else in the Bible) are literal, infallible truth. Although their main concern in this book is with the Flood, they also have much to say about the creation that is typical of the fundamentalist approach:

Since God's revealed Word describes this Creation as taking place in six "days" and since there apparently is no contextual basis for understanding these days in any sort of symbolic sense, it is an act of both faith and reason to accept them, literally, as real days.

And in another place they advise the reader,

It is important to remember that whatever may have been the sources employed by Moses in the composition of Genesis—whether written records, oral traditions, or direct revelation—verbal inspiration guarantees its absolute authority and infallibility.

These quotations are the more apposite because Morris is one of the most prolific and influential creationist writers and *The Genesis Flood* one of the most successful creationist books. What is most singular about the creationist viewpoint is its superficiality and lack of scholarship. Just as many biologists and anthropologists espouse a naïve materialism that is completely uninformed about developments in physics and parapsychology, biblical fundamentalism proceeds as if no one else had written anything about the Bible in the last 130 years. Regarding the six days of creation, for example, Morris and Whitcomb state that "there apparently is no contextual basis for understanding these days in any sort of symbolic sense. . . ." Even the slightest nodding acquaintance with Hebrew cosmology discloses that the traditional Jewish day is defined from sunset to sunset, that is, from evening to evening, whereas the six days of creation are defined as "evening to morning." So there is on the face of it a direct contextual basis for supposing that these "days" are something other than conventional twenty-four-hour periods. One of the more plausible interpretations of these days is found in the notes of an undated Cassell's Family Bible, which cannot be later than about 1900. The "evening to morning" periods, it is suggested, were a series of successive *visions* in the night, revealing to the author of this part of Genesis the major epochs or events in the formation of the earth and its biosphere.

Such an approach is too supercharged for Morris and Whitcomb, however. They deal with the contradiction concerning the creation of man in approximately the same way that Johanson deals with the high degree of specialization implied by Lucy's extra-long arms: they sidestep the issue. Although they quote practically every other line of the first two chapters of Genesis somewhere in *The Genesis Flood,* they give the incriminating portion of Genesis 2:5 a total miss.

If this were the only textual difficulty in Genesis, the creationist view might appear less extreme. But biblical scholars concerned with accounting for the actual form of the text as we now have it—as opposed to defending a simplistic, preconceived version of "the truth"—long ago noticed that there are many other indications of two or more distinct sources having been woven together to produce the books traditionally ascribed to Moses. The existence of these separate strands is still apparent because, as in the case of the creation, there are often two or more men-

tions of many details, and the editor or editors who brought
these differing versions together were apparently so much in
awe of their sources that they often did not have the temerity to
reconcile their differences.

For example, in the story of the deluge (Genesis 6:5–9:17),
Noah is told in one place to take seven pairs of all clean animals
and of birds, and a single pair of all unclean animals (Genesis
7:2–3); a few lines later (Genesis 7:8–9), reference is made to
only a single pair of all animals, both clean and unclean. Many
scholars descry a parallel situation with the duration and cause
of the flood. In Genesis 7:12 and 7:17 we have a flood enduring
for forty days of rain; but from references in 7:11 and 8:14 we
find that the flood endures for one year and eleven days, with
the water rising for 150 days (7:24) and receding for 150 days
(8:3). In one tradition the flood is due to excessive rain; in the
other it seems more like a collapse of the entire cosmos, with
"the fountains of the deep" bursting forth. Similarly, there are
two differing genealogies of the antediluvian patriarchs (Genesis
4 and 5); two presentations of the Ten Commandments (Exodus
20 and Deuteronomy 5); and perhaps most significantly of all,
even the Deity is called by two different names throughout the
Pentateuch: El (or Elohim) and Yahweh.

Here I have noted only a few instances of these double and
sometimes triple mentions. The Pentateuch contains many
more. Not all are contradictory, but when these repeated sections
of narrative are set alongside one another, it becomes evident
upon detailed analysis that certain common features of vocabu-
lary and style appear in various groups. Informed scholarly
opinion now recognizes that there are four distinct sources that
were woven together to form what we have today as the Bible's
first five books. These are called the Jahwist, Elohist, and Priestly
sources or traditions, with a fourth and distinct source for Deuteronomy. The Priestly tradition is the most recent. Many scholars think this element was incorporated as recently as 400 B.C.,
approximately eight hundred years after the time of Moses. Even
the oldest tradition, the Jahwist, is thought to date no earlier
than the era of David and Solomon (1,000–920 B.C.).

This obviously brings us some considerable distance from the
concept of Moses as the single inspired author of these books.
Of course it is possible in these enlightened times to find trendy
liberal theologians who will say practically anything to capture

a headline, even that God is dead or missing in action. But it is not the trendy liberals who have come to these conclusions about Genesis and the Pentateuch. This analysis rests upon more than a century of accumulated scholarship by the most learned bibliophiles in Christendom and is presented and endorsed by such voices as the Rev. John L. McKenzie, S.J., in his *Dictionary of the Bible* (1966), an 800,000-word tome of remarkable erudition.

McKenzie is as convinced as Thumpwell of the divinity of Christ, the fatherhood of God, and the revelatory significance of Scripture. But he is sufficiently sophisticated that he does not find this significance in a crassly literal reading of every line. "The arrangement of the works of creation in six days followed by a Sabbath of divine repose is not intended to indicate the time elapsed during the formation of the universe," McKenzie says. This description of the creation has much more to do, he suggests, with sanctifying the Sabbath and providing man a model by which to structure his own activity. The biblical story of creation also served the purpose of attributing the generation of the world to the Lord God, as opposed to seeing it as a result of the combat of the gods Marduk and Tiamat, as the contemporaneous Babylonians believed.

McKenzie's style of interpretation yields results dramatically different from those of the fundamentalists right down the line. The chronology of patriarchs from which Morris and fellow travelers deduce that the earth is only six to ten thousand years old is an "artificial chronology" as far as McKenzie is concerned. Morris and colleagues are attempting to establish "creation science," as a vindication of their interpretation of Genesis. As a serious Catholic, McKenzie also believes that the Bible is infallible—with respect to certain truths and dimensions. But this inerrancy must take account of literary forms (such as the parable); the character of Semitic languages; and the fact that the Bible uses popular, nontechnical language, figures of speech, paradox, approximation, telescoped narrative, inexact quotations, folklore, legends, and myths. As a consequence, McKenzie views the apparent conflict between science and the Bible this way:

The difficulties raised against inerrancy from the natural sciences show that the language of the Bible is unscientific and that its conceptions of physical realities are those of its times. We now see that "scientific truth" and "scientific error" are modern conceptions; neither appears in the Bible, which makes no "scientific" assertion of any kind, true or false.

This does not diminish the Bible for McKenzie. It is still the revealed "history of salvation" as far as he is concerned. But he looks beyond the literal surface to the underlying message, thereby avoiding having to defend the indefensible. For Morris, Whitcomb, and other fundamentalists, everything in the Bible has the same surface value.

It is really rather pathetic to find Morris and Whitcomb still defending the literal character of the book of Jonah. Aware that no fish or whale has a throat large enough to swallow a man whole (to say nothing about the prospect of a man surviving for three days in a fish's or whale's stomach, even if he could be swallowed), Morris and Whitcomb suggest that God specially created a unique creature in order to accomplish that particular "miracle." In contrast, McKenzie says,

It is not merely the fish which is wonderful in the story, but the entire story is motivated by wonders from beginning to end: the storm, the fish, the gourd, and the greatest wonder of all, the instantaneous conversion of Nineveh. A search therefore after the species of fish which swallowed and regurgitated Jonah or for parallels to this wonder is idle; the fish is the creation of the author. The literary type of the book is didactic fiction or parable.

The point of the parable is that God's compassion and forgiveness extend even to the bloody, aggressive, and plundering Assyrians, the most hated nation in the entire ancient Middle East. This was an extremely important statement of the universality of the Deity in an Israelite community which at the time often conceived the purposes of God in narrowly nationalistic terms. As McKenzie remarks, "Hence Jonah marks one of the greatest steps forward in the spiritual advancement of biblical religion. It is unfortunate that so much discussion of its historical character has obscured the meaning of the book for many readers."

The weakest aspect of the creationist position is not that it is bad science, but that it is even worse as biblical scholarship. They literally do not know a parable when they see one, which is the more curious in that it was Jesus' favorite form of instruction. It would seem they put themselves in the category of those who confuse the letter of the law with its spirit, who see but do not perceive, and hear but do not understand. Since the letter of the law kills and only the spirit gives life (cf. II Corinthians 3:6), a really old-line Christian might argue that those who take every word in the Bible at its literal, surface value are more deadly bone peddlers than any overly ambitious paleoanthropologists.

II.

Of course, these considerations do not faze Thumpwell in the slightest. As highly sectarian as contemporary Christianity is, the fundamentalists take little or no notice of the scholarship of other sects and denominations, no matter how reasonable, well documented, or widely endorsed elsewhere. In terms of the wider scene in other countries, American creationists are even more insular than American evolutionists. Thumpwell is perfectly willing to believe that everyone else has missed the boat. He has the Truth in plain American English and an unshakable belief that no matter how many special miracles his interpretation of the book requires, the Power of God is Absolutely First Class and equal to the task. Hallelujah and Amen. Isn't it fine to have a God like that?

Simple faith in divine omnipotence is one thing. The difficulty is that when Thumpwell recruits the Almighty to produce a giant fish or a six-day creation, he does not stop there. The sense of power goes to his head; his self-righteousness becomes inflated, and he begins passing out judgments on everything from political candidates to the definition of a family, the role of women in society, abortion, homosexuality, and the content of biology classes and television programming—all based on the same elevated scholarship that cannot distinguish a parable from a piece of history. Of course, given free speech, Thumpwell can say what he wants, and if, as it seems, creationist pressure was instrumental in determining school board policy in Texas (requiring that evolution be presented as theory rather than fact), then one might acknowledge that such pressure has provided a valuable corrective. But if the Texas state school board has arrived at a policy that is just about right, this is more a tribute to compromise and the democratic process than to Thumpwell's enlightenment. The tone and content of many fundamentalist pronouncements provide the sharpest possible contrast to Jesus'

recommendation that we judge not, lest we be so judged ourselves, and the authoritarian attitude Thumpwell conveys carries associations reminding one of much terrible history. Little
wonder that many evolutionists overreact, drop their scientific
cover, and chant in unison, "There is no doubt . . . ." Little wonder that the alternative to evolution seems to be "intellectual
barbarism." It is a pity that instead of indulging their own hys-
teria, they cannot find a single, confident man well enough
versed in Scripture to tackle Thumpwell on his own ground. It
would certainly improve the quality of the debate.

III.

As it is, the creationist challenge consists of more than Bible-
thumping. They attack the highly vulnerable evidence for evolution, often with considerable cogency, and smelling blood,
move on to besiege the geologists. If the earth is only six or ten
thousand years old, then something must be very wrong with
modern geology, which now suggests that our planet is about 4.6
billion years old. Well, there *is* something wrong with modern
geology, and the difficulty is such that it plays neatly into
Thumpwell's hand.

Ever since Charles Lyell (1797–1875) founded modern geology with the publication of *Principles of Geology* in 1830, most
devotees of this discipline have assumed that all known geological formations and deposits can be explained by presently ob-
servable processes operating at their present rates. This is known
as uniformitarian geology. It has attracted many critics other
than creationists because there is much provocative evidence
that even if the earth's history has been slow and tranquil for
great stretches of time, it has not always been so.

Among this evidence is the well-known case of the Siberian
mammoths. Remains of tens of thousands of these giant mammals have been found quick-frozen in the permafrost; they were
so well preserved that in some cases the fodder in their mouths
and stomachs was still fresh. In 1900 such a mammoth was
found at Berezovka; it was still standing and had not had time
to swallow its last meal of buttercups. It seems obvious that the
animals did not starve to death; that the climate of the region in
which they are found must have been significantly different than
it is today; and that they died very suddenly.

Even many geologists acknowledge it is not easy to explain how the mammoths could have arrived in their present condition as a result of slow and gradual processes. In *The Earth's Shifting Crust* (1958) and *The Path of the Pole* (1970) Charles Hapgood argues that the mammoths were exterminated by a shifting of the earth's poles caused by the entire crust of the earth slipping over the inner mantle. This moved Siberia much further north than it had been, freezing the mammoths and some sixty other species. It is worth mentioning that *The Earth's Shifting Crust* is one of the very rare works to be personally endorsed by Albert Einstein, who wrote a foreword for it.

Of course Morris and Whitcomb see the Genesis flood as the cause of the mammoths' extinction. There are many other deposits and formations, they argue, that could not have been formed gradually but only through some sudden catastrophic agency. They point to huge bone beds in Nebraska where millions of fossilized skeletons of many different animals are found compacted together. It is quite as if these animals were all drowned at once and deposited as at the bottom of a sink that afterward lost its water.

There are indeed many more indications of prehistoric catastrophism than uniformitarians like to discuss, and the creationists can make as much use of these as other critics. Where the creationists part company with other critics is on the question of the earth's age; and where they run into the most trouble is with the dates provided by the decomposition of radioactive elements like carbon 14, various isotopes of uranium, and potassium 40.

This is not to say that the well-informed creationist cannot criticize radiometric dating in both theory and practice. In theory all these dating systems rest upon a number of unproven assumptions. It is merely assumed, for example, that the production of carbon 14 in the atmosphere by cosmic-ray bombardment has been constant throughout all time. If it were not constant, this would greatly affect the estimated ages of materials dated by this system. Similarly, these methods also assume that the rate of radioactive decomposition has also been constant over millions or billions of years. It is not difficult to imagine any number of events that could have affected the rate of decomposition: Reversals of the earth's magnetic field, of which there have been several over the last few million years, could affect this rate. So could the explosion of a nearby supernova. And who knows? There may well be pockets of unusual "local conditions" through which the earth passes as our solar system slowly moves around the center of the galaxy. For all we really know, there have been many alterations in the rate of decomposition over the last hundred thousand or billion years. It is a remarkably sanguine assumption that atomic processes have behaved with absolute constancy over 4.6 billion years.

In practice, radiometric dating has produced a number of gaffs. In the flush of euphoria following the first employment of carbon 14, some archaeologists spoke enthusiastically of "the absolute chronology" of the atomic clocks. A couple of decades later, they are more sober. We have already seen how two different laboratories gave potassium-argon dates for 1470 that varied by a million years. Other results are a good deal less "absolute" than this. The shell of a living oyster was carbon-dated to 600 B.C. Perhaps most outrageous of all, a 180-year-old lava flow in Hawaii was dated by the potassium-argon method to be no less than 2.96 billion years old! Not terribly precise.

Creationists are quite right in saying that paleontologists and geologists attach too much importance to particular radiometric dates. These systems are obviously quirksome and inexact. But to maintain that radiometric dates have no significance at all because of a relatively few flukes is to generalize too much. No particular date may be as precise as the laboratory readout suggests, but there are still good reasons to think that as a general indication of age, radiometric readings usually give a better sense of magnitude than, say, the Genesis chronology.

One of the best of these reasons is that recently the accuracy of the carbon 14 method has been substantially verified by comparing its results with dendrochronology—the art of counting tree rings. Trees add one ring a year. The thickness of that ring depends largely upon the amount of rainfall in the area in which the tree grows. Rainfall varies in cyclical patterns over periods of years, and the rings of all the trees in an area show the same cyclical pattern. With certain kinds of long-lived trees, such as the bristlecone pine of California, overlapping samples of tree rings can be found so that a continuous sequence may be constructed reaching back six or seven thousand years.

This was actually done, and then the oldest part of the sequence was dated by carbon 14. The true, absolute age of the sample could be determined simply by counting the number of rings. When that count was compared with the results by carbon 14, it showed that the radiometric method is indeed not entirely accurate. But the error does not favor the creationist position, according to which the disputed dates are said to be too old. The comparison showed, rather, that the carbon 14 dates were too young. Where carbon 14 read 5,500 years, the ring count might show 6,000 years. Moreover, a whole series of comparisons done with various rings showed that the percentage of error becomes greater the older the sample is.

Those favoring a recent origin for the earth can still argue that carbon 14 has the least range of these dating techniques (about fifty thousand years) and that the correlation with dendrochronology proves nothing about the potassium-argon and uranium methods. The tree-ring experiment does seem to show, however, that the concept behind these techniques is basically sound. And it is worth remembering that even if uranium dating were found to have an error factor of 75 percent on the high side, the earth would still be over a billion years old.

IV.

Scientists almost invariably overstate the case for evolution, and creationists have as much access to the critical literature as anyone else. But when it comes to defending their own theory, creationists do not have a strong case in terms of biblical scholarship or for a recent creation of the earth. And yet the creationists are stronger in the 1980s than they have been in many decades, and their influence appears to be still on the increase. This puzzles, annoys, and frightens the evolutionists, who tend to think that science, logic, history, and truth are all on their side. They cannot understand why the creationists do not simply blow away. They have no better explanations than ignorance, irrationality, and dark conspiracies.

The most peculiar aspect of the debate is that the creationists are sustained by events completely outside the question of evolution. The Bible of course does not end with Genesis. Scattered throughout the Old and New Testaments are a number of prophecies indicating that the nation of Israel would be reborn with Jerusalem as its capital and that there will eventually be a great, final, and dramatic last battle between Israel and an alliance of various nations, including one "from the uttermost parts of the north," (Ezekiel 39:2), a reference many see as pointing to Russia.

As everyone knows, Israel has in fact been reborn. As recently as 1980, the Israelis proclaimed Jerusalem as their eternal, indivisible capital. And almost every week the political realities in the Middle East can be seen falling ever more precisely into the pattern required for consummation of the ancient prophecies that are yet to be fulfilled.

This obvious and enormous fact hardly ever enters the argument, and yet the contemporary Middle East situation probably has more to do with the resurgence of fundamentalism than any other factor. The creationists instinctively sense that the tide of history is running with them. Perhaps more than any other reason, and despite their simplistic interpretation of Genesis, this is why they have not retreated from the stings and arrows of the opposition.

Naturally, even if the Jerusalem prophecies are completely and literally fulfilled, this would not alter the parabolic character of Genesis. But there are in fact deep reasons for Thumpwell's enthusiasm. As long as Israel exists surrounded by enemies, and as long as some of those enemies, like Syria, are supported by the Soviet Union, the Thumpwells of this world will continue to roar that the end is near, desolation is nigh, the truth is set down in black and white, and the argument over our origin will not go away.

In a broad view, this may be just as well, because there is a much stronger case to be made for the involvement of some kind of spiritual agencies in the emergence of man than can be guessed if one hears nothing but obsolete chronologies and monstrous fish stories.

6: Creation According to Broom

IT IS IRONIC, but at this point perhaps not unexpected, that the strongest case I have found arguing for directing, spiritual influences behind the emergence of man, animals, and plants was put forward by a notable evolutionist. In addition to Alfred Russell Wallace, science since Darwin has produced a number of evolutionary renegades, among them Robert Broom of South Africa.

As a collaborator of Raymond Dart, discoverer of Australopithecus africanus, and himself the discoverer of the species now called Australopithecus robustus, Robert Broom was a dedicated evolutionist in the thick of the fray. But Broom was more than a fossil hunter. He was a man of many parts, being an anatomist, a practicing physician of wide medical experience, and a man with broad experience of life in general. Fully aware that the theory of human evolution in particular carries tremendous philosophical implications and raises profound questions, he candidly addressed the most fundamental of these questions in

1933 with a book called *The Coming of Man: Was It Accident or Design?*

In stark contrast to Carl Sagan and others, Broom had potent reasons for concluding that man's emergence was not by accident and that the development of man and the rest of creation was influenced by spiritual agencies. Today the vast majority of evolutionists offer purely materialistic theories, and while they may occasionally allude to Broom's beliefs, they do not discuss them. Yet today more than ever there are deep problems with all the mechanisms that have been proposed to explain evolution. There are genuine puzzles in the fossil record and innumerable unsolved mysteries concerning the often extraordinary precision with which plants and animals are adapted to their environment or to each other. And now there is also significant, empirical evidence developed by scientists in other fields for the kind of spiritual agencies Broom thought might be involved.

For all these reasons, and because Broom himself was both an evolutionist and highly trained in the art of scientific observation, it is appropriate to air the factors that led him to adopt the view that he did. Written a few years after the Scopes trial, the mention of "the people of Tennessee" refers to the outcome of that trial, which went against the schoolteacher who had been teaching evolution:

It is hardly to be expected that any evidence will convince the people of Tennessee or those fundamentalists who believe they already know the truth, but the evidence for evolution is sufficient to convince anyone who examines it with a perfectly open mind. The difficulty is not whether there has been evolution, but what has brought about the evolution. . . .

Darwinism, the theory that evolution has come about by the survival through natural selection of the fortuitous variations most suited to the environment, has had the support of many of the greatest zoologists. . . . But there have always been those who were dissatisfied with the theory. . . . [However,] many . . . who are apparently dissatisfied with Darwinism do not seem very willing to express their opinions. Curiously enough, Darwin himself was not an extreme Darwinian, and was inclined to believe that use and disuse were important factors, and that acquired characters were inherited. Of course all Darwinians have to admit that nothing is known of the cause of the variations which they believe nature selects, and it is now known that most of the variations which they believed could be inherited are not inherited at all.

The geneticists have shown that they can produce variations of con-

siderable magnitude which they call mutations and that these mutations breed true. If such mutations occur in nature, the suitable ones
would doubtless be selected; and at the present time most zoologists
in America believe that evolution has come about by natural selection
of mutations. Unfortunately, while mutations do occur in nature, they
are very rare, and there is the strongest evidence from paleontology
that evolution has been by extremely minute changes—changes so
minute that it is inconceivable that they could have had any survival
value.

F. B. Sumner, who has devoted years to the study of species and
sub-species of the deermice of America, has come to the following
conclusion: "We are not yet prepared to frame any adequate general
hypothesis as to species formation. The Mendelian mutation system
of facts and theories appears to me to be no more successful in this
respect than its predecessors."

The Lamarckians [followers of zoologist Jean Baptiste de Lamarck,
1744–1829] believe that change of habit is the fundamental factor in
evolution. To the writer Lamarckism appears to be far more satisfactory
than Darwinism; and one feels there must be something in it, though it
may be perhaps wrongly expressed. For the origination of new organs,
Lamarckism invokes a psychic factor. . . . The lengthening of the leg of
the greyhound or the antelope may not be due to the increased use of
the leg in running but to the increased stimulation by some psychic or
mental agency. There are so many cases where the development cannot
be due to use at all, that one is inclined to believe that there is something behind the use even in those cases where use or disuse would
appear to be a factor. No use, for example, ever produced the peacock's
tail or the wonderful . . . plumage in the birds of paradise. . . . The
flowers of the orchids . . . the almost endless devices for cross-
fertilization by insects, and the many ingenious plans for the wide
distribution of the seeds all seem to suggest some psychic agency. If it
has been some psychic or spiritual agency that has evolved the flowers
and the plumage of birds, it is difficult to decide whether such agency
or agencies are in the animals or plants or mainly apart from them.
Perhaps there are two distinct agencies. It looks like it.

In animals, and probably also in plants, there seems to be some
controlling and coordinating agency. It almost seems necessary for
many physiological processes to call in something of the sort. And in
medicine we see many things taking place that are hard to explain
unless we assume some controlling agency. We have a host of interesting cures of disease, usually spoken of as mental healing, faith healing,
divine healing, Christian Science, which cannot be explained by physical laws. Those who have never seen such cases deny that they occur.
Or if they see what looks like a miraculous healing they say they cannot

understand it, and try to forget it. A medical man myself, I have no hesitation in stating that I have seen many healings that seemed little less than miraculous. Such apparently miraculous cures are generally assumed to be the result of the exercise of some divine power. It may be. But perhaps it may be due to the re-establishment of some controlling agency in the patient which had been temporarily disorganized.

The mechanist holds that there is no evidence in living matter of anything that cannot be interpreted in terms of physical laws. The vitalist believes that there is something else not found in dead matter, and this is the Entelechy of Driesch and others. Smuts, like many others, wishes if possible to avoid the appearance on the scene of a *deus ex machina* like Entelechy or Clerk Maxwell's demon. But whatever it is, there is reason to believe there is something in life which is not governed by the laws of physics and chemistry.

Haldane has shown that in the ordinary physiological processes there are coordinating factors that cannot be explained by physics; and the work of the experimental zoologists also seems to show that there is something of a non-physical nature that controls development.

It has long been known that if in a developing tadpole the hind limb bud is cut off and the developing tail grafted on to its place, the developing tail will be converted into a limb. And if the limb bud be grafted on to the place from which the tail bud was cut off, the developing limb will grow into a tail. When the growth is a little further advanced, the transformation no longer occurs. . . . It would seem as if in development there is something controlling the growing organism.

But the experiments of Spemann are far more remarkable.

Broom then describes these experiments in which similar graftings of tissues in frogs' eggs were transposed. These transpositions were made at an earlier stage than in the tadpole experiments and showed that even tissues that were to grow into fundamentally different kinds of cells could be interchanged and the embryo would still develop normally. Material that was to have become skin could be cut out and grafted to the appropriate place so as to become spinal cord, and vice versa.

From this it would seem that there was something controlling the development and able to mold any growing tissue to the requirements of the animal.

But if a piece of the lip of the blastopore [the most critical part of the egg] is cut and grafted into the side it does not form skin but a new medullary plate [which becomes the brain and spinal cord] and ultimately grows into a nearly complete embryo, and it compels all the surrounding tissue to form the right parts of the new embryo. Apparently there is in the piece of the blastopore lip something that can organize the other tissue. Spemann calls it an "organizer."

It is generally held that in animals the vital processes are controlled by the nervous system—brain, spinal cord, and nerves—but here we have something acting like a brain at a time when neither brain nor nerves have been developed. And the organizer situated near the blastopore seems to control development at a distance, though there are no nerves. . . .

Here we have some rather remarkable agency that directs development, and the thought is forced on one—does this agency disappear after development has gone on at least as far as the brain, spinal cord, and nerves? Perhaps—and perhaps not. There is much in life that is by no means clear. In fact, it seems to me that in life there is far less that is clear than there is that is mysterious.

The mysterious we are considering at present is—what is behind evolution? What is it, for example, that leads to the increased molar in the evolution of the horse? Increased action, say the Lamarckians; the more likelihood of those with slightly large molars surviving, say the Darwinians. To me neither explanation is satisfactory. Sudden mutations, say the geneticists. But all the evidence of paleontology is dead against it; and even if it were not so it would be no explanation at all.

Can it be that there is retained in the organism something like the "organizer," which we find in early ontogeny, that controls the whole economy and can increase and decrease the vitality of a part? Take the case of the flightless bird. May it not be that the organizer braces all the parts of the bird that are functionally active and partly at the expense of the unnecessary wings? . . .

There are many developments far too subtle to be explained as a result of any change of innervation [nerve development] brought about by any conscious or unconscious nerve activity. The strange lemur of Madagascar, the Aye-aye, has a slender finger on each hand which is used for passing into the holes made by grubs in wood and for pulling the grubs out. No other animal has ever developed a finger of the same type. . . . There seems little doubt that the peculiar finger in the Aye-aye was evolved for the special purpose of pulling grubs out of wood. It is difficult to see how any change in innervation could effect the development, for the finger is not reduced in length but only changed in becoming extremely thin. One feels driven to the conclusion that some intelligent power has played a part in the evolution.

There are no nerves in the zoological sense in plants, and no conditioned reflexes, though Sir Jagadis Bose has shown that plants respond to outside influences as if they had some sort of nervous structure and even some degree of mentality. . . .

And when we look at the adaptations that have been evolved in

plants we find them quite as remarkable as anything found in the
animal kingdom. Let us consider only a few cases.

The orchids are among the most wonderful flowers ever evolved. . . .
In many cases the development is such that the flower and insect
[which fertilizes it] fit each other like glove and hand. In some cases
the device is so ingenious that the bee or other insect is attracted by
the fragrance and nectar into a chamber from which there is only one
way of escape, and in escaping the insect must first touch the stigma
and then the stamen, and as it passes to the next flower it carries the
pollen to the next stigma. But the devices are almost endless. There are
over seven thousand different species [of orchids] known, and it is
very remarkable that this, the most specialized group of the flowering
plants, should have more species than any other family except the
Compositae.

Broom then notes that "the devices found among plants for scat-
tering the seeds are as ingenious as those for effecting cross-
fertilization," and he provides examples. Then he continues:

Now it seems to me difficult to avoid the conclusion that behind the
various devices for cross-fertilization in flowers, and the various arrangements for seed dispersal, there is intelligence somewhere. Fortuitous mutation or variation seems too far-fetched.

But the question is whether the intelligence is in the plant or outside.
To fit a flower to the structure of a bee, or a nectary tube to the probos-
cis of a moth or butterfly, seems to imply some knowledge of the
insects, and we can hardly believe that flowers can study insects. Then
the development of burrs would seem to imply some knowledge of
mammalian fur, and whatever agency invented the spear grass would
seem to have had some knowledge of the structure of the mammalian
skin. . . .

To suggest the possibility of a spiritual agency in evolution will of
course evoke a vigorous protest from most scientists; but if physicists
and philosophers are considering the possibility of a spiritual view of
the physical universe a biologist may perhaps be excused for considering whether some spiritual agency or agencies may not be largely concerned in the processes of evolution. When we have a very definite
effect we may claim the right to consider all possible causes even
though at first sight they may appear improbable. Even those who
believe in mutations great or small have to admit that they know nothing of what may have produced them; and Darwin had to admit that
what was behind variations was quite unknown.

When Broom mentions "physicists and philosophers . . . considering the possibility of a spiritual view of the physical uni-

verse," he is referring to the sudden collapse and transformation of classical, mechanistic, nineteenth-century physics into mystical, twentieth-century quantum physics, which took place between 1900 and the time Broom wrote, 1933.

In 1803 an Englishman named Thomas Young demonstrated (through the production of interference patterns in his famous "double slit" experiment) that the nature of light was wavelike. This understanding rested secure until 1900, when Max Planck noted that the heated objects emit radiation in discontinuous chunks he called *quanta*. According to the wave theory of light and the model of the atom then widely accepted, a heated object (a black body) should emit or radiate large amounts of ultraviolet light. Planck found that it did not. This observation became known as the ultraviolet catastrophe of classical physics.

After Planck's work in 1900, the nature of light was more puzzling than ever. Then in 1905, the same year in which he published the Special Theory of Relativity, Albert Einstein published another scientific paper. In this he put forward a theory that a beam of light may be described as a stream of particles, called photons. This photon theory won Einstein the Nobel Prize in 1921. It proved to be essential in explaining something called the photoelectric effect, an effect observed when light hits the surface of a metal, jarring loose electrons from the atoms in the metal. According to the wave theory of light, the electrons in the metal should only start to oscillate when they are first struck by light. They should not start flying out of the metal until they have had a chance to warm up. But this isn't what happens. The electrons start flying off as soon as the light is turned on. Hence Einstein's idea of photons as a stream of particles.

Einstein's particle theory of light would have been revolutionary if it simply meant that Young's earlier wave theory were now outmoded and known to be in error. It was a good deal more extraordinary in that Young's wave theory of light is still perfectly valid and still just as necessary to explain interference patterns as the particle theory is to explain the photoelectric effect.

How can light be *both* particles *and* waves? Reality had suddenly become a good deal more complex, and soon reality became stranger still. Around 1924, a young French prince named Louis de Broglie formulated a simple equation derived from those of Planck and Einstein. Even as other physicists were attempting to explain how waves can be particles, de Broglie's equation, in effect, proposed that particles are also waves. The equation specifies the wavelength of the matter waves that correspond to matter. It posits a simple relationship between momentum and wavelength: the greater a particle's momentum, the shorter is the length of its associated wave.

As Zukav says in *The Dancing Wu Li Masters*, this "demolished what was left of the classical view." It also brought a certain completeness to the famous wave-particle duality, which is now recognized as fundamental to quantum physics. Only two years after de Broglie presented this hypothesis, it was confirmed by accident by Clinton Davisson and Lester Germer of the Bell Telephone Laboratories. Davisson and Germer noticed that electrons—which are particles—were reflecting off a surface as if they were waves (electron diffraction). For this they too received Nobel prizes.

De Broglie's theory was demonstrated in its simplest case: The wave-particle duality applies to the smallest particles as well as to light. However, his equation shows that the wave-particle duality applies to more than this: It applies to *everything*—from light, to electrons, protons, living organisms, and freight trains.

The implications of the wave-particle duality produce a watershed in the history of science as momentous as the Copernican revolution or the discoveries of Galileo and Newton. The two sets of experiments that establish the wave-particle duality but which seem to disprove each other have one crucial element in common; this is the "we" that does the experimenting. Sheer force of logic has driven most modern physicists to conclude that the wave-like behavior in Young's double-slit experiment is not a property of light itself, but of our *interaction* with light. Naturally, the same must be said of the particle-like characteristics that we observe in the photoelectric effect. They also are a property of our *interaction* with light rather than being somehow intrinsic to light itself. Zukav underlines the same conclusion: "Wave-like behavior and particle-like behavior are properties of *interactions*."

Another way to emphasize the central and definitional role of these interactions is to think of them instead as "transactions" and to look at transactions in ordinary life. For example, there cannot be a seller without a buyer, nor a buyer without a seller. An individual is a buyer or seller by virtue of his role in a particular transaction, not because he is somehow intrinsically one or the other. (What he buys today he may sell again tomorrow.)

This emphasis on our knowledge as a property of transactions or interactions has a tendency to turn the universe inside out. Zukav narrates,

Since particle-like behavior and wave-like behavior are the only properties that we ascribe to light, and since these properties now are recognized to belong . . . not to light itself, but to our interaction with light, then it appears that light has no properties independent of us! To say that something has no properties is the same as saying that it does not exist. The next step in this logic is inescapable. Without us, light does not exist. . . .

This remarkable conclusion is only half the story. The other half is that, in a similar manner, without light, or, by implication, anything else to interact with, *we do not exist!*

This may sound extreme, but many or most physicists today would agree with it. Neils Bohr, one of the founders of modern physics, wrote in *Atomic Theory and the Description of Nature* in 1934,

. . . an independent reality in the ordinary physical sense can be ascribed neither to the phenomena nor to the agencies of observation.

Now, the spookiest thing about recognizing our knowledge and our identity as a function of our interactions is that these interactions are developed and designed by human consciousness, by a mind in action. In this sense, physics has become the study of the structure of consciousness. Robert G. Jahn, dean of the School of Engineering and Applied Science, Princeton University, commented in the February 1982 issue of *Proceedings of the IEEE* (International Electrical and Electronics Engineers),

Quantum mechanics may be more than a system of physical mechanics; it may be a more fundamental representation of human consciousness and perceptual processes, and the empirical pillars of this formalism, such as . . . the wave/particle dualities may be as much laws of consciousness as laws of physics.

However, as in all transactional or interactional situations, the implications feed both ways. (A buyer creates a seller.) If we are discovering something about human consciousness, we are also discovering something about the universe; and we very quickly arrive at the view that behind the veil of matter and light that covers the world, we find mind-stuff, awaiting re-cognition. The noted British astronomer, Sir Arthur Eddington, wrote of these developments in the 1920s and '30s,

> The whole of those laws of nature . . . have their origin, not in any special mechanisms of nature, but in the workings of the mind. . . .
> All through the physical world runs that unknown content which must surely be the stuff of our consciousness. . . .
> Where science has progressed the farthest, the mind has regained from nature that which the mind has put into nature. . . .
> We may look forward with undiminished enthusiasm to learning in the coming years what lies in the atomic nucleus—even though we suspect that it is hidden there by ourselves. . . .
> The stuff of the world is mind-stuff.

This makes the world an unexpectedly mysterious place in which the activity of mind seems, ultimately, to disclose patterns governed by—the activity of mind. Or as Einstein remarked in his 1936 essay, "On Physical Reality," "The most incomprehensible thing about the world is that it is comprehensible."

Such was the background in physics and the climate this generated at the time Broom wrote. When Broom stressed the apparent role of intelligence somewhere in the processes resulting in nature's multitudinous marvels and "adaptations," he was not indulging an antiquated mysticism but was suggesting in effect that living creatures could hardly be less complex, less the products of mind-stuff, than light and elementary particles.

Or, to come to the same conclusion from a slightly different angle, many of the relations and interrelations among and between subatomic "particles" and our perception of them appear to be of that intimate and dynamic variety which, as Zukav says, "coincides with our definition of the organic." The philosophical implications of quantum physics, he writes, "is that all of the things in our universe (including us) that appear to exist independently are actually parts of one all-encompassing organic pattern. . . ."

Organic means "living."

Possibly Broom's breadth of experience fostered a broadmindedness that enabled him to see the implications earlier than most of his colleagues. A generation later, David Bohm, a theo-

retical physicist of Birkbeck College, London, outlined the same
implications in terms so parallel to those of Broom that they
might have come from his pen:

... physics has really totally abandoned its earlier mechanical basis.
Its subject matter already, in certain ways, is far more similar to that of
biology [sic!] than it is to that of Newtonian mechanics. It does seem
odd, therefore, that just when physics is thus moving away from mechanism, biology and psychology are moving closer to it. If this trend
continues, it may well be that scientists will be regarding living and
intelligent beings as mechanical, while they suppose that inanimate
matter is too complex and subtle to fit into the limited categories of
mechanism. But of course, in the long run, such a point of view cannot
stand up to critical analysis. For since DNA and other molecules studied by the biologist are constituted of electrons, protons, neutrons, etc.,
it follows that they too are capable of behaving in a far more complex
and subtle way than can be described in terms of the mechanical concepts. (Towards a Theoretical Biology, Vol. 2, 1969, C. H. Waddington,
ed.)

As Broom said, more of his contemporaries in the biological
sciences were dissatisfied with Darwinism than gave vent to
their feelings. But he was far from being an isolated voice.

Among others of the same generation, we have the interesting
case of Lecomte du Nouy (1883–1947), a scientist of broad experience in medicine and physics, inventor of many scientific
instruments, who was known as the father of biophysics. His
career spanned professional appointments with major institutions in both the United States and his native France. While
attached to the Rockefeller Institute of New York from 1920 to
1927, he created the world's first physiochemical laboratory entirely devoted to biological problems. From 1927 to 1936 he
supervised the erection of Europe's first laboratory of biophysics
at Paris' Pasteur Institute and was director of the school of Advanced Studies at the Sorbonne from 1935 to 1942.

Du Nouy was an agnostic at the beginning of his scientific
career. With his interests at the crossroads of physics and biology, however, he came to appreciate better than most the implications of the new developments in physics upon the latter field.
In a 1941 essay, "The Future of Spirit" (in Between Knowing
and Believing, 1966), du Nouy criticized the evolutionary materialists in much the same terms as David Bohm did in 1969 and
as one may still do in the 1980s:

The sincere materialists and positivists are, alas . . . ignorant. They still rely on the physics, chemistry, and biology of 1880. But there have been important upheavals in those realms since then, and we can state without exaggeration that the proud intellectual edifice which at that time represented the picture of the universe has crumbled and only the stones remain. These stones are the scientific facts which when they have been well observed are indestructible. But we have already known for . . . years that the edifice which is being built at present with the help of the same materials will not in any way resemble the former one.

Like Broom and others, du Nouy became convinced that science did not imply materialism. As we have heard, various critics of neo-Darwinism have spoken of the enormous odds against highly structured organisms arising by the accumulation of chance variations. This led the astronomer Eddington to speak of an "anti-chance" factor. Following Eddington, du Nouy went one step further and said that this "anti-chance" was just a euphemism for God. His view of the new findings of science, without being specifically Christian, implied the existence of spirit and a creation whose ultimate source is a Creator. Du Nouy says the role of man is an integral part of this creation. He called his version of teleology (the study of final causes) *telefinalism* and suggested that man's physical evolution was at an end and that man was now embarking on his moral, spiritual, and intellectual evolution. Du Nouy's last book, *Human Destiny* (1947), enjoyed a worldwide success, which he did not live to see.

In terms of its general conclusions, du Nouy's work also parallels that of his more famous countryman, Teilhard de Chardin. Teilhard, of course, started from the other end of the court than the youthful agnostic du Nouy. As a priest devoted to the Church and its concepts of Christ, Teilhard was concerned that the rapid expansion of scientific research would overwhelm the comparatively small-scale academic image of Christ most Christians had to work with. Science was continually making the universe larger and more detailed, more challenging and satisfying for man's mind and spirit, producing a sort of natural religion of the universe. By contrast, the center of Christianity seemed to be contracting and diminishing in importance. The only salvation for the Church, he felt, was a style of Christianity that incorporated the results of scientific research, not only accommodating concepts like evolution, but actively employing them to explain the development of the spiritual forces unleashed by Christ in the world today.

Teilhard did this with a great deal more sophistication than most other writers, and with many finely wrought distinctions. But the basic concepts he elaborated are remarkably similar to Eddington's mind-stuff and to Broom's emphasis on intelligence and personalities.

For Teilhard the phenomenon of man was not simply a subsidiary or anomalous element of the universe, but "the supreme phenomenon of nature." "One of the principle acts of universal evolution is not only experienced but lived by us," he wrote. For Teilhard the cutting edge of cosmic evolution is the global network of material organization, communications, and thought that man is now evolving. Just as the earth is composed of layers, envelopes, or zones of activity like the lithosphere, the atmosphere, the biosphere, Teilhard dubbed this "zone of thought" the noosphere. This was the vehicle of the spiritualization of man and the earth, which was ultimately tending—enriched, elaborated, and tested—back to the source from which it came.

Teilhard's influence has been considerable. (Marshall McLuhan's "Global Village," for example, seems but a step away from Teilhard's noosphere.) It is regrettable that most mechanistic evolutionists who are happy to cite his testimony on Peking man neglect to outline his larger philosophical position. Even in the 1980s, Teilhard is still one of the leading thinkers on the intersection of Christianity and evolution. For all his sophistication, however, what seems to stand out in Teilhard's thought are not unique ideas but his similarity to others of his generation.

Broom demonstrates that it is both possible and necessary to come to very similar conclusions without any religious or doctrinal preconceptions. In the concluding section of his book, Broom places the appearance and meaning of man in a very much larger perspective than is usual among today's scientists and draws some remarkable conclusions. Here he has just recounted the evidence from paleontology showing that most animals and plants evolved into specialized types very long ago:

There is ... no doubt that evolution, so far as new groups are concerned, is at an end. That a line of small generalized animals should have continued on till in Eocene times the primates originated and then ceased, and that except for specializations of Eocene types there has been no evolution in the last forty million years, and that the evolutionary clock has so completely run down that it is very doubtful if a single new genus has appeared on earth in the last two million years, seems to drive us to the conclusion that there was no need for further evolution after man appeared, and that the evolution of man must have been deliberately planned by some spiritual power. . . .

While others will doubtless consider that the conclusions to which the writer is inclined to come are not justified by the facts, there seems no harm in quite frankly indicating what may be a possible explanation, especially as most of those that have previously been advanced seem to break down. Perhaps that here indicated may also prove to be unsound, but it seems at least worthy of consideration.

The great religions of the world—the Jewish, the Christian, and the Mohammedan—all believe that a supreme Spiritual Power has created and rules the universe. But they believe also in other spiritual beings —archangels, angels, devils, and a variety of less clearly defined types. How they have arrived at these conclusions we need not consider. And further, they believe that in man at least there is a spiritual element, the soul.

Now it seems to the writer that the facts of science not only do not contradict the main conclusions of those religions, but are possibly in considerable harmony with them.

Much of evolution looks as if it had been planned to result in man, and in other animals and plants to make the world a suitable place for him to dwell in. It is hard to believe that the huge-brained thinking ape was an accident. But if we become convinced that man is the result of the working out of millions of years of planning, we seem forced to the further conclusion that the aim has not been merely the production of a large-brained erect walking ape, but that the aim has been the production of human personalities, and the personality is evidently a new spiritual being that will probably survive the death of the body.

When one has come to the conclusion that the evolution of man has been planned by some great spiritual power, it would almost seem natural to further conclude that the same power had planned all evolution, and that all plants and animals had arisen through the will of the same power. But there are many difficulties if we accept this conclusion.

The great artist-poet, Blake, when apostrophising the tiger, says, "Did He who made the lamb make thee?" And the same thought must come to anyone who looks at the different forms of life. It hardly seems possible that the same agency that evolved the turtle dove also evolved the cobra and the mamba. And it seems incredible that the power that resolved to make man, also planned the evolution of the germs of tuberculosis, diphtheria, tetanus, and typhoid.

If one admits the possibility of spiritual agencies in evolution, then we seem forced to the conclusion that these agencies are very numerous and very different.

Obviously, this view is very different from the simplistic notion that God created everything at a stroke. Broom certainly does not deny the existence of a supreme Deity; on the contrary, he seems to suggest it is more than probable. But as he is aware, this deepens the mystery rather than solving it, because to wave the wand by claiming that God can do anything has no more explanatory power than claiming that natural selection can do anything.

To explain everything with a single slogan is to explain nothing. Given the diversity of nature, it is necessary to suppose as great a variety of spiritual agencies as there are and have been forms of life on earth. Broom notes that the great monotheistic religions also believe in other spiritual beings—archangels, angels, devils, "and a variety of less clearly defined types." Broom has said a lot with few words, but he is careful not to say too much. Archangels, angels, and devils are familiar classical stuff, even if for many people today they seem part of a completely outmoded cosmology. He draws up rather short with the "variety of less clearly defined types." At these even conservative Jews, Christians, and Mohammedans may raise their eyebrows, but Broom has to mention them because we cannot attribute radishes to angels and moles to devils; both are too grand for the job.

In taking this stance, Broom at least faces the problem squarely. In terms of human psychology, one of the great arguments against attributing the various productions of nature to a single supreme Creator is that to do so invites the question, Did God goof? Not only do we live in a world where there are poisonous snakes, noisome insects, and numerous diseases, but it is also a world where an estimated 95 to 99 percent of all species that have ever lived are now extinct. Many people still ask why, if God made this world, we have creatures venomous, troublesome, and deadly, and why an all-knowing Deity apparently "blundered" when nineteen species out of every twenty now seem to have been false starts.

Of course it is a mistaken assumption to begin with that the activities of the Deity should be judged by human standards. But if there is an answer comprehensible to human reason, it is the one articulated by the ancients and reiterated by Broom: There are hosts of spiritual agencies. Not all answer directly to the supreme spirit; and not all are benign.

As refreshing as Broom's open-mindedness is, the most alarming aspect of his creation is that it cracks the door on one gigantic fairy tale. With hosts of spiritual agencies "very numerous and very different," we have in fact reentered the ancient realm of nature spirits. Expressed thus, this might seem the most far-fetched theory of all. But before we are frightened off by the pukka in the park, we should note that there is a lot else in Broom's creation. Following his own path, he too has brought us back to Plato's universe, that world interlaced with form and living intelligence in which man has soul and spirit. The noosphere is heating up. In the last few decades there have been a rather amazing number of researches that all seem to indicate that it is only a cosmos of these dimensions that is large enough to contain man and to account for a great variety of human experience, both early and late, beyond the bonds of matter.

7: Into the Realm of Spirit

In any discussion of evidence for spiritual agencies, it is first necessary to look at what we mean by the term *spiritual*. For some people, the idea of a spiritual being, body, energy, or pattern is so far removed from the world of conventional reality that, by definition, it has nothing to do with the physical world and thus could never be scientifically detected. To speak of something spiritual in this conception is to posit two completely different levels of reality, implying that spiritual reality can only be experienced and known after death, if it can be known at all. This is extreme, classic dualism.

Obviously, if one starts from this kind of assumption, we are not likely to get very far. There is another view of *spiritual*, however, that sees it not as a distinct, separate reality but as a continuation of the same spectrum of energies and forces of which the physical world is a part. In this conception spiritual bodies or energies bear something of the same relation to the ordinary physical world as ultraviolet radiation does to infrared radiation. They are not necessarily perceptible to the same instruments and organs, but they are still part of the same conceptual universe. The spiritual dimension becomes a continuation of nature, not an alternate reality.

This is a nondualistic approach to the spiritual realm. It is especially appropriate in an age when the science of physics has become very largely concerned with metaphysics—literally, "that which is beyond the physical." Many of the investigations of modern physics into subatomic particles, quarks, and patterns of energy and number are quite as removed from surface reality as the pursuits of medieval alchemists. In smashing the atom, modern physics also smashed philosophical distinctions and obstacles that had separated the physical and the metaphysical since the rise of rationalism in the late eighteenth century.

Another powerful development working in the same direction has been the rise of modern technology. Science is a function of its instruments. It is no use trying to calculate longitude without a chronometer. We now live in a world where there are instruments of such incredible sensitivity that they are literally changing our view of reality. The Hughes Aircraft Company has developed a tilt meter so delicate it can measure lunar tides in a teacup. There are instruments that can detect fluctuations of one ten-millionth of a volt in the electrical currents produced in the human brain. Supersensitive strain gauges have actually detected the "astral" or "second body" described in thousands of accounts as a vehicle of consciousness during out-of-body flights, certain altered states of consciousness, and near-death experiences.

In short, we can now measure many kinds of transactions and events that were completely undetectable only a few decades ago. And many of these transactions and events occur in that narrow intersection between the so-called physical and the metaphysical where the activities of the kind of agencies Broom mentioned must operate, if they operate at all. Recent works such as *The Secret Life of Plants* by Tompkins and Bird leave little doubt that, as Broom suggested, even plants "respond to outside influences as if they had some sort of nervous structure and even some degree of mentality." The case of a philodendron that registered emotion on a lie detector (polygraph test) in response to an investigator merely *thinking about* burning one of its leaves is now famous, and it is by no means an isolated example.

Many serious investigators have now moved to a view of nature that brings them nearly full circle with the ancient proposition that everything from the most humble plants to stars have some kind of spirit or intelligence. Whatever the difficulties and merits of this view, the one really crucial case is man himself. And, in an era when even philodendrons are suspected of having guardian angels, it is not surprising that the question of a spiritual element in or associated with man should be receiving closer scientific scrutiny than it has since the rise of the modern analytic mentality.

It's about time. Across all history, from the earliest pyramid texts and Hebrew prophets down to stories in contemporary magazines and newspapers, human experience is replete with accounts of paranormal and psychic experiences: telepathy, clairvoyance, and precognition via voices, visions, and dreams. There are even folks who will tell you of awakening in the night and noticing a glimmering image of dear departed Uncle Frank hovering near the ceiling. Such episodes are now especially interesting because of the numerous tales of out-of-the-body consciousness experienced by accident victims and other temporarily dead people that have lately reached the mass-market paperback shelves. Between the moment of impact (or cardiac arrest) and their revival by modern medical techniques, they tell of their consciousness separating from the physical body and often of a second, very light, floating body—an ethereal duplicate of the physical body—that separates as well.

This light, ethereal body, they tell us, acts as a vehicle of consciousness, and in this vehicle they can travel anywhere. Like Superman, they can leap tall buildings in a single bound. They can pass right through ordinary terrestrial matter as if it weren't there. Faster than a speeding bullet, they can fly at the speed of thought thousands of miles around or above the earth. If we are to believe the texts chiseled into the interior walls of pyramids at Saqqara, Egypt, ancient initiates perfected the techniques of out-of-body travel to journey millions of miles into deep space. According to the texts, they actually reached the stars.

II.

The beginnings of the attempt scientifically to document and study psychic or parapsychological events in modern times may be traced to the founding of the Society for Psychical Research in London in the latter half of the nineteenth century. A counterpart was later formed in the United States, called the American Society for Psychical Research. The journals of these two organizations have long been and continue to be important forums for the description and analysis of paranormal events, and over the years they have published thousands of cases that cannot be explained adequately by naïve materialism. The following is a provocative example published in *Proceedings of the Society for Psychical Research* (London) in 1891–92:

Mr. S. R. Wilmot, a manufacturer of Bridgeport, Connecticut, sailed on October 3rd, 1863, from Liverpool for New York, on the steamer City of Limerick, of the Inman line, Captain Jones commanding. The night following a severe nine-day storm he had the first refreshing sleep since leaving port. "Toward morning I dreamed that I saw my wife, whom I had left in the United States, come to the door of my stateroom, clad in her nightdress," he reports. "At the door she seemed to discover that I was not the only occupant of the room, hesitated a little, then advanced to my side, stooped down and kissed me, and after gently caressing me for a few moments, quietly withdrew.

"Upon waking I was surprised to see my fellow-passenger, whose berth was above mine, but not directly over it—owing to the fact that our room was at the stern of the vessel—leaning upon his elbow, and looking fixedly at me. 'You're a pretty fellow,' said he at length, 'to have a lady come and visit you in this way.' I pressed him for an explanation, which he at first declined to give, but at length related what he had seen while wide-awake, lying in his berth. It exactly corresponded with my dream."

This gentleman was William J. Tait, a sedate fifty-year-old man who was not in the habit of practical joking. From the testimony of Mr. Wilmot's sister, Miss Eliza E. Wilmot, who was also on board ship, he was impressed by what he had seen. She says: "In regard to my brother's strange experience on our homeward voyage in the *Limerick*, I remember Mr. Tait's asking me one morning (when assisting me to the breakfast table, for the cyclone was raging fearfully) if I had been in last night to see my brother; and my astonishment at the question, as he shared the same stateroom. At my, 'No, why?' he said he saw *some* woman, in white, who went up to my brother." Miss Wilmot said her brother then told her of his dream.

Mr. Wilmot continues: "The day after landing I went by rail to Watertown, Connecticut, where my children and my wife had been for some time, visiting her parents. Almost her first question when we were alone together was, 'Did you receive a visit from me a week ago Tuesday?' 'A visit from you?' said I. 'We were more than a thousand miles at sea.' 'I know it,' she replied, 'but it seemed to me that I visited you.' 'It would be impossible,' said I. 'Tell me what makes you think so.' "

His wife then told him that on account of the severity of the weather she had been extremely anxious about him. On the night in question she had lain awake for a long time thinking of him, and about four o'clock in the morning it seemed to her that she went out to seek him. Crossing the wide and stormy sea, she came at length to a low, black steamship, whose side she went up, and then descending into the cabin, passed through it to the stern until she came to his stateroom.

"Tell me," she said, "do they ever have staterooms like the one I saw, where the upper berth extends further back than the under one? A man was in the upper berth, looking right at me, and for a moment I was afraid to go in, but soon I went up to the side of your berth, bent down and kissed you, and embraced you, and then went away."

The description given by Mrs. Wilmot of the steamship was correct in all particulars, though she had never seen it. Mrs. Wilmot states that she thinks she told her mother the next morning about her dream; and "I know that I had a very vivid sense all day of having visited my husband; the impression was so strong that I felt unusually happy and refreshed, to my surprise."

The case of Uncle Frank is not quite as unusual as one might think. The Wilmot story is a classic example of what is now called an out-of-body experience (*OOBE* for short). It has been quoted by others before me because it contains virtually all the elements associated with these experiences. It is typical in that unlike perceptions in ordinary dreams, Mrs. Wilmot had a clear and definite sense of having left her body; and she gave an accurate account of events and objects at the distant place to which her consciousness was projected—information to which she did not have access through normal channels. This account is somewhat unusual, but by no means unique, in that the presence of the out-of-body traveler was sensed in some manner by people at the location she visited. It is rare, but again not unique, in that Mrs. Wilmot was visually perceived in bodily form at the location to which she traveled.

Naturally, the skeptic can point out that this story is merely anecdotal and that in this case, as in so many others, we have no scientific evidence that the related experiences were not due to hallucinations, coincidence, or fraud. Of course these particular events are beyond verification today, but there is now ample evidence that all the elements in the Wilmot case are genuine phenomena. In the first place, putting aside the unusual elements in the Wilmot account, it is now recognized that OOBEs are far more common than once thought. See, for example, the 205-item bibliography in *Psi: Scientific Studies of the Psychic Realm* (1977) by Charles T. Tart, professor of psychology at the Davis campus of the University of California and past president of the Parapsychological Association. Many of these bibliographic entries deal exclusively with OOBEs. In the second place, it is not so easy to dismiss the account of Carl Gustav Jung, probably the greatest psychologist of the twentieth century, concerning his own OOBE, which he described in *Memories, Dreams, Reflections* (1963). Jung broke his foot in early 1944 and shortly thereafter he suffered a heart attack. Unconscious and on the edge of death, he experienced "deliriums and visions" which he described as follows:

The images were so tremendous that I myself concluded that I was close to death. . . . I had reached the outermost limit, and do not know whether I was in a dream or an ecstasy. At any rate, extremely strange things began to happen to me.

It seemed to me that I was high up in space. Far below I saw the globe of the earth, bathed in a gloriously blue light. I saw the deep blue sea and the continents. Far below my feet lay Ceylon, and in the distance ahead of me the subcontinent of India. My field of vision did not include the whole earth, but its global shape was plainly distinguishable and its outlines shown with a silvery gleam through that wonderful blue light. In many places the globe seemed colored, or spotted dark green like oxydized silver. Far away to the left lay a broad expanse —the reddish-yellow desert of Arabia; it was as though the silver of the earth had there assumed a reddish-gold hue. Then came the Red Sea, and far, far back—as if in the upper left of a map—I could just make out a bit of the Mediterranean. My gaze was directed chiefly toward that. Everything else appeared indistinct. I could also see the snow-covered Himalayas, but in that direction it was foggy or cloudy. I did not look to the right at all. I knew that I was on the point of departing from the earth.

Later I discovered how high in space one would have to be to have so extensive a view—approximately a thousand miles! The sight of the earth from this height was the most glorious thing I had ever seen.

Few would accuse Jung of inventing this story, and it is symptomatic of Western scientific awareness at midcentury that this renowned psychologist confessed that he "would never have imagined that any such experience was possible."

A generation later, books such as *Life After Life* (1975) and *Reflections on Life After Life* (1977) by Raymond Moody and *Return from Tomorrow* (1978) by George Ritchie, both medical doctors, have documented that OOBEs happen to a great many people—especially those who, like Jung, are in near-death situations. Moody's books in particular became very popular, and although they were largely anecdotal in style, the fact that they were penned by a physician seems to have put the onus on skeptics and those desiring more precise details to make their own investigations.

Subsequently, Kenneth Ring, a parapsychologist (author of *Life at Death*, 1980), and Michael Sabom, another medical doctor (author of *Recollections of Death*, 1982), have done just this. While Moody was basically concerned to document the existence and nature of the experience, Ring and Sabom are very much more analytical and statistical. Possibly one of the most interesting statistics they produce is that both Ring and Sabom found that approximately 40 percent of the hundred or so people each interviewed—all of whom had been near death or "clinically dead" due to cardiac arrest, and so on, in hospital situations—had had an out-of-body experience during the emergency. Sabom began his five-year study as a complete skeptic, simply not believing Moody's reports; but his skepticism was overwhelmed by the testimony he received.

Possibly the greatest number of medically detailed cases have been collected by Dr. Fred Schoonmaker, chief of cardiovascular services at Saint Luke's Hospital in Denver. Since 1963 he has documented over 2,000 case histories of patients who came close to death. As reported in the March 1981 issue of *McCall's* magazine, Schoonmaker found that 70 percent, or some 1,400, of these had near-death or out-of-body experiences. In a number of Schoonmaker's cases, the electroencephalograph readings that report on the brain's activity had been "flat," or nonexistent, for from thirty minutes to three hours. This is well beyond the time at which a person is considered medically dead and another indication that we are in fact looking at disembodied mental activity, not at abnormal brain function.

Again and again the most important effect of these experiences is stated by the subject along these lines: "I no longer *believe* in life after death; I *know* there is life after death." And those who have been there and back also frequently declare that they are no longer afraid of death.

This confidence derived from direct personal experience that man is something more than flesh and bone could not contrast more strongly with Darwin's assumption, still held by Gould and many others, that all mental or psychic processes are inseparable from and completely dependent upon the physical brain. Actually, for many scientists it is more than an assumption; à la Simpson and Monod it has become a controlling, unquestionable methodological principle.

So how do we know that these out-of-body experiences are what they seem? How can we be certain that they are not mere hallucinations, a snap, crackle, and pop in the cerebral cortex induced by the stresses of traumatic injury or illness, or in cases where there is no injury or illness, perhaps by a surfeit of peculiar chemical secretions?

III.

The strongest indication that these experiences are not mere hallucinations is the fact, repeatedly reported in the literature, that often the out-of-body traveler accurately perceived events or objects to which he or she otherwise had no access. As noted, this was an important element in the Wilmot case. In more recent instances, it is not unusual for a "temporarily dead" person to describe in detail the medical procedures employed to revive his lifeless, unconscious body as it lay in the hospital.

Hallucinations do not provide accurate descriptions of the instruments, personnel, and action in the operating theater. Repeated instances of this kind of easily corroborated description, as well as other consistent features, such as autoscopy (seeing one's own body from a vantage point outside or above the body), which emerged as predictable elements in the interviews, confirmed the reality of the OOBE for Ring and convinced the skeptical Sabom.

Further testimony that the human mind is not synonymous with the physical brain but merely resides temporarily therein, lighting up the higher circuitry when at home, comes from other sources in the medical community. In what he termed a "final examination of the evidence" after a lifetime of distinguished neurosurgical research into the structure and function of the human brain, Dr. Wilder Penfield concluded that the separate existence of mind and brain was "the more reasonable of the two possible explanations."

Mind comes into action and goes out of action with the highest brain-mechanism, it is true. But the mind has energy. The form of that energy is different from that of neuronal potentials that travel the axone pathways. (*The Mystery of the Mind*, 1975)

If we widen our view and include clairvoyance, telepathy, and similar experiences in which human consciousness has gathered veridical information unimpeded by distance and matter, one can find hundreds or thousands of examples in the literature. While these experiences frequently convince the person involved that the mind has an existence and energy of its own, it is only fairly recently that such experiences have been monitored under highly controlled scientific conditions. Perhaps the most noteworthy work of this kind has been described by Russell Targ and Harold Puthoff in *Mind-Reach* (1977). Significantly, Targ and Puthoff are not parapsychologists but physicists, senior researchers at Stanford Research Institute with experience in ultra-high vacuum technology, optics, lasers, plasma, and quantum physics.

It is now possible for physicists to be interested in parapsychology for reasons directly related to their own field. In 1935 Albert Einstein, Boris Podolsky, and Nathan Rosen published a paper entitled, "Can Quantum Mechanical Description of Physical Reality Be Considered Complete?" The burden of their paper was that quantum theory was not complete, and they sought to demonstrate this by describing what has come to be called *the EPR effect.*

As demonstrated by physicist David Bohm, the EPR effect involves the behavior of a pair of electrons in a two-particle system. One of the attributes of subatomic particles is their state of angular momentum, called *spin* (although nothing is actually spinning). The spin of any particular particle may be said to be "up," "down," "right," or "left." In the two-particle system, the spin of each electron is equal to and opposite that of its companion. The spin state of the two-particle system is thus zero.

The spin of a subatomic particle can be oriented by a magnetic field. If we separate the electrons in the two-particle system and send one of them through a magnetic field (called a Stern-Gerlach device), it will come out with one of those four spin states. The spin of its separated twin particle (which did not go through the field) will be opposite.

The question is, How did the separated second particle "know" what the spin state of the other particle was after passing through the field? Einstein, Podolsky, and Rosen wanted to show that quantum theory was not complete because it did not account for this kind of transaction. Inadvertently they also showed that the behavior of these particles is somehow connected in a way that transcends our usual ideas about causality.

Put another way, what the EPR effect did was to call into question one of the primary assumptions of traditional physics, namely the principle of local causes. As Zukav has aptly expressed it in *The Dancing Wu Li Masters*,

The principle of local causes says that what happens in one area does not depend upon variables subject to the control of an experimenter in a distant space-like separated area. The principle of local causes is common sense. The results of an experiment in a place distant and space-like separated from us should not depend on what we decide to do or not to do right here. (Except for the mother who rose in alarm in the same instant that her daughter's distant automobile crashed into a tree—and similar cases—the macroscopic world appears to be made of local phenomena.)

It was this kind of "exception" that interested Targ and Puthoff. The connection between mother and daughter resembles the connection between the separated particles in the EPR effect. It appears to be instantaneous, yet no signal between them can be detected. Although some physicists would still shun the term, it appears to be telepathic, implying a faster-than-light or "super-luminal" connection.

During the 1930s, '40s, and '50s most physicists shied away from these implications, believing that the theory of local causes was still valid, that quantum mechanics was nevertheless complete, and that the difficulties raised by the EPR effect would be satisfactorily explained at a later date without violating those theories.

What happened instead was that around 1964, J. S. Bell, a

physicist at the European Organization for Nuclear Research (CERN) in Switzerland, addressed the problem of this strange connectedness in a mathematical proof which has come to be called Bell's theorem. According to Zukav, some physicists are convinced that Bell's theorem is the single most important work in the history of physics. Bell's theorem proves that if the statistical predictions of quantum mechanics are correct—and they always are—"then our commonsense ideas about the world are profoundly deficient." It means that the principle of local causes *must* be false, and not only on the subatomic level. As physicist Henry Stapp wrote, "The important thing about Bell's theorem is that it puts the dilemma posed by quantum phenomena clearly into the realm of macroscopic phenomena. . . ." In other words, the theorem applies to the world of everyday reality as well, to the world of human beings, automobiles, and trees.

So we may indeed live in a nonlocal universe characterized by superluminal connections between apparently separate parts. This is one step from saying (as some physicists already have) that at the most fundamental level there are no separate parts, only an unbroken wholeness.

Superluminal connections in a universe of unbroken wholeness means that modern physics has caught up with the phenomena of parapsychology, not in the sense of being able to explain telepathy, clairvoyance, and other psychic experiences, but as Targ and Puthoff have said, "these phenomena are not at all inconsistent with the framework of modern physics. . . ." They define their area of investigation in *Mind-Reach* as "quantum-biological physics." They were appropriately first concerned to test the alleged ability of some individuals to accurately perceive events or objects beyond the line of sight and to do this using the conceptual and physical apparatus available in state-of-the-art physics. Targ and Puthoff chose the neutral term *remote viewing* to describe this ability, whether it occurs during an OOBE, as a function of simple clairvoyance (without the individual losing consciousness through the physical body), or in other ways.

For some of their experiments, many distinct locales within a radius of ten miles or so of their laboratory were preselected. A test subject, closeted with an experimenter at the lab, was to describe one of these sites being visited by a "target team" at a prearranged time. Both the lab experimenter and the subject

were kept in ignorance of the chosen site, which had been selected at random from those available. This eliminated the possibility of the experimenter cueing the hopeful "remote viewer."
As the subject honed in on the scene, he recorded his impressions on a tape recorder and provided drawings. Typically, nine
different targets might be tried with a single subject. The tapes
were later transcribed and were submitted along with the drawings to neutral or skeptical judges, who used an exact statistical
procedure to determine if the results were better than that expected by chance. In addition to this tight protocol and double-
blind technique, Targ and Puthoff employed their considerable
experience in physics to implement sophisticated shielding systems to detect the transmission of information to the subject via
radio waves or other means.

Under the most controlled conditions imaginable, Targ and
Puthoff repeatedly demonstrated that extrasensory perception
and remote viewing in particular are undeniable realities. Of
course, not everyone possesses these abilities to any significant
degree, but in some individuals they are so developed that one
would think they could save the Defense Department and the
CIA a lot of work. Targ and Puthoff's research is so clear and
well documented that, as far as they are concerned, "the burden
of proof with regard to excluding the possibility of paranormal
functioning now lies with the skeptics." Any larger explanation
of these phenomena, they conclude, must take account of Bell's
theorem.

... it must permit physically separated events to interact with each
other in a manner that is contrary to ordinary experience. This aspect
of modern theory, which has been experimentally tested and confirmed, reveals that parts of the universe apparently separated from
each other can nonetheless act together as parts of a larger whole, a
statement perhaps more expected to be found in mystical writing than
in a theory of physics.

IV.

We see, then, that the noosphere is getting hotter all the time. In
the nature of things, it is far more difficult to determine whether
OOBEs are a purely mental experience, or whether, as in the
classic teachings, there is an actual "second body" of some kind

that acts as the vehicle of consciousness and sensation. Lately, even this most elusive of questions has received attention from parapsychologists using techniques and equipment at the frontiers of technology, and here again the evidence confirms the thousands of anecdotal accounts and the classic descriptions positing an ethereal "second body."

In *Psi* Charles Tart narrates his experiments with a young woman, referred to as "Miss Z" in order to protect her anonymity:

... She told us that ever since her childhood it had been a routine experience for her to awaken in the middle of the night, often several nights a week, and find herself floating near the ceiling of her bedroom, looking down at her sleeping physical body lying in her bed. The experiences generally lasted less than a minute, then she would fall asleep again. After the surprise of the first few experiences, Miss Z became rather bored with them: After all, it's not very exciting to watch yourself sleeping over and over again for years!

This points up the great variety in OOBEs: Some people can "fly" thousands of miles and are able to target their flight to a specific destination (like Mrs. Wilmot); others (like Miss Z) seem unaware of these possibilities and remain within a few feet of the physical body. What is immediately at question, however, is the reality and nature of the experience, and here Miss Z proved to be a very valuable subject. As a preliminary test Tart suggested to Miss Z that she put the numbers 1 through 10 on randomized pieces of paper and that these be placed in a box near her bed. After lying down for the night, she was to reach blindly into the box, take a piece of paper, and without looking, lay it on her bedside table, where it could not be seen from the bed. If she had an OOBE, she was to look for this number, memorize it, and check it in the morning. Several weeks later Miss Z told Tart she had done this experiment successfully seven times in a row.

Tart then decided to test Miss Z in a laboratory. She was to sleep in a bed in the lab and was wired up so that her brain waves, eye movement, and autonomic nervous system could be monitored. After this was done, Tart placed a random five-digit number on a shelf near the ceiling: If Miss Z had an OOBE, she was to try to see this number, then awaken and report it to Tart. She reported several OOBEs, and these were associated with "a unique brain wave pattern" of a kind Tart had not seen before;

but she had not been able to float high enough to see the number on the shelf and so did not even guess at it. Then,

On the one occasion when Miss Z reported that she had floated high enough to see the target number, she correctly reported that it was 25132. The odds against correctly guessing a five-digit random number, making only one guess at it, are 100,000 to 1. . . .

Tart reports no evidence indicating that Miss Z had any clairvoyant ability in a normal waking state. Taking all factors into account, Tart concluded that Miss Z's experiences fit the theory "that something does indeed leave the physical body" very well.

Further evidence to the same effect comes from even more recent experiments, in which the elusive second body was actually detected with instruments. The experiments are reported in the July 1980 issue of The Journal of the American Society for Psychical Research. Dr. Karlis Osis and his colleague, Donna McCormick, placed highly sensitive "strain gauges" in a sealed room containing pictures that were targets for Alex Tanous. Tanous, who claimed many OOBEs and whose psychic abilities had been previously demonstrated in controlled studies, was instructed to attempt a standard out-of-body perceptual task of reporting on details of the pictures in the sealed room. So that Tanous would not attempt to affect the strain gauges intentionally, he was told that they were not part of the experiment but that they would only be used in a later series of experiments to test psychokinesis. Out of 197 attempts to perceive details of the hidden pictures during out-of-body flights, Tanous scored 114 hits and 83 misses. The supersensitive strain gauges consistently detected significantly more vibrations and movement in the room during the hits than during the misses.

V.

So there is hard evidence, if not of the soul itself, then at least of the ethereal covering of the soul, the elusive second body described in both ancient and modern accounts of out-of-body experiences. Considering the traditional belief that the soul is immortal and the many indications in ancient cosmologies that the soul was created first, before the development of the physical body, one would think these developments might influence current speculations on the nature of man's emergence on earth.

The progress of parapsychology has confirmed the beliefs of many people, but despite its relevance it has not entered the public debate between the creationists and the evolutionists. Most biologists and paleontologists are not really interested in evidence for any theory but their own. They give parapsychology a wide berth and seem totally uninfluenced by the "mystical" trend in modern physics. Most still operate under G. G. Simpson's dictum that only "physical" explanations should be considered. They have maintained this posture with such rigid and undivided attention for so long that they are conceptually paralyzed.

Unbending literal fundamentalists are no more receptive to the advances of parapsychology than the biologists and bonemen. They sense that these advances compromise the uniqueness of Jesus—or their conception of the uniqueness of Jesus. This comes about because several of the "miracles" of Jesus turn out to be merely examples of clairvoyance and telepathy: Jesus "seeing" Nathanael under the fig tree before they met (John 1:48–50); Jesus telling the Samaritan woman at Jacob's well that she had had five husbands (John 4:5–30). In fact, many of the "miracles" and prophecies of the Scriptures are indistinguishable in kind, if not in degree, from broadly documented psychic phenomena happening in the world today. Of course, the really determined fundamentalist is not going to have anyone compromising the miraculous nature of his "true religion," so the least educated clear the boards by declaring that if it isn't a miracle, it's witchcraft and the work of the devil, into which category they consign the saints of other faiths and the millions of other people who have some measure of psychic ability.

Not all creationists are afflicted with this kind of ideological desperation, but none that I know of plays the excellent cards dealt him by the parapsychologists and physicists. The findings of parapsychology tend to confirm rather than deny the reality of certain of Jesus' feats. Jesus' uniqueness is not really at stake, because this is defined by his mission rather than his miracles. And—on the theory that what upsets orthodox scientists should be good for the creationists—they should take another look at just how hysterical certain orthodox scientists recently became when seasoned professional physicists finally nailed down the reality of extrasensory perception in the laboratory.

A case in point is the performance of Martin Gardner, author of a regular column on mathematical games in *Scientific American*. Among the experiments Targ and Puthoff conducted were some involving a "random-target generator," sometimes also called an ESP teaching machine. Volunteers attempted to guess the targets generated by this machine over a series of twenty-five trials, in an effort to determine whether individuals could "learn" to improve their performance of ESP in a controlled and limited system. One such volunteer named Elgin achieved scores "at odds of better than 1,000,000:1." In October 1975, Gardner published an article in *Scientific American* alleging fraud on the part of the subjects, "who, he suggests, probably turned in the good runs and threw away the bad." Targ and Puthoff point out that this was impossible because all results were recorded on continuous fanfold paper tape, which ensured the recording of *all* the results in sequence for each trial of each subject. Not only that; these tests were also recorded on videotape. This information was available to anyone who cared to inquire. In January 1976, *Scientific American* published Targ and Puthoff's inevitable reply, which stated in part, "Gardner's major criticism of the experiments is based on an error in fact, namely his misconception of the manner in which data were collected." And they go on in precise detail to recount exactly how the data were collected and how superficial and irresponsible Gardner's criticisms were.

In response to this, Gardner says simply that someone told him that the tapes were turned in in bits and pieces. So we have a major U.S. science publication presumably exposing the inadequacies of a major research effort on the basis of a piece of erroneous hearsay, anonymously authored!

It was not just Gardner and the editors of *Scientific American* who behaved irresponsibly; similar gross misrepresentations appeared in the British journal *New Scientist*. In fact, various "authorities" were so alarmed by Targ and Puthoff's work that they exerted considerable pressure on SRI to terminate the two physicists. Targ and Puthoff were so amazed by these responses that they devote an entire chapter of *Mind-Reach* to them. More than one of their critics, they say, began with the incredibly unscientific assumption that "we know in advance that telepathy, etc., cannot occur." These intellectual giants, it would seem, have not really got their teeth into the lessons to be drawn from the history of science. At least I fail to see how their stance is an improvement on that of the French Illuminati of the 1790s, who "knew in advance" that rocks cannot fall from the sky.

Clearly, this anti-ESP reaction demonstrates that the tendency for certain spokesmen for science to shoot from the hip and ask questions later is not confined to the issue of evolution per se but is a more general problem. It is important for evaluating the overall state of affairs to realize that many who don the scientific cloak are not really scientific about many of the matters on which they presume to speak. Everyone has a belief system of some kind, and all too often faith comes before evidence for the "practical materialist" as much as it does for the fundamentalist. Perhaps it is healthy that rather than merely refuting Gardner's groundless criticism, Targ and Puthoff do get around to calling a spade a spade:

Gardner fell back on the "believerism" approach, the taking of a position on the basis of an a priori belief, in this case a belief in the nonexistence of paranormal functioning. All this is not very encouraging to researchers like ourselves who dream of a world in which observations count, not belief structure.

Part of the larger problem is the extraordinary specialization and compartmentalization of modern science. Someone may be a world expert on fossil pollen or a wizard with mathematical games and be almost completely oblivious of the bases for the revolution in parapsychology. Naturally, if he "knows in advance that paranormal experiences do not exist," he will not bother acquainting himself with the now-voluminous literature documenting that it does. And yet, if his belief structure is threatened, he will use the forums available to him to comment on developments about which he has no expertise and in the name of science offer the public a piece of critical quackery.

Unencouraging as this response is, it should not distract us from the center of the action. One branch of modern inquiry has come face to face with one of the world's great questions, and Charles Tart has phrased it as well as anyone:

The slightest possibility that we can scientifically show that OOBEs are what they seem to be makes them a fit subject for an immense amount of scientific investigation. After all, good answers to questions of whether this life is all there is or whether we go on to something else, whether religions are just arbitrary belief systems that are useful for promoting social order or whether they are dealing with a vitally important reality, are very important to each one of us.

More than this, the issues raised by out-of-body experiences are central to the whole question of the nature and origin of man and to the style, tone and confidence of our entire culture and civilization. As we look back on the pervading sense of order and serenity of ancient Greece and Egypt, we might find that they derived these qualities from crucial knowledge about the human condition, knowledge that we are only now redis-covering.

8: The Voice of Tradition

I.

As IMPORTANT as the laboratory studies of out-of-body experiences are in themselves, they are only the tip of an enormous iceberg. Their significance is magnified manyfold by other bodies of information with which they connect. Accounts of these experiences are not confined to the modern era; OOBEs were well known to the ancients and are a crucial element in many of the oldest philosophical and religious writings. For example, in "The Dream of Scipio," the conclusion of *De Republica* (54 B.C.), a treatise by the important Roman statesman, orator, and philosopher Cicero, we find an account of such an experience rather similar to that of C. G. Jung, except that Cicero describes a scene a much greater distance from the earth than the thousand miles Jung managed to soar:

From thence, as I took a view of the universe, everything appeared beautiful and admirable: for there, those stars are to be seen that are never visible from our globe, and everything appears of such magnitude as we could not have imagined. . . . The globes of the stars far surpass the magnitude of our earth, which at that distance appeared so exceedingly small, that I could not but be sensibly affected on seeing our whole empire no larger than if we touched the earth as it were at a single point.

Descriptions of and references to out-of-body flights are also found in Hesiod, Plato, Lucius Apuleius, Empedocles, Virgil, Plutarch, Egyptian pyramid texts, *The Tibetan Book of the Dead*, and Saint Paul, to limit ourselves to some of the better known ancient sources. The integral role of these experiences in ancient philosophical and religious ideas has been almost entirely overlooked by the modern world. Yet there is a clear continuity between the contemporary laboratory research into this phenomena and the ancients' considerations of it—a continuity that is perhaps best illustrated by that other major bloc of information, the lived experiences of thousands of ordinary, contemporary people who have neared or passed the threshold of clinical death and, like Jung, returned to tell about it. Beginning with contemporary accounts of those who have returned from death, it is fascinating to follow the continuity back in time to some of the oldest memories of our race. We will then see why certain researchers have found potent reasons to reassess ancient systems of thought and how the lab work, near-death experiences, and the voice of tradition together provide a larger context of direct relevance to the origin of man.

II.

On several crucial points, contemporary accounts of near-death experiences not only agree with each other but parallel descriptions of the after-death state in ancient religious literature. Here are a few examples concerning the nature of the ethereal second body in which people have said they traveled when their physical bodies were "clinically dead." This is a typical account of an accident victim recorded by Raymond Moody in *Life After Life:*

People were walking up from all directions to get to the wreck. I could see them, and I was in the middle of a very narrow walkway. Anyway, as they came by they wouldn't seem to notice me. They would just keep walking with their eyes straight ahead. As they came real close, I would try to turn around, to get out of their way, but they would just walk *through* me.

Moody, a veteran medical doctor, collected hundreds of such stories from patients and colleagues over the years, and when *Life After Life* proved its interest for the public, Moody had plenty of material left for a second volume, *Reflections on Life After Life* (1977). In this work there is an account by another woman, describing the departure of her consciousness from her physical body as she was attended by a doctor and nurses while lying in a hospital:

I became separated. I could then see my body. . . . I stayed around for a while and watched the doctor and the nurses working on my body, wondering what would happen. . . . I was at the head of the bed, looking at them and my body, and at one time one nurse reached up to the wall over the bed to get the oxygen mask that was there and as she did she reached *through* my neck. . . .

Among the most extensive and interesting such accounts is the one provided by George Ritchie in *Return from Tomorrow* (1978). Ritchie, a medical doctor and psychiatrist, narrates what happened to him as a twenty-year-old when in 1943 he was pronounced dead of double-lobar pneumonia and nine minutes later returned to life. During those nine minutes it took Ritchie some time to realize that he was no longer connected to his physical body, and he was amazed at his power to fly:

Almost without knowing it I found myself outside, racing swiftly along, traveling faster in fact than I'd ever moved in my life. . . . Looking down I was astonished to see not the ground, but the tops of mesquite bushes beneath me. . . . My mind kept telling me that what I was doing was impossible, and yet . . . it was happening. A town flashed by beneath me, caution lights blinking at the intersections. This was ridiculous! A human being couldn't fly without an airplane—anyhow I was traveling too low for a plane. . . . An extremely broad river was below me now . . . and on the farthest bank the largest city I had come to yet. I wished I could go down there and find someone who could give me directions. Almost immediately I noticed myself slowing down. . . . Finding myself somehow suspended fifty feet in the air was an even stranger feeling than the whirlwind flight had been. . . . Down on the sidewalk toward [an] all-night cafe a man came briskly walking. . . . I thought I could find out from him what town this was. . . . Even as the idea occurred to me—as though thought and motion had become the same thing—I found myself down on the sidewalk. . . .

Not only are these and hundreds of other modern accounts remarkably uniform on these aspects of the experience, but comparison with ancient texts and ideas shows that these experiences have been consistent in nature for thousands of years.

For untold ages human beings have pondered the great questions of if and how we survive bodily death, whence comes the soul before the body's birth, where it goes after quitting the body, and how we may prepare for the journey. For almost all ancient and archaic peoples of whom we have record, knowing how to die was the supreme question of life; without knowing this, whatever else could be done in life might be in vain. Modern man has largely forgotten how to die. For many people, death is not an adventure of entering another world; it is an embarrassment and an obscenity. But it was not always so: Answers were found to these great questions and handed down in the stories, myths, and liturgies of the various cultures of the earth.

Among the most explicit instructions for guidance of the dying are found in *The Tibetan Book of the Dead*, translated by W. Y. Evans-Wentz and first published in English in 1927. These instructions were actually read aloud during a person's death throes, or shortly after he had succumbed, the belief being that the soul remained close to the body for a certain interval after death. Just as George Ritchie discovered, *The Tibetan Book of the Dead* tells the deceased that after death he will travel in a "desire body," a body commanded by one's wishes—a body in which it will indeed seem, as Ritchie put it, "as though thought and motion had become the same thing." This is a body in which it is possible to traverse cosmic distances at the speed of thought, because as the book declares, the desire body "is not a body of gross matter, so that now thou hast the power to go right through any rock-masses, hills, boulders, earth, houses and Mt. Meru itself without being impeded."

It is just this condition that so amazed those out-of-body accident victims when other people passed *through* them. Naturally, the mere awareness of this condition indicates that consciousness continues after death, but more than this, again as Ritchie and others have found, this state of consciousness includes heightened sensory perceptions. The Tibetan document counsels the deceased that even if when living he had been "blind of eye, or deaf, or lame, yet on this After-Death Plane thine eyes will see forms, and thine ears will hear sounds, and all other sense-organs of thine will be unimpaired and very keen and complete."

When parapsychologist Karlis Osis recently detected the activity of the desire body instrumentally, he did not discover anything new but merely confirmed a traditional belief. Not only do descriptions in ancient systems of thought closely resemble modern stories about this ethereal body; equally significant is that the geography of the otherworldly realms sometimes attained by contemporary out-of-body travelers matches the exotic descriptions found in the Tibetan and Egyptian books of the dead, Egyptian pyramid texts (especially the text from the Pyramid of Unas), classical Greek and Latin authors, and even Dante's *Divine Comedy*. Contemporary accounts as well as these ancient texts all refer to various "rivers" on the afterdeath plane. (The river described earlier by Ritchie is not one of these "heavenly" rivers but an ordinary earthly river.) Some out-of-body travelers, especially those experiencing a profound crisis with their physical body, venture far from the earth, penetrating not only the depths of the solar system but another dimension or level, in which they can see things invisible to normal vision. These "rivers" are often associated with the boundaries of certain territories or realms; to "cross the river" often means to pass into the next world on a more or less permanent basis. In other words, in terms of life on earth, it means to die; thus many contemporary soul travelers report that they were turned back by a guard as they attempted to cross these rivers. Their time had not yet come; they were brought back to life on earth.

Detailed studies of the ancient metaphysical texts in which these rivers are described show that on the basis of direct identifications as well as a host of secondary clues it becomes apparent that the geography of this otherworldly realm matches the geography of the physical solar system. The rivers are actually the circuits of the planets.

While the same basic extraterrestrial geography underlies most of the ancient texts, there are distinct cultural differences in the way these various realms and their inhabitants are depicted. It amazed psychologists Stanislav Grof and Joan Halifax, authors of *The Human Encounter with Death* (1977), to find that many people who returned from clinical death actually reported sequences and symbols as they were presented by the long-vanished sages of other cultures, of whom they had no conscious knowledge whatever:

European and American subjects do not necessarily follow the canonic rules of the Judeao-Christian religious tradition, as one would expect. On occasion unsophisticated individuals have described detailed sequences from Hindu, Buddhist, and Jain mythology, or complex scenes from the little-known Egyptian *Book of the Dead.* . . . In many instances, the sophisticated structure of such sequences transcends the education of the experiencer.

Among other things, this led Grof and Halifax to a radical reevaluation of traditional religious ideas.

We are now beginning to learn that Western science might have been a little premature in making its condemning and condescending judgments about ancient systems of thought. Reports describing subjective experiences of clinical death, if studied carefully and with an open mind, contain ample evidence that various eschatological mythologies represent actual maps of unusual states of consciousness experienced by dying individuals. Psychedelic research conducted in the last two decades has resulted in important phenomenological and neurophysiological data indicating that experiences involving complex mythological, religious and mystical sequences before, during and after death might well represent clinical reality.

Thus we see how contemporary experience of these phenomena integrates with the voice of tradition and how together they constitute excellent evidence for the kind of spiritual agencies to which Broom referred, at least in the case of man himself.

III.

The next question to be clarified is whether these spiritual elements of man could have existed independently before the emergence of the human body and thus influenced its development. Perhaps the most relevant and intriguing studies suggesting the preexistence of the spirit are those by the internationally renowned scholar Mircea Eliade, particularly his works *Shamanism* (1964) and *Myths, Dreams and Mysteries* (1967).

In its most narrow sense shamanism is a body of archaic religious belief and practice of the peoples of Siberia and north-central Asia. Chief among these beliefs is the idea that various orders of spirits govern the operations of nature and that man also is first of all a soul and spirit temporarily resident in a physical body. The religious leaders of these peoples are the shamans. Although there were also priests, "medicine men," and healers, the shaman alone possessed the ability to leave his physical body at will and travel in spirit to determine the location of prey or to intercede on behalf of his people with the spiritual forces of heaven and earth. In short, the shaman's distinguishing characteristic was his ability to undertake what was called "the magical flight." The magical flight is the same thing as an out-of-body flight, except that through fasting and meditation the shaman learned how to achieve this voluntarily.

Mircea Eliade is a leading scholar on comparative religion and widely respected for his researches on shamanism. From a lifetime's research Eliade found that the distinctive characteristics of the shamans were not restricted to Siberian and Asian peoples but that they existed alongside more organized forms of religion in virtually all the ancient and archaic cultures of the earth. Eliade found it particularly intriguing that the shamans—those who could undertake the magical flight—were almost everywhere the most important individuals in the religious life of a community, even though they were often independent of the organized religious fraternities.

The universality of shamans and shamanism made this phenomenon of prime importance for a student of comparative religion. Quite independently of the researches of parapsychology, Eliade sought to determine the nature and reality of the magical flight, a task of considerable difficulty if one was working solely with the reports of ethnologists and cultural anthropologists, because by the beginning of the twentieth century, shamanism had become degenerate in many cultures, and often the shaman merely "staged" his magical flight. The question was further confused because very few of the European and American scholars who interviewed shamans were intellectually prepared to accept the reality of the magical flight, even if they found a shaman who could actually carry it out.

Through a triumph of cautious, comparative scholarship Eliade concluded that while many shamans no longer possess genuine powers, a few still do and that in earlier centuries most practitioners were genuine. The shamans were of unique importance in the life of their communities because in earlier times the magical flight was greatly prized, studied, and directed to accomplish much more than mere stunts, such as reporting an inaccessible five-digit number or the details of pictures locked in a sealed room. The magical flight was the basis of man's cosmic identity and was thus the heart of his ancient religions. From the accounts of out-of-body flights in the Egyptian pyramid texts, *The Tibetan Book of the Dead*, and the classic literature of Greece and Rome it becomes clear that to be "initiated" meant to undergo an induced out-of-body experience precisely for the purpose of knowing the spiritual condition firsthand. Thus across all human time, from the earliest cultures and records down to the present, the out-of-body flight is the common denominator of what it means to be human; it is knowledge of the cosmic life of man. More than this, it is also a reminder of our larger history and of the nature of our emergence on earth. As Eliade has expressed it in *Myths, Dreams and Mysteries,*

It is not possible here to pass in review all the species and varieties of this "flight" and of the communications between Earth and Heaven. Let it suffice to say that the motif is of universal distribution, and is integral to a whole group of myths concerned both with the celestial origin of the first human beings and with the paradisiacal situation during the primordial illud tempus when Heaven was very near to Earth and the mythical Ancestor could attain to it easily enough by climbing a mountain, a tree or a creeper. . . . In short, the ascension and the "flight" belong to an experience common to all primitive humanity.

The key phrase here is "the celestial origin of the first human beings." To put this matter in context, it must be said that Eliade is most definitely *not* suggesting that physical human beings descended from the heavens. Just as the magical flight is a metaphysical or an ultraphysical phenomenon, so is this "celestial origin." In other words, there are a whole group of myths from all over the earth that in one way and another imply that man's soul and spirit had their origin somewhere beyond the earth long before the development of man's physical body. It is important to note that this idea is not derived from one or two particularly imaginative cultures but may truly be said to be "transcultural," since it is of universal distribution. Since man "flew" into the earth, just as out-of-body travelers today may be said to "fly" in their desire bodies, in the earliest, primordial times man could again leave the earth as easily as he had come to it—hence the many myths of the first ancestors ascending to heaven in one way or another.

But this "two-way" traffic did not continue indefinitely. The spirits became fascinated with the mysteries, treasures, and beauty of the earth, and in pursuing knowledge of this, the densest planet in the solar system, they gradually became more attracted to it than the realm from which they had come. This is the legendary "fall" of man. This event is symbolized in the mythologies of many peoples, perhaps finding its most elegant encapsulation in Japanese mythology, much of which is structured to trace the celestial origin of the Japanese royal family, who descended from a line of "gods." Formerly, earth was linked with heaven by a floating bridge, which allowed the gods to go to and fro. One day when the gods were all asleep, this bridge or stairway collapsed into the sea, stranding the gods on earth.

Surveying the oldest myths and legends of mankind, we find that the motif is ever the same: Man came into materiality from outside it; his spirit preexisted the beginning of his terrestrial adventures and the emergence of his physical body. Many mythologies distinguish the creation of the physical body as a separate and last act. Almost always, this body was formed from the most prosaic of materials: dust, clay, grass, wood, maize, and even excrement. Then the preexisting spirit is breathed into it or infused in other ways by various spiritual powers.

The volume of scholarly literature that might be called upon in testimony of these points is so tremendous that to do nothing more than list it would require a bibliography of many pages. Suffice it to say that when Broom concluded from his own observations that spiritual agencies seemed to have played a part in the evolution of man, he had the voice of tradition behind him chanting like a Greek chorus that it was so—whether he was aware of it or not. It remains, then, to apply this information directly to a closer analysis of the biological facts concerned with man's emergence.

9: Psychogenesis

I.

WITH AMPLE EVIDENCE that the human spirit is more than folk-lore and with some solid indications that the psychic elements of man preexisted the development of his physical body, the next step is to ask to what extent mind and spirit can influence the processes of living mammalian bodies.

We recall that Robert Broom, the South African anthropologist who suggested that spiritual agencies were behind evolution, was particularly impressed with mental and faith healing and that as a medical man of wide experience he had personally witnessed many healings "that seemed little less than miraculous." Psychic or mental healing, at least in part, is mind over matter, or in parapsychological terms, psychokinesis (PK). Religious fundamentalists, of course, are familiar with spiritual healing, such healers being as perennial as the grass and represented of late by Kathryn Kuhlman, Olga Worrall, and Oral Roberts, among many others. But PK is also a part of the secular world, and the effects of the mind's influence on organic and inorganic matter are now being explored in scientific studies.

Sporadically, a Daniel Dunglas Home or Uri Geller comes along to call attention to dramatic psychokinetic feats. Home was a nineteenth-century medium who levitated at will before witnesses on several hundred occasions. Some credible witnesses claim Geller did bend keys in their possession through pure mental power. However, such individuals are too rare to serve as bases for broad scientific examination.

If PK exists on a more general level throughout the population, it is likely to manifest through relatively small-scale events. Much of the early scientific testing for PK, for example, involved throwing dice. While J. B. Rhine and others did find occasional gifted subjects who could will the dice to produce certain numbers far beyond their normal probability, even this sort of skill is quite unusual.

Thus scientists interested in this question have been led inexorably toward the microscopic and atomic levels in designing both organic and inorganic systems for detecting PK. It seems a reasonable assumption, after all, that PK will affect a system most readily when the scale of events is so small that they approach the level of indeterminacy—the world of subatomic fragments awash in particle-wave duality, which some physicists believe represents the interface between the physical world and consciousness.

Today highly sophisticated random-event generators (REGs) and random-number generators (RNGs) designed specifically for testing psi abilities utilize such small-scale events, but their development did not come easily. As early as 1952 parapsychologists tried to employ computers to generate random events—such as momentarily lighting one of four lights in a display panel, and then another, and another, and so on, in a purely fortuitous sequence. In tests for precognitive ESP, the subject, of course, was to guess which light would next be lit. There were, however, real difficulties in ensuring that such a series of targets was truly random. It was not until the space race, the accompanying electronics boom, and the development of integrated circuits that highly sophisticated REGs came into use.

By 1969 Dr. Helmut Schmidt, then a senior research scientist at the Boeing Research Laboratories in Seattle, had utilized the randomness of the time intervals between electron emissions produced by the radioactive decay of strontium 90 to construct machines for testing both precognition and PK. These machines also automatically record the subject's guesses and calculate the deviation, if any, from normal probability. Schmidt's machines are fraudproof and operate according to such rigorous criteria that they satisfied even some of the severest critics of parapsychology. They gave the whole field of parapsychology a new scientific respectability.

Yet even when the activating source was a process of radioactive decay, Schmidt found subjects who demonstrated not only significant precognition but significant psychokinesis as well, with one subject affecting the pattern of radioactive decay to such an extent that the odds against this happening by chance were 30,000 to 1.

As biologist John Randall has commented, "In so far as it is humanly possible to prove anything in this uncertain world, the Schmidt experiments provide us with the final proof of the reality of both ESP and PK."

Schmidt's experiments are especially interesting for their indications that human psychokinetic influence is goal oriented. For example, in certain of his tests, Schmidt arranged his testing device so that if the subject were to influence the pace of radioactive decay, he would see the results indicated by the lighting of one of nine lamps arranged in a circle. The subject's direct task was to make the light move in either a clockwise or a counterclockwise direction. (He could only do this by affecting the radioactive decay.) Yet even when Schmidt reversed the circuitry without telling the subject, gifted individuals still accomplished the original goal (moving the lights clockwise) even though unknown to them the psychokinetic effect required was now opposite what it had originally been. There have been other experiments as well that suggest that no matter how complicated or how skillfully manipulated the machine circuitry may be, this presents no difficulty for gifted, goal-oriented PK subjects.

Since decaying atomic nuclei are one of nature's most intractable phenomena, it is indeed not surprising that physicists such as Targ and Puthoff should have become involved in parapsychological investigation, which, as we have seen earlier, they called quantum biological physics. Using Ingo Swann, an artist and gifted psychic with a strong track record, as their subject, Targ and Puthoff have reported psychokinetic effects on the rate at which an oscillating magnetic field in a shielded magnetometer slowed down when Swann tried to influence it. They have also reported that short-lived magnetic fields were generated inside a magnetometer where no magnetic field existed previously.

With psychokinetic influence demonstrated at this level in the inanimate realm, it would be quite remarkable if a PK or healing influence were not detectable with living organisms, which, one suspects, might be more sensitive and easier to influence. There are indeed innumerable accounts of the effect one's mental attitude can have upon one's own or another's body. Of course, just as only the tiniest fraction of out-of-body experiences happen in a laboratory, very few instances of mental healing take place in circumstances where objective scientific analyses may be made. But there are researchers who have developed programs to test the reality of healing influences possessed by certain people.

Bernard Grad of McGill University tested a faith healer who worked by the "laying on of hands" method. Grad found that of three hundred mice with identical injuries, those held by the healer for fifteen minutes a day recovered more rapidly than those held by other people. Grad then carried out a more ingenious and precise experiment. He had barley seeds baked and salted sufficiently so that they were injured but not killed. The seeds were then planted twenty to a pot and watered daily. Ordinary tap water was put into two sealed bottles, one of which was held by the healer for half an hour each day. The experiment was conducted in such a way that those watering the plants did not know which plants received the treated water. After two weeks it was evident that the plants in the pots receiving the healer's water were more numerous, larger, and produced better yields than the others.

Grad next performed another barley-seed test that confirmed that the healer's effect was real and not due to some overlooked factor. In this second run he had a normal individual handle one bottle, while two psychiatrically disturbed people with deep depressions each handled another. The water handled by the normal individual produced the same results as in a control group, but that handled by the depression-ridden patients produced plants that were greatly retarded.

These startling results are the more thought-provoking when we consider that the human body is minimally 65 percent water.

Today there is increasing documentation of phenomena of this type. Recently Dr. Howard R. Hall, assistant professor of psychology at Pennsylvania State University, announced results of a study showing that mental influence can even produce a biochemical reaction in the body's immune system. The study sprang from preliminary work by Dr. Carl Simonton, a radiation oncologist, and Dr. Stephanie Matthews-Simonton, a psychotherapist. By way of augmenting conventional therapy, they had been using a "mind over matter" technique of teaching cancer patients to relax and visualize their white blood cells attacking their cancer cells "as sharks attack meat." The enhanced survival rates of these patients suggested that the therapy bolstered the body's immune system.

In the first study of its kind, Hall and his colleagues decided to test this hypothesis by hypnotizing twenty healthy subjects and telling them to visualize the same shark imagery the Simontons employed. Blood samples were drawn from each subject before hypnosis and again one hour later, to monitor any changes in the white-cell count. The subjects were also taught self-hypnosis and told to practice it with the same visualization twice a day and then return in a week for another blood test. Healthy people under the age of fifty who were easily hypnotizable showed significantly higher counts of white blood cells after the procedure than before it. (This story was reported by the Associated Press, October 19, 1981, under the dateline State College, Pa.)

There are of course a great many other cases involving mental or faith healing and related influences that could be cited. Those mentioned here are neither unique nor especially rare, but they are useful for their illustrative value and because those documenting these cases employed a scientific methodology. In addition to the healing experiments with mice, injured barley seeds treated with healer-held water, and increased white-blood-cell counts among "right-thinking" cancer patients, similar effects have been scientifically monitored on enzyme activity and human hemoglobin as well as bacterial and fungal cultures.

What is especially important about PK and living organisms is that the subjects do not have to be extraordinarily gifted in order to produce significant results. As we move from affecting atomic processes in Schmidt's REGs to increasing white blood cells or raising hemoglobin levels (as nurses did with hospital patients by using a technique called "therapeutic touch"), we move from rare to much more generalized abilities. In fact, some of these psychokinetic effects are so far beyond dispute and so generalized that they are increasingly employed in the realm of applied medicine. The study, dissemination, and application of such techniques is now part of applied laboratory courses in some universities and in the healing regimes employed by some physicians. We are already in an era when biofeedback devices are used to teach people how to alter their own pulse rates, expand or contract capillaries, and affect other biological processes.

It is also worth noting that this generalized PK illustrates the same goal-oriented principle seen in Schmidt's experiments. For example, the subjects do not have to understand how white blood cells or hemoglobin are created in biochemical terms, nor how to repair or treat damaged barley seeds; they just have to "picture" the end result.

Even this brief recapitulation of scientific developments in recent years shows that mental or spiritual influence on living organisms is well established. While there is sufficient evidence to conclude that the human body can indeed be altered by mental influence, some people might argue that this kind of mental influence is not the same thing as the spiritual agencies suggested by Broom. But how is it possible to distinguish between them? A rose by any other name would still get the job done. Mind is only superficially a function of the brain; we know many cases where it continued to exist independently of the brain when life signs in the latter were absent. Mind has all the elusive characteristics of spirit, except that the mere fact of consciousness makes it impossible to question its existence. It might be an oversimplification to say that mind and spirit are the same thing; it is perhaps better to say that mind is one of the aspects or manifestations of spirit.

II.

We are now very close to having all the basic elements of an entirely logical solution to the origin of man's body. We have first of all the undeniable fact that man shares a basic skeletal structure with the primates and with certain extinct hominids in particular—Homo habilis, Homo erectus, and Neanderthal. We have the fact that many species appear suddenly in the fossil record and then continue unchanged for great lengths of time. We have the fact that the existence of a spiritual element or "body" in man (or associated with man) has been verified experimentally and empirically.

Then we have two other very interesting discoveries that have long been known and that are undisputed by biologists and anatomists. As indicated by Broom and others, it is in the early stages of ontogeny—that is, the earliest stages of the embryo—that we have the strongest evidence of some sort of "organizer" at work, some extra factor that ensures that a budding tail grafted to where there should be a leg becomes a leg, and a budding leg, grafted to where there should be a tail becomes a tail, just as if no material had been transposed.

The second interesting discovery concerns what has been called the fetalization of the human skeleton as compared with the skeletons of apes. Numerous paleoanthropologists and anatomists have pointed out that the infants of all presently existing apes are far more human in appearance than the adult forms into which they grow. The resemblance is even more marked in embryonic forms, as we hear in the account of G. R. de Beer, taken from his book *Embryos and Ancestors* (1958):

Bolk has shown that many of the features of the adult structure of man show resemblances to those of the embryonic structure of the anthropoid apes, and the same point of view has been expressed by Devaux. These features include the relatively high brain-weight, the position of the foramen magnum and the cranial flexure, the retarded closure of the sutures between the bones of the skull, the dentition, the flatness of the face (orthognathy), the hairlessness of the body, the light color of the skin, the position of the vagina, the big toe, and a number of other features.

The axis passing through the front and back of the head forms a right angle with that of the trunk in the embryo of all mammals (and of nearly all vertebrates, for that matter), and this bend is known as the cranial flexure. Whereas in mammals other than man the axis of the head is rotated during the later development so that the animal's head points in a direction which is a continuation of the line of its backbone, in man the cranial flexure is retained so that his head points in a direction at right angles to the axis of his body. . . . Since the direction in which his head points, i.e. his line of sight, is horizontal, the position of the body will be vertical; and so man's erect attitude is associated with the retention during ontogeny of a condition which in other mammals is embryonic and temporary, as it must have been in man's ancestors.

In the latter part of the nineteenth century and the early decades
of the twentieth, there was a theory, still occasionally repeated
by people who have not kept up with the progress of science,
that ontogeny recapitulates phylogeny, meaning that in the
course of its development an embryo recapitulates the evolutionary history of its species. This idea was fathered by Ernst
Haeckel, a German biologist who was so convinced that he had
solved the riddle of life's unfolding that he doctored and faked
his drawings of embryonic stages to prove his point. But Haeckel
was not the only man in the world with a microscope. Despite
its occasional repetition by uninformed people, the recapitulation idea has long been discredited by other biologists and
anatomists.

(Amazingly, in The Dragons of Eden, 1977, Carl Sagan en-
dorses the recapitulation theory and refers to the "fish stage" of
human embryology, stating that "the fish stage even has gill
slits." It has been known for almost a century that at no stage of
its development does the human embryo have gill slits. There
are simple folds in the tissue in the region which later becomes
the neck, but to refer to these as gill slits is about as accurate as
referring to hands as antennae.)

The examination of human and other embryos does not show
a fish evolving into an ape, which then evolves into a man, but
instead, as recounted by de Beer (and taken for granted by Gould
in Ontogeny and Phylogeny, 1977), something quite the opposite: The ape embryo starts out very similar to a human, but then
evolves past this condition in a specialized direction. In Gould's
phrase, man is a neotenous creature. (Neoteny means "the retention of formerly juvenile characters by adult descendants.")

In other words, if something intervened to retard the specialization process, the unbending of the cranial flexure and the loss
of the hairless, light-skinned condition, an embryonic ape would
grow into a much more humanlike creature. Obviously, an embryonic Neanderthal, Homo erectus, or Homo habilis would
have borne an even closer resemblance to modern man than
embryonic apes do.

Now, if we accept all these data as genuine, and if we take
them all into account, it seems to me that a solution to the origin
of man's body fairly springs from the data themselves: Assuming
that the spiritual element(s) of man preexisted the development
of the physical body, we are very much invited to conclude that
this spiritual agency (whether we call it the mind, the soul, the

spirit, or the desire body does not matter at this point) directly intervened in the embryonic development of certain hominid forms then existing on the earth. By retarding some processes and modifying others, they may have effected a more profound transformation in the resultant offspring than could otherwise have been produced in millions of years. What might be called the extreme plasticity of the early stages of ontogeny—as indicated by experiments transposing legs and tails, and so forth—implies that intervention by mental or spiritual agencies of a high order could have produced a fundamentally new creature at a stroke.

Other anatomical facts also point in this direction. In "Tools and Human Evolution" (1960) S. L. Washburn describes the relationship of certain specialized features, such as heavy brow-ridges, to the adrenal glands:

One of the essential conditions for the organization of men in co-operative societies was the suppression of rage and of the uncontrolled drive to first place in the hierarchy of dominance. Recently it has been shown that domestic animals, chosen over the generations for willingness to adjust and for lack of rage, have relatively small adrenal glands, as Curt P. Richter of Johns Hopkins University has shown. But the breeders who selected for this hormonal, physiological, temperamental type also picked, without realizing it, animals with small brow ridges and small faces. The skull structure of the wild rat bears the same relation to that of the tame rat as does the skull of Neanderthal man to that of Homo sapiens. The same is true for the cat, dog, pig, horse, and cow; in each case the wild form has the larger face and muscular ridges. In the later stages of human evolution, it appears, the self-domestication of man has been exerting the same effects upon temperament, glands, and skull that are seen in the domestic animals.

As we have seen with Neanderthal's tools, the culture of this creature was completely static for forty thousand years, a most unhumanlike characteristic and one that does not argue well for his gradual "self-domestication." If Neanderthal had any place in human ancestry, it seems at least as likely that some external factor intervened in their culture—or in their embryonic development. Washburn's description is especially valuable in the present context, however, because it indicates how a mere change in the level of glandular secretions can have a profound effect on skeletal structure, and it is noteworthy that the adrenals are particularly subject to mental influence.

III.

Quite a few facts seem to cluster neatly around the possibility that mental or spiritual agencies intervened in the embryonic development of certain hominids to produce man. It is not necessary to suppose that these mental or spiritual agencies reengineered the structure of DNA in the way that genetic engineering is imagined today. If we recall the goal-oriented character of some of the most rigorous PK experiments, it is more appropriate to imagine these mental or spiritual agencies working toward an ideal form and to see subsequent DNA structural changes *as a result* of changed levels of hormonal activity, or whatever. It may be nevertheless significant that in *Molecular Biology of the Gene* (1965) James D. Watson, one of the decoders of DNA, makes the point that many DNA structures are formed by weak biochemical bonds, implying their susceptibility to alteration under certain circumstances. Thus in the case of man's origin, as in others, once the goal is envisioned, the circuitry seems to take care of itself.

This theory might be called *psychogenesis*, meaning "the initiation of a novel form of creature through the activity of a psychic—that is a mental or spiritual—agency." Something very close to this was suggested by British biologist A. C. Hardy in *Science and ESP* (1965):

Perhaps our idea of evolution may be altered if something akin to telepathy . . . was found to be a factor in moulding the patterns of behavior among members of a species. If there was such a non-conscious group behavior plan, distributed between, and linking, the individuals of the race . . . it might operate through organic selection to modify the course of evolution.

To be sure, a gaggle of anthropologists tell us that there never was a time when a Homo erectus mother gave birth to a Homo sapiens child. But how do they know this? Such statements are predicated on the assumption that in all cases evolution proceeded very slowly, through the mechanics of accident, and that any line we might draw between these species, assuming we had a smooth continuity of forms, would be arbitrary. But perhaps it happened in a very different fashion. It is just as easy to interpret the fossil record supposedly pertaining to man as showing discontinuities and strange accelerations in the rate of change.

In any case, we do not have to be quite so extreme. A Homo habilis, Homo erectus, or Neanderthal mother could have given birth to a being significantly closer to modern man than to her own species, a creature perhaps governed by a spiritual agency of a totally different character than her own, but a creature who still retained enough resemblance to the parental stock so as not to be rejected as a monster. Now, if hundreds of thousands or millions of these human spirits came down to earth together and acted in the same way at the same time, a whole generation of fledgling human beings could have been produced at once. Thereafter they could have interbred, and still other human spirits, waiting in reserve, could again modify the early stages of ontogeny and thus within only two or three generations man as he is today could have arisen from a biochemically related but very different creature.

The reader will of course recall that in the opinion of leading paleoanthropologists Neanderthal was already too specialized to become modern man; Homo erectus seems to have been at an evolutionary standstill for a million years and does not fit easily between 1470 and modern man; and 1470 itself, while really hair-raising, is in the final analysis nothing more than problematic. But these kinds of problems disappear with psychogenesis, because we are positing a goal-oriented, psychically initiated, neotenous change affecting embryonic development *before* the specializations leading away from man expressed themselves.

It is appropriate to point out that the theory of psychogenesis does enable us to account for a great deal of the data relevant to the origin of man, and it solves a host of evolutionary problems along the way.

It accounts for why we share skeletal and biochemical structures with the primates, and with certain hominids in particular.

It accounts for why there are few or no intermediate forms between modern man and Homo habilis, Homo erectus, or Neanderthal.

It accounts for the sudden appearance of man in the fossil record and solves the problem of how man so quickly acquired his outsized brain, so unlike every other brain on earth; and it explains whence arose all those abilities far in advance of the needs for mere survival pointed out by Wallace and others.

If we extend the principle of psychogenesis to all living species, with lesser spiritual agencies accomplishing what human spirits have in the case of man, we have an explanation for why so many species appear suddenly in the fossil record, and we have an inkling of why the products of nature are replete with pattern and seem to be the work of designing intelligence.

It enables us to abandon the ostrichlike and rather schizophrenic posture that ignores a whole body of evidence and an entire world of discourse, both of which testify that there is a spiritual dimension to man and the universe.

It enables us to retain the essential dignity and singularity of man; for in this hypothesis there was never a time when man was an animal, with purely animal passions and instincts.

This theory also seems to me to have the admirable feature of retaining much that is oldest and best in Western tradition—of employing some of the best elements of contemporary science while not neglecting the crucial element of our ancient metaphysics, which so many people still find strong reason to accept.

In a sense, psychogenesis is a perfect compromise between evolution and creation, retaining the best features of both. Philosophically speaking, materialistic, accidental evolution is as extremist a doctrine as is a completely literal reading of Genesis. Both positions ignore scientific fact, building their respective cosmologies on half-truths. The full truth is rarely found in any extremist position on any question, and it would be surprising if it were otherwise with the basic question of man's origin. Psychogenesis enables us to affirm the spiritual nature of man while also affirming the validity of the concept of evolution. The theory of psychogenesis is not a substitute for evolution, but rather the mechanism behind it. And it profoundly extends the concept of evolution to apply to the human spirit itself. The creationist can have his way, if it is his claim that the essential man, spiritual man, was created directly by God. That seems to be the claim of the Scriptures of many religions. The advocate of psychogenesis can point out, as does Broom, that the ultimate purpose of intervention by spiritual beings in the ontogeny of an ancient hominid could hardly have been merely for the purpose of converting that hominid to a man. The purpose must have been to provide a vehicle suitable to the further development, refinement, or evolution of those spirits. And if we entertain the possibility of reincarnation, it is possible to see this spiritual evolution as an ongoing and dynamic process that is very much alive and continuing in the world today.

Perhaps that is why many people find the concept of evolution attractive: At some level they can feel it happening. But the level at which it is proceeding might be something other than what they thought.

IV.

Unlike most aspects of standard evolutionary theory, psycho-genesis has both real explanatory power and the requirement for a truly scientific proposition that it can be proved or disproved. Psychogenesis implies that from whatever stock we arose, we separated from it far more quickly than would seem possible through the "normal" course of nature. In decades hence, when, it is hoped, we will have a far more complete reading from the fossil record than we do at present, the relative suddenness of our emergence should be even more apparent than it is today.

A final factor supporting the theory of psychogenesis is its great simplicity. Simplicity is a virtue in a theory. The main points of this theory seem so obvious and straightforward as to arise spontaneously from the data without requiring further elucidation.

The only trouble with this little theory is that it is not harmo-nious with certain consistent features in ancient creation stories. There are some rather good reasons to give these creation stories serious consideration, and if we do, we require a somewhat more electrified theory than the one just proposed.

10: Life in the Cosmic Egg

I.

WE LIVE in interesting times. From a vantage point a few centuries in the future, certainly one of the most hilarious aspects of our era will be the current belief of some of our scientists that we can learn more about man by studying chimpanzees than we can from the ancient writings of our own race.

Chimpanzee watchers are convinced they can learn something about human origins by studying these apes because some scientists have long believed the chimps are our closest living relatives, because protein analyses can be interpreted as indicating the same conclusion, and because the social life of these creatures is thus presumed to cast light on our own beginnings. It is not difficult to follow the chimpanzee watchers' reasoning, but as good an idea as it may seem at the moment, it is all too likely to prove to be another of those evanescent crazes that infect academic thinking for a while and then die out.

Intellectual history, it seems, does not proceed so much in a straight line as it does in circles or spirals. For some time the ancient creation stories and cosmologies of our race have been in disrepute among many scientists, who have tended to regard them as childish fantasies. But now researchers who are directly and foremostly inquisitive about *human* experience are coming to recognize that ancient systems of thought encapsulate much more genuine experience and knowledge than is usually assumed at present.

In fact, there is already a bit of a tide running in this direction. One of the most ancient and widespread beliefs of man is that something human survives the death of the physical body, and we now have a great deal of testimony from those who have experienced clinical death to corroborate that. We have seen provocative descriptions in *The Tibetan Book of the Dead* and other classic sources featuring all the essential elements of present-day out-of-body experiences. We have heard how psychologists Grof and Halifax have revalued ancient systems of thought because those descriptions of the soul's progress after death now appear to be clinical reality. And we have heard the renowned scholar Eliade point out the amazing unanimity in ancient myths concerning "the magical flight" and the celestial origin of the first human beings.

These are not the only indications that ancient systems of thought are very different in source and kind than most Western academics have portrayed them. One of the most important of these indications in this century reached the streets in 1969 with the publication of *Hamlet's Mill,* an investigation of science and myth before the Greeks by Giorgio de Santillana and Hertha von Dechend, historians of science at Harvard and the University of Frankfort, respectively. They have documented the remarkable discovery that many of the gods and places of myth, previously thought to have been the stuff of imaginary earthly adventures, are actually compressed descriptions of celestial phenomena. For example, in many ancient myths and legends the earth is described as flat. In deciphering all the associated references accompanying this description in the legends, they have shown that this "earth" does not correspond to what we now call our planet but refers instead to the plane of the ecliptic—the plane in which the earth revolves around the sun and in which all the other planets also revolve—and which is indeed flat.

This instance illustrates a profound shift in scale and meaning that is not confined to a few examples; the whole body of mythic discourse is replete with similar instances. De Santillana and von Dechend assemble massive evidence (reflected in thirty closely printed pages of bibliography and thirty-nine appendices) that these systems have a common origin in a prehistoric celestial cosmology; not so much "a star religion" as a workable, accurate "geography" of the heavens, a cryptic, encapsulated science, sometimes much disguised in its numerous retellings.

De Santillana and von Dechend, I might add, are not exactly flaming radicals. When they started out on their quest to make better sense of the myths many years ago, they had no intention of abandoning the terrestrial interpretations of their colleagues. Von Dechend says that "there existed 'in the beginning' only the firm decision never to become involved in astronomical matters, under any condition." But after years of research, the evidence that astronomical matters were involved became overwhelming, and they reversed themselves. It is significant that they did this late in their careers, with two lifetimes of scholarship behind them.

One wonders what the relationship might be between their discovery and those of Eliade: the reality of "the magical flight" and the universality of myths about the celestial origin of the first humans. Hamlet's Mill is not only an interesting companion volume to Eliade's Shamanism and Myths, Dreams and Mysteries, it also constitutes an important additional example of the kind of revaluation of ancient systems of thought Grof and Halifax achieved.

These leading researchers in several different fields have independently come to conclusions that all point in the same direction: The oldest records and relics of man now seem to suggest that human consciousness appeared suddenly and full blown. We have no indications of gradual development. I emphasize that we are not here concerned with technology and tools but with direct symptoms of consciousness, such as language. Amazingly, the simpler languages are the less ancient. Even language becomes more complex as we go back in time! This is truly a mystery and is compounded by several studies indicating that the letters of the alphabet did not arise haphazardly but were first used as a numbering system.

These considerations contrast starkly with orthodox evolu-

tionary assumptions about the development of culture and consciousness. Harvard's G. G. Simpson acknowledges the pattern
of language development, but is unable to digest it. "It is incredible," he says, "that the first languages should have been the
most complex," and then simply abandons the subject. De Santillana and von Dechend, on the other hand, face a contradiction
when they see one. They are highly outspoken and critical of
gradual, step-by-step evolution as an explanation for the patterns of development they have uncovered. Evolution has become a "platitude," a "soporific," they say, "which it is no
longer thought necessary to examine." They call *evolution* a
"lazy word" that has blinded us to the real complexities of the
past. In their view, evolution has been so grossly misapplied to
man's cultural development as to create questions about our own
collective sanity:

When, riding on the surf of the general "evolutionism," Ernst Haeckel
and his faithful followers proposed to solve the "world riddles" once
and for all, Rudolf Virchow warned time and again of an evil "monkey
wind" blowing round; he reminded his colleagues of the index of
excavated "prehistoric" skulls and pointed to the unchanged quantity
of brain owned by the species Homo sapiens. But his contemporaries
paid no heed to his admonitions; least of all the humanists who
applied, without blinking, the strictly biological scheme of the evolution of organisms to the cultural history of the single species Homo
sapiens.
   In later centuries historians may declare all of us insane, because
this incredible blunder was not detected at once and was not refuted
with adequate determination. Mistaking cultural history for a process
of gradual evolution, we have deprived ourselves of every reasonable
insight into the nature of culture.

Indeed, we are now so deprived that such insights "into the
nature of culture" as we are usually offered are the sort Leakey
and Lewin provide in *Origins*. With perfectly straight faces, they
regard it as somehow an edifying and significant revelation that
"there is clearly more to chimpanzee life than anyone ever suspected." Well, except for the chimpanzees themselves, I'm sure
that this is so. But it is increasingly apparent that there is a great
deal more again to *human* life than these and other evolutionary
writers *presently* suspect, or are likely to discover given the assumptions under which they are operating.

II.

If the ancient myths and creation stories reflect full-blown consciousness and encapsulate genuine experience and knowledge,
then the modest little theory of psychogenesis outlined in the
previous chapter is not very adequate. No ancient mythology of
which I am aware describes the emergence of man by the transformation of an apelike creature through the intercession of
human spirits. If many ancient myths actually record the primordial descent of human spirits from heaven to earth, they
should be of sufficient age to recount the process of transformation I have suggested, but we find no significant mythic evidence
in this direction. Instead, we find many stories of a much more
magical kind of emergence and transformation, as in this famous
passage in Plato's *Symposium:*

... the primeval man was round, his back and sides forming a circle;
and he had four hands and four feet, one head with two faces, looking
opposite ways, set on a round neck and precisely alike; also four ears,
two privy members, and the remainder to correspond. He could walk
upright as men now do, backwards or forewards as he pleased, and he
could also roll over and over at a great pace, turning on his four hands
and four feet, eight in all; this was when he wanted to run fast. . . .
Terrible was their might and strength, and the thoughts of their hearts
were great, and they made an attack upon the gods. . . . Doubt reigned
in the celestial councils. Should they kill them and annihilate the race
with thunderbolts, as they had done to the giants, then there would be
an end of the sacrifices and worship which men offered to them. . . .
At last, after a good deal of reflection, Zeus discovered a way. He said:
". . . I will cut them in two and then they will be diminished in
strength and increase in numbers. . . ." He spoke and cut men in two
. . . as you might divide an egg with a hair. . . . After the division the
two parts of man each desiring his other half, came together, and
throwing their arms about one another, entwined in mutual embraces,
longing to grow into one. . . . And . . . the male generated in the female
in order that by the mutual embraces of man and woman they might
breed, and the race might continue. . . .

Of course very few people today take this story seriously, the
fashionable interpretation being that it is merely a quaint tale by
an old philosopher grasping for an explanation. We are apt to be
distracted by the references to Zeus, giants, and gods and to
jump to the conclusion that Plato's twin-sexed, undivided man

is a physically impossible creature. And so it is. But is Plato really talking about physical bodies or about something more akin to what *The Tibetan Book of the Dead* calls "the desire body," before it took on physical substance?

If we keep this question open and strip away the veneer of Greek culture (Zeus, giants, and gods), the really interesting thing is that the same basic image occurs again and again in other ancient cultures—some of which were not likely influenced by the Greeks or by each other. Consider this image from the *Brihadaranyaka Upanishad*, recorded in India about 700 B.C. several centuries before Plato. There it says of the first man,

He was exactly as large as a man and woman embracing. This Self then divided itself in two parts; and with that, there was a master and a mistress. Therefore this body, by itself . . . is like half of a split pea. And that is why, indeed, this space is filled by a woman. The male embraced the female, and from that the human race arose.

Even more extraordinary, the same basic image occurs in creation myths halfway round the world. In the creation stories of the natives of the Society Islands in the southwest Pacific, men did not at first have human shape, but were like balls on which arms and legs developed later. Likewise among Australian tribes, the first men were said to be of a rounded shape with only rudimentary appendages and organs, which were later developed by deities or supernatural beings. Additionally, various scholars have noted that the division of the sexes described by Plato and the *Brihadaranyaka Upanishad* is also alluded to in Genesis. The creation of Eve from Adam's "rib," which is more accurately translated as Adam's "side," brings the biblical account into substantial agreement with these other images. At the least, the biblical story certainly emphasizes the theme of "two-from-one" found elsewhere.

The split-pea image—to mix a metaphor—wraps up the whole idea in a nutshell. It is a hauntingly organic image and in some respects is remarkably reminiscent of the process of division in the DNA molecule, in which the two sides are said to "unzip," forming two halves, each of which acts as a "template" for the production of its missing half.

These descriptions of peas, balls, and other ovoid images containing male-female halves locked in sexual embrace are actually all metaphors for the "cosmic egg," a concept of much greater proliferation and antiquity than I could possibly indicate here. But even the few examples cited show that it was scattered throughout the world. This is significant. We are not dealing here with a peculiar national image such as that of the Egyptians' dung beetle or the Americans' Mickey Mouse, but with a concept of virtually universal distribution expressed through a variety of cultural motifs. It is a very old idea. If Vertesszollos man was indeed Homo sapiens, it could well be half a million years old. Those stories of magical flights in the desire body, of their celestial origin and descent to earth, are probably of equal age.

It is only through researches that have come to fruition in the last few decades that we can now see that there was in fact a universal prehistoric cosmology, a group of ideas and stories about the nature and origin of man that were once recognizable by peoples everywhere. Significantly, not all the concepts in this ancient complex of thought have died out. Among them are a couple that form the essence of the Judeo-Christian tradition: the belief in a supreme Lord God and in a special leader or "son" (cf. Adam, the Messiah, Christ), who acts as his agent in dealing with the earth. Even cultures like the ancient Egyptian, which we now think of as grossly polytheistic, were basically mono- theistic. There was in ancient Egypt long before and after Moses and Akhenaten (Ikhnaton) a persistent belief in a single supreme God above and beyond the numerous "lesser gods" or manifes- tations of deity we now associate with that culture. The Nesi- Khonsu Papyrus of about 1,000 B.C. describes the supreme deity in terms that would be acceptable to many Christians, Jews, and Moslems today and makes clear that the sun (the Divine Disc) was not worshiped for itself but as a symbol or substitute for the "One One":

This holy God [is] the Lord of all the gods . . . the holy soul who came into being in the beginning, the Great God who lives by truth, the first divine matter which gave birth unto subsequent divine matter! [He is] the being through whom every [other] god hath existence; the One One who hath made everything which has come into existence since pri- meval times when the world was created; the being whose births are hidden, whose evolutions are manifold, and whose growths are un- known; the holy Form, beloved, terrible and mighty . . . the Lord of wealth, the power . . . who created every evolution of his own exis- tence, except whom at the beginning none other existed; who at the dawn in the primeval time was Atennu, the prince of rays and beams of light . . . whose substitute is the Divine Disc.

It is perhaps even more astonishing that before Christian missionaries ever set foot on the Hawaiian Islands, the aboriginal Hawaiians were recounting the relationship between Teave, the father-mother regent of the kings of heaven, and his son, Tane, in terms that exactly parallel Christ's relationship with the Father in the Gospel of John. The gospel begins,

In the beginning was the Word, and the Word was with God, and the Word was God. He was in the beginning with God; all things were made through him, and without him was not anything made that was made.

The Hawaiians simply said,

All that emanated from the Father flowed hither via his Son.

There is a similar relationship in the legends of the Hopi Indians between Taiowa, the Infinite Deity, and his "nephew" and agent, Sotuknang, whom he created first. The same basic concept was found among many other ancient peoples.

A meaningful alternative to the theory of evolution is properly sought not in a narrow, literal interpretation of a single scriptural tradition, but in this oldest body of ideas that crop up in ancient cultures all over the world. How is it that behind the various cultural accretions we find such a primeval body of fundamental ideas that were shared by people everywhere? This is a profound question, and with increasing understanding of ancient systems of thought, and in some cases contemporary verifications of crucial elements of those systems, it is becoming increasingly difficult not to entertain the possibility that the ancients knew what they were talking about.

III.

Let us now follow the ancient conception of the nature and origin of man a bit further. In metaphysical tradition, the nature of man is sometimes likened to an onion with various layers or shells. At man's innermost center is a spark or spirit. The layer immediately surrounding this spark is the soul—what today we might describe as an ultra-high-frequency plasma body. It is extremely unlikely that these elements will ever be detected by instruments. The spark and soul are of direct, divine origin. These are the elements of man—not his physical body—of which it is said that they were made in the likeness and "image" of God, because God also is spirit. Both the soul and the inner spark are said to be immortal. The soul is sentient. It has intelligence, free will, and memory. The human mind is not the most recent manifestation of man, but one of the earliest. The mind is channeled and constrained by the physical body and its development, but we have ample evidence that the mind is not dependent upon the body. It seems more likely that the body is actually dependent upon the mind. No one knows when the soul and spirit were created. Ancient systems of thought uniformly imply that this took place long before their descent to earth, probably making us older than the oldest bone on the planet.

Working outward, the next shell is what the Tibetans call the desire body, what others have called an astral or etheric body, what the Germans call a doppelgänger, and what in contemporary parlance we might call a very-high-frequency plasma body. It is operating on a lower frequency than the soul, but it is still higher than the physical body. The desire body is not as permanent as the soul and spirit. It is more like a radiation or field set up by the higher frequency elements. Today this field seems to be saturated with the physical body, so that it resembles it, so that it carries enough mass with its energy to be detectable with very sensitive instrumentation, and so that occasionally it may flicker into visibility when divorced from the physical body, as in the case of Mrs. Wilmot.

I have suggested that the level on which Plato and the *Brihadaranyaka Upanishad* are speaking when they describe the human cosmic egg that divided into male and female halves is that of the desire body. We are encouraged in this belief because, as mentioned earlier, many mythologies explicitly distinguish the formation of man's physical body as a separate and last stage in the process of emergence. Typically the physical body is said to have been formed from dust, clay, grass, and so on. The "spiritual" elements do not arise with the body, but are usually "breathed into" it in some way or other, as if the desire body, mind, and soul were outside and preexisting the physical form.

In ancient systems of thought, the physical body is often referred to as a designed product. It is said to have been produced the way a potter fashions a vessel; the body is almost regarded as a piece of sculpture or a water jar. In most traditions the potter is not God Almighty but a "genius" in the hierarchy of lesser beings, often a craftsman god. In some schools of Judeo-Christian mysticism the potter is Adam or Christ (according to taste), the primeval leader of the race.

The tradition that man's body was intentionally designed could hardly be further from current evolutionary speculations alleging the natural selection of accidental mutations. But it harmonizes very well with one observation of practically everyone who has considered the puzzle of man: Our species is peculiarly unspecialized in a world in which everything else is highly specialized. In terms of evolution, the generalized, unspecialized creature is the more primitive. Some have gone so far as to say that anatomically man is more primitive than the gorilla—from the point of view of specialization. Quoting Julian Huxley, Norman Macbeth arrives at one of the more startling observations concerning man's generalized form:

The foot of an antelope, the wing of a bat, the flipper of a sea lion, and all the other multitudinous forms known to comparative anatomy "can all be reduced to a common plan—one bone in the upper arm, two in the lower, a number in the wrist, and five fingers. The variations are brought about by the enlargement of some parts, as with the bat's fingers, the reduction or loss of others, as in the side toes of the antelope, or the joining of originally separate parts into one, as in the antelope's cannon bone. The plan is the same, though one is used for running, one for grasping, one for flying, and one for swimming."

Macbeth then adds,

If we are looking for a form possessing the forelimb structure in a simple and primitive form, perhaps it is staring at us in the human hand.

Macbeth also suggests that "if a few biologists would brood on these strange facts . . . they might find new insights occurring to them." One insight that does occur, whether we are biologists or not, is that if man's body is actually a designer's product, the designer has not gone out of his way to hide the evidence.

Now, whether the human body was designed after earthly patterns or whether the "pea" or cosmic egg that split into male and female existed long before there were earthly patterns is not so important as the question, How did man's physical body actually come into existence? In contrast to the idea that human spirits intervened in the life history of certain hominids, activating hormonal changes or whatever to produce unspecialized offspring, the alternative concept implied in ancient systems of thought seems to be that after the cosmic egg split in two, the fully formed male and female halves simply materialized or solidified as though through a process of reverse evaporation. These sexually charged desire bodies had the power to draw into themselves finely dispersed elements of matter in the earth's environment, somewhat the way magnets "materialize" a magnetic field if iron filings are spread on a paper above them.

In other words, in this scenario men first appeared as "wraiths," gradually becoming more solid, so that eventually they "blinked" into visibility in somewhat the same way that Mrs. Wilmot became visible for a moment or two aboard that ship in the middle of the Atlantic, or, for that matter, in somewhat the way that other apparitional phenomena (from Fatima and Lourdes to possibly "UFOs" and conceivably "Big Foot") manifest at present. I use the word *somewhat* advisedly, because this conception implies the manifestation of "permanent" physical bodies, until these outer skins or vessels became subject to physical death. This version of man's materialization might be called the apparition theory.

So in the end we are right around the corner from a miracle of special creation, having not too craftily sneaked up on it from behind. Such an emergence of man could have happened far more suddenly than anything currently dreamed of in the bone-rooms. Yet it is not a miracle of the wave-the-wand variety, in which God or the natural selection of mutations is said to be capable of anything, with no further explanations offered. What looks like a miracle of special creation is actually the result of a cause-and-effect process with identifiable components, a history, and a motivation. Like television, the results of the apparition theory only seem miraculous to one who is unaware of the inner explanation. Likening the nature of man to the structure of an onion is admittedly quaint, but the image is highly organic. Much in this world, from trees to snails to man himself, seems to grow from the center outward, springing from an invisible organizing kernel.

A great deal more could be presented in support of the apparition theory, but all that can be done in a work of this scope is to survey the known and the unknown broadly and to show that there really are alternatives to evolving man from an ape via the mechanics of accident. Suffice it for the moment to say that there are adequate examples of relevant phenomena in nature, sufficient structures in the new physics, and considerable evidence from parapsychology and ancient systems of thought so that quite as strong a case can be made for this magical version of man's emergence as any other. In a dispassionate overview it is obvious that the accumulated, direct evidence for the independent existence of mind is many times greater than the direct fossil evidence for man's evolution from the apes. And given the overwhelming consensus of antiquity on the celestial origin of the first humans, an impartial judge could well conclude that this was the best theory of all.

IV.

If the apparition theory can be deduced directly from diverse ancient sources and has so much else to support it, why, then, even bother with the theory of psychogenesis, which was proposed in the previous chapter as an explanation of the human emergence in particular?

There are several reasons, the first of which is that it is best to follow where the evidence leads, and as we saw, there are suggestions from paleontology, embryology, and parapsychology that all point in that direction. The second is that the emergence of man is an especially complicated case, and if we are really open-minded, we should not automatically assume that all men originated in the same way—even if according to Thomas Jefferson it is supposed to be "self-evident" that all men were created equal.

The possibility that all men did not originate in the same way has suggested itself to many people, who have noticed the phrase in Genesis about "the sons of God" and "the daughters of men," perhaps indicating two fundamentally different strains of humanity. The same suggestion emerges from other ancient sources, as in the Greek myths, where "gods," "demi-gods," and larger-than-life heroes coexist and interact with mortal men and women. If there were two races, it may be that only the "higher" one developed traditions recounting its emergence. The legends of two races may not be as undemocratic as they at first appear, because the two strains have obviously been long genetically homogenized. This conception also reminds us of Louis Leakey's two strains of Neoanthropus and Paleoanthropus, so even the evidence of paleoanthropology can in some measure be seen as supporting this idea.

We recall that that advocate of common sense, Norman Macbeth, remarked that the whims and caprices of nature frustrate all attempts to generalize. Mankind alone is a large subject, and it may well be that in this case also we crave too much simplicity to trust everything to a single explanation.

It is certainly doubtful that a single explanation will suffice to account for the rest of the biosphere. The appearance of life in the beginning, as well as the emergence of all the great distinct types of plants and animals, may be due to a process like that described in the apparition theory. It is not necessary to suppose that rhinoceroses and bulldogs have souls on the same order as or individualized to the extent that they are in man; but they may well be possessed of less high-powered spiritual components (possibly a group soul) allowing them to express something like the human desire body. To take the most extreme cases, it is fairly indisputable that whales and porpoises are highly intelligent, enjoy some sort of consciousness, and may therefore have a mental life as independent of corporeality as man's. Animism, the belief that all life was produced by spiritual forces such as the dryads of the Greeks and the devas of India, was once universal. Recent studies on the "awareness" of plants suggest that there is some reason for such thinking even when applied to the vegetable kingdom. The occasional use of the plural form *Elohim* (singular *El*) in Genesis when referring to divine being(s) and reflected in the phrase, "Let us make man . . . ," shows that this conception may not be irreconcilable with Judeo-Christian tradition. Given numerous cases like that of the bat, where evolutionary theory requires "impossible" intermediate forms between it and its flightless ancestors (impossible because half-evolved wings would be too weak for flight and too cumbersome for running), we seem required to postulate that some forms came into existence virtually all at once. With the apparition theory, it might be imagined that the vertebrate skeleton is an ideal, platonic form that various animal intelligences have first modified in thought to suit their particular goals before solidifying as physical creatures. In this conception, vestigial organs such as pelvic bones in the whales may be more like neglected ideas than signs of ancestry.

Once the relatively few primeval types were established, a great deal may be attributed to microevolutionary species radiation. We do not need anything as magical as the apparition theory, for example, to explain the transition from the three-toed to the one-toed horse. And in many of those cases where chance variations seem too improbable to account for very specific and peculiar adaptations—such as the finger of the Aye-aye mentioned by Broom or the panda's thumb made so much of by Gould—a process more like psychogenesis may be involved.

I certainly agree with Gould that we do not need God Almighty to design the panda's thumb. They probably could have done a better job at Ford. But to empty the universe of all possibilities other than natural selection and ignore the laws of probability is to make natural selection the biggest fairy of them all. Why not acknowledge that in this case just a bit of directive intelligence seems to be involved? Is it not at least equally cogent to suggest that the consciousness of the notoriously playful panda did it? Given the repeated demonstrations that psychokinesis is goal oriented, we do not have to suppose that the panda must understand comparative anatomy to have brought this about.

And as with the panda, so with much else. Indeed it seems that spirit and intelligence are the missing components in many biological problems. The more deeply we investigate, the more materialistic explanations break down. In providing evidence for many hypotheses, we are continually thrown back to the position where we can only say that the evidence rests with some still-undiscovered specimen or missing regulator genes. And even now it is apparent that if those genes are found, we will still have to explain what regulates the regulators.

V.

The history of science has repeatedly shown that major innovative ideas arise more than once, independently and often at the same time. They seem to be "in the air," as it were. And so it may be with the concepts behind psychogenesis and the apparition theory. There is today a great deal of intellectual ferment among the vigorous minority who are pushing out the boundaries in physics, biology, parapsychology, and the history of science itself, and it all seems headed in the same general direction. In a shock of recognition, physicists probing ultimate forces and connections find mind-stuff. D'Arcy Thompson found the products of mind in the geometry of organisms. Researchers such as Grof, Halifax, de Santillana, von Dechend, and Eliade find reasonable cause for reevaluating the reality content of ancient systems of thought and metaphysics. Another singular instance of this synchronicity is the appearance of *A New Science of Life: The Hypothesis of Formative Causation* (1981) by Rupert Sheldrake, a British plant physiologist.

I became aware of Sheldrake's work after this text was largely complete. Sheldrake alludes to a strange effect involving the crystallization of organic chemicals that have never been synthesized before. Every such chemical has a characteristic crystalline structure. New compounds are generally difficult to crystallize, but once the first crystals have been made for any particular compound, they tend to form more easily as time goes by—even in laboratories on other continents.

Sheldrake suggests that there is a "morphogenetic field" associated with each crystalline pattern. This field has a life of its own, and through "action at a distance" across space and time it guides the patterning of subsequent crystals made from the same compound. In addition to crystals, morphogenetic fields may also determine the characteristic form taken up by molecules, cells, tissues, organs, and organisms. In extending the concept to living creatures, Sheldrake is in effect saying that these morphogenetic fields are the "organizers" mentioned by Broom that control development. They perform the function of the missing regulator genes. Although he does not mention it, they also resemble Plato's ideal forms and the Tibetans' desire body.

Sheldrake suggests that his hypothesis may also explain the acquisition of new behavior by animals. In an article in *Science Digest* (October 1981) he cites the findings of Harvard's William McDougall, who began putting rats through mazes in 1920. McDougall found that successive generations of rats learned the maze more quickly, just as the crystals later form more easily. Controlled studies demonstrated that his behavior did not correlate with genetic inheritance. Sheldrake says, "To this day [McDougall's results] have not been satisfactorily accounted for in conventional terms. . . ."

Immediately following Sheldrake's article in *Science Digest* we have "The Quantum Monkey," a short piece in which Lyall Watson recounts somewhat similar behavior involving an isolated colony of monkeys on the Japanese island of Koshima. It seems that these monkeys subsist largely on sweet potatoes, introduced to the island by scientists, and that they long found it difficult to remove sand from their food. Then in 1952 one bright little female started carrying the potatoes to a stream and washing them. This behavior gradually spread throughout the colony, so that by 1958 all the juveniles were doing it. The bright little female next discovered that if she washed the potatoes in the salt water of the sea, they tasted even better. This behavior too slowly spread, but then, Watson writes, at a certain point it was as if a critical mass had been reached. Suddenly almost all the monkeys in the colony were doing it. "Not only that, but the habit seems to have jumped natural barriers and to have appeared spontaneously, like glycerine crystals in sealed laboratory jars, in colonies on other islands and on the mainland."

Of course, one may as easily attribute this kind of behavior to telepathy or clairvoyance as to morphogenetic fields, but Sheldrake's idea carries many other resonances. He likens mechanistic biology to an attempt to explain the operation of a television set without taking into account the existence of the transmitter. Many scientists, it seems, are now on the verge of reinventing the platonic universe.

The noosphere is imploding and has now reached a temperature where not everyone is able to adapt gracefully. Since Sheldrake's inquiries have led him a step beyond solid materialism and since parapsychological investigations are much less numerous in Britain than in the United States, it is not surprising that Sheldrake's book was greeted in his own country with the same medieval shrieks that Targ and Puthoff's work elicited from certain quarters in the States. The prestigious British scientific journal *Nature* called Sheldrake's book "pseudoscience" and "a candidate for burning." They all but accused him of worshiping false gods.

The attack in *Nature* was so outrageous that many top British scientists rose to Sheldrake's defense, including Nobel laureate Brian Josephson. Noting that Sheldrake's concept of "morphological fields" was rejected as "pseudoscience" because Sheldrake did not prescribe their nature or origin, Josephson replied that "the properties of heat, light and sound were investigated long before there was any understanding of their true nature, and electricity and magnetism originally had exactly the same status. . . ." The Nature critics had said that a theory was only legitimate if all its aspects could be tested. Josephson retorted, "Such a criterion would bar general relativity, the black hole and many other concepts of modern science from being regarded as legitimate scientific theories." It would certainly bar evolution itself.

The truly medieval aspect of Nature's response was described by Josephson as "a failure to admit even the possibility that genuine physical facts may exist that lie outside the scope of current scientific descriptions." And then we have that wonderfully enlightened description of Sheldrake's book as "a candidate for burning." It seems we have come full circle from the days when inquisitorial priests dispensed such judgments. Long ago T. H. Huxley wrote, "It is the customary fate of new truths to begin as heresies and to end as superstitions." This has obviously been the fate of evolution and that magic phrase natural selection. Like "God's Will," they are invoked as the explanation for everything. Today anyone so bold as to seek additional explanations is the heretic.

No doubt rediscovering the multiple dimensions of man and the universe is not a journey everyone may accomplish without some degree of intellectual motion sickness. For many, their entire world view is undermined by the documentation that mind is a discrete reality, not dependent upon the physical brain, or that there is anything in the universe not susceptible to materialistic explanation. Earlier I poked fun at Professor Nettlebottom (an archetypal figure if there ever was one) for having built his career on the bones of Sinanthropus. Yet his investment is minute compared with the investment many people have in equating mind and brain. As we have seen, Darwin based everything on a naïve materialism and the assumption that mind is a "secretion" of the brain. Gould and thousands of others profess the same faith. Yet it is now obvious, though little remarked, that this assumption rested upon negative evidence. Negative evidence, as Gould himself has noted in another context, "is notoriously prone to invalidation by later discovery." And so it has been with the equation of mind and brain. It may be reiterated that the accumulated evidence for the independent existence of mind is now many times greater than the questionable fossil evidence for man's supposed evolution from the apes. And in the context provided by modern parapsychology, it is surely less of a leap in the dark to admit myths of universal distribution recounting the celestial origin of the first humans into the discussion of the origin of man than it is to extrapolate the bases of the human condition from the social life of chimpanzees. The very nature of psychic experience is such that for many people the independence of mind is not a matter of argument, belief, or interpretation, but according to their testimony, an item of knowledge born of direct personal experience. This does not mean that we should accept their descriptions uncritically, but certainly we should be willing to listen.

Living the neatly compartmentalized lives they do, Gould and others of the Darwinist faith have not yet noticed the sea change that is overtaking them. Gould's case in particular is deeply ironic. As the most eloquent advocate of punctuated equilibrium, with its sudden emergence of new forms, he is endorsing a rate of biological change that accords well with the model implied by psychogenesis and the apparition theory.

This kind of convergence illustrates the greatest intellectual need of our time—the need to study man and the universe holistically and to integrate knowledge from supposedly disparate disciplines. Are we to suppose, for example, that the Newtonian physics of Darwin's time is still an intellectual imperative for today's biologists? Why shouldn't their theories of consciousness be judged in light of the new physics, in which there is room for clairvoyance, superluminal connections, and mind? Why shouldn't we presume that scholars like Eliade and parapsychologists like Tart have as much to contribute to the study of man as paleontologists like the Leakeys and biologists like Mayr?

Really, what are we to think? Are these parapsychologists, ethnologists, and historians of science and religion all wasting their time? Is the testimony of virtually all the world's ancient traditions a mere chimera, even when part of that testimony has now been verified in the laboratory? Are those who deny the spiritual dimension for purely a pirori ideological reasons better qualified in the assessment of out-of-body experiences than the thousands of people who have direct personal knowledge of them?

It is far more likely that we have completely misread our own ancient traditions and that if anyone is wasting his time, it is those researchers who believe we are going to learn more about man by watching chimpanzees than by studying the words of the ancients. Yet even chimpanzee-watchers may have something to contribute in further documenting the ubiquity of intelligence.

Whatever one may think of psychogenesis and the apparition theory, it should at least be clear that the tired alternatives of Darwin or Genesis no longer serve: Too much else has come into the picture. Yet a truly holistic approach requires that we do not overreact to partial explanations. Parapsychology practiced with the rigor employed by a Targ and Puthoff supercedes Darwin's philosophical materialism (at least in the case of man) the way quantum mechanics supercedes Newtonian physics. Yet Newtonian physics still adequately accounts for a tremendous range of phenomena, including, for example, the element of celestial mechanics involved in landing a man on the moon. What the discoveries of quantum mechanics have shown is that Newtonian concepts do not fully account for various transactions on the subatomic level. In short, those discoveries show that Newtonian physics is not a *complete* description of physical reality.

Similarly, what the parapsychologists have done (especially those documenting out-of-body flights) is to show that the old hypothesis of mechanistic materialism can no longer be considered adequate to provide a complete description of human nature and experience. The innumerable assertions of the type that man is nothing but an accidental animal—as well as all others predicated upon the assumption that materialism *is* a complete description—are now scientifically untenable. Those proselytizing the soulless mid-Victorian monkey business are now in the stance of peddling the bones of a dead paradigm. Yet the new physics, parapsychology, and the reevaluation of ancient systems of thought does not change the structure of DNA, nullify the considerable evidence for microevolutionary species radiation, or lessen the necessity to explain as much as we reasonably can through physical postulates alone.

Much the same selective approach is appropriate in comparative religion and biblical studies, where a century of critical scholarship has been largely corrosive of traditional notions of the nature and authorship of the Scriptures. As we have seen,

Genesis may still contain profound truths about the origin of man—if it is read as synoptic myth and not as literal, historical chronology. It is a unique expression of those truths, but it is not the only one. All around the world there are other old tales of similar age and implication. The stories of the primeval days were already so old by the time they were recorded in Genesis, Plato, or one of the Upanishads that they are all fragmentary and strained through the imaginations of particular cultures and writers. But they all share certain themes and are like pieces of a mosaic.

If we can detach ourselves from our own piece of the mosaic long enough to glimpse the larger picture, it is quite a spectacular view. And, yes, there is even a pattern in the mosaic called evolution. This larger view is not incompatible with the secure truths of science. Evolution is not the total explanation for all species, but it is almost certainly part of the explanation for many of them. It is apparent that Darwin was a great naturalist. *The Origin of Species* set in motion a great and continuing debate stimulating innumerable investigations that have enormously enlarged our understanding. A century after his death, it does Darwin no disservice to suggest that the world in which we now find ourselves is discovered to be so large, varied, and complex that both he and Plato may be considered men of knowledge in their respective spheres.

VI.

Finally, with the emphasis I have placed on the relevance of ancient and archaic systems of thought to the problem of man's origin, and with deep resistance in many quarters to the idea that Western, high-technology man has anything to learn from such peoples, it is appropriate to point out that excellent precedents exist for invoking the testimony of other cultures in solving contemporary scientific problems. One of the most relevant has been provided by none other than Ernst Mayr and Stephen Jay Gould, who addressed the problem of the reality of species by employing the taxonomic distinctions of aboriginal peoples.

The problem is as old as evolutionary theory itself. If ceaseless evolutionary change is a fundamental fact of nature, how can our division of organisms into discrete types be anything more than arbitrary? Darwin, Lamarck, and many others wrestled with this problem, which continued to be debated by biologists until recent times. Broadly speaking, opinion fell into two camps. Some argued for a "commonsense" approach, pointing out that we do distinguish and define species as a matter of everyday necessity and that these definitions and distinctions are valid. Species, therefore, are real. The other camp held that a species is a fiction, a mental construct without objective existence, a mere concession to our linguistic habits.

In an essay in *The Panda's Thumb* entitled "A Quahog Is a Quahog" Gould suggests,

. . . we have a way to obtain valuable information about whether species are mental abstractions embedded in cultural practice or packages in nature. We can study how different peoples, in complete independence, divide the organisms of their local areas into units. We can contrast Western classification into Linnaean species with the "folk taxonomies" of non-Western peoples.

This line of reasoning and research was suggested to Gould by Mayr, who lived with a tribe of Papuans in the mountains of New Guinea and found this people to have 136 names for the 137 bird species he distinguished. The Papuans confused only two nondescript species of warblers. Mayr concluded,

That . . . Stone Age man recognizes the same entities of nature as Western university-trained scientists refutes rather decisively the claim that species are nothing but a product of the human imagination.

Gould then proceeds to cite other studies, both formal and informal, of the folk taxonomies of other non-Western peoples and shows how they converge with Mayr's observations. Gould thus proclaims a victory for the "realists," concluding, "We live in a world of structure and legitimate distinction. Species are the units of nature's morphology."

Yes, a quahog is a quahog, and what's good for the goose is good for the gander. If the testimony of aboriginal Papuans is relevant to establishing the reality of what we call species, then the testimony of that and other archaic and ancient peoples is also relevant to establishing the reality of what we call mind, soul, spirit, and life after death. Comparing Dr. Ritchie's account of his out-of-body experience with descriptions in *The Tibetan Book of the Dead* is exactly parallel to comparing Linnaean classifications with Papuan taxonomies.

There are differences, however, in the two situations. As Gould says, "the literature on non-Western taxonomies is not extensive, but it is persuasive." The literature containing ancient, archaic, and non-Western testimony on these metaphysical questions, on the other hand, is enormous and includes not only hundreds of "folk" traditions of the kind studied by Eliade but also the products of great minds and civilizations—such as Plato. If approached with an open mind and read in light of the findings of de Santillana, von Dechend, Grof, Halifax, Rhine, Targ, Puthoff, Tart, Osis, and others, it too is persuasive.

There is another brief, ironic point worth the reader's attention. The terms in which those who denied the reality of species are virtually identical to the terms in which Gould denies the reality of mind, spirit, and God. Outlining the position of those who thought species were imaginary, Gould writes,

J. B. S. Haldane, perhaps the most brilliant evolutionist of this century wrote: "The concept of a species is a concession to our linguistic habits and neurological mechanisms." A paleontological colleague proclaimed in 1949 that "a species . . . is a fiction, a mental construct without objective existence."

In his earlier work, *Ever Since Darwin* (1977), Gould used the same argument in this other context:

Matter is the ground of all existence; mind, spirit, and God as well are just words that express the wondrous results of neuronal complexity.

The implications are, I trust, clear.

11: THE Woodlouse Connection

I.

IN A BROAD VIEW it is not difficult to see why, as Broom put it, there is reason to believe there is something in life that is not governed by the laws of physics and chemistry—at least insofar as these laws are conventionally understood. It should also be clear that there *is* something to evolution. It is easy to see why scientists find examples like the Galapagos finches, the New Guinea kingfishers, and the horse highly significant. If anything, it looks as if the origin of species generally consists of a three-stage process: (1) creation of spiritual beings and energies; (2) the physical manifestation of basic types; and (3) the modification, evolution, and proliferation of species from *some* of these basic types.

So, in a wider perspective, it appears that both creationists and evolutionists are correct to some extent, but there is little movement toward accommodation and compromise. Instead we seem to be witnessing an ever more sharply drawn confrontation between contrasting world views. This confrontation has assumed the form of an ongoing media debate with so much momentum that extroverts in both camps get caught up and carried away whenever the other side scores a point. But somehow this does not result in an even exchange. The selling of evolution is backfiring in a big way, and it is instructive to see why this is happening.

On one level, we find that evolutionists value the media and realize they need to use it. Thus, following minor creationist media victories in late 1981, Samuel P. Martin of the Department of Anthropology, University of Illinois, felt compelled to suggest in a letter to Science ("Confronting Creationism," February 5, 1982) that large science organizations such as the AAAS and the National Academy of Science (NAS) use their funds "to initiate a major media assault on the creationists now—before the cracks in the dike turn to fissures."

On the level of actually debating with a live creationist before TV cameras, evolutionists are less enthusiastic. On October 13, 1981, Duane Gish of the Institute for Creation Research debated biologist Russell Doolittle of the University of California. According to spokesmen for the scientific community itself, Gish routed Doolittle. Unfortunately for the biologists, the debate was recorded for broadcast on national television at a later date. In the November 6, 1981, edition of Science Roger Lewin was making excuses beforehand. Members of the NAS and the National Association of Biology Teachers (NABT) were "appalled" by the debate. They describe Gish's presentation as "slick" and "timed to the last second." Doolittle's is said to have been "heavy, labored and poorly organized." But they aren't going to admit that the creationist won that debate fair and square. Doolittle, they concluded, "had been trapped." They complain that "the creationists are well practiced in this kind of presentation. Scientists are not." Lewin reports that at an NAS meeting at which the debate was discussed, "all but one voice" agreed that "debating with the creationists should be avoided."

Such is the fearless progress of science. Apparently it has been a shock to discover that some of the creationists are actually intelligent. But there is a deeper reason for such embarrassments. By the very nature of their specialization, most biologists and anthropologists operate in an insulated environment largely devoid of radical criticism and unconcerned with developments in other fields. Even the reasonable, relevant, and purely secular criticisms of Macbeth have been excluded so as not to disturb the ongoing extrapolations. It is not likely that many in this protected ecosystem are aware of the strange facts emerging from parapsychology, the history of science, and archaeology in recent years. And if open-minded professionals such as Tart, Targ, and Puthoff actually verify and document the reality of extrasensory perception—or anything else that throws standard assumptions about human nature open to question—then a host of self-selected colleagues chant in unison that they know in advance these things cannot be. As suggested earlier, this pattern of behavior is indeed very similar to that of the Académie française in 1790, who knew in advance that meteorites could not fall from the sky.

There is a price to be paid for the insulated, self-reinforcing atmosphere. The "educated few" appear foolish in the eyes of the many who know from experience. And in the present case, the scientists are ill prepared to parry with a fundamentally different perspective, which is especially damaging in an era of mass media. Nor in refusing direct debate does one really answer the argument. Historically there have been few direct debates; and usually the urge to explain has been transferred to the pages of professional journals and books.

Superficially, parrying with an invisible opponent who cannot offer an immediate response might seem a safer contest than live debate. But it doesn't work out that way. The extreme insularity in which many scientists now work often operates against the evolutionist in this situation as well. Because of this insularity, many evolutionists seem prone to a breakdown of professional discipline, and as a result they not infrequently sound as extreme as their adversaries.

A particularly diagnostic example of this breakdown of discipline emerges in *Evolution* (1978), a book by Colin Patterson. Patterson is a specialist on fossil fishes and is on the staff of the British Museum (Natural History). Even though Patterson is a Briton, his book qualifies as an example of the problems in American evolutionary discourse because it was published in the United States and was sufficiently acceptable to find its way into public libraries in Virginia.

Evolution is a popularization of modern evolutionary theory designed for high school students and the general public. The book relies heavily on genetics and protein analysis and is more technical than most such popularizations. On many questions it is careful, thoughtful, and balanced. Patterson is well-enough read, for example, to have noticed the work of Karl Popper, the influential philosopher of science, and to note the relevance of Popper's criticisms to evolutionary theory: "Popper warns of a danger: 'A theory, even a scientific theory, may become an intellectual fashion, a substitute for religion, an entrenched dogma.' " Patterson agrees with this, saying, "This has certainly been true of evolutionary theory." Yet only twenty-some pages later in the concluding section of his text, entitled "Human Nature," Patterson offers these lines:

It is true that evolutionary theory is no substitute for religion, though some have tried to make it one. But it does contain a message about our relationship to the rest of nature that is more positive than the Old Testament message: that man is unique, made in the image of God, and that the rest of creation is there for him to exploit. It will take us a long time completely to lose this attitude, although its results are daily more obtrusive. The message of evolution is that we are not unique. We are animals, members of the same lineage as the woodlouse and the shrew.

There are several problems here. One of them is that Patterson seems to be taking the Bible on hearsay. Nowhere does the Old Testament teach that the rest of creation is there for man to exploit. Man is given dominion over the animals, and every green herb bearing seed for food; but man is also held responsible for the creatures over whom he has dominion, as is reflected in the command to Noah to save the animals from the flood.

A more startling problem is Patterson's statement that we are members of the same lineage as the woodlouse and the shrew. One hopes that what Patterson is trying to convey is the romantic sentiment that all creatures are children of the earth, but he comes within an ace of saying that we are evolved woodlice. Indeed, it is difficult or impossible to exclude that implication. If one accepts a connection between man and the apes, we can then attempt to trace the apes back to earlier mammals, shrews or whatever, and then—if one gets carried away with protein analysis, as Patterson does—back to woodlice or anything you please. Patterson's statement is sufficiently ambiguous that younger readers may well take its message to be that we *are* evolved woodlice—a proposition guaranteed to amaze and delight "concerned" parents everywhere.

The remarkable thing about Patterson's formulation is not that it is clumsy and unfortunate, but that it is completely unnecessary. He is not required by the scope of his book or public demand to speculate on "human nature." His book would be informative and useful without it. But like many other scientists, he cannot resist the cosmological imperative, the need to explain the meaning of life (assuming that evolution *is* universally applicable), and that is where his discipline breaks down. He may be a whiz with fossil fishes, but he is decidedly weak as a philosopher. He fails to distinguish between facts and assumptions, and then—in the name of science—he marches his assumptions past the limits of credulity.

Patterson has truly reached that magical point when evidence no longer matters. If even the supposed transition from Homo erectus to Homo sapiens is full of pitfalls and hurdles, watching a man dance between mammals and crustaceans is entertaining indeed. But this is no longer science. When evidence no longer matters, science has been replaced by superstition and dogma.

I do not mean to pick on Patterson, but he does provide a wonderful example of a pervasive problem in the scientific community. Evolutionists persistently assume too much, extrapolate too much, and cannot restrain themselves from indulging in philosophical and cosmological speculations that are not infrequently preposterous. The breakdown in discipline is so profound that they do not seem to be conscious of what they are doing. Patterson can tell us in one breath that evolutionary theory is no substitute for religion and in the next claim (mistakenly) that it offers a more positive message than the Old Testament. If he is not offering a substitute, what is he offering?

Patterson is the only writer I have found who goes so far as to allege our kinship with woodlice, although Sagan is operating in the same vein when he says that oak trees are our relatives. Increasingly, pop-evolutionists write as if human evolution from the animal kingdom is proven and as if evolution is the sole explanation for all life. Once one's mind is tilting in this direction, it easily slides off into peculiar and narrow speculations on man's place and meaning in nature. Willy-nilly, we have hundreds of biology and anthropology texts whose authors have succumbed to the cosmological imperative, offering not just the

facts of biology and anthropology, but also their own philosophical beliefs. They have indeed mixed up their science with their
religion and can no longer tell where one ends and the other
begins.

If these ill-starred speculations were merely chaff in professional journals, no one would care. Instead they have been in-
jected directly into the cultural bloodstream. The problem
assumes a different dimension, for example, when someone's
impressionable teenager brings a book like Patterson's home
from the school library. Into what state of mind is the protective
parent led as he weighs the virtues of having little Suzie taught
that she is of the same lineage as the woodlouse? Whom can he
sue and where can he vote? He finds he cares not if Mr. Patterson
does have a degree in fossil fishes. The woodlouse connection is
either a Kafkaesque joke or it is the encapsulation of a profound
loss of perspective.

One needn't be a creationist, a Christian, or religious in any
way to find the woodlouse connection and similar notions absurd or objectionable. At this level, the dissonance is not between "science" and one particular interpretation of the Bible,
but between enormous extrapolations from a theory of limited
application and the larger collective experience of the human
family. Few evolutionists seem aware how poorly their materialistic pronouncements fit the larger life experiences of the public. The voluminous literature now in print about life after death
and out-of-body experiences, for example, is itself only a symptom, a tiny reflection of a larger pervasive reality that millions of
people actually experience. Patterson at least senses that his pronouncement is uninspiring:

Some people find it profoundly depressing. They read genetic and
evolution theories as proof that we are the products of blind chance,
nothing but pointless experiments in protein chemistry. My reply is
that I find it no more depressing to be a chemical experiment than an
experiment in ethics, which is the Christian message read from the
same nihilist or "nothing but" viewpoint.

Attempting to be more positive, Patterson then offers the typical
palliative that "our uniqueness lies in our brains, tongues and
hands, that have allowed us to accumulate knowledge. . . ." Yet
if Patterson and others really paid due attention to the knowledge that *has* accumulated, they might better appreciate that the

ancient definition of man's uniqueness—the existence and quality of man's spiritual aspect—is better documented today than
in many centuries.

In addition to acquainting themselves with developments in
parapsychology and the history of science, it may also be worth
the attention of many scientists, I suggest, to take note of current
cultural trends in the United States. While innovative developments at the forefront of science and philosophy may take a
generation to percolate "down" throughout society, cultural historians have long recognized that major trends seem also to
emerge from "below," manifesting as it were in the lowest cultural denominators as early as or even before they have been
formalized at the top. Thus it was with some interest that I noted
the content of a recent Saturday morning television cartoon
show for children. Scantily clad, well-developed heroes and her-
oines in a prehistoric setting were having out-of-body flights and
doing much magical battle with demons. (This is a far cry from
the Saturday morning cartoon shows I attended as a child.) And
there is little doubt that this is part of a trend. There have been
dozens of recent motion pictures, some of them very successful,
on themes involving discarnate entities. While the events they
depict may be sensationalized, exaggerated fiction, and not infrequently thoroughly debased, they are also indications of the
premises involved in a culture's world view. Similarly, Superman, always a good metaphor for the old shamanic powers, has
recently been promoted, leaping from comic books to multimil-
lion-dollar productions for the big screen. Spirit has even reentered the materialistic genre of science fiction, evoked in the
salutation of the heroes of *Star Wars:* "The Force be with you."

With Ring and Sabom both finding that about 40 percent of
the victims of medical crises they interviewed reported out-of-
body experiences, it is not surprising that the trend shows up in
other numbers as well. A case in point is a new study by the
Gallup Organization described as "the most comprehensive survey on beliefs about . . . the afterlife that has ever been under-
taken." As reported in the June 1982 issue of *McCall's* and in a
book, *Adventures in Immortality* by George Gallup, Jr., and William Proctor, published the same month, this study showed that
two-thirds of Americans believe in life after death. Significantly,
college-educated Americans were found to be more likely to
hold such beliefs than those with a high school education or

less. Age, on the other hand, does not appear to be a factor. Eighteen-year-olds were just as likely to believe in life after death as those over fifty. Surprisingly, the poll found that almost one American in four believes in reincarnation. Among those described as "leaders in medicine and science," however, the study disclosed a sharp contrast to the attitudes of the general public. Only 32 percent of the physicians and 16 percent of the scientists believe in life after death.

Earlier I suggested that the origin of man is not a popularity contest to be decided by paleoanthropologists. One might rejoin that neither is the nature of man and the question of life after death to be so decided; 50 million Frenchmen or 150 million Americans *can* be wrong. In principle, I agree. But as we have noted, there is a significant element of direct personal experience involved in such beliefs, which is a rather different matter than sitting around a table contemplating which fossil best serves a particular theory.

The reality is that there is a deep tide running in the direction of things of the spirit. Unless and until anthropologists and related scientists are able to develop a more holistic approach, studying the whole man and taking into consideration the full depth of human nature, they will soon lose their wider constituency. As it is, many are now discrediting themselves, behaving more like bone peddlers than scientists. They imagine their opponents are the fundamentalists, but the cultural currents flowing through the United States today—and a great deal else— suggest instead that their deeper problems arise from their lack of appreciation of the multiple dimensions of man himself.

Bibliography

Ardrey, Robert, *African Genesis*. New York: Atheneum, 1961.

Attenborough, David, *Life on Earth*. Boston: Little, Brown and Co., 1979.

Barnett, S. A., ed., *A Century of Darwin*. London: Heinemann, 1958.

Bird, Christopher. *See* Tompkins, Peter

Bird, Roland T., "Thunder in His Footsteps," *Natural History*, May 1939.

———, "We Captured a 'Live' Brontosaurus," *National Geographic*, May 1954.

Birdsell, J. B., *Human Evolution*, 2nd ed., Chicago: Rand McNally College Publishing Co., 1975.

Bohm, D., *Causality and Chance in Modern Physics*. Philadelphia: University of Pennsylvania Press, 1957.

———, and B. Hiley, "On the Intuitive Understanding of Non-locality as Implied by Quantum Theory." London: preprint, Birkbeck College, University of London, 1974.

———, see Waddington, C. H., ed.

Bohr, Neils, *Atomic Theory and the Description of Nature*. Cambridge, England: Cambridge University Press, 1934.

Boule, Marcellin, and Henri V. Vallois, *Fossil Men*, translated by Michael Bullock. New York: Dryden Press, 1957.

Bowles, Norma, and Fran Hynds, *Psi Search*. New York: Harper & Row, 1978.

Brace, C. Loring, and Harry Nelson, Noel Korn, Mary L. Brace, *Atlas of Human Evolution*. New York: Holt, Rinehart and Winston, 1979.

Brace, Mary L. *See* Brace, C. Loring

Brandon, S. G. F., *The Judgement of the Dead*. New York: Charles Scribner's Sons, 1975.

Brashler, William. *See* Janus, Christopher

Bronowski, Jacob, *The Ascent of Man*. Boston: Little, Brown and Co., 1973.

Brooks, J., and G. Shaw, *Origins and Development of Living Systems*. New York: Academic Press, 1973.

Broom, Robert, *The Coming of Man: Was It Accident or Design?* London: H. F. & G. Witherby, 1933.

Brown, Dale. *See* White, Edmund

Budge, E. A. Wallis, *The Book of the Dead*, 3 vols. London: Kegan Paul, Trench, Trübner & Co., 1901.

Burbank, Luther, quoted in Macbeth, *Darwin Retried*. *Also see* Wilbur Hall, *Partner of Nature*, Appleton-Century, 1939.

Campbell, Bernard G., *Human Evolution*, 2nd ed. Chicago: Aldine Publishing, 1974.

Campbell, Bob. *See* Leakey, Richard

Campbell, Joseph, *The Masks of God: Oriental Mythology*. London: Condor/ Souvenir, 1973.

Cerminara, Gina, *Many Mansions*. New York: Wm. Sloan, 1950.

Cherfas, Jeremy. *See* Gribbin, John

Cicero, *De Republica*, translated by C. D. Yonge, in *Cicero's Nature of the Gods*. London: George Bell & Sons, 1907.

Clark, R. E. D., *Darwin: Before and After*. London: Paternoster Press, 1950.

Cohane, John Philip, *Paradox: The Case for the Extraterrestrial Origin of Man*. New York: Crown, 1977.

Darwin, Charles, *On the Origin of Species*, A Facsimile of the First Edition with an Introduction by Ernst Mayr. Cambridge, Mass.: Harvard University Press, 1964.

———, *The Descent of Man and Selection in Relation to Sex*, 2nd ed. Akron, Ohio: Werner Co., 1874.

———, *The Origin of Species and the Descent of Man*. New York: Modern Library, 1936.

Davidson, H. R. Ellis, ed., *The Journey to the Other World*. Cambridge, England: D. S. Brewster, 1975; Totowa, N.J.: Rowman and Littlefield, 1975.

Davis, Whitney M., "The Ascension-Myth in the Pyramid Texts," *Journal of Near Eastern Studies*, Vol. 36, no. 3, July 1977.

De Beer, Sir Gavin R., *Embryos and Ancestors*, 3rd ed. London: Oxford University Press, 1958.

———, *Homology, an Unsolved Problem*, Oxford Biology Readers, 1971.

Delfgaauw, Bernard, *Evolution: The Theory of Teilhard de Chardin*. New York: Harper & Row, 1969.

De Santillana, Giorgio, and Hertha von Dechend, *Hamlet's Mill*. Boston: Gambit, 1969.

Dewar, Douglas, and H. S. Shelton, *Is Evolution Proved?* London: Hollis & Carter, 1947.

Du Noüy, Pierre Lecomte, *Human Destiny*. New York: Longmans, Green and Co., 1947.

———, *Between Knowing and Believing*. New York: David McKay Co., 1966.

Eddington, Arthur S., *Space, Time and Gravitation: An Outline of the General Theory of Relativity*. Cambridge, England: Cambridge University Press, 1920.

———, *The Nature of the Physical World*. Cambridge, England: Cambridge University Press, 1928.

———, *Relativity Theory of Protons and Electrons*. New York: Macmillan, 1936.

Edey, Maitland A., et al, *The Missing Link*. New York: Time-Life Books, 1972.

———, *See* Johanson, Donald

Einstein, Albert, B. Podolsky and N. Rosen, "Can Quantum-Mechanical Description of Physical Reality Be Considered Complete?" *Physical Review*, 47, 1935.

Einstein, Albert, "On Physical Reality," *Franklin Institute Journal*, 221, 1936.

Eiseley, Loren, *The Immense Journey*. New York: Vintage, 1958.

———, *The Firmament of Time*. New York: Atheneum, 1960.

———, *Darwin's Century*. New York: Doubleday, 1961.

———, on Piltdown, *see* McKern, T. H., ed.

Eliade, Mircea, *Myths, Dreams and Mysteries*. New York: Harper & Row, 1960.

———, *Shamanism*. Princeton, N.J.: Princeton University Press, 1964.

———, *Patterns in Comparative Religion*. New York: New American Library, 1974.

———, *Death, Afterlife and Eschatology*. New York: Harper & Row, 1974.

Evans-Wentz, W. Y., *The Tibetan Book of the Dead*. London: Oxford University Press, 1927.

Faulkner, R. O., "The King and the Star Religion in the Pyramid Texts," *Journal of Near Eastern Studies*, Vol. XXXV, no. 3, July 1966.

Fix, Wm. R., *Pyramid Odyssey*. New York: Mayflower, 1978.

———, *Star Maps*. New York and London: Octopus/Mayflower, 1979.

Ford, E. B., ed. *See* Huxley, Julian

Fox, S., "In the Beginning . . . Life Assembled Itself," *New Scientist*, February 27, 1969.

Gallup, George, Jr., and William Proctor, *Adventures in Immortality*. New York: McGraw-Hill, 1982.

Gamow, George, and Martynas Ycas, *Mr. Tompkins Inside Himself*. London: Allen & Unwin, 1968.

Goldschmidt, Richard, *The Material Basis of Evolution*. Paterson, N.J.: Pageant Books, 1960.

Goodall, Vanne, *The Quest for Man*. New York: Praeger, 1975.

Gould, Stephen Jay, *Ever Since Darwin*. New York: W. W. Norton & Co., 1977.

———, *Ontogeny and Phylogeny*. Cambridge, Mass.: Harvard University Press, Belknap Press, 1977.

———, *The Panda's Thumb*. New York: W. W. Norton & Co., 1980.

———, "The Piltdown Conspiracy," *Natural History*, August 1980.

Greenhouse, Herbert B., *The Astral Journey*. New York: Doubleday, 1974.

Gribbin, John, and Jeremy Cherfas, The Monkey Puzzle. New York: Pantheon Books, 1982.

Grof, Stanislav, and Joan Halifax, The Human Encounter with Death. New York: E. P. Dutton, 1977.

Guthrie, W. K. C., Orpheus and Greek Religion, 2nd ed. London: Methuen & Co., 1952.

Halifax, Joan. See Grof, Stanislav

Hapgood, Charles, The Earth's Shifting Crust. New York: Pantheon, 1958.

——, The Path of the Pole. New York: Chilton Book Co., 1970.

Haraldsson, Elendur. See Osis, Karlis

Hardy, A. C., Science and ESP. London: Routledge & Kegan Paul, 1967.

——, ed. See Huxley, Julian

Harris, John. See White, Timothy

Henderson, Joseph L., and Maud Oakes, The Wisdom of the Serpent. New York: Collier Books, 1971.

Hiley, B. See Bohm, D.

Himmelfarb, Gertrude, Darwin and the Darwinian Revolution. New York: W. W. Norton & Co., 1959.

Hitching, Francis, The World Atlas of Mysteries. London: Pan Books, 1979.

——, The Neck of the Giraffe. New York: Tichnor & Fields, 1982.

Howell, F. Clark, et al, Early Man. New York: Life Nature Library, 1965.

Howells, William, Mankind in the Making, rev. ed. Garden City, N.Y.: Double-day, 1967.

Hume, Robert Ernest, trans., The Thirteen Principle Upanishads. London: Oxford University Press, 1921.

Huxley, Julian, Evolution, the Modern Synthesis. London: Allen & Unwin, 1942.

——, A. C. Hardy and E. B. Ford, eds. Evolution as a Process, 2nd ed. London: Allen & Unwin, 1958.

Hynds, Fran. See Bowles, Norma

Ingrasci, Rick. See Taylor, Peggy

Jahn, Robert G., "The Persistent Paradox of Psychic Phenomena: An Engineering Perspective," Proceedings of the IEEE, Vol. 70, no. 2, February 1982.

James, William, The Varieties of Religious Experience. New York: Longmans, Green and Co., 1911.

Janus, Christopher G., and William Brashler, The Search for Peking Man. New York: Macmillan, 1975.

Johanson, Donald C., and Maurice Taieb, "Plio-Pleistocene Hominid Discoveries in Hadar Ethiopia," Nature, 260, March 1976.

Johanson, Donald C., "Ethiopia Yields First 'Family' of Man," National Geographic, December 1976.

Johanson, Donald C., and Timothy White, "A Systematic Assessment of Early African Hominids," Science, January 26, 1979.

Johanson, Donald C., and Maitland Edey, Lucy: The Beginnings of Humankind. New York: Simon & Schuster, 1981.

Jung, Carl Gustav, Memories, Dreams, Reflections. New York: Random House, 1963.

Keith, Arthur, *The Antiquity of Man*, 2 vols. Philadelphia: J. B. Lippincott, 1929.

Kennedy, G. E., *Paleo-anthropology*. New York: McGraw-Hill, 1980.

Kletti, Roy. *See* Noyes, Russell

Koestler, Arthur, *The Ghost in the Machine*. London: Hutchinson, 1967.

Korn, Noel. *See* Brace, C. Loring

Krutch, Joseph Wood, *The Great Chain of Life*. New York: Pyramid Publications, 1966.

Kübler-Ross, Elisabeth, ed., *Death: The Final Stage of Growth*. Englewood Cliffs, N.J.: Prentice-Hall, 1975.

Kurten, Björn, *The Age of Mammals*. New York: Columbia Univeristy Press, 1972.

———, *Not from the Apes*, New York: Pantheon/Random House, 1972.

La Barre, Weston, *The Human Animal*. Chicago: University of Chicago Press, 1954.

———, *The Ghost Dance*. London: Allen & Unwin, 1972.

Leakey, L. S. B., *Adam's Ancestors*, 4th ed. New York: Harper Torchbooks/ Harper & Row, 1960.

———, ed., and Jack and Stephanie Prost, *Adam or Ape*. London: Schenkman Publishing Co., 1971.

Leakey, Mary D., *Olduvai Gorge: My Search for Early Man*. London: William Collins Sons & Co., 1979.

Leakey, Richard E., and Roger Lewin, *Origins*. London: Macdonald and Jane's, 1972.

Leakey, Richard E., and Bob Campbell, "Skull 1470—New Clue to Earliest Man?" *National Geographic*, June 1973.

Leakey, Richard, and Roger Lewin, *People of the Lake*. London: Collins, 1979.

Leakey, Richard E., *The Making of Mankind*. New York: E. P. Dutton, 1981.

———. *See* Walker, Alan

Le Gros Clark, Wilfred, *Man-Apes or Ape-Men?* New York: Holt Rinehart & Winston, 1967.

Lewin, Roger. *See* Leakey, Richard E.

Long, Max Freedom, *The Secret Science Behind Miracles*. Los Angeles: Huna Research Publications, 1954.

Lowenstein, J. M. *See* Zihlman, A. C.

Lyell, Charles, *Principles of Geology*, 4th ed. London: John Murray, 1835.

Macbeth, Norman, *Darwin Retried: An Appeal to Reason*. Boston: Gambit, 1971.

McAtee, W. L., "Effectiveness in nature of so-called protective adaptations in the animal kingdom, chiefly as illustrated by the food-habits of nearctic birds." Washington: Smithsonian Miscellaneous Collection, 85, 7:1– 201, 1932.

McKenzie, John L., *Dictionary of the Bible*. New York: Macmillan, 1965; London: Geoffrey Chapman, 1968.

McKern, Thomas, ed., *Readings in Physical Anthropology*. Englewood Cliffs, N.J.: Prentice-Hall, 1966.

MacKinnon, John, *The Ape Within Us*. London: William Collins Sons & Co., 1978.

Macrobius, *Commentary on the Dream of Scipio*, translated by Wm. H. Stahl. New York: Columbia University Press, 1952.

Matson, Archie, *Afterlife: Reports from the Threshold of Death*. New York: Harper & Row, 1975.

Mayr, Ernst, "Change of Genetic Environment and Evolution," in J. S. Huxley, A. C. Hardy, and E. B. Ford, eds., *Evolution as a Process*. London: Allen & Unwin, 1954.

———, "Darwin and the Evolutionary Theory in Biology," in *Evolution and Anthropology: A Centennial Appraisal*, B. J. Meggers, ed. The Anthropological Society of Washington, 1959; reprinted in McKern, *Readings in Physical Anthropology*.

———, and William B. Provine, eds., *The Evolutionary Synthesis*. Cambridge, Mass.: Harvard University Press, 1980.

Melville, Leinani, *Children of the Rainbow: The Religion, Legends and Gods of pre-Christian Hawaii*. Wheaton, Ill.: Theosophical Publishing House, 1969.

Michell, John, *City of Revelation*. London: Abacus, 1973.

———, "The Darwin Myth," *Resurgence*, no. 83, Nov./Dec. 1980.

Monod, Jacques, *Chance and Necessity*. New York: Fontana Books, 1974.

Montagu, Ashley, *Man: His First Two Million Years*. New York: Columbia University Press, 1969.

Moody, Raymond, *Life After Life*. Covington, Ga. Mockingbird Books, 1975.

———, *Reflections on Life After Life*. St. Simon's Island, Ga.: Mockingbird Books, 1977.

Morris, Henry, and John C. Whitcomb, Jr., *The Genesis Flood*. Philadelphia: Presbyterian & Reformed Publishing Co., 1961.

Nelson, Harry. *See* Brace, C. Loring

Nesi-Khonsu Papyrus. *See* Budge, E. A. Wallis

Noyes, Russell, and Roy Kletti, "The Experience of Dying from Falls," *Omega*, Vol. 3, 1972.

Oakes, Maud. *See* Henderson, J. L.

Oakley, Kenneth P., *Man the Tool-Maker*. Chicago: University of Chicago Press, 1959.

———, "Dating the Emergence of Man," 1961 Address at Norwich Meeting of the British Association; reprinted in McKern, *Readings in Physical Anthropology*.

O'Connell, Patrick, *Science of Today and the Problems of Genesis*. St. Paul, Minn.: Radio Replies Society, 1959.

Osis, Karlis, *Deathbed Observations by Physicians and Nurses*. New York: Parapsychology Foundation, 1961.

———, and Elendur Haraldsson, *At the Hour of Death*. New York: Avon Books, 1977.

Osis, Karlis, article in *The Journal of the American Society for Physical Research*, July 1980.

Oxnard, C. E., article in *Scientific American*, Vol. 234, February 1976.

Paley, William, *Natural Theology*, 6th ed. London: 1803.

Panati, Charles, "Quantum Physics and Parapsychology," *Parapsychology Review*, Vol. 5, no. 6, Nov./Dec. 1974.

Patterson, Colin, *Evolution*. New York: British Museum (Natural History) and Cornell University Press, 1978.

Pelto, Gertrude, and Pertti J. Pelto, *The Human Adventure*. New York: Macmillan, 1976.

Penfield, Wilder, *The Mystery of the Mind*. Princeton, N.J.: Princeton University Press, 1975.

Pfeiffer, John E., *The Emergence of Man*, rev. ed. New York: Harper & Row, 1972.

Piankoff, Alexandre, *The Pyramid of Unas*, Vol. 5 of *Egyptian Religious Texts and Representations*. Princeton, N.J.: Princeton University Press, 1968.

————, *The Wandering of the Soul*, Vol. 6 of *Egyptian Religious Texts and Representations*. Princeton, N.J.: Princeton University Press, 1974.

Pilbeam, David, *The Evolution of Man*. New York: Funk and Wagnalls, 1970.

Plato, "The Myth of Er," in *The Republic*, translated by Francis MacDonald Cornford. New York and London: Oxford University Press, 1945.

————, *The Symposium*, in *The Dialogues of Plato*, translated by B. Jowett. New York: Random House, 1937.

Plutarch, "On Exile," in *Plutarch—Selected Lives and Essays*, translated by Louise Ropes Loomis. New York: Walter J. Black, 1971.

Podolsky, B. *See* Einstein, Albert

Popper, Karl R., *Conjectures and Refutations*. London: Routledge & Kegan Paul, 1963.

Proctor, William. *See* Gallup, George

Prost, Jack and Stephanie. *See* Leakey, L. S. B.

Provine, William B. *See* Mayr, Ernst

Puthoff, Harold. *See* Targ, Russell

Randall, John L., *Parapsychology and the Nature of Life*. New York: Harper & Row, 1975.

Rensberger, Boyce, "Ancestors, A Family Album," *Science Digest*, Vol. 89, no. 3, April 1981.

Ring, Kenneth, *Life at Death*. New York: Coward, McCann & Geoghegan, 1980.

Ritchie, George, *Return from Tomorrow*. Waco, Tex.: Chosen Books, 1978.

Romer, Alfred Sherwood, *Vertebrate Paleontology*, 3rd ed. Chicago and London: University of Chicago Press, 1966.

————, *The Procession of Life*. New York: World Publishing Co., 1968.

Rosen, N., *See* Einstein, Albert

Sabom, Michael B., *Recollections of Death, A Medical Investigation*. New York: Harper & Row, 1982.

Sagan, Carl, *The Dragons of Eden*. New York: Random House, 1977.

————, *Cosmos*. New York: Random House, 1980.

Schmeidler, Gertrude, ed., *Parapsychology and Its Relation to Physics, Biology, Psychology and Psychiatry*. Metuchen, N.J.: Scarecrow, 1976.

Shapiro, Harry L., *Peking Man*. New York: Simon & Schuster, 1974.

Shaw, G. *See* Brooks, J.

Sheldrake, Rupert, *A New Science of Life: The Hypothesis of Formative Causation*. Los Angeles: J. P. Tarcher, 1981.

————, article in *Science Digest*, October 1981.

Shelton, H. S. *See* Dewar, Douglas

Simak, Clifford D., *Prehistoric Man*. New York: St. Martin's Press, 1971.

Simons, Elwyn, "On the Mandible of Ramapithecus," *Anthropology*, Vol. 54, 1964.

Simpson, George Gaylord, *Tempo and Mode in Evolution*. New York: Columbia University Press, 1944.

———, *This View of Life*. New York: Harcourt Brace and World, 1964.

———, on language: *Biology and Man*. New York: Harcourt Brace and World, 1969.

Standen, Anthony, *Science Is a Sacred Cow*. New York: Dutton, 1950.

Stanley, Steven M., *The New Evolutionary Timetable*. New York: Basic Books, 1981.

Steiner, Rudolf, *Life Between Death and Rebirth*. New York: Anthroposophical Press, 1968.

Stern, Jess, *Edgar Cayce—the Sleeping Prophet*. Garden City, N.Y.: Doubleday, 1967.

Swann, Ingo, *To Kiss the Earth Good-bye*. New York: Hawthorn Books, 1975.

Taieb, Maurice. *See* Johanson, Donald

Targ, Russell, and Harold Puthoff, *Mind-Reach*. New York: Delacorte Press, 1977.

Tart, Charles T., "Psychophysiological Study of Out-of-the-Body Experiences in a Selected Subject," in *Journal of the American Society of Psychical Research*, Vol, 62, no. 1, January 1968.

———, *Psi: Scientific Studies of the Psychic Realm*. New York: E. P. Dutton, 1977.

Taylor, Peggy, and Rick Ingrasci, "Out of the Body: A New Age Interview with Elisabeth Kübler-Ross," *New Age*, November 1977.

Teilhard de Chardin, Pierre, *The Phenomenon of Man*, translated by Bernard Wall. New York: Harper & Brothers, 1959.

———, *The Appearance of Man*, translated by J. M. Cohen. New York: Harper & Row, 1965.

———, *The Vision of the Past*. New York: Harper & Row, 1966.

———, *Man's Place in Nature*, translated by Rene Hague. New York: Harper & Row, 1966.

———, *Science and Christ*. New York: Harper & Row, 1968.

Thompson, D'Arcy Wentworth, *On Growth and Form*, 2nd ed., 2 vols. Cambridge, England: Cambridge University Press, 1942.

Thorp, W. H., *Science, Man and Morals*. London: Methuen, 1965.

Tompkins, Peter, and Christopher Bird, *The Secret Life of Plants*. Harmondsworth, England: Penguin Books, 1975.

Vallois, Henri V. *See* Boule, Marcellin

Virgil, *The Aneid*, translated by W. F. Jackson Knight. Baltimore, Md.: Penguin Books, 1965.

Von Dechend, Hertha. *See* De Santillana, Giorgio

Waddington, C. H., ed., *Towards a Theoretical Biology*, Vol. 2. Edinburgh, Scotland: Edinburgh University Press, 1969.

Waechter, John, *Man Before History*. New York: E. P. Dutton, 1976.

Walker, Alan, and Richard Leakey, "The Hominids of East Turkana," *Scientific American*, August 1978.

Ward, Henshaw, *Evolution for John*. London: 1926.

Washburn, S. L., "Tools and Human Evolution," *Scientific American*, Vol. 203, no. 3., 1960.

Waters, Frank, *The Book of the Hopi*. New York: Viking, 1963.

Watson, James D., *Molecular Biology of the Gene*. New York: W. A. Benjamin, 1965.

Watson, Lyall, *Supernature*. London: Hodder and Stoughton, 1973.

Weidenreich, Franz, Apes, Giants and Man. Chicago: University of Chicago Press, 1946.

——, "Facts and Speculations Concerning the Origin of Homo Sapiens," *American Anthropologist*, April/June 1947.

Wendt, Herbert, *In Search of Adam*. Boston: Houghton Mifflin, 1956.

——, *From Ape to Adam*. New York: Bobbs-Merrill, 1972.

Whitcomb, John C. *See* Morris, Henry

White, Edmund, and Dale Brown, *The First Men*, The Emergence of Man Series. New York: Time-Life Books, 1973.

White, Timothy D., and John M. Harris, "Suid Evolution and Correlation of African Hominid Localities," *Science*, 198:13–21, October 1977.

White, Timothy. *See* Johanson, Donald.

Williams, B. J., *Evolution and Human Origins*. New York: Harper & Row, 1973.

Williams, George C., *Adaptation and Natural Selection*. Princeton: Princeton University Press, 1966.

Ycas, Martynas. *See* Gamow, George.

Zihlman, A. L., and J. M. Lowenstein, "False Start of the Human Parade," *Natural History*, August 1979.

Zuckerman, Solly, "Correlation of Change in the Evolution of Higher Primates," in *Evolution as a Process*, Julian Huxley, A. C. Hardy, and E. B. Ford, eds. London: Allen and Unwin, 1954.

Zukav, Gary, *The Dancing Wu Li Masters*. New York: William Morrow, 1979.

Index